Czechoslovak
Academy
of Sciences

BLACK AFRICA/Literature
and
Language

Czechoslovak
Academy
of Sciences

Scientific Editor
Professor Dr. Zdeněk Vančura, DSc.

Scientific Adviser
Professor Dr. Josef Vachek, DSc.

BLACK AFRICA

Literature
and
Language

VLADIMÍR KLÍMA

KAREL FRANTIŠEK RŮŽIČKA

PETR ZIMA

1976

D. Reidel Publishing Company
Dordrecht — Holland/Boston — U.S.A.

Library of Congress Cataloging in Publication Data

Klíma, Vladimír
    Black Africa: Literature and language.

    Modified and enl. English version of the authors
Literatura černé Afriky.
    Bibliography: p.
    Includes indexes.
    1. African literature — History and criticism. 2. African languages. I. Růžička, Karel František,
joint author. II. Zima, Petr, joint author. III. Title.
PL8010.K54   809'. 8967   74-83869
ISBN 90-277-0531-3

Sold and distributed in the U.S.A., Canada, and Mexico
by D. Reidel Publishing Company, Inc.
Lincoln Building, 160 Old Derby Street, Hingham, Mass. 02043, U.S.A.

Published by D. Reidel Publishing Company, P.O. Box 17,
Dordrecht, Holland in co-edition with ACADEMIA, Publishing House
of the Czechoslovak Academy of Sciences, Prague

Printed in Czechoslovakia

Contents

I. FOREWORD

In October 1972, our Czech-written book *Literatury černé Afriky* (Literatures of Black Africa) was published in Prague, presenting a survey of an extensive field. The publication, which was signed at that time by all three authors, differed from most contemporary introductions to the study of African literatures in a threefold way:

a) The authors attempted to cover various literacy and literary efforts in the area roughly delimited by Senegal in the west, Kenya in the east, Lake Chad in the north and the Cape in the south. We were well aware—even at that time—that neither technically nor linguistically would it be possible to cover all literary efforts within that area. We did try, however, to include in our survey both the literacies and literatures written in the Indo-European linguae francae (English, French, Portuguese) and in at least several of the major African languages of the area. We did not attempt an exhaustive description, but wished, rather, to show the mutual relationships which emerge, if the literatures of this area, written either in the major linguae francae or in the African languages, are studied not as isolated phenomena, but as mutually complementary features.

b) As two of us were linguists and one was a literary historian, we did not limit our analysis of the developing literacies and literatures to the purely cultural and literary aspects. Our intention was to deal—where and if it was relevant—not only with the process of African literary development, but also with the simultaneous, complementary process of literary language development and of the standardization of languages for literary and other cultural purposes.

c) Neither ideological, cultural or religious barriers nor such external symptoms of these barriers as the usage of particular scripts were neglected within the area in question; rather, a tendency to analyze African literatures as entities within the areas delimited became one of the leading criteria for us, even at that time.

When preparing, in 1971, the draft plan for a revision of the original text for the purposes of this English edition, we felt that more emphasis should be placed upon the scholarly character of this version. Some chapters, therefore, had to be completely rephrased and expanded. Also bibliography had to be considerably extended. It soon became obvious that a complementary analysis of the phenomena of literature and language, which had begun by mere coincidence, having originated from the composition and professional capacities of the authors' team, was worth considering within the context of the English edition.

When preparing this modified and enlarged English version, we were aware of the relative incompleteness of our information. Since, however, our work was not intended to serve as an encyclopaedia of African literary life—which, it should be pointed out, would be a rather rewarding task for future literary historians—we had to determine the purpose of the publication more precisely than we had done for the Czech version. While reckoning with the fact that the book would be also read by those having only a slight knowledge of our subject, we nevertheless respected more the needs of those readers who wish to become familiar with the general and special characteristics of these literatures, the development of which can be analyzed from a number of different standpoints, while various methods may be attempted in such efforts.

In order to avoid any misleading one-sidedness, we decided to combine different approaches, fully realizing the mutual influence and dependence of literature and language. The present study, therefore, is based on the idea that African (and other) imaginative writing may profitably be interpreted in terms of the interrelationships between the two. For these reasons, the theoretical passages which in the Czech version were comparatively short had to be included in the present English version. In the authors' opinion, a thorough clarification of broad problems connected with the development of Black African writing is not only desirable, but also necessary.

The reader who may not find mentioned herein a particular writer or novel may be disappointed. However, he will undoubtedly be able to find the information he seeks in encyclopaedic surveys or bibliographies. For our part, we are mainly concerned with research in this new field and the experience gained thus far indicates that it has been possible to achieve some progress in this respect by establishing a definition of overall tendencies and general lines of development.

Black Africa in itself represents a rather controversial concept; many previous studies discussing it acknowledged certain limitations not only in terms of geography, but also in terms of race. The present book, therefore, attempts to include also non-black authors living in or coming from the area in question. The writing of the Malagasy Republic is also mentioned in one chapter, since Madagascar has had a sort of cultural affinity to the black continent.

In the initial stages of drafting the English edition of this work, a possible extension of the authors' team was considered, but subsequently this did not prove to be realistic, owing to the limited time available for the preparation of the manuscript. On the contrary, we are sorry to say that destiny weakened the original authors' team by the premature and unexpected death of Dr. Karel František Růžička. As a result, most of his chapters, which were translated by Dr. Vladimír Klíma, had to be left in their original form and were only occasionally shortened.

The Czech-written version is a popular science series and, with respect to its requirements, included also certain extracts, mainly from poetry and oral folklore, hitherto untranslated into Czech. Owing to a relatively large amount of such anthologies in English, we found such extracts redundant for the present publication. Literature is generally studied as one of the written forms of language. Hence, apart from Chapter IX, preserved for obvious personal reasons, oral traditions are analyzed chiefly in relation to written literature.

We thank Professor Dr. Zdeněk Vančura, DSc., and Professor Dr. Josef Vachek, DSc., who, having officially read the full text, kindly made a number of inspiring comments, Mrs. Leonora Strádalová for her generous revision of our English and many other friends and colleagues both in this country and abroad.

August 1974   Vladimír Klíma   Petr Zima

II. LANGUAGE AND SCRIPT IN BLACK AFRICA

0. Introduction

A century ago (or even less), any attempt to present or analyze an inventory of scripts or other symbols used for the graphical recording of languages in Black Africa might have appeared vain and unnecessary. Today, however, the situation appears different, as we find ourselves obliged to modify previous statements about Africa as a scriptless continent. Intensive research accomplished in this field by various authors has opened new perspectives, especially as far as the scripts and graphical symbols of a supposed or real local origin are concerned (Klingenheben, 1933; Dugast-Jeffreys, 1950; Dalby, 1967, 1968, 1969; Monod 1958; Schmitt 1963). On the other hand, however, one cannot escape the feeling that despite this intensive interest of both cultural anthropologists and linguists, most research into script in Black Africa has been focused so far on a search for a possible (or impossible) local origin, history, or design, whereas comparatively little interest has been shown in the problem of the real written usage and existence (or non-existence) of a script as a basic precondition for the development of the written form of any language in that area. Although the tendency to stress an analysis of the historical or artistic origin of scripts in Black Africa is perfectly understandable within the entire defensive context and in the search for a certain self-identity of all African cultures against the "Europocentrism" of the past, a contemporary sociolinguistic approach to written language communication, including an analysis of their graphical form, also seems important. One of its aims must be an attempt to bridge the still largely existing gaps between the linguistic, literary and social analyses of written language communication. Although it would have to take into account problems connected with the possible history, origin and design of local scripts, such an attempt would obviously have to respect the whole inventory of scripts used by the languages of that area. From this point of view, however, any cript which effectively serves the languages of the area must be considered important (whatever its origin, history or design), providing it serves them in a linguistically and socially acceptable way. As a consequence, two scripts, the history and design of which were clearly foreign and which were imported into Black Africa (at least in recent centuries) must be included in the inventory, and their respective functions must be considered: These are the Arabic and the Roman scripts. Whereas their origin, history and usually even typology of designs differ considerably from those of other scripts used for the writing of the languages of Black Africa, their functions in the contemporary written communication of the languages in that area should be analyzed within this same context.

The process of the application and adaptation of these two "imported" scripts into the written language communication of Africa south of the Sahara has, however, been described and analyzed in a rather unbalanced way. Research into the sub-Saharan usage of the Arabic script for the writing of African languages is scattered over various contributions on such usage in individual—though important—languages, and attention is devoted occasionally even to one single manuscript or one genre of manuscripts and written documents. Thus, with respect to West Africa, there exist important contributions on this written usage in Hausa (Taylor, 1929; Na'ibi Wali, 1959; Olderogge, 1960), Fula (Taylor, 1929) and Kanuri (Benton, 1911). In East Africa, research has been focused on this type of usage in Swahili (Velten, 1908). On the other hand, African usage of the Roman script has also been analyzed on a more general and comparative level (Berry, 1958; Tucker, 1971), with particular attention being devoted to the various types of this written usage found in different languages in all areas of Black Africa.

It should be emphasized, however, that whereas works on local scripts devote little or no attention to the two "foreign" scripts, the above-mentioned sources on Arabic and Roman characters and their usage for writing the languages of Black Africa also devote little attention to texts written in these so-called "local" scripts. Most authors are probably well aware of this situation and an explicit remark by Tucker in this sense (1971, p. 618) perhaps only formulates a sort of common feeling on the subject. One of the aims of the following section is also to consider what similarities or contrasts—if any—exist in the present functions of both groups of scripts.

1. Inventory

1.0 The symbols for the graphical and other recordings of language communication in Black Africa are neither poor nor scarce. As revealed by the present state of research and in the light of possible further unanticipated findings in this field, Black Africa can possibly measure up to certain other areas of the world. However, a basic distinction must be clearly made when any such inventory is undertaken: a systematic graphical recording of language communication by representative social groups (even though they may be a minority within the given language communities) must be considered in contrast to the individual or occasional usage of relatively isolated graphical symbols. Though we are fully aware of the difficulties involved in drawing a possible, and always complex, borderline between such embryonic or half-writing (or, as they are sometimes called simply mnemonic devices for memorization—see Diringer, 1948, p. 21) and scripts as systems of graphical symbols, typical groups must be considered of importance on both sides of the borderline. From this point of view, Africa offers no exception, but rather a confirmation of the rules established in other areas as well.

1.1 Isolated graphical symbols and mnemonic devices used with a different degree of sophistication appear scattered through various language areas of Black Africa. A precise map and inventory of them has never been drawn, nor does it seem probable that it will be drawn in future. One of the reasons for such a situation is the fact that most such symbols or devices are an inherent part of the whole context of the traditional forms of culture and, as a result, they ultimately share their fate in the present process of changes going on in Africa. Earlier reports on the usage of such symbols and devices by Meinhof (1911—partly based on Spieth's findings) and Westermann (1907) were rightly placed within the context of an analysis of the development of the usage of scripts and written languages in Africa south of the Sahara, generally. Although we may not share many of Meinhof's evolutionary opinions, it is undoubtedly his merit that he was among the first scholars to realize the possible links between unsystematic recording devices (whether graphical or even non-graphical is of limited importance in this context) and scripts as graphical systems, especially in the area of sub-Saharan Africa. He analyzes the script as a dynamic, not static, system, and discusses, at least from this standpoint, the non-systematic usage of graphical and other isolated symbols in Ewe, in the same context (though in a different function) as the two African script systems known in his time, the Vai and the Bamum systems (Meinhof, 1911, p. 7).

Westermann and Meinhof by no means limited their analyses to the symbols used by various African communities for transmitting and recording communications of importance—that is, to the mere graphical or picto-graphical sphere. Apart from analyzing pictorial symbols, they also devoted attention to the usage of such devices as the sending or preserving of concrete objects hung from a stick, as symbols, the placing of symbolic objects in a net, and certain other types of symbolism. A possible theoretical link was, perhaps sub-consciously, established at that time by Westermann (1907, p. 12) between such devices and various sign languages (*Zeichensprachen*), including the usage of pantomimic dances in a "narrative" context. He called such symbolic devices of communication "speaking by dancing" (*Sprechen in Tanzen*, l.c.). Apart from dancing and pantomime he also mentioned certain forms of musical usage, including the so-called talking drums. These non-graphical means of symbolism in communication obviously share certain functional similarities with written language communication in general (some of them are also a sort of reduction of language messages), although the very nature of the symbols used is completely different from those in the purely graphical field. This is why Nketia (1971) was completely correct in analyzing the whole field of such non-graphical symbolism as "surrogate" forms of African languages.

Various other forms of symbolism in the recording or transmitting of language communications, mostly of a semi-systematic character, have relatively recently been reported, described and analyzed in various areas of Black Africa by such authors as Griaule and Dieterlen (1951), Zahan (1950) and some others. Valuable descriptive remarks, linked, however, to certain rather audacious and far-reaching hypothetical conclusions, may be found in the numerous contributions of K. Hau (1959, 1964, 1967). All these contributions, which are different in nature and style of approach, nevertheless indicate a relatively extensive usage of such symbolic devices of differing natures in various parts of Africa: the Bozos, Bambaras, Dogons, and perhaps even the Binis and Yorubas are reported to use them, at least occasionally. If remarks on possible symbolic interpretations of the famous rock-painting are taken into consideration in this context, then there is no doubt that attempts to create a symbolic usage, comparable to such symbolic devices at least in function if not in nature or design, may have existed (and perhaps exist even today) in many areas of Black Africa. Only the recently increasing number of research projects in African linguistics and cultural anthropology may help to fulfil the task of their description and inventorization before these devices fade away altogether. Dalby (1967, p. 2—3; 1968, p. 158—59) believes that it is primarily the contextual character of such symbolic usage (he even considers such usage to be a graphical system) which contrasts them to real scripts which should be considered textual in character. Although we share with him his ideas concerning such a fundamental text — context dichotomy, we doubt whether these contextual graphical symbols can ultimately be considered to be systems altogether. Thus, in our opinion, the primary distinctive criterion between such half- (or embryonic) scripts and real scripts lies, rather, in their systematic character, as opposed to the unsystematic character of the former devices. Moreover, we consider that this principal criterion could be extended to the sphere of non-graphical devices. A line could be drawn even here between the unsystematic and isolated usage of symbols and various forms of "surrogate" languages, the basic character of which is systematic. A comparison between the occasional symbolic usage of musical drumming and the systematic usage of talking drums (based usually upon a sort of imitation or reduction of an existing language system, or at least its prosodic features) could perhaps be used as an illustration of the possibility of applying this criterion to a broader field.

1.2 In contrast to the individual non-systematic usage of graphical and other symbols, which are dealt with in the preceding section, the following authentic systems of a graphical recording of the languages of Africa south of the Sahara have thus far been reported, described and analyzed (in keeping with the geographical delimination of this area, as defined in the introductory section of this book):

Vai, Mende, Loma, Kpelle (plus the Bassa-VAH script), Bete
Wolof, N'ko (Manding), Dita (plus the other Fula script), Bamum, Bagam
Obɛri Ɔkaimɛ, Nsibidi, the Yoruba "Holy" script
Arabic script, Roman script

It should be stressed, in this connection, that it is highly probable that the present inventory of scripts, which are known at this stage to be used or to have been used for the writing of African languages, may not be complete. Further additions to this inventory are not out of the question, especially in the light of the "magical" character of certain scripts and the resulting justifiable hesitation of some representatives of traditional African cultures to discuss with first-generation expatriate researchers these and related problems (cf. the similar opinion of Dalby in 1968, p. 190). The role of new generations of academically-trained linguists and social anthropologists of local origin may be crucial in this respect.

Most up-to-date sources tend to analyze this inventory in terms of

(a) origin and design, or

(b) script type

As our analysis is oriented principally towards the usage of script for the writing of the languages of this particular area, we shall include three further criteria in our consideration of script -language relations in sub-Saharan Africa, i.e.:

(c) zone of influence of particular scripts

(d) adaptation of a script to a particular language for which it was not designed or created

(e) social and literary functions.

2. Design and Origin of Scripts Used for the Languages of Black Africa

2.1 The question of the design of scripts used in this area, important as it is paleographically (and within the general context of the history and development of script in general) has been the subject of a relatively recent, thorough analysis (Dalby, 1967, 1968, 1969). From our standpoint, however, as we study the actual functioning of the scripts for the writing of texts, the problem of design is not of major importance. The question of origin, however, is of certain importance, even in our context, especially since it entails the question of the basic dichotomy of local-foreign scripts. This dichotomy matters not so much because of its cultural or prestige repercussions, mentioned in Section O., but because of the language-script relationship dealt with in detail in Section 5. of this chapter. It is evident that a script which has been created for a particular language system, or at least used by a particular language system for a long historical period, is usually much more suitable for registering the structural features of the respective language system than some other script which was invented for another language system and hence is less applicable to a foreign (and structurally different) one. This was perhaps the main factor which incited most authors dealing with this problem to use the only partly correct local-foreign dichotomy (even we have proceeded in such a way in the past: cf. Zima, 1969, p. 212).

It is true, however, that the usage of the local-foreign dichotomy, though useful within the context of script adaptation and orthography, is rather absurd in the cultural and literary sphere not only because of the fact that most world literatures are written in "foreign scripts". Very few language communities in the classical area of Europe in fact use a script which could be termed "local" from the standpoint of national, and particularly continental, affiliation. Is the Roman script, after all, a European creation? The same argument can also be used, however, the other way round, as these same world and national literatures of Europe have proved to be capable of developing excellent writing in a script which was originally foreign but which, for better or worse, has been adapted to the needs of the particular languages in question. As shown by Berry (1958, p. 752), factors of social acceptance may prevail over factors of linguistic suitability, at least in the case of scripts.

This is an important realization, even within the context of the newly-developing literary standards of Africa south of the Sahara, especially in the light of a possible classification of the Arabic and Latin scripts and an evaluation of their eventual linguistic and social destinies within the entire context of writing in Africa south of the Sahara. In the light of the relatively large inventory of both literary and non-literary texts written in this area in these scripts, and in view of the adaptation processes described in Section 5., one necessarily hesitates before labelling them as sociolinguistically foreign. When their overall usage and literary importance are taken into account, they might be considered local in their own right—perhaps more so than some of the above-mentioned scripts of an obviously local cultural origin.

2.2   In contrast to the two preceding scripts, the position of the following group of scripts used for the writing of various languages in the area under consideration is different, not only from the standpoint of their origin. We have in mind the Bamum, Bete, Bagam, Obɛri Ɔkaimɛ, N'ko, Dita (and other Fula scripts), and also perhaps the Bassa VAH script. One of their common characteristics, as far as their origin is concerned, lies in the fact that their immediate origin (and, in most cases, even the main individual creator or inspirer) is known with a reasonable degree of certainty. Although an inspiration from other unknown sources or roots cannot be, even in their cases, altogether excluded, it does seem that these scripts constitute a relatively recent innovation in African cultures, and that they should be considered in the general context of the rising prestige of writing under the direct or indirect influence of both the Arabic and Roman scripts. This does not mean, however, that most of such scripts follow the two above-mentioned scripts with respect to their type or language-script relations, nor do they serve identical social or literary functions.

2.3   The position of the Vai script, which curiously enough belongs to those earlier known in Black Africa (and perhaps also the position of the Mende script), seems to be different. Many authors (Hair 1963, Dalby 1967) have suggested that the origin of this script is perhaps also connected to some extent with outside influences. According to Dalby (1968, p. 168), Hair plans to publish a paper on the existence of possible historical links between the Vai script and the syllabaries of the American Cherokee Indians, the two respective areas having been served by the same American board of missionaries. But the position of the Vai script in a Mande area, where both geographical and cultural factors may have been favourable to the earlier existence of either a graphical system or at least a pre-script symbolism, might not have been a pure coincidence. Moreover, the Vai script reflects an initial consonantal mutation which is grammatically irrelevant in the contemporary Vai language itself but is highly important in other Mande languages of that area. This might also speak in favour of an older existence of a written tradition in this case. Dalby (1967, p. 16) thinks that this situation might perhaps be explained by the fact that the inventor of the Vai script was acquainted with, and perhaps influenced by, another Mande language. One may, however, consider even other solutions: as our knowledge of the historical development of the Vai language is scarce, one might suppose that such an initial consonantal mutation, which has been documented today only in the genetically related languages, existed in the Vai grammatical system some time ago as well. Subsequently, the script, as a more conservative feature, might have preserved a phenomenon which was lost in the oral form of the language a long time ago, as has happened in so many languages the historical development of which is known and supported by graphical evidence. Comparative studies of Vai and other Mande languages might bring to light more facts and help us to reconstruct not only the historical development of this language; they might also simultaneously assist us in either supporting or dismissing such a possibility.

Even today, however, one cannot escape the feeling that the whole "mystique" connected with the "invention" of the Vai, and perhaps other scripts of that area, as well, represents a sort of graphical "folklore", and that it is highly doubtful whether the whole story of the Vai script really started with Momolu Duwalu Bukele and his dreams to devise a script sometime around 1833. In spite of the fact that he is so sceptical of Delafosse (1899), who thinks that the Vais' belief in a long previous historical development of the present script is correct, Dalby himself appears, especially in his second paper, more inclined to accept the possiblity of at least certain local roots of this script (1968, 168). Moreover, the typological character of certain African scripts also speaks in favour of their having local roots.

3. Typology of Scripts

If conventional typological criteria are applied to the inventory of scripts used for languages in Black Africa, these scripts may be basically subdivided into two unequal groups:

a) phonemic scripts (alphabets): Bassa-VAH, Oberi Ɔkaimɛ, N'ko, Dita (plus the other Fula alphabet), Wolof, the Yoruba "Holy" alphabet, the Roman and Arabic alphabets.

b) syllabic scripts: Vai, Mende, Loma, Kpelle, Bete, Bamum, Bagam.

The typological question which has retained the attention of those who have analyzed these scripts is the predominantly syllabic character of most scripts having a probable local origin; the curious typological similarity of the Liberian-Sierra Leonian scripts with such a remote and historically different invention as the Bamum script raises a question which has been dealt with by all scholars from Meinhof (1911, p. 7) to Dalby (1968, p. 168): is this the result of a mere coincidence, a situation resulting from the best possible language-script adaptation, or does it indicate a possible historical link? To complicate the situation even further, the Djuka script of the Surinam Negroes, the descendants of African slaves imported into that part of Latin America, appears to be also of a syllabic origin.

It may be that—apart from some possible chance similarities or historical ties — this syllabic character testifies to an optimum spontaneous languages-script adaptation. Indeed, it fits extremely well the structure of the languages of that area, not only because of a frequent syllable-morpheme coincidence (the majority of syllables are of an open CV structure), but because it serves also to record languages with distinctive tones on the syllable level. One cannot exclude the possibility that the inventors of these syllabic scripts (the historical period in which they actually lived is of no importance in this connection) were perhaps better transcribers of their respective language structures than the 19th or 20th-century phoneticians and linguists, for the most part of European origin or training: the difficulties met by all orthographies based on the Arabic or Latin script, which attempt to transcribe most of the languages of that area and type, provide effective proof of this situation.

In conclusion, we should stress that such a conventionally-based typology of scripts is far from perfect or exhaustive, particularly in the case of the African scripts or scripts used in Africa. Most syllabic types of scripts have ideographic (or even pictographic) elements in their structure; on the other hand, some of the "alphabetic" scripts manifest features of other types. Moreover, if some of the critical remarks formulated by A. A. Hill (1967) about conventional script typology are accepted, then elements of what he calls "discourse" script type can be discovered in some of the attempts at establishing a more systematic graphical symbolism classified here in the conventional manner, under half-scripts in Para. 1.1. The case of Nsibidi symbolism appears to be very close to a sort of discourse script in this sense.

4. Zones of Influence of Different Scripts

4.1 The zones of influence of all scripts enumerated in Para. 1.2. (apart from the Roman and Arabic scripts) are more or less concentrated in certain areas of Black Africa. This clustering of scripts appears to be most typical in at least two areas of West Africa: the Liberia-Sierra Leone and the Nigeria-Cameroons regions. The most ancient and locally-adapted scripts appear in the former region: the Vai and Mende scripts can certainly be classified as their most typical representatives. The Nigeria-Cameroons area seems to be—at least in this respect—secondary. The Bamum script and its history might confirm this hierarchy, although some features of the Obɛri Ɔkaimɛ and perhaps even Nsibidi scripts (if included in the inventory as a system) might have older roots than is today supposed. Other zones of influence of this category of scripts outside these two cluster areas are scarce: the Bete script, the two Fula scripts, the N'ko script, and the Wolof script are both recent and more or less considerably restricted in usage, covering very limited writing areas and communities in the Ivory Coast, the Republic of Guinea, Mali and Senegal.

4.2 The problem of texts in the African languages written in the Arabic script is a complicated one, and surprisingly little research was done in this direction until quite recently. No clear-cut identity can be established between the language areas where this form of written African language exists and the Islamic zones of Africa, including the zone of occurrence of texts in the Arabic language, although definitive ties between these factors obviously exist. It is true that such important African languages as Hausa, Fula and Swahili, spoken by people who have been relatively long in contact with Islam, have developed a comparatively large number of vernacular texts written in the Arabic script (called *Ajamiya*, derived from "foreign", i.e. non-Arabic sources). Apart from the use of the Arabic script for texts in these important African languages which were acknowledged at an early date (see e.g. Robinson, 1896), recent research has revealed that vernacular texts in the Arabic script occur in a surprisingly vast but rather incoherent range of other African languages as well. Apart from such important languages as Kanuri (cf. Benton 1911, Prietze, 1930; Lebeuf and Rodinson 1958), such texts also occur in Dagbani, Mamprule, Gonja, Dyula, Manding and other African languages (cf. *Research Review*, Legon, 1965). It is not yet clear how many languages in the zone of Islamic influence in Black Africa have actually developed vernacular literatures, or at least some written texts in the Arabic script, since apart from Fula, Hausa and Swahili, this kind of research is still in its initial stages and there is much exploration yet to be done. It seems that although the influence of Islam was an essential factor and inspiration, other—probably local—factors may have been decisive for the development or non-development of this type of written text in the African languages, or even of texts of a literary character.

4.3   The usage of the Roman Script for the writing of African languages obviously came about in modern times as a result of cultural, religious and — last but not least — administrative contacts with Europeans. The early stimulus for using the Roman script for African languages came from Christian missions, but later certain colonial administrations joined the missions in their effort to introduce written forms of African languages in the Roman script, at least in some areas and in some functions. The missions were intent upon reaching the average African primarily with religious texts, but their efforts were in fact never limited to the propagation of such texts alone (cf. Rowling—Wilson, 1927 and supplements). Owing to the fact that they started their activity long before the definitive creation of colonial administrative units, they never acted strictly within the limits of these artificial territorial areas, but were usually oriented towards certain genuine African language communities. Later efforts by the administrative organs of the newly-formed territorial units took the form of what were called "language and literature (or translation) bureaux and committees", etc. These activities were largely devoted to certain territories (this was the case of the language and literature bureaux in the former British West African territories). On the other hand, certain institutions of this type in the former British territories of East Africa attempted to effectively cover, at certain periods of their existence, all of these territories. This happened especially in the light of the linguistic situation, which clearly offered simpler solutions in language questions in this area. The Inter-Territorial Language (Swahili) Committee, organized in the 1930's, later known as the East African Swahili Committee, offers evidence as to how useful such an inter-territorial, and later, in fact, even inter-state, approach to common language problems could be. More details on the activity of this organ may be found in various detailed papers and are summarized in Whiteley (1969, p. 79 ff.).

A fundamental difference existed, however, between the language policies of different colonial administrations. In the British zone, the African languages, or at least some of them, were accepted as written in the Latin script for certain purposes of education, mass communication and public life (cf. Berry, 1952; UNESCO Report, 1952). In the French zone, however, only the French language was accepted for writing in the Latin script, even for the basic purposes of all these areas of communication, and the written vernacular usage was neither encouraged nor even generally tolerated (Alexandre, 1963, p. 53). Only the last decade brought certain major changes in this sphere.

Initial attempts to foster and support the writing of certain major African languages (in the Roman script, of course) arose both in East and West African territoires under the German colonial administration before World War I, but owing to well-known historical circumstances these attempts were never completed. Interesting details about this stage in the Ewe territory are analyzed in Chapter VII. of this book; Whiteley (1969, p. 57 ff.) shows that even in the Swahili area, the steps undertaken by the early German administration in East Africa in the field of active indirect language policies left rather deep roots.

Both in the former Belgian Congo and in Rwanda-Urundi attempts were also made to introduce a sort of written form of certain African languages (also in the Roman script), at least for initial, primary education and lower levels of administration and other services. In the Union (now Republic) of South Africa, the language policies of the originally British-influenced administration permitted, or even encouraged, certain types of written usage of African languages in the Roman script. These tendencies are being perpetuated in certain forms even today, although the ultimate goal of such language policies is now apparently different.

The final result of these and other local factors was that although by the middle of this century the theoretical zone of influence of Roman characters extended over most of Black Africa, this did not mean—as in the case of the Islamic zone and African languages texts in the Arabic script—that these texts in the Roman script existed in all language communities. The activities of the missions seem to have covered the largest linguistic areas, but they did not affect certain language communities in Africa, either because of their affinity to Islam, or because of their small size and relative unimportance in the sphere of communication. On the other hand, the administrative language and literature bureaux and committees covered the zone of British influence, for the most part, although they also penetrated the Islamic zone with some success and established the written usage of African languages in the Roman script, even for certain languages which were already employing the Arabic script.

5. The Process of Language-Script Adaptation

5.0 The result of the historical co-existence of the zones of influence of different scripts in Africa south of the Sahara seems to be a certain measure of interference and interaction: the usage of the Arabic and Roman script penetrates into the zones of languages where indigenous, "local" scripts already exist, but not vice versa. The marginal exception in this direction, noted by Stewart (who discovered that the Vai script has been also used to record Arabic texts: see Stewart 1967, p. 71—4), could be mentioned perhaps as a curiosity. If we take into consideration the fact that despite the influence of all the above-mentioned scripts, there are still many languages in the area under consideration which have no scripts, then we may conclude that theoretically the number of scripts, and hence the number of written forms of a particular African language, may vary from three to zero.

While all such possible combinations of language-script relationships in Africa south of the Sahara are academically interesting, by no means all of them actually exist; many of them are limited to a few, almost theoretical cases and have little, if any, linguistic, literary, cultural or social significance. The upper extreme (i.e. the co-existence of three scripts—that is, of an indigenous script together with the written usage of the same language in the Arabic script and Roman script) is rare and restricted in usage. The lower extreme (no existing script) and the co-existence of two different scripts for writing one and the same language are important. This latter alternative is of particular importance, especially in those cases in which both types of written usage show tendencies to develop into a literature, in the true sense of this term. We would use here the term *digraphia* for such situations (see Zima, 1974), in a sense parallel to the term and notion of *diglossia* initiated by Ferguson (1964, p. 429). Both the case of languages without any script and that of languages with two co-existing scripts exceed the narrow limits of mere adaptation problems, as they manifest broader cultural, literary and even social phenomena unknown in other language communities. In such cases, we are confronting not so much the problem of the adaptation of a script as the more crucial problem of the choice of a script, shifts in the use of a script or co-existences of scripts. The script, therefore, should often be considered as a mere external, though important, symptom of a broader and deeper stratification within a given language community. Particular cases of such development in Black Africa, which are perhaps of more general significance, are dealt with in Chapter VII.

The crucial problem at the origin of any process of script adaptation is that of a possible application of a script created for a different language to another language system which is different both typologically and genetically from the original script-bearing language. Whereas, as we have indicated, the application of the various "local" scripts in Africa to languages outside the original language areas is scarce and marginal, this phenomenon does apply in the case of the adaptation of the Arabic and Roman alphabets to the written usage of African languages.

5.1 A graphical system, used heretofore for a genetically foreign and structurally different language system, is often applied to another language as a result of linguistically arbitrary or accidental factors, including those of historical, cultural or other significance. Since, in such cases, the two systems (i. e. that of the script and that of the language) are ultimately different, many features and elements—or even whole complexes of features of the respective language system—have no counterparts on the level of the graphical system. On the other hand, however, many elements or features of the graphical system used for transcribing a different language may be redundant in the new situation. As a consequence, the need arises for the adaptation of one of the systems, if at least some degree of suitability for communication is to be achieved in the script-language relationship. As the arbitrary system of a script can be modified much more readily and with less harm for communication, the problem of the adaptation of the script arises. This particular problem obviously arose when both the Arabic and Roman scripts came into use for African languages, and two factors seem to have played different roles in the process of their adaptation: the spontaneous, traditional factor of this process seems to have been much stronger in the case of the Arabic script, although even the arbitrary factor was not completely absent in this case. The reverse seems to be valid for the process of adaptation of the Roman script.

5.2 The degree to which the Arabic script has been adapted for the writing of various African languages seems to vary considerably. In the case of Hausa and Fula, a certain traditional norm, although vague and inconsistent, has developed, at least in some areas and probably for some traditional schools of scribes only. The importance of this type of script and its long establishment, as well as the large number of texts occurring, especially at certain historically pertinent periods, seem to be the cause of this relative stabilization of a written form. Additional general rules for the adaptation of the graphic system of the Arabic script to these two languages have been established on the basis of an analysis of relatively large corpuses of texts. (Robinson, 1953, p. 172—91; Taylor 1929, *passim*; Na'ibi Wali, 1959, *passim*). They include the principle of a more or less consistent vocalization based on a triadic system of notation of vowels. This system has given way in some areas and scribes' schools to a four-vowel marking system both for Hausa and Fula. The distinction of vowel quantity seems to have been much more respected and marked, especially in the case of Hausa, than that of tonality. There is a considerable variation in the usage of symbols for diphtongs, and the same is true of the notation of consonants which are non-existent in classical Arabic, especially where these have no similarity to analogous sounds in that language. Although some kind of traditional norm has developed for the use of the Arabic script in Hausa and Fula—vague, traditional, spontaneous and inconsistent though it may be—texts using the Arabic script in other languages of this area seem to be much less adapted, and even less consistent.

5.3   As has already been pointed out, the adaptation of the Roman script to African languages has been much more a matter of arbitrary decision than of traditionally developing norms. Three approaches have characterized this process: the varied application of Lepsius' standard alphabet (see Lepsius, 1863, 1880), the application of the orthographic rules valid for the various European languages of the missionary and administrative centres, and the application of the phonetic principles of the IPA (International Phonetic Alphabet). The use of Lepsius' alphabet and orthographic rules applicable to a European language (especially English and French) were characteristic of the earlier African language texts in the Roman script; the IPA principles of phonetics have penetrated into usage only relatively recently. Even the application of the orthographic rules of a single European language sometimes introduced the element of division, where the African language community was divided into zones of interest of the different missions and administrations. This situation was a considerable help, however, in the process of transition from writing in the respective African language to writing in the European lingua franca. The application of certain IPA rules and symbols, which was realized by D. Westermann and I. C. Ward and a group of phoneticians and linguists associated with the International African Institute (Orth. Mem., 1927) helped to express particular features of African vernaculars, especially phonetic features. However, the detailed expression and description of phonetic features at the language and dialect level ignored many phonemic and morphophonemic rules. This introduced obviously other difficulties. Where linguistic norms of the standard usage were not yet clearly described or defined, the detailed phonetic transcription of dialectal differences led to a certain disintegration, rather than to an integration of the written norm. In deference to classical sociolinguistic situations, in which the introduction of writing and the creation of a widely accepted literary standard led towards the strengthening of the standard norm and started, or at least supported, the process of dialect integration, such a phonetically precise transcription of dialects in writing, if introduced into literary usage, automatically recorded dialect differences or congealed the existing ones into a written form. The detailed sociolinguistic consequences of such a process, where they affect the development of new literary standard languages, are described in Chapter III. The emphasis on special characters, rather than on diacritics, for transcribing sounds or features which are non-existent in Latin and other European languages, and the usage of diacritics for transcribing or marking tones introduced additional difficulties. "Exotic characters" were difficult to find, type and print; consequently, various practical measures have been taken since their introduction in attempts to avoid them (see Berry, 1958; Swadesh, 1965; Tucker, 1971). The discussion on the marking of tones by diacritics and the marking of tones in writing and printing various African language systems, in general, is interesting even psychologically. In most cases which are perfectly justified linguistically, the marking of tones in the writing or printing African languages became the subject of an earnest discussion. In these discussions linguists were usually on one side, the majority of the practical language-users (readers, writers, editors, teachers etc.) on the other side. The latter were usually against this marking of tones in general, the former obviously in favour of it. As spontaneous adaptations of the Arabic script for writing various African languages were dealing often with a similar problem, the whole question appears as inherent strictly in alphabetic (phonographic) scripts used in Black Africa. No such problems appear to exist in other, typologically different scripts used in this same area. It may be that the syllabic (or even morphemic) types of script are better suited to the transcribing or writing of languages in which the tone is distinctive at the syllable (or morpheme) level. As Hill (1967, p. 97) stated: "...all phonemic systems (i.e. writing systems, P. Z.) are to some extent partial, in that all slight or omit the suprasegmental phonemes." One may say that it is perhaps not by chance that most "local" West African scripts are syllabic (or morphemic) in character. They are certainly linguistically much more appropriate for writing the languages of that area, as no tone-marking problems would have arisen in their usage. Social and cultural factors, however, have thus far acted against them and in the favour of the phono-graphic (alphabetic) scripts. This is not a unique case of such a conflict between the linguistic and social factors influencing the choice of script (see Berry, 1958, p. 752).

Generally speaking, no adaptation of the Roman script to the written usage of African languages complies entirely with both the theoretical and practical principles of good orthography in that area. Two such principles were established by H. Wolf (1954) in his attempt to unify the adaptations of the Latin script to the written usage for various languages in Northern Nigeria. The first principle is to unify the orthography of the local vernacular and area vernacular, in order to facilitate educational transition in literacy projects. The second principle is then to unify principles of all vernacular orthographies with the main principles of the respective European lingua franca of the given area, in order to facilitate the transition from basic to higher levels of education. A third problem arises, however,—in our opinion—in the case of the so-called "divided" language communities. By "divided" in this sense we mean language communities divided either between zones having different European administrative languages (Hausa in Nigeria and Niger, Yoruba in Nigeria and Dahomey/Togo, Manding in Gambia and the adjacent French-speaking territories, etc.) or language communities divided between different areas of missionary or administrative language policies. Tucker (1971, p. 628) reports such a situation of an orthographically divided South Sotho community. The South African authorities have introduced a phonetically (IPA) based orthography, issued according to the main principles of the Africa script (cf. Orth. Mem., 1927). The same language community is using in Lesotho (former Basutoland) another orthographical system, introduced by the Swiss Missions. Similar cases of such di-orthographia are well-known in West Africa, notably in the Akan and Ibo language areas (concerning this point, see also Chapter VII). In the case of divided language communities, a third principle must be added: that of unifying the principles of adaption and usage of the Roman (or any other) script for the *whole* language community. Such attempts at a uni-fication are not always easy, especially since in the case of language communities divided between zones having different European linguae francae, the third principle may contradict the two preceding ones. Recent mass-scale adult education and literacy campaigns based on areally important African languages in the rural areas have been undertaken with the assistance of UNESCO in several West African states and have had to tackle some of these interesting problems. Problems conected with the appearance and existence of such "divided" language communities are not, however, limited to the adaptation of the script and orthographic rules; they often exceed even the context of the script-language relationship and the whole process of the development of the newly-arising standard literary norm is strongly influenced by such a division. Certain problems having to do with such a situation are dealt with in Chapter III.

Alongside all these arbitrary, official attempts to adapt the Roman script to the needs of the written usage of the vernaculars in Black Africa, a certain amount of spontaneous adaptation has developed as well. Bad and inconsistent teaching, as well as no teaching at all, has always left room for such spontaneity. Unusual, extreme effects of such spontaneous adaptation are reflected not only in individual written usage in the African languages by people who have not been taught the official adaptation systems, but also in the usage of those who know something about Roman characters or know how to write the European lingua franca. Examples of this type are provided not only by the particular correspondence models, wall inscriptions, lorry inscriptions and slogans, but also frequently by public announcements, warnings, traffic directions, etc. A particularly interesting case is the written usage of an African language in a country where it is not taught, although an "official" adaptation of it exists in another, not too distant African country. This is the rather frequent case of written Hausa outside Nigeria, at least that of Hausa written in Roman characters (the tradition of Hausa written in Arabic characters does not differ, however, in French-speaking countries outside Nigeria from that which used to appear in Ghana); the same can be said about the occasional written usage of Yoruba in Dahomey. Some observers report a slightly comparable situation with respect to Swahili written outside Tanzania, and especially outside former British East Africa. Whiteley (1969, p. 76—77) reports on the usage of Swahili (the Ngazija variant) in the marginal area of the Comoro Islands. Although the official language of these islands is French, the above-mentioned variant of Swahili subsists even in writings: "... notices aimed at the general public are issued in French and Ngazija, usually in the Arabic script..." (*ibid.*).

All such situations probably reflect the process of the spontaneous adaptation of any "foreign" script whenever daily usage creates the necessity or opportunity of using a written text in the "local" language. However, psychologically, socially and even culturally relevant material on such a spontaneous adaptation of both the Roman and Arabic scripts in Black Africa confirms this thesis which has already been illustrated in the "classical" areas: after a transitional period of contact, any script is affected by the process of adaptation and accommodation to the system of the language for which it is newly being used. Such spontaneous, initial "writing" and adapting in Africa could perhaps be identified with the initial stage of the development of the written form of any language (the transcription stage), as defined by Vachek (1959, p. 13). It may be compared to the unsystematic attempts at writing and the existence of written records dating from the early periods of writing in the languages of Europe and of all other "classical" areas. African material, however,—unlike comparable material from the classical areas—has the advantage of its living presence. Whereas written records represent the main, and almost exclusive, evidence of this complicated sociolinguistic situation, which led to such usage in the historical past of writing in the classical areas, similar or comparable written records from contemporary Africa may be analyzed *in statu nascendi;* the whole complex of the language-society correspondence in question may be analyzed as the theoretical background of such written records. From this standpoint, a comprehensive analysis of the entire inventory of writing (including "bad" and marginal writing), as well as a thorough analysis of all written texts in the African languages would undoubtedly be of broader linguistic and literary significance. Moreover, it might well cast additional light, theoretically at least, even on the early history of writing as well as on the process of the creation and development of the written form of languages in general.

6. Function

6.0   Until now, the corpuses of written texts in the African languages have been assumed to be homogeneous. If, however, we proceed to analyze the functions of the respective texts and their quantitative occurences, a rather different picture emerges.

6.1   The situation is relatively simple with regard to written texts in the so-called "local" African scripts. Although the functions and quantity of written texts in such languages as Vai, Bamum, etc., are by no means as restricted as they might have appeared to be some years ago, the corpus of written texts in these languages using "local" scripts is still somewhat different from what might be called "normal" written usage. According to Ferguson (1962b, pp. 8—15), it is more or less a "restricted literacy" (using the term initiated by Goody, 1968, p. 11). Basic epistolary usage and written records do exist. Occasional efforts to record oral literature, or even attempts at mass distribution, continue to be, however, only marginal. Thus we may speak of a basic restricted literacy utilized on an individual, not a mass-scale, level. Unless a drastic change in "language" or "script engineering" or script policies occurs, it is difficult to foresee the necessary preconditions for the further development in these scripts of a literature in the proper sense of the word.

6.2   African language texts written in the Arabic script can be divided essentially into two groups, according to their main function and quantitative basis.
   The texts written in such languages as Gonja, Mamprule and Dagbani, and also texts in such relatively important West African languages as Dyula (Manding) and Kanuri, seem to fulfil only a limited function similar to that of texts in the "vernacular" scripts. Correspondence and historical records, etc., do exist, but few other types of texts may be found. Possibly many other written documents in various African languages, which have heretofore been left entirely unrecorded scientifically, would fall into this category. However, the quantity of such texts in each language seems to be limited.

In the cases of Hausa and Fula in West Africa, as well as Swahili in East Africa among others, texts in the Arabic script are much more numerous and cannot be said to be limited to basic epistolary and recording functions. In these cases, not only local chronicles, lists of chiefs, local histories, etc. exist, but attempts have also been made to record traditional oral literature, especially poetry, and to paraphrase classical Arabic poetry. These two types of written texts in particular reveal rather important characteristics of the transition towards genuine literatures. We believe that e.g. a true popular Hausa literature could have developed from the previous recording of oral literature in much the same way as the so-called "classical" or "Islamic" Hausa literature and poetry, in particular, developed from a long co-existence with analogous forms in the Arabic language: one must, of course, assume the continuing influence of Arabic over the process of growth of Hausa literature, with the Ajami variant of the Arabic script being used. In any case, the character of Hausa texts written in the Arabic script has not been limited to usage by individuals alone, even though relatively little research in Ajami has been undertaken thus far. Copying by hand and reciting in public places have helped to strengthen the mass basis of this written usage; in many aspects, this would seem to be valid for other African language communities in comparable cirumstances.

6.3 The difference between various African languages written in the Roman script, from the standpoint of their functions and quantitative occurence, are even greater than among those written in the Arabic script. In fact, the scale of transitional features seems even broader. Languages with no or very little written usage, which are limited mostly to basic individual or restricted educational, religious and epistolary functions, obviously comprise numerically small and unimportant language communities such as some of the Jos Plateau languages in Nigeria, the so-called Togo remnant languages in Ghana and Togo, etc. (cf. East, 1941, *Works on Ghana Languages*, 1967).

Not all numerically minor languages have failed to develop a broader written usage and a more extended literacy. On the other hand, some numerically important language communities belong to this group. Various transitions—from the restricted, almost individual, written usage towards complete "basic" written usage on a mass scale—obviously exist. Some communities have had a restricted but rather stable corpus of texts, which were distributed on a mass scale (Gã, Nupe, etc.), although the distribution of written texts may have been limited only to certain periods of time. There are also large language communities with considerable corpuses of texts having many literary functions, which are also widely disseminated. This seems to be the case of Yoruba, Ewe, Akan, etc. All these communities indicate tendencies towards the development of a literature, in the modern sense.

Curiously enough, the intersections of zones comprising the two major scripts, Roman and Arabic, have created notable cases of digraphia, in which two corpuses of written texts—one using the Arabic script, the other the Roman script—have arisen. Since these differences parallel other, functional differences between the texts with respect to style, form, content and even language—especially on the lexical level, the question arises of the amalgamation of the two literacies or literatures virtually co-existing within a single language community. This problem is exemplified with a detailed analysis of the case of Hausa (see Chapter VII.).

6.4 In conclusion, it should be pointed out that the complex interrelationships between scripts, languages and vernacular written texts having various functions offer an extremely intriguing picture in Black Africa. Studies of the relationships between scripts and languages, the functions of written texts, and interrelations between the oral and written forms of languages are producing satisfying results, at least with regard to two aspects. First, new light is being thrown on the analogies and differences between the functions of the oral and written forms of the languages concerned. The same can be said of the analogies and differences between the systems of script and the systems of languages for which the scripts are being used. This in turn could throw still more light on the question of the creation and growth of literatures in the African languages, as a process of the fixation of a written form of the vernacular in certain specific functions. A script is obviously the basic precondition for the existence of the written form of a language, just as the written form of a language and subsequent literacy is a precondition for the development of a given literature. A developing literature is, then, a precondition for a literature, in the classical sense of this term. From this standpoint, the relationship between script and language and its analysis constitutes only the initial phase of a complex analysis of the written form of African languages, the inherent and specific form of which African literatures represent.

III. LANGUAGE AND LITERATURE IN BLACK AFRICA

0. Introduction

The question of the mutual relationship between the language and literature of Black Africa has been the subject of a relatively wide discussion during recent decades. Linguistic or sociolinguistic arguments have been frequently combined with social, racial, political and even religious argumentation, while reason has been mingled with emotion, and scholarly criticism with enthusiastic partiality. Some earlier or later contributions, written by expatriates with a long experience in the African field (Berry, 1953 and 1970; Alexandre, 1963 and 1972) appeared side by side with the pioneer African contributions (Anta Diop, 1954) and the modern African scholarly approach (Ansre, 1971; Amonoo, 1963 and many others). Moreover, African data were considered for the purposes of a further theoretical abstraction (Kloss, 1968; Fishman, 1971). The prevailing common aspect of most of these contributions is their stressing of the arbitrary, artificial factor in the establishment of a mutual relationship between the language and literature of this area. In fact, most (though not all) of these contributions tend to ask (or even answer) the basic question: which language or languages are to be used as the languages of the literatures of Black Africa? Within the rapidly changing cultural and political context of the Africa of the 1960's, these questions undoubtedly had a very profound justification. Even this author has contributed a short paper on the subject, of a similar orientation (Zima, 1961). Although the arbitrary politico-cultural implications of the language-literature question cannot be underestimated in any society or culture, in this section we deliberately prefer to study the relationship between languages and literatures not simply as sets of arbitrary (good or bad) human decisions and social acts; rather, we prefer to stress—among other factors—that the language-literature relationship is also the result of a spontaneous, often lengthy process of language (society and language) culture correspondences, which may (and must necessarily, in our opinion) have deep historical sociolinguistic roots.

Although the possiblity of the standard language development under the conditions of a scriptless society may exist (and particular cases, especially in Black Africa, prove this fact beyond any doubt), the study and analysis up to now of the development of standard and literary languages in the "classical areas" have resulted in a certain analytical symbiosis of these two processes, at least in those cases in which (and if) the development of a standard language has occurred under conditions of a writing (or later printing) society. In spite of the fact that in the most recent period a certain shifting of popularity from the written (printed) mass media of language communication towards the spoken (or even visuographical) form has been noted, in certain highly-industrialized societies, and that—at least in the long run—another reverse shift of social interest from the graphical to the spoken form of the languages in question cannot be totally excluded, close ties between the two processes, i.e. that of the development of a standard language and the creation of a literary language, undoubtedly exist.

In multilingual areas (and Black Africa clearly represents such an area), the development of a standard language and the creation of a literary language (or the usage of a language in literary functions) represent two closely-related, though analytically different, stages of the same process. The problem of a language choice represents the first stage of selection, the prevailing character of which is interlingual: the selection and choice is made from among two or more languages used in a particular area or areas. The development of a standard language on the other hand, represents that stage of selection in which the intralingual aspect prevails; in other words: a choice from among two or many language systems is confronted (and often occurs in a parallel way) with the choice of features and phenomena from within one language system. Since, however, no language choice for cultural and social literary communication may be considered as an ultimate and final one, languages rarely if ever develop in a vacuum. Apart from the extralinguistic factors (i.e. social, cultural and other realities), co-existence and contact with other languages play an important role throughout the establishment of a relationship between a language and a literature and result in language interference, which also affects literature.

Hence, this chapter dealing with the problems of language and literature in Black Africa is analytically sub-divided into the three following sub-sections:

a) Language Choice
b) Language Development
c) Language Interference

1. Language Choice

1.0 The factors affecting the choice of a language for the purposes of literature in Black Africa may be studied according to:

a) the opportunities prevailing with respect to a language choice (potential or real);

b) the actual operation of the language choice.

Similarly, distinction must be drawn between a multidimensional choice (one from among many) and a more or less bilateral choice (either-or).

Although particular correspondences between certain historical, sociolinguistic and socio-cultural or even political periods of the development of languages and literatures in Black Africa can certainly be observed, these criteria have mutually interfered and intersected each other in different periods of language and literature development.

1.1   The opportunities prevailing in the lengthy and often slow process of a spontaneous choice of literary languages were obviously different in the pre-colonial and colonial periods. The post-independence periods have changed the situation only in certain areas so far.

1.1.1   The prevailing aspect of the choice of literary languages (and hence, the transition from writing or recording languages towards writing the first stages of literatures) in the pre-colonial period was the obvious predominance of internal, African linguistic factors and opportunities.

If the existence of a certain script in that period can be presumed for certain areas (see Chapter I.), the literacies thus created—unless further research produces evidence to the contrary—served only one language community on the whole. Enclosed as it probably was within its own language barriers (evidence concerning possible translations at that stage is scarce), and sometimes only within the barriers of a section of a given language community, such a literacy hardly had to confront the problem of a language choice. The price paid for such an easy solution to the problem, to become so painful for future generations, was, however, a certain isolation and even a sort of intraversion of such a tribal literacy.

On the other hand, such isolation was probably never total; it was mostly literacy and literary works in the pre-colonial period which felt the increasing influence of external cultural and linguistic factors. Alongside the "mythological" literacies in the presumably "local scripts", literacies in the Arabic script appeared together with the spreading influence of Islam in certain areas, especially during the last four centuries. The factors affecting the choice of a language immediately manifested a different dimension, as the literacies and literatures in the African languages co-existed and competed not only with each other (i.e. Hausa and Fula, for example), but also with the literature or literacy written in the Arabic language and script, though often by local (non-Arabic) writers for local (non-Arabic) readers. Thus, the multidimensional and the bilateral opportunities for the choices of the languages of Black Africa literatures seem to have been long and deeply rooted in the pre-colonial period of that area. The often difficult choice of a language is frequently the price which must be paid for the broadening of these peoples' social, cultural and even technological horizons.

1.1.2   The colonial period brought with it—at least in its final stages, when new territorial, political and cultural entities were established—a further complication of a twofold character:

The important Indo-European (IE) languages of the respective administrations competed not only with the African languages of the areas in question, but in the Islamic areas with Arabic as well. Owing, however, to the particularly strong position and prestige of their technologies and cultures in the late 19th and early 20th centuries, their influence became so strong that in a certain way, and in certain areas, they ultimately simplified the question of a language choice, at least in the short run and for written literature. This was the case of those territories in which the language policies of the last six or eight decades clearly favoured the exclusive written usage of the IE linguae francae. Apart from sporadic missionary or literacy efforts, whole areas of Black Africa became—at least for the time being and in a socially restricted sense—literally (or sometimes merely graphically) monolingual. Such a superficial solution of the language choice problem continued to be valid (or even more strictly valid) in the early post-independence years of most French-speaking areas; they could perhaps be labelled as "French-writing". In the oral sense, these areas are mostly still bilingual or multilingual.

Moreover, the colonial powers' "scramble for Africa" influenced the opportunities for a choice of language for literacies and literatures in another, indirect way as well. It often—though not always—cut across old frontiers, barriers and communities frequently creating new ones in a completely new and different way. It reoriented in these areas the cultural (and hence ultimately also literary) life toward new centres, while the ancient centres were either abandoned or fell into partial oblivion. The whole question has thus been oriented towards a new framework and context. Under these new circumstances, the ancient choice of a language or languages for literary purposes, the roots of which had been objectively, spontaneously prepared by numerous pre-colonial generations, was rendered either unworkable or became acceptable only for a part of the original community. One may speak about the rare case of a one-to-one correlation between the African mother tongue and a new political entity (such as Somalia), a partly one-to-one correlation (the Malagasy Republic), the correlation between several major important languages (often regionally distributed) and a new state entity (Nigeria and its major languages: Hausa, Yoruba, Ibo, Fula, Bini and several others), or of the correlation between a state entity and many splitter languages, but with a single "surface" lingua franca. Tanzania became a famous example of such a type of correlation, especially owing to its courageous post-independence language-policy decision. Other correlations, most of them created by the reshaping of new geographical entities in the last decades of the 19th century or early years of this century, might be mentioned as well. A factual analysis of the sociolinguistic map of contemporary Africa could provide detailed conclusions, as suggested in a general way by the language-nations typology proposed by such authors as Kloss (1968) and Fishman (1971); especially the latter typology includes data from Africa. Most recent attempts to focus such a typology on Africa (Brauner, 1973, Ohly, 1974) are very successful.

1.2 But apart from the long-term opportunities of a language choice, even its daily operation with respect to the writing and reading of a literacy or literature has profound literary importance. This is especially true of those areas in which a competition between and co-existence of literacies or literatures in different languages exists. The relationship between a literature in English (with its Standard and local varieties) and literatures in the African languages, which has been characteristic of certain periods of the literary life of particular African areas, appears to offer a rich field for the study of such an operation (known sometimes as the switching of languages for literary purposes).

1.2.1   The operation of the choice of a language for literary purposes does not seem to be reducible to a merely linguistic factor in this context, although language capacities and opportunities obviously also play a decisive role. In our opinion, the operation of a language choice must be analyzed in certain respects also as an external phenomenon of the general differences of the entire cultural orientation, tastes, style of life and habits of either the authors' community or the readers' community, or both.

Curiously enough, the dividing-line would seem less profound, as far as the authors are concerned. True, the majority of authors of today's so-called vernacular literatures come either from pedagogical circles clustered around village and city schools (teachers, head-masters, former educational officers or missionaries); these are, however, not the only authors preferring such a language (and hence ultimately also such a literary) choice. New literates and also "modern" intellectuals have appeared side by side with Muslim dignitaries or traditional scholars, contributing occasionally to this type of literature mostly in their mother tongues. Exceptions in the reverse sense ("vernacular" authors writing in a language which is not their mother tongue) are limited usually to those authors who write in an areal lingua franca (e.g. Alhaji A. Tafawa Balewa in Nigeria). The exceptional cases of intellectuals who have started their literary activity with a contribution in the vernacular (or local African variety of English) and who later became renowned authors, preferring the standard form of English, are well known.

Most authors writing in an African Language under such conditions have been at least partly bilingual. As they have realized that many of the vernacular publications are (or were) produced by small administrative or missionary printing-shops and editing centres or local printers, and are available only to certain sections of the community in question (see further remarks on the distribution problem), they have always tended to produce their works either bilingually or to publish subsequent English abridgements and re-editions for the broader public. Moreover, most of these authors have had at least a reasonable knowledge of African literature published in English. The reverse is, however, only partly valid: those writers who have produced most of their African literature in Standard English and who knew at least something about the so-called "vernacular" literature (even about literature written in their mother tongue) have been—at least until fairly recently—very rare. Hence, the possiblity of an introduction of so-called "vernacular" topics into modern intellectual literary circles was also scarce: Ekwensi's attempt to translate from Hausa literature must be considered an exception in the past; thus the most recent translation of Fagunwa's book into English, by W. Soyinka, clearly represents an encouraging reverse phenomenon in this respect.

It should be noted, however, that the need to create "bridges" between the "vernacular" and "Standard English" (official) literatures was also felt by some authors who started from the vernacular to become top-level academic or research and cultural personalities (Nketia in Ghana, Babalọla in Nigeria and several others).

The differences between reading communities are probably more profound. In fact, when the actual reading communities are taken into consideration, the choice of languages for literary purposes implies in certain areas a switching over to a substantially different audience. From this standpoint, African literature written in the vernacular languages is addressed to and read by not only new literates who are ignorant of the essentials of English, but also to considerable sections of the rural reading population and last but not least to the majority of those comprising "the man-in-the street" group in the large and small towns: petty clerks, messengers, night-watchmen, lower-rank policemen (the former so-called N.A. police in Nigeria, sometimes called "escort" police in the former Gold Coast, later Ghana), members of the working class and even (or especially) petty-traders at markets. Such people have rarely read "official" intellectual literature in the more or less standard form of English. This form has always been preferred, however, by intellectuals, students, senior clerks, officials, teachers and members of the higher technical staff and also—one might be tempted to say—by all university gradutes, but this would be a sort of over-simplification.

The gap between the readers of "vernacular" literatures and Standard English literatures is actually not so very wide. Such an S.E. literature, if good, cheaply-published and well-distributed, may easily find its way to such people. On the other hand, the gap between the vernacular literature and intellectual readers of Standard English is much more profound. Apart from several professionals, this author rarely discovered in the Africa of the 1960's an intellectual who was proud of and—to some extent at least—fond of the literature in his own "vernacular".

Economic factors, and also the mere administrative or commercial organization of book distribution, are to some extent responsible for such a situation. The cost of Standard English literature—even in paper-back editions—is still mostly beyond the economic possibilities of the "man-in-the-street". This in itself illustrates the fact that these books are simply oriented toward other readers. On the other hand, vernacular publications (which are usually subsidized by certain sources) cost pennies instead of the shillings, and shillings instead of the pounds listed on the back covers of Standard English African books.

Even mere access to books has been differently stratified in most areas (although our own actual field experience has been restricted to West Africa only): vernacular publications, produced by various literacy or language bureaux, have been obtainable either from the book-vans run by such bureaux directly in the field, which come periodically to the villages in the bush to reach their readers, or they may be obtained from small, low-cost bookshops or stationers in the town. If, however, direct distribution is abandoned and left to the huge, usually uninterested corporations, the resulting lack of direct contact may be disastrous (cf. Otoo, 1969, p. 44). Occasionally one may obtain them at the market-stalls, around well-known "chop-bars" or near petrolstations (the latter offer "vernacular" publications, or at least the most popular of them, alongside market literature in English). Conversely, however, one can rarely obtain "romance" booklets in most academic or university bookshops or in the book- and magazine-stalls of the large department stores in the cities.

Substantial differences also exist in the field of literary criticism and public reaction. Intellectual literature written in Standard English is created in the general framework of the international literacy criticism published in this language. The African atmosphere penetrates into such criticism of this sort of African literature only through the personal experience of authors, readers or critics of African origin. Non-intellectual African readers have little influence on such criticism, while the African intellectual is by far the most determining voice of such criticism. Contacts between non-sophisticated and specifically non-literarily-oriented African readers and authors have been largely based upon personal communication; few details about such contact have penetrated the field of published literary criticism.

Vernacular literature, on the other hand, has little if any opportunities to receive "official" literary criticism. Critical columns have always been rare, even in the best "vernacular" periodicals, but letters to editors expressing the personal opinions of literarily unschooled readers constitute an interesting and very intensive form of contact between such writers and their readers, if such periodicals exist.

It seems unnecessary to characterize here the main differences in both the form and substance of these two types of literature, which are described in detail in the respective sections of this book.

1.2.2 The factors affecting the choice of a language for literary purposes appear, therefore, in a much broader light. One may be tempted to correlate the language abilities and capacities of readers in the situations analyzed with the social and economic stratifications of African communities; such a correlation is undoubtedly at least partly responsible for the stratification of the two types of literatures. But while this criterion would seem valid for the rural areas where a general knowledge of English (and the IE languages in general) is usually much poorer, the urban situation is more complicated, especially due to the existence (at least in some areas) of so-called market literature in English (for details on this manifestation, see Section 3.2.2). While written in a sort of English (and hence constructed upon the general assumption of a certain knowledge of this language on the part of the anticipated readers), this literature is in some respects not too remote from the style, tastes and genre of most popular vernacular books. Moreover, both its reading and writing communities manifest certain particular characteristics which are common not so much to literature in the standard form of English, but rather to non-pedagogical vernacular literature. This would confirm our thesis that the choice of a language and the switching of a language for literary purposes are indications of a certain fundamentally different orientation of the two literatures in question. While both vernacular and market literature are aimed at the style and tastes of a certain readership, Standard English literature still largely remains oriented toward an entirely different audience.

1.3 The study of the choice of a language for literary purposes and of language-switching in literature is therefore important not only from the sociolinguistic standpoint, but primarily also from the social and literary standpoints. Most contemporary intellectual African literary criticism and history (whether written by Africans or expatriates is as yet unfortunately of little concern) ignores these differences; it usually considers the language barrier as a plausible excuse. We think, however, that their differences run deeper. The language should be seen merely as the symptom of such a difference. This does not mean that these two types of African literature are contradictory in character: in our opinion, they represent two complementary views of African cultural and literary life as a whole. When official literary criticism neglects or refers ironically to the literarily inferior values of a "vernacular" literature, it may be right in one sense: Achebe's novels cannot be compared with, say, certain booklets produced by E. A. Akintan in Yoruba as two equally excellent literary works. They can, however, be compared as complementary evidence of the differing literary life of contemporary Black Africa. In this sense, the study of African literature in Standard English, occasional Krio and Pidgin literary attempts, the so-called market literature in English and "vernacular literature" may be compared to K. L. Pike's matrices in linguistics (cf. Pike, 1960): only a complementary analysis of the data through all such matrices may bring us closer to an understanding of the reality concerned. If the literary history and literary criticism of Black Africa is to achieve its task in this sense, it must approach certain aspects of African literature, hitherto unrecorded in "official" literary magazines and critical columns, through direct field research comparable to the methods used in Africa (as in other areas) by researchers into language and oral traditions. The factors affecting the choice of a language for literary purposes and language-switching in certain parts of African literature will thus become not the obstacles, but the sources of further inspiration.

2. Language Development

2.0 If a language is to serve the aims of a literacy or literature sufficiently adequately, it must undergo the process generally known and analyzed as standard language development (SLD). Although the literary functions of a language may not be exclusively tied to its standardization (as discussed in the introduction to the preceding section), in the present-day period one may still conceive of a standardized language without any literature, rather than vice versa.

2.0.1 The development of standard languages has been analyzed in different parts of the globe. The classical areas, and Europe in particular, have offered many valuable data for an analysis of this process, but non-European areas have also contributed considerably, especially during recent decades, towards broadening the inventory of the relevant characteristics of this sociolinguistic process (Gukhman, 1960; Garvin, 1964; Haugen, 1966; Ray, 1963; Yarzeva, 1969 and 1970; most modern Czech contributions to this problem have been reprinted in Beneš—Vachek, 1971). Africa south of the Sahara has also attracted particular attention of linguists during recent decades (Berry, 1953 and 1958; Whiteley, 1969; Ansre, 1971). Our analysis is also mainly based upon data from this latter area (cf. Zima, 1968) and upon our attempt to define a broader theoretical analysis for a general sociolinguistic typology (Zima, 1975).

Certain general features of language development have been defined by Ferguson (1968, 28—33) with respect to three variables:

Graphization (reduction to writing),

Standardization (the development of a norm which overrides regional and social dialects),

Modernization (the development of intertranslatability with other languages in a certain range of topics and forms of discourse characteristic of industrialized, secularized, structurally "differentiated" "modern" societies).

Haugen (1966) offers a four-dimensional schema of language development: selection of a norm, codification, elaboration of the norm, acceptance. The origins of these and certain other theoretical conceptions were at least partially influenced at the outset by the theories formulated in the early 1930's by several Czech linguists (notably V. Mathesius and B. Havránek). They were reformulated as a concise conception of the norm and codification by M. Dokulil in the 1950's and reprinted in a German translation in Beneš—Vachek, 1971).

2.0.2 In the present chapter, we attempt to analyze certain features and types of standard language development in Black Africa. As data from African areas offer an opportunity to broaden the concept of the more general features of any standard language development, our basic concept of such features is not identical with those formulated by the many works of the above-mentioned authors. The main differences are twofold:

a) The three main variables are understood not as a linear set, but rather as a hierarchy of factors, all three being potential, but not obligatory features of the standard language development

b) None of these variables must necessarily be always binary in character (+ —); a certain binarism was evidently inspired by the nature of the data available in most "classical" areas. The value of African data is that, among other things, they indicate the inventory of the actual manifestations of these variables as being much broader. Thus they confirm the thesis concerning the certain multidimensional character of these variables as a fully possible and justifiable one. Moreover, different standardization features co-exist and overlap in different cases of natural languages.

2.1 Thus, the general features of standard language development used from such a standpoint for the analysis of African data are as follows:

2.1.1 Graphization—in our conception—implies not only a mere reduction of any language to writing, but also to the systematic usage of a given script for the language in question. This in turn leads to the establishment of a written form of this language, in contrast to an introductory or occasional transcription (in the latter distinction, we are in agreement with Vachek, 1959, 13). Moreover, African data require the drawing of a distinction between a simple graphization (one script being used for one language) and a double, or even multiple, graphization: two or more scripts may be used in the latter cases involving one, two or more orthographic systems for one and the same language. The terms digraphia, multigraphia (or di-, multi-orthographia) are used in such a case. On the other hand, the existence of the frequently appearing cases of languages without any existing script, which are still developing some sort of more or less commonly accepted standard norm (a sort of oral standard) confirms the need for a theoretical separation of the graphization feature, as potential (and frequent) in the standardization process, but not obligatory. This need for an analytical differentiation between the concept of a standard norm and any written norm in general has been recently stressed both by Havránek (1971, 23) and Ansre (1971, 680). (More details on this subject may be found in Chapter 1.)

2.1.2 The concept of standardization as established by Ferguson and others corresponds roughly to the two-fold, partially differing aspects of the process of development of a standard language (SLD): the development of a standard language norm which is basically spontaneous and independent of direct individual, institutional or group interference, and that of a codification which is characterized mostly by some sort of interference from the community or its representatives. A specific feature of some African language communities (and of certain other language communities in the Third World) is, however, a transitional phenomenon between standardization and codification in this sense. In these areas, certain natural correspondences between language systems and social or cultural systems have often been artificially interrupted, principal communication channels reoriented, and new social groups or constitutions imposed upon social entities which had existed for centuries within other frontiers. In such cases, the natural process of standardization in its spontaneous sense (i.e. the integration of dialects, the development of a standard norm gradually imposed upon territorial or social dialectal norms, etc.) did not always proceed according to the real requirements of social communication. Perhaps one of the reasons for this was that the former correspondence between language and social structures were disrupted or restricted, while the new correspondences did not have sufficient time to develop. At any rate, the resulting social situation required a type of universally-accepted standard, but the existing language situation was not adequate enough to provide an obvious choice of such a standard. As a result, attempts at an "arbitrary" standardization were begun, which came into being usually as a result of the spontaneous needs of the society or entity in question, but which resulted ultimately in various sorts of interference on the part of linguists, educationalists and administrators, into the sphere of language/society correspondences. The ultimate effect was usually an artificial attempt to select and impose a certain norm in the position of a standard. As this process, which implies the arbitrary selection of the very basis of the future standard, must be distinguished from that of a mere codification interference into some sort of actually existing spontaneous standard, we shall distinguish henceforth between:

a) Spontaneous standardization.
b) Standardization based on arbitrary interference and choice (arbitrary standardization).
c) Codification of the existing spontaneous base of a standard.

2.1.3 Modernization clearly appears to be one of the most debatable of all the features thus far analyzed. Apart from the timebound meaning and validity of the term "modern", "modernity" or "modernization" themselves (cf. Ferguson, 1968, 32), the relativity of which is obvious from all standpoints, one may also discuss the quantitative aspect of this process. In current linguistic usage, modernization has been understood primarily as a process of expansion or growth, both in the sphere of lexicon and in the sphere of discourse styles in general. Field research into certain African languages, both in their original and in their "transformed" social and cultural environments, leads us to believe that this quantitative growth and expansion should be understood as only *one* aspect of this entire process. In our opinion, while important new areas of lexicon are being added and new discourse styles are being created, the entire process of "modernization" cannot be characterized by growth alone, since simultaneously with this process of growth a parallel (and virtually necessary) process of loss in the lexicon, and even in the inventory of discourse styles, is taking place. This concerns most areas of the lexicon which are directly or indirectly related to the ancient (or traditional) style of life and work and the traditional culture generally. In such a way, the growth and increase in the lexicon and inventory of discourse styles incurred by the process of "modernization" is often almost offset by a symmetrical reverse process affecting the same language spheres (for details, see Zima, 1975).

Thus, the entire process of modernization, the very concept of which no one doubts, should be seen as a shift in both the centre and the periphery of a lexicon and in the inventory of discourse styles as a whole. We prefer, therefore, to call this process the *reorientation,* rather than *modernization,* of a language. Moreover, the complex social and cultural conditions of language development in Africa south of the Sahara have created situations in which some language systems have been subjected not to one, but to two (and possibly even more) reorientations in different periods and under different cultural influences. On the other hand, this same complexity in this area offers evidence of languages which have not been subject, until fairly recent times, to such a process of reorientation.

2.2   In general, we may say that both the three main features of "language development", as formulated by Ferguson, Haugen and other authors, as well as the norm-codification dichotomy inherent in Czech general linguistics, are subject to various modifications, if confronted with the relevant features of the standard language development (SLD) in Black Africa. In the following section, we shall attempt to formulate certain basic types of such sociolinguistic processes in that area, and we may find that the validity of such types may well exceed the strict geographical frontiers of that part of the world. We are, however, well aware that any such typological abstractions will not correspond precisely to most concrete examples. It seems impossible to establish any precise dividing-line between the characteristics of the different types of sociolinguistic processes; some of them undoubtedly overlap two or more types, so that—as in any typology—transitional phenomena are frequent.

2.2.1   Generally speaking, we feel that the following three basic types of standard language development emerge in Black Africa:

a) Languages manifesting a double graphization, double reorientation (mainly successive in time) as well as spontaneous standardization;

b) Languages manifesting a single graphization (with the possibility of di- vs. tri-orthographia within a single given script), single reorientation and spontaneous standardization often based on the oral form of the developing standard;

c) Languages with a single graphization and reorientation (if these have occurred at all), with an arbitrary standardization.

2.2.2   The first type obviously resembles in certain features the classical sociolinguistic features of the development of standard literary languages in the areas outside Africa, including Europe and the Middle East. The two most widely used languages in Africa south of the Sahara—Hausa and Swahili*—though different in their genetic origin and the typology of their respective systems, offer important sociolinguistic features which entitle us to make a comparison, if not an identification, within the scope of this sociolinguistic type.

2.2.2.1   The original impetus for the spreading of Hausa and Swahili over relatively vast areas of Africa south of the Sahara in their function as linguae francae was obviously similar, being essentially economic in character (cf. Whiteley, 1969; Westermann, 1950). Hausa, like Swahili, was primarily accepted in vast regions as the language of the market and trade. It should be stressed, however, that both these languages and their economic importance were directly or indirectly linked with the importance of pre-colonial inter-African trade, commerce and markets. The importance of Hausa, moreover, was extended during some periods along the trans-Saharan economic routes into several areas outside sub-Saharan Africa proper, i.e. into the otherwise Arabic-speaking areas of North Africa, Egypt and the Sudan, or even into the pilgrimage centres of the Arabian Peninsula. Non-economic factors also appeared in the earlier periods of the dissemination of these languages. Such factors seem to have been more intensive in the case of Hausa, where the identification of the language with its ethnical background played a role. Religious and marginally other ideological factors were also of importance in both cases, especially in their broader cultural reperscusions, thereby influencing the graphization and reorientation (or rather, initial graphization and reorientation) processes· A spontaneous standardization (or development of a literary standard) took place in both

---

* The idea of a sociolinguistic comparability of the two main African linguae francae grew out of a discussion held by the present author with Professor Jack Berry, Lyndon Harries, Ali Mazrui, John Paden and the late W. H. Whiteley in 1966, and on some later occasions. The formulation of the following paragraphs owes much to them in various ways, although the final responsibility for them is that of the author. A more sociologically oriented attempt to analyse the types of the 'linguae francae', was published recently by B. Heine (1970). Owing to the character of the present book, which studies languages in Africa predominantly in their relation to writing nad literature, we did not restrict our sociolinguistic comparison to the 'lingua franca' usage, but we included into our consideration also the native language communities, speaking the respective languages as mother tongues.

cases, although its development was slow and irregular. In both cases, the developing norm which was superceding the regional and social dialects reflected the competing rivalry of dialectal factors emanating from centres having differing socio-cultural and politico-economic importance. In the case of Hausa, this is to be seen in the competing dialectal features of Kano and Sokoto during various periods of the development of Standard Hausa, while in the case of Swahili similar factors have appeared in the Zanzibar-South Kenya areas and perhaps in other centres as well. We should stress, however, that some degree of spontaneous standardization occurred in both cases, without any outside interference. Moreover, these integrational factors were not identical with the economic factors which were the basis of the spreading of both these languages as linguae francae. This was of particular importance during the late pre-colonial and early colonial periods, when the economic basis of the inter-African commercial exchanges and markets which used these languages as their media of communication was considerably decreasing. Thus, the gradual deterioration of the traditional inter-African commercial and trade routes did not have the immediate consequence of a decreased usage of the respective language in their central domestic areas. In the peripheral and remote areas, however, this situation obviously occurred, so that the usage of Hausa in North Africa, which was apparently quite considerable even in the early years of this century, is no longer as extensive today. One may well ask to what extent Hausa is still in use in the oasis area of the ancient trans-Saharan routes.

2.2.2.2 In the spheres of culture and ideology (and their respective administrative bases) both the Hausa and Swahili language communities also manifest certain curious similarities and common differences. Both have been subjected to three partially different cultural factors, though these factors influenced them in somewhat different chronological periods. The traditional African systems of thought and culture constitute the origin of the cultures corresponding to both language communities, although they may reveal a differing and heterogenous picture in West and East Africa respectively. The Islamic religion, ideology and culture influenced both areas in succession in different historical periods, and partly also in different forms. The impact of the Middle East (but also that of certain other, more remote Islamic areas) was felt simultaneously with this influence of Islam. It included language interference with the main "prestige" language of the Middle East, which is also the language of Islam, i.e. Arabic. The impact of Europe in these two areas was not, on the other hand, so directly connected with the influence of Christianity, at least in the main centres of both Hausa and Swahili-speaking language communities. The European cultural and ideological influence, however, became the predominant influence, due to the fact that it was backed up by the impact of contemporary technology and education (and last but not least, by the colonial administration which inspired it). All these multiple cultural, economic and social factors therefore created a situation in which these two languages developed differently from the classical European pattern. They were subjected to a double graphization and double reorientation.

The graphization of both Swahili and Hausa by the Arabic script occurred under different conditions. The orthographic conventions and habits acquired by both languages were also different. The European influence also ultimately led to a second graphization in Roman characters. In both cases, this literacy in the Roman script is restricted territorially (it was applicable in the case of both Hausa and Swahili only in certain colonial territories) as well as functionally. This latter, functional restriction creates a situation in which the literacies in both the Arabic and Roman scripts are limited to certain styles and types of texts. The final result of this double graphization is, however, different in the Hausa and the Swahili language communities. In our own opinion (expressed in detail in Chapter VII.), in the case of Hausa, the usage of the Arabic script persits in certain functional styles and in some literary genres, while the written usage in the Roman script seems to be also subject to a certain functional specialization. The final result in such a case seems to be the different functional load of both scripts. Moreover, under such conditions the script is becoming a relevant feature of functional discourse styles. Owing to partly differing sociolinguistic conditions, the situation of Swahili does not appear to be identical, at least from this standpoint.

Analogical features appeared even in the process of the double reorientation (or modernization) of the two languages. Both languages were, in fact, subjected to two successive, different reorientations or "modernization" processes: the criteria of "modernity" were imposed in the chronologically earlier case by the general framework of Islamic culture and the Middle Eastern style of life at that time, whereas in the latter case they were adapted in conformity with the conditions of European social life and technological progress. Although abundant parallelism exists in the spheres of chronology, the influence of religious and ideological trends as well as language contacts with the Arabic language, the respective IE languages, and English in particular, in some areas and in some social groups lead one to believe that these reorientation processes may have been received with differing responses. We must assume, accordingly, that the double process of reorientation (or "modernization") did not affect both language systems in the same way. Some marginal territorial dialects may have been affected by this process differently than the dialects in the central areas. The following example may well illustrate such a non-similar influence of a reorientation process in the case of marginal and central dialects. A comparison of the lexicon of a WNW marginal Hausa dialect*) with Standard Hausa reflecting mainly the usage of the central Kano-Sokoto dialects with repect to the active usage of loanwords from Arabic which were undoubtedly one of the symptoms of the Islamic reorientation of Hausa, provides the following results:

a) Entire important areas of Hausa lexicon, which have been borrowed from Arabic and incorporated into Standard Hausa usage in the central areas, are practically

---

*) This comparison is based upon this author's material collected during field research into the WNW marginal dialects of Hausa in the area of Dogondoutchi, Republic of Niger, in 1963 and 1967—68 (see Zima, 1969 a, 1970 e.a.). These field trips were suported by the Oriental Institute of the Czechoslovak Academy of Sciences, the CNRS, CNRSH and the University of Ghana. We are grateful to these institutions for their support and encouragement.

unknown in the marginal WNW dialectal areas. Instead, older or different Hausa lexical elements or loanwords from other African languages function in their place. This is true not only of substantial parts of the abstract and cultural terminology, religious terminology, etc., but also of such words as the names of days of the week, the names of the months, periods of time, etc.

b) Some of the Hausa loanwords from Arabic, which are otherwise quite usual in the Standard Hausa of the central areas, are little known in the WNW dialectal area, or are used parallel with old, different or local dialectal Hausa expressions; such is the case of the higher numerals, basic units of weights and measures, certain administrative terms, and some common names of both domestic and bush animals.

The same area of the WNW marginal Hausa dialect is, however, characterized by a much greater number of French loanwords in Hausa than is the case in the central areas. Conversely, certain English loanwords are much rarer than they are in the same central Nigerian Hausa areas.

This brings us to the preliminary conclusion that—at least in the Hausa area—these reorientation processes may have influenced differently the central (Standard) norm of the language and certain peripheral dialects. Moreover, the effects of these two reorientation processes may well have been different. The results of the earlier reorientation might have influenced broader areas, but some peripheral (marginal) dialects may still have remained unaffected by them. On the other hand, however, dialects closer to the central area may have been influenced by the earlier reorientation, but not yet by the latter. Moreover, as the second reorientation has affected both language communities in at least two variant forms (English and French; the case of Swahili is more complicated from this point of view, as the German linguistic factor was very noticeable in that area) with a certain degree of reorientation being initiated from the marginal, rather than central, areas, the latter reorientation may have affected certain peripheral areas sooner than the central ones. In such marginal areas, the effect of the former reorientation may well have been "skipped over" (for details, see Zima, 1964).

2.2.2.3 Thus, although differing in their linguistic structures and genetic origins, Hausa and Swahili offer a very rich field for sociolinguistic comparison, both as developing standard forms of languages and as languages of wider communication and understanding (linguae francae). This double graphization and double reorientation also appear in the case of other languages of Africa south of the Sahara. The languages which came under the Islamic influence in the past and which during the colonial period were subjected to some form of "indirect language policies" are mostly of this type, although by no means all the language communities, which due to historical chance happened to fulfil these conditions, have followed indentical or even similar paths of development in terms of their standard literary forms. Some of them never achieved such importance in communication as Hausa and Swahili (this seems to have been the case of such languages of West Africa as Gonja, Dagbani and even Kanuri). Some other languages did not develop a single literary norm; in other cases, one graphic form has remained a more or less unaccepted, dead, graphical system for the language in question. This was mainly the case of Fula, the rich literary usage of which is to be found even today written mainly the Arabic script. The subsequent reorientation of this language was also mainly achieved in the Islamic sphere. The overlapping of such features of language development with other, subsequently described and analyzed types of development is, however, frequent.

2.2.3 As stated in Section 2.2.1, the second, and perhaps more general, type of development of a standard form of language in Africa south of the Sahara may be characterized by a single graphization and a single reorientation, while some form of spontaneous standardization has taken place in this case. These are mostly the languages of those communities which—until the time of the early missionary efforts and the colonial partition of Africa—were not written, or if some sort of literacy did exist, it was restricted to certain very narrow social groups. If, through non-linguistic (or rather historical) chance, these language communities, or at least important sectors of them, happened to be situated in territories having some sort of "indirect" language policies, they were subjected to a relatively recent single graphization (mostly in Latin characters or their derivatives) and a reorientation toward the European style of life and technology.

2.2.3.1 In spite of the lack of any graphization until fairly recently, the languages of this type spontaneously developed at least a few basic features of a supradialectal standard form. This is probably a sociolinguistic type of developing standard which may also have existed in many "classical" areas as well, especially in the past. In such areas, initial tendencies to establish a supradialectal sort of "oral" standard might have existed, but the later emphasis on the written form of the language and graphization of the standard form has perhaps overshadowed this fact. Actually, the very term "literary standard" was created on the basis of materials adhering to classical European standards, in which the standard was always parallel to the written form of the language. Africa south of the Sahara offers dynamic evidence for the theory that a sort of dialectal integration, developing perhaps from a supradialectal koinē, may constitute the basis for a supradialectal, more or less generally accepted standard form of the language, even in those language communities which have no script. The existence of only the oral form of a language may have influenced the rate of development of the standard language, the degree of its acceptance by speakers of different dialects, and the limits of its validity. In spite of this, it seems to us that social, economic or cultural factors, if favourable to the development of such a standard form of a language, were not, in fact, contraindicated by the absence of the written form of the language and the subsequent lack of any literacy. Whether these were supratribal tendencies to form more advanced state units (as seems to be the case of the Yoruba language community, for example) or common economic and ideological bonds, these supraregional tendencies nevertheless clearly occurred in many areas of the development of an "oral standard' in Africa south of the Sahara.

2.2.3.2 Both the late graphization and late reorientation of the respective languages of this type had, therefore, very solid, objective sociolinguistic roots, so that these short-term language policies acquired objectively favourable long-range perspectives. Certain problems arise in Black Africa, however, in this particular type of development of a language standard, for two reasons:

a) either two or more different orthographical systems for one single graphization of one single language have been introduced,

b) or these and deeper problems arise in connection with the situation of so-called "divided" language communities (i.e. original African language communities divided by the arbitrary character of new administrative frontiers into two or occasionally, more zones of differing language policies).

A single graphization with successive, interfering or simultaneous double ortho-graphization is not particularly rare, especially with respect to what might rather vaguely be called the West African Coastal Type. In some other cases, a double orthographization reflects here an administrative division (e.g. the double or triple orthographization of Hausa), but this sometimes occurs even within the political frontiers of a single administrative unit. The former Gold Coast—today the Republic of Ghana—un-doubtedly offers a rich inventory of di- or multi-orthographia, which is based, moreover, on different dialects of the same language (this seems to be the case of Akuapem and Asante-Twi) or on efforts to orthographically unify two closely similar languages: Twi and Fante. Two or more different missionary centres, or a missionary centre and an administrative centre (which sometimes initiate their graphization attempts from two opposite dialectal areas), might have been at the origin of such a complex situation which in some cases also reflects previous feuds or segmentation problems (cf. Ward, 1945). Such cases of di- or multi-orthographia in connection with possible administrative or religious divisions have obviously not been restricted to the West African coastal belt alone. Tucker (1971, 628) reports interesting comparable cases from South and South-Eastern Africa—(see details in Chapter II., paras 5.3. ft.)

The divided approach to some African language communities, which in the pre-colonial period might have developed certain tendencies towards a single standard language form, is, however, affecting—apart from script and orthographies—their lexicons and occasionally even their grammar, as well. The existence of two variants of reorientation (each centred around a particular variant of a European style of life and system of values) creates problems, even in the fields of education, culture, literature, etc., if communication between members of a single language community is required (for details, Zima, 1958).

2.2.4 A third, sociolinguistically rather complicated type of standard language develop-ment in Africa south of the Sahara can be characterized by the absence of any marked spontaneous tendency toward a dialect integration and the development of any supra-dialectal norm, at least, during recent periods. Such dialect clusters (the term was introduced into African linguistics by Diedrich Westermann and Margaret Bryan, 1952) often do not manifest, at least in their present form, any tendency towards spontaneous standardization, in spite of their obviously close genetic relationship and usually high degree of mutual understandability. The present lack of any such tendency towards integration may not always correspond to the lack of such a process in the past, since in fact the very existence of such closely-related dialect clusters (in contrast to clusters of mutually-related languages) testifies to certain previous integrational tendencies. But the present nature of such a sociolinguistic type of language development points to the fact that such integrational tendencies which must have affected these language communities in the past were probably replaced—under historically, socio-politically, economically or culturally unfavourable circumstances—by opposite, disintegrating tendencies. Instead of a further integration of dialects and the creation of a supra-dialectal standard norm, this development must have halted and a disintegration of the already partially integrated dialects must have taken place. It seems to us that the so-called Malinke-Bambara-Dyula dialect cluster in West Africa could be cited as one of the possible typical examples of such a sociolinguistic development, at least in the last period of colonial administration and the early years of independence. In recent years, however, Bambara appears to become a sort of integration center and focus, at least within the confines of the Mali Republic (see Brauner, 1968, 1973).

On the other hand, however, the particular conditions of certain Third World areas, and especially those in Africa south of the Sahara, might have created—at least during the last two centuries—certain special circumstances of development within this socio-linguistic type. One of the features of the process of the colonization (and conversely also de-colonization) of Africa was undoubtedly a sometimes rather drastic restructuring and re-delimiting of entire social, political and even cultural units and communities, as well as their respective frontiers. As a result of such a process, the ancient language/society correspondences, which had developed during the centuries-long process of a mutual co-existence of natural languages and social communities, were either brought to a standstill or else interrupted altogether. As a consequence, both language and social communities appeared in new contexts (and within new frontiers), with respect to which only some of the previous language/society correspondences could retain a certain degree of their previous validity. New language/society correspondences were created, but they had to build upon the results of the previous, centuries-long correspondences, one of which was the existence of some of these dialectal clusters. One can imagine that, as a result of rapid social changes, such dialectal clusters must have been confronted with situations which required a sort of integrated, supradialectal standard norm. Arbitrary standardization was therefore one of the possible solutions; it was enforced by social, administrative and educational needs for communication. However, as arbitrary linguistic, educational or even administrative interference had to create or choose such standard linguistic norms altogether, the spontaneous bases of which had not even been produced by natural language/society correspondence processes, the results of such "language engineering" were not based upon a natural choice, nor were they the spontaneous result of integration. The results of such language engineering have always been problematic, although some degree of success has been achieved in certain areas. (One may contrast in this respect the well-known tendencies to develop a Union Ibo in West Africa and a Union Shona in South-East Africa.)

2.3 These three basic types of standard language development in sub-Saharan Africa do not, obviously, entitle us to describe the entire wealth of the inventory of standardization features, even in that area with all its richness and variety. Particular varieties of this standard language development process are described and dealt with in various sections of this book, in connection with the factors affecting literary development in various areas of Black Africa. On the other hand, an analysis of certain similarities and dissimilarties of these "paths" towards standardization within the broader context of language/society correspondences—especially at the level of large social communities and entire language systems—enables us to modify or verify certain sociolinguistic patterns which are common in other areas and which were supposed, until fairly recently, to be generally valid. From this standpoint, at least, our analysis exceeds the strict limits imposed by a study of language and literature.

3. Language Interference

3.0 While language choice and language development have always played a primary role in the establishment of literary standards or in the complex process of the borrowing of foreign (imported) languages for the role of new languages for literatures, no language exists in a vacuum. In particular, the cultural position of a literary language always enhances contact with other languages. Such language contacts and language interference may in some cases have only marginal literary repercussions; however, the most intensive contacts are manifested by a high degree of interference of the two language systems. Although contemporary linguistics advocates much caution with respect to the classical notion of language "mixing", which was studied even on the basis of African linguistic data a long time ago, the processes known as "pidginization" and "creolization" clearly reflect that stage of the mutual interference of two language systems in which—to use Labov's words (1971, p. 447)—"we have yet to develop a procedure for arguing 'one system or two...'" Much data from such "classical" areas as the Balkans in Europe have been reanalyzed recently in the light of contemporary linguistic theories (cf. Havránek, 1966), but Africa (together with the Caribbean area) still provides the basic stock of material for the analysis of this particular linguistic process. (Berry, 1962, 1971; Hall 1966; Hymes et al., 1971). While earlier research was focused very much on the interference of non-European, and particularly African, language systems with the concrete Indo-European languages in the area, and while some recent contributions develop this line of analysis in a new way (e.g. Bamgboṣe, 1971; Boadi, 1971; Kirk-Green, 1971), the interference of IE languages into the African language systems is also becoming increasingly an object of linguistic interest (Berry, 1971; Ansre, 1971). The interference of Arabic and certain languages of Islamic literatures into Black Africa clearly constitutes a comparable although historically and chronologically different case (see Greenberg, 1947, Hiskett, 1965b).

Language interference among various non-European and African language systems is also being studied and the very notion of "pidginization" and "creolization" is being liberated—at least in linguistic terminology—from its strict analytical ties with English, French or other IE languages. Research into the "pidginization" or "creolization" of various regional or areal African linguae francae is increasingly coming into the foreground of the approach of the sociolinguistic field to language in Africa (Swahili, Hausa, Sango, Bemba etc.).

The purpose of this section is not, however, to draw up an inventory of language interference features in Black Africa; rather, its aims are more specialized. What we are confronting is the relatively little analyzed question of the possible or real literary usage and repercussions of language interference in this area.

3.1 The penetration of language interference features into a literacy or a literatury may, at least theoretically, originate from two partly different sources:

a) either writing (and script) are introduced into and applied to a particular existing "interference" (mixed) language, which has hitherto been only oral in form,

b) or the parallel co-existence and contact of two (rarely more) languages in their written forms (and possible literary language switching) leads to particular interference on a "mass" scale.

From the stylistic standpoint, language interference features may also appear within the context of a literary work in two unequal roles:

a) either the "mixed" language is used as the stylistically neutral language of the whole literary text,

b) or the literary text is written in another language system (with a substantially lesser amount of interference features), which then functions as the basic stylistically "neutral" language of the text, while the language system with a greater amount of interference features is used as a stylistically non-neutral feature, deliberately illustrating particular literary functions.

A certain correlation between the two above-mentioned sources and the two subsequently described different stylistic functions clearly exists, at least in some cases, but this correlation is neither simple, nor can the two sources be identified with the two subsequent stylistic functions. Sometimes a possible misunderstanding or different understanding of either the source or the stylistic function of interference features may lead to a partly different evaluation or understanding of an entire literary text. Thus, one of the bases of misunderstanding between Amos Tutuola, his West African readers and his Standard English readers abroad is apparently the fact that the interference features considered stylistically netural by Tutuola (and by many of his West African readers) are felt to be non-neutral (exotic) by the latter. The lack of contrast might have been particularly responsible for such an understanding of Tutuola's language in his early books. Ekwensi's *Jagua Nana* represents, however, a completely opposite case: the contrast between the pidginized and Standard English forms enables any reader to distinguish the stylistic function of the pidgin-written parts. Ibo proverbs and short quotations (mostly translated or explained somehow) in Chinua Achebe's otherwise more or less strictly Standard English books also represent an extreme example of such differences.

3.2 Three different types of literary usage of language interference in Black Africa will be briefly analyzed within the context of this section: attempts at a literary beginning in Krio (Sierra Leone), the so-called popular "market" literature to be found especially in certain areas of West Africa, and above all the rather special case of the literary activity of Amos Tutuola as manifested in the interference features of his early works. Interesting attempts to introduce various forms of West African pidgin into the usage of the different mass communication media, including printed or spoken forms of journalism and literature (as reported e.g. by Mafeni, 1971, p. 100), remain, however, for the moment, outside our consideration.

3.2.1 The linguistic and social context of Krio, the language which has developed from the interference of African (and occasionally other) languages into English, principally in Freetown and the adjacent parts of Sierra Leone, has been discussed on a number of occasions, including its present-day usage and possible cultural perspectives (Berry, 1969). Various papers also report on early and recent literary work in this language (Eldred Jones, 1957, 1964, 1971; Thomas Decker, 1964, 1965, 1966).

Krio has been primarily considered within the general sociolinguistic context of Sierra Leone which uses Standard English as its official prestige language—to be a sub-standard form of this language. Hence, its cultural and social prestige (and therefore the prestige of writing or printing in it) have rarely been very high. On the other hand, however, its value for disseminating information among much broader communities than those speaking only the standard form of English, has never been doubted. The same seems to be true of its stylistic value for an immediate imitation of popular forms of language communication, which has been appreciated for a relatively long time. The official newspaper *The Sierra Leone Weekly News* (which is otherwise written and published in SE) is reported to have published a 59-line poem in Krio, describing a reception at the Freetown Governor's mansion, back in 1882 (Eldred Jones, 1964). Other poems in Krio (some of them signed only "J.") have followed. A tendency to criticize the administration—at least in a humorous way—has appeared, while taxation has become the most obvious target of such critics. In one such poem (reported by Eldred Jones, 1964, p. 25), the author invokes all activities for which the administration has prescribed taxation: for getting married, being buried, keeping dogs, selling grog and other drinks, etc. He concludes with a typical West African comparison: *Tenk de lord den mor able for tax foofoo* (ibid.).

Krio has also been used for occasional short articles, feuilletons and marginal "columns" in this same and some other newspapers; most such marginal journalistic attempts have been unsigned. The partly regular "column" published by C. L. Pritt in the early decades of this century in the same above-mentioned weekly entitled "Five Minutes Chat" also displayed a certain amount of Krio usage.

However, an author who was to decisively establish himself as the founder of Krio literary usage exceeding the stylistically functional, humoristic and journalistic genre appeared only later in the person of Thomas Decker. He, too, started his activity in journalism; during the early 1930's he regularly contributed to the so-called "Relaxation Corner" published in another Sierra Leone newspaper *The Daily Guardian*. This corner, later rebaptised "Loosbodi Coona", constituted a further contribution to the journalistic development of Krio.

Thomas Decker's main merit is, however, in introducing Krio into other genres and styles and thereby attempting to exceed the otherwise stylistically limited usage of Krio. His Krio dramatic sketches *Wahalla* (The Trouble, 1939) and *Boss Coker Befo St Petr* (1939) met with relatively favourable responses. Moreover, he has attempted to introduce Krio even into poetic usage. His patriotic poem *Plasas* (The Palaver Sauce) compares the tribes of Sierra Leone to various condiments necessary for a sweet sauce: both must be melted, if the result is to be good. Some of his poems manifest reflective or even lyrical sub-tones: "Yestadey Tidey and Tumara", "Slip Gud", etc.

According to Decker, Krio should no longer be considered a mere sub-standard stylistic form of English, but rather a Sierra Leonian form of English: only from this standpoint can we understand his attempts to translate the dramatic works of such a classical Standard English author as Shakespeare into Krio. His Krio translation of *Julius Caesar* is reported to have been very favourably received when performed on the occasion of the festivities marking the third anniversary of Sierra Leone's independence, in Freetown in 1964. He has also translated *As You Like It*, giving it the Krio title *Udat Di Kiap Fit,* and various short prose.

The poetic usage of Krio, Decker notes, has been further developed by Gladys Hayford, although her poetry has never been published in full (See Eldred Jones, 1971, p. 89).

In the early 1960's, a Sierra Leone Journal having the Krio title *We Yone* (Our Own) published from time to time occasional shorter or longer literary efforts and articles in Krio; various other attempts to use Krio, at least for literacy purposes if not for real literary usage, are reported occasionally. It is still difficult, however, to decide whether Krio will follow the path of literacy and literary development started by Thomas Decker and some other, younger authors, or whether it will remain an "oral", sub-standard variety of Sierra Leone English. The pressure of high-prestige Standard English is apparently much greater in the case of Krio than in other (African) languages, owing particularly to the close structural and genetic ties between the two systems. One may wonder, however, whether it will not be precisely this close similarity but not identity of structures which may lead—at least in the long run—to the creation of a sort of literacy or literary development in this language.

3.2.2.1 The so-called "popular" or "market" literature appearing especially in certain areas of West Africa shares with the literature or literacy in Krio (or at least with some phases of its development, as represented by the activity of Thomas Decker and similar authors) one common feature: a language system which is heavily influenced by interference features from another language or languages is also used as a stylistically neutral literary language. Unlike the Krio literature, this is not an attempt to use an orally existing creolized, and not even pidginized, language in writing and literature. Similarities with Krio, or even the different spoken forms of local pidgin English, are due, rather, to the general fact of the similarities of the systems being interfered with, but the language of market literature is certainly not identical with either Krio or with any pidgin. In fact, this type of literature is occasionally claimed to be written in "Standard English", in the opinion of its authors. One might better call its language "an attempted Standard English"—at least from the standpoint of the language capacities of its authors; as, however, the authors' attempts to utilize Standard English may be—in their average performance—very close to that of the reading community toward which their booklets are oriented, the differences between the English in these booklets and real English Standard could be considered a phenomenon valid for comparative linguistic or literary purposes only. Both the authors and the average reader of these booklets share certain vague ideas about Standard English, and the norm valid in intellectual communities (whether geographically close or remote) is of little importance for them. Some authors therefore tend to characterize the language of these booklets as a "new mad English" (Warner, 1963).

3.2.2.2 Representative collections of such booklets have already been analyzed in their literary and stylistic contexts, mostly on the basis of data collected from the former well-known large Onitsha book-market (Beier, 1964; Nwoga, 1965). Our remarks are in substantial agreement with most of their conclusions, as far as the Onitsha material is concerned.*) The topics, composition and style of these booklets reflect to a considerable extent the style, tastes and cultural behaviour of the average West African urban man-in-the-street. A night watchman, petty trader, labourer or craftsman displaced in the city, far from his native willage to which he still feels deep social, cultural and even emotional ties certainly discovers in these booklets (providing he is able to read to some extent in English) the world of his daily realities and evening dreams. Certain romantic stories and love-dramas may occasionaly remind an outside reader of the cheap love-stories produced by the hundreds for the European and American book-market in paperback editions. In this sense, the popular African reader shares the invasion of such literature of European or American provenience even with his intellectual compatriots. While Young (1971, p. 179) considers that "... a further factor of importance is the increase in the amount of light popular reading among certain sections of the community" and that "Few students are unfamiliar with Cheyney, Charteris or Ian Fleming...", one might say that this is even more valid for the non-intellectual members of the West African communities. Instead of Cheyney or Fleming, illustrated fashion magazines and comics should

---

*) Apart from a study of the two above-mentioned analytical surveys, we have been able to collect some material in the West African field; a collection of booklets from the Onitsha market was kindly recently made available for our analysis by Mr. B. C. Bloomfield, Librarian at the S.O.A.S., University of London, to whom we are much indebted.

perhaps be considered a factor in the case of this average urban-dweller. Examples of sentimental dramas such as *Veronica, My Daughter* written by a certain O. A. Obagi, or stories like *My Seven Daughters are After Young Boys (My Seven Girls are Good For Nothing)*, written by Nathan Njaku, illustrate one such tendency in this genre. The features of crime stories often interfere with overt social criticism and naked pictures of the conditions in which the readers live and the problems they must solve. Example: *The World is Hard* ("Counterfeit policeman runs away. Catcham, catcham, shouted the true policeman..."). The problem of living conditions and accommodation so relevant especially for the migrant city-dwellers is almost politically reflected in a booklet written by Ezekiel Uta and Aaron Aganweze entitled *Landlords and Tenants*. The following, rather attractive and promising short characterization of the book is given: "The fat landlord warns his tenants, who look at him with ferocity mixed with laughter. Such occurrence often leads to fighting and consequently police intervention. Landlords should regard their tenants as fellow equals and neighbours..."

Sexual and sentimental problems are often dealt with either in the "cheap romantic" style, or else occasionally exploit their rationalization and commercialization. Thus, the booklet *Husband and Wife Who Hate Themselves* has the following revealing sub-title: "It was a forced marriage, made by the Chief Monger; as a result of this, everyday so-so quarrel, so-so talk, so-so fight, no peace." Another sub-title speaks about relations between men and women in a rather sober tone: "Money hard to get, but some women do not know..."

Financial and economic questions confronting the ordinary man at each step of his urban life and presenting him with almost unsolvable problems to which he may not have been in the least accustomed in his original village are reflected in the various forms of pedagogically and practically-oriented instruction and advice. Examples: *Money Palaver* ("written by Master of Life, who obtained the title M.L. [Master of Life] at the Common-sense College, where he passed very hard lessons in money-mastering and life problems"). A similar example is represented by the booklet *Lack of Money is not the Lack of Sense* by F. N. Stephen.

A certain pedagogical or even applied character of particular booklets within this genre is rather frequent. Textbooks for learning languages and practical daily subjects of activity are not rare. Thus, a *Modern Hand Book in Business* (Letter Writing, Composition...) offers the following initiation and blessing: "The possesor of this small book will not regret what he spends for it. In fact it can be called and rightly a dictionary of Good English..." Textbooks are by no means limited to the English Language only; a publication entitled *Learn to Speak English, Hausa, Ibo and Yoruba* was prepared by G. Oji (Master of English and Ibo), R. A. Salami, Master of English and Yoruba, and Mallam B. Umaru, Master of English and Hausa. The preface to this work incites one to learn languages in the following way: "I can assure you that you will enjoy this book from the beginning to the end. We must be very happy for this book how to learn Ibo, Hausa and Yoruba, because we do not know them. Oh, buy, how to learn..." (p. 1).

The popularity of oral cultures and folklore in particular is reflected by several collections of proverbs, riddles, sayings and folk-stories published in this same genre and style. For example, *Learn to Speak 360 Interesting Proverbs* ("and know your true Brother") prepared by C. N. Eze is a good example of this type. Moreover, history (or African history, in particular) and especially modern politics are by no means lacking from among the titles of such booklets. Biographies of African politicians are published, regardless of their political opinions—witness the biographies of Patrice Lumumba, Kwame Nkrumah, Joseph Kasa-Vubu, Sylvanus Olympio and others.

3.2.2.3 Up to now, most such booklets have been analyzed as a more or less local phenomenon of the famous Onitsha book-market in Eastern Nigeria. It is certainly true that most of those analyzed in the preceding sections originated either directly or indirectly in that fascinating cultural and commercial centre. One cannot, however, escape the notion that a tendency to publish similar or comparable booklets and literature is more generalized throughout Black Africa.

Two facts cannot be overlooked in this connection:

a) A certain similarity between this popular market literature and particular forms of the so-called vernacular literature exist.

b) Tendencies have appeared under favourable circumstances to publish unofficial cheap "popular" booklets, which are at least comparable, if not similar, in size, topics, style and types of distribution to those in other parts of Black Africa. Missions have sometimes been the responsible and inciting factor, or else various voluntary and commercial organizations and agencies. From the pidgin-based commercial advertisment texts (the popularity of which makes them also a marginal sort of literacy) to the French-written, "popular" missionary booklets which could be obtained at small bookshops in such cities as Dakar or Lomé in the early 1960's—all these publications testify to the fact that though Onitsha represents the foremost literary centre for such production thus far, the soil seems ripe in Africa for the expansion of this sort of reading. Such a situation may well persist until the human, intellectual and social gap between the SE (or Standard French) African literature and the "man-in-the-street" as a reader is bridged in some way.

Comparable publications have begun to appear—for instance, in Ghana in late 1966, more or less immediately after the partial lifting of the press bans and censorship. Such booklets as *When Heart Decides* (continued under the title *Who Killed Lucy?*) written by E. K. Mickson share many features in common with the Onitsha booklets as described and analyzed above, the place of edition (Accra) being not too relevant in this context. The case of the booklet *Don't Leave Me Mercy* by K. A. Bediako (s.a.) is similar, as one might hesitate to state that some of the early works of the Ghanaian author Samuel Asare Konadu (b. 1932) should be included in this genre. Such books of his as *Shadow of Wealth* (1966) or *Come Back, Dora!* (1967), published in Accra during that same period, certainly share several common characteristics with most similar types of "popular" literature. This is not the case of various later books of his (such as *The Woman in Her Prime*, 1967), but in this sense Konadu's development does not seem to be an isolated case, as the transition from "popular", "market" literature towards "standard" literature is characteristic of many well-known West African writers. The case of Cyprian Ekwensi is the best known.

If, however, famous "official" writers such as Konadu or Ekwensi have developed from the "popular" type of literature towards the intellectual standard (incidentally shifting the place of publication and distribution of their books from Africa to Europe or America), at least one West African author has become famous, not owing to the loss of his "popular" style and language interference, but precisely because of having kept these in his literary and language program during the initial periods of his activity. This is the case of Amos Tutuola.

3.2.3 Born in Abeokuta (1920)—a traditional centre of Yoruba crafts, especially wood-carving—he has always remained a typical representative of the common man, despite the fact that his books have been translated into French, German, Russian, Serbo-Croatian and many other languages. (A Czech translation of his first and basic work, prepared by this author and Vladimír Klíma, appeared in 1966.) His books have been circulated among the intellectual communities of Africa and other continents, but Tutuola as a human being seems a stranger in such communities, being personally much closer to the world of petty clerks, messengers, porters and market-traders in the contemporary West African cities. A brief summary of his life illustrates this situation: having started primary school with some success, he was sent to a missionary school in Lagos. The death of his father obliged him to earn his living somehow: he tried to cultivate cacao, to help with manual work and crafts and during the Second World War got a job as an auxiliary worker at an RAF base in Nigeria. After the war, he once again had similar difficulties in finding the right job, but eventually found a suitable junior post at the Colonial Labour Office. His knowledge of English being generally found unsatisfactory even for junior posts, he faced the problem of how to improve it. Thus, various adult literacy booklets played an important role in his life for a time. This might have led him to appreciate the value of the written and printed word, and especially that of stories. Knowing the richness of the Yoruba folk-stories and oral literature from his youth, he was soon tempted to try his own literary luck. With an unsatisfactory knowledge of English, his language heavily influenced by interference from his native Yoruba and everyday pidgin, and with a vague idea of literacy and literatures in general, he started to write his first book. He sent it to a London publisher Faber and Faber who courageously decided to publish it after some basic adaptations. This—in a word—was the simplified path of *The Palm-Wine Drinkard* (1952) into the book-markets of the English-speaking world. As Gerald Moore put it, (1962, p. 38) "... Amos Tutuola was unfortunate enough to be the first famous Nigerian writer..." This was certainly true, as at the time that Tutuola's first book was first published the obvious tendency developed to identify him, his style, his language and his composition with the Nigerian, or even African, style in general, as literary works from Nigeria and Africa were extremely scarce at that time.

Tutuola's first and still basic work is primarily a narrative, combining folk-tales and myths with stories of the daily life of a simple West African in the mid-20th century—a combination of dreams and realities. Such a combination may occasionally reach the stage of a more or less complete interference, when the borderline between the former and the latter becomes indistinguishable both for the reader and perhaps even for the author himself.

The Drinkard's palm-wine tapster, who had procured for him daily portions of his favourite liquor, had fallen from a palm tree and died immediately. What shall the poor Drinkard do? His obvious decision is to follow his tapster to the Deads' Town and bring him back to the world of living people. His journey and quest, trials and suffering lead him through the whole world of myths, ghosts and jinns, intermixed with the world of realities. He must confront ghosts issuing orders like RAF corporals, witches giving instructions in the style of junior colonial clerks, and monsters making noises comparable those of World War II bombers or artillery. Certainly, this is the most remarkable literary syncretism of African (and perhaps also foreign) mythology—a syncretism of oral folklore with some of the features of both world literatures and of the grey, sober, everyday reality of West Africa in the mid-20th century. The language of the book supports or even stresses such a literary syncretism by its typically interference character. Tutuola must be considered a pidgin-writer. He simply writes his English as he is accustomed to speaking it, and this—once more—stresses the narrative character of *The Palm-Wine Drinkard*. Its English is much closer—at least idiomatically—to that which one may hear spoken by an African scribe writing his letters at a market-place, behind his huge, old-fashioned typewriter, or even by a local policeman in a small far-off place in the West African bush. One may be inclined to conclude that at least in syntax and idiomatic constructions the interference features of Yoruba and pidgin clearly prevail over the general English construction. Subsequent parts of the text with "official" or "bureaucratic" hyper-correct phrases stress the contrasts resulting from such a situation.

The book was a great success in two respects: outside Africa it was accepted—mistakingly at that period, undoubtedly—as something exotic and special, inherent in Africa. In Africa itself, however, the only positive reaction we were able to discover on the spot was the reaction of "popular readers" and intellectuals who had kept fresh their contacts with the world of the ordinary individual. The reaction of African literary critics and writers (also to a certain extent some critics and writers outside Africa), was, however, rather harsh. To quote Gerald Moore once again; "In introducing My Life in the Bush of Ghosts, Dr. Parrinder wrote of Tutuola's style: 'It is a beginning of a new type of Afro-English Literature...' It is, of course, nothing of the sort," Moore goes on (1962, p. 57). "The beginning of Afro-English literature is to be sought, if anywhere, in the works of men like Onuora Nzekwu, Chinua Achebe or Wole Soyinka. Tutuola's books are far more a fascinating cul-de-sac than the beginning of anything directly useful to other writers... The cul-de-sac is full of wonders, but it is nonetheless a dead end..."

Although sharing the first half of Gerald Moore's judgement (Tutuola certainly can by no means be considered a model for any modern African writer), in our opinion, the latter part of his judgement is based upon a sort of misunderstanding common to most literary critics dealing with *The Palm—Wine Drinkard* within the context of modern African literature, primarily in the context of the literature written in Standard English (whether in Africa or elsewhere). If it is not a dead end, then it is at least an isolated island among such intellectual writers as Achebe, Ekwensi or Soyinka. Tutuola's work (and especially his first book) is by no means isolated within its own context, which is not identical with theirs. He appears isolated among them as only by chance have his works been edited, printed and distributed in a literary milieu which is not his own and where he has actually gained popularity by the mere luck of having been one of the first Nigerian authors to have his works printed in London. However, if analyzed and evaluated within the sphere to which he organically belongs, i.e. within the literary context of the popular "interference" literature of West Africa, he can be said to be one of its outstanding phenomena. This can be illustrated by the early literary criticism dealing with the parallels and possible sources of Tutuola's inspiration. Various authors have tended to discover different literary origins of Tutuola's inspiration, including classical Greek mythology and Dante Alighieri, despite the fact that it has been increasingly difficult to demonstrate what possible access these literary works might have had into the intellectual life of a junior clerk in a West African colonial administration, who was just beginning to learn English.

Recent studies of Yoruba mythology, and especially of Yoruba literature (including D. O. Fagunwa's work), have shown a much more intensive and real possibility of a direct inspiration. Thus, although he is an isolated phenomenon within the Standard English literature of West Africa, Tutuola is one of the major contributors to the "popular" literature of West Africa, the only difference between him and his less favoured fellow authors being that his books started out right from the London book-market toward the literary magazines and critical columns, instead of following the usual paths of market-stalls, petrol pumps and small missionary bookshops.

The fame Tutuola acquired following the warm reception of *The Palm-Wine Drinkard* was, however, not followed by a comparable reaction to his rapidly following later books: *My Life in the Bush of Ghosts* (1954), *Simbi and the Satyr of the Dark Jungle* (1955) and *The Brave African Huntress* (1958). Though their English became gradually increasingly standardized and their style and composition less strange and "exotic", they did not contribute many new elements, nor did they introduce any substantial innovation into his basic genre. The further they departed from the immediate "popular" matrix and model, the looser became their ties with their popular roots and audience. As a result, they reached a sort of cultural no-man's land: neither intellectual circles nor the "popular" audience accepted them as their own. The short stories written subsequently by Tutuola ("Ajantala, the Noxious Guest", "Ajayi and the Witch Doctor"), refreshing though they may be, offered little alternative to this general fate of his literary work, which represents one of the foremost examples of the literary, cultural and language interferences of the popular milieux of present-day West Africa with the English language and the literature or culture associated with it.

IV. THE IDEOLOGY OF THE BLACK AFRICAN LITERARY MOVEMENT

Contacts between black artists and white artistic circles in Europe and America have always been fruitful. But only the present century has clearly revealed the fact that such cultural influences are mutual. As the black man became increasingly active in both the economic and ideological spheres, the absurd assumption of his inherent inferiority began to break down. The special qualities of Black African art gradually won a certain amount of recognition between the two world wars among the colonialists who, however, were convinced that the domain of politics and economics in the countries under their control should be left to the white man, "in order that the African might develop his own genuine culture".

Thus, modern expansionism has been disguised by romantic-sounding appeals aimed at the conservation of old traditions. These appeals have met with a positive response among certain African intellectuals. Owing to their educational level, this black élite has adopted an essentially foreign way of life, very different from that of the broad masses of the people. Moreover, these black intellectuals' idealization of their peoples' tribal customs and ancient traditions has been further intensified by their comparison with the exploitation, egoism and extreme individualism existing in contemporary bourgeois societies. This idealized approach to the past, which has also been reflected in African creative writing is, however, erroneous; the course of history can hardly be held back, since the development of society may justifiably be regarded as a continual process.

Technological progress is today penetrating those regions where social relationships have not yet advanced sufficiently to ensure its smooth absorption. The lack of realistic attitudes on the part of black African conservatives in such regions is explained by the conflict between the old and the new elements in African social and economic life. If the Africans were to leave research, management, trade and transport in the hands of the white man, they would not be able to sufficiently influence their countries' future development. They would remain dependent, even though the formal independence of many of their countries has already been achieved. In such cases, traditional beliefs and ancient customs would be accompanied by economic dependence and spiritual isolation in contradiction to emancipatory efforts, leading eventually to a general decline and indifference.

However, the new African states have opted for the principle of active participation in political and economic life, thus initiating the process of Africanization. They have endeavoured to develop multilateral relations with other countries, in order to overcome their numerous handicaps. But it is precisely these intense relations that have revealed more distinctly the differences existing between the various countries of Black Africa, as well as the characteristics which contrast with those of the European countries. On the other hand, the formers' economic integration requires the overcoming of tribal differences, the abandoning of old superstitions, a more flexible distribution of labour force and a generally increased standard of education. It is apparent that these tasks cannot be fulfilled all at once. Characteristic tribal particularities have persisted, often leading to internal crises. Moreover, tribal traditions cannot be eliminated through expatriation, intermarriage, discussions, or propaganda. On the contrary, all truly tolerant cultural policies must respect such traditions.

Differences with respect to nationalities may be successfully utilized by the so-called nationalist propaganda, which has acquired exceptional significance in the period of the African revival. African nationalists, however, have rightly understood that they should emphasize those characteristics which the various tribes have in common, rather than seeking those factors which separate them. In this way, they hope to intensify feelings of patriotism in their native countries. The main difficulty of this approach consists in the fact that the ethnic nations resulting from this conception are often not identical with the existing states, the majority of which originated under colonial rule. Furthermore, the concept of nationalism is contradictory to the concept of Pan-Africanism, which is oriented toward forming broader entities that will surpass the frontiers of present-day states. The more powerful countries can undoubtedly become more stable units in the arena of international affairs, but particularist and separatist tendencies, which sometimes assume violent forms, have not as yet permitted the formation of many large African political federations. The uneven, unequal economic development of their countries constitutes a serious handicap, preventing these Pan-Africanists from realizing their aims in this respect. Their opponents feel that in large suprastate entities the economically underdeveloped and backward regions would be privileged, at the expense of the more advanced ones. Linguistic, financial and other difficulties also exist in the sphere of culture. Thus, while nationalism has made itself felt in modern Black African writing, the concept of Pan-Africanism as such has appeared only marginally and sporadically.

These nationalist attitudes have been in accordance with contemporary historicism. The fact that the African countries have their own histories—and in some cases even what is sometimes referred to as their "great pasts"—is greatly encouraging national pride. Scholars and artists have been interested in the gradual discovery of historical data, with some of them going even rather too far in this respect. In the realm of art, an overestimation and idealization of former times has emerged in that part of the world, while a concept which ascribes almost the entire world's culture to the black man has been propagated in certain academic circles. The intellectuals of modern Black Africa understand today better than preceding generations their spiritual affinity to the Caribbean and American blacks, those descendants of slaves exported from Africa centuries ago. This spiritual affinity is chiefly due to an awareness that black-skinned people are also living outside Africa, where they have frequently achieved considerable success.

The emergence of the Negro literary movement before World War II was directly influenced by Marcus Garvey's Negro Zionism, the Cuban *negrismo* movement, and the activities of black Haitian writers. These trends had a common feature in that they emphasized the exclusivity of the black man as a human being set apart from the general cultural context of both North and South America. Since the 1930's, this tendency has become increasingly apparent in the black literary movement whose members, however, had adopted not only certain European languages, but also a good many creative methods developed in the major colonial countries. Particularly the writers of French-writing Africa were strongly influenced from the 1930's to the 1950's by the ideas of European symbolism, surrealism and existentialism. The emphasis they tended to place on the racial aspects gave rise to certain complications, however, particularly during the cultural revival following the Second World War, when it became necessary to adopt more constructive attitudes toward non-black artists. In those countries having large European minorities this imperative was by no means easy. Moreover, racial dogmas sometimes required distinguishing mulattos from pure blacks, etc. The Africans' natural aversion to colonial oppression tended to idealize everything that was black and reject all that was white. This "inverse racism' was partly misused by non-African reactionaries who observed only the "change of colours" and realized the basically unaltered character of this conception. Belief in the black man's superiority and the white man's inferiority is, of course, just as absurd as the old colonial prejudice. Although this belief has occurred in modern African writing only exceptionally, progressive critics, authors and philosophers have found it advisable to warn against this dubious approach.

The conception of nationalism is in accordance with the efforts to form nationalities through the unification of tribes. Essentially it coincides with the political standpoints of most African governments. But a completely opposite tendency can be found in modern African writing, as well. So-called tribalism represents the most powerful opposition to any governmental centralism. Tribalists have often argued that the existing state frontiers are vestiges of the colonial era, that specific tribal qualities are being sacrificed in the formation of new national cultures, and that political ideas should not be injected into culture in such a direct manner. Tribalist concepts have sometimes delayed the formation of national cultures in the modern sense of the term; moreover, they are usually very conservative. These concepts are based on an idealization of the African past, on religious rites devoted to ancestor worship and on a desire to preserve the traditional way of life. The tribalists apparently attempt to persuade the general public outside Africa that only their concept is entirely in accordance with the real needs of the African continent, which, in their opinion, can best be satisfied by themselves. They also underestimate scientific and technological progress and its importance for the development of the African economies. Their conservative approach is perpetuated more easily in the sphere of culture, where—unlike in the economic sphere—certain illusions still exist regarding the presumed self-sufficiency of the African "closed system", or the African system of cultural values.

The tendency to hold to ancient norms is most sharply criticized by those with a socialist outlook. As most countries of Black Africa are dominated by their national bourgeoisies, there are only a few elements in their cultural policies which are directly or indirectly influenced by Marxism. Attempts to apply socialist concepts in various spheres have been made in Guinea, Mali and Ghana (under Nkrumah) where the principles of socialist realism have been more or less successfully accepted and used by a few proletarian writers.

Other authors sometimes refuse to relate their work to contemporary social development: they consider certain present-day regimes rather unstable, and do not wish to have their works affected by any abrupt political changes. They base these views on a demand for artistic freedom and proclaim the need for a differentiated creativity which is closely connected with such freedom. At a time when a great deal of African literary production was decisively anti-colonialist, the first voices were already protesting against uniformity and stereotypes. Some critics recommended that prose writers should devote more attention to psychological analyses of their characters, and that they should limit their portrayals of social situations. If applied to the extreme, this recommendation would have led to sheer individualism and escapism.

Some African authors became escapists mainly for two reasons: either they failed to observe the usefulness of direct attacks on colonialism in the sphere of literary activities, or else they chose to turn their attention to history, which tendency was being manifested in other countries as well. Some South Africans realized that their long, protracted protest against apartheid had not brought any valid results and so they began to analyze the black man's spiritual life. Others did not cease protesting but they were obliged to disguise their radicalism by resorting to allegories, similes, etc. This is particularly true of those authors who still live in South Africa under harsh political pressure—but not of the numerous emigrants living in London and other cities.

A more significant influence is historicism, which exerted a strong influence even at the time of the origins of the black literary movement. Generally speaking, it played a positive role in the first stage of the development of modern African writing as it enhanced the self-awareness of the black writer. Moreover, it helped to define the specificity of his creativity in contrast with that of the highly-developed cultures of Europe and North America. Historicism has often been linked with the evolution of African nationalism. The African past, so long unappreciated by European historiography, is often alluded to by many African poets. Historicism had a special function in francophone Africa, where it neutralized assimilationist policies in education and effectively destroyed the false idea of a close cultural relationship between the French area and the inhabitants of their colonies.

Cheikh Anta Diop of Senegal (b. 1923) in his works *Nations nègres et culture* (Black Nations and Culture, 1955), *L'unité culturelle de l'Afrique Noire* (The Cultural Unity of Black Africa, 1959) and *L'Afrique Noire précoloniale* (Pre-Colonial Black Africa, 1960) stresses the success of the old African civilization. In the first-mentioned book, Diop tries to prove that the ancient Egyptians, whose cultural standard is marvelled at by the whole world, were of Negro origin. This fantastic statement should serve the purpose of encouraging the present-day black man, who, in Diop's opinion, can build his contemporary culture on the cultural foundations of his Egyptian ancestors.

Tendencies towards extreme individualism have occurred in Black Africa less often than in Europe or the United States, but thus far they have always been objected to by the critics. Ideological questions were discussed at the writers' conference in Kampala in 1962. At that conference, the Nigerian poet Christopher Okigbo stressed that creative works must derive from African experience, which is more important than theme or race. The black American poet Langston Hughes emphasized subject-matter, while the Cameroonian critic Bernard Fonlon said that emotion and experience are universally human and cannot form a basis of African specificity. He saw in the concept of *négritude* an expression of chauvinism and a restriction of literary creativity.

Before we begin to analyze *négritude* in some detail, we should make a few historical observations. World War I undeniably revealed the fact that not all white people are colonizers and that some of them are not "masters" at all. The prestige of the white man became drowned in large-scale bloodshed, while the existence of black troops constituted an encouragement of African self-awareness. Complicated interrelations among nationalities were being solved in post-revolutionary Russia and the Soviet doctrine of racial equality and the right to self-determination proved attractive to Africa as well.

Meanwhile, white thinkers and creative artists were searching urgently for the roots of the moral decline that had made itself felt since the last quarter of the 19th century and which was to reach its climax in the horrors of the war. Precisely during the period of colonial triumphs, sceptical warning voices were heard, criticizing the white man's "civilizing mission" in Africa, and especially the methods he was using there. And then the world witnessed the disaster that had been brought about by the most civilized countries, and it began searching for something to counterbalance this omnipotent technology. But in vain—although more interest was henceforth to be shown in the life and culture of primitive ethnical groups, as well as in the philosophy, religion, painting, music, folklore and customs of the Black African peoples.

The popularization of Negro culture in North America and Western Europe was also furthered by Pan-Africanism. The movement, headed by William Burghardt Du Bois, organized five congresses between 1919 and 1945 which stressed the idea of Negro unity throughout the world. Even the 1920's, well-educated Negro authors in the United States were proudly aware of their affinity with the black African masses. Although Marcus Garvey, the founder of Negro Zionism, failed in his attempts to transport his black compatriots from America back to Africa, he nevertheless helped to concentrate public opinion on the intricacy of the black man's position. Writers, not only in the United States but also in the Caribbean islands, dealt with this problem. The well-known American author Claude McKay (1860—1947) came from Jamaica, and René Maran (1887—1960) of Martinique wrote *Batouala* (1921)—the famous novel awarded the Goncourt Prize. Black writers had begun to win international recognition.

At the end of the 1920's and beginning of the 1930's, extraordinary literary activity was carried on by Negro authors in Cuba and Haiti. While the Cuban *negrismo* movement (dating from 1927) emphasized mainly the authenticity of artistic expression, Haitian writers, grouped around the journals *La Nouvelle Ronde, La Revue Indigène* and *La Revue des Griots,* strived to preserve the traditions of Africa's popular bards. Jean Price-Mars struggled for the recognition of the so-called cultural heritage, but the most practical application of these ideas can be found in the prose works of Jacques Roumain (1907—1944). Among the Cuban poets, probably the greatest name is that of Nicolas Guillén (b. 1902), who became a Communist.

Another centre of the Negro literary movement originated in Paris where young undergraduates from the colonies could meet. In 1932, they founded *Légitime Défense,* a short-lived review whose single issue was influenced by French surrealism. Two years later, the journal *L'étudiant noir* appeared, carrying a sharp criticism of the cultural assimilationist policies being applied by the French colonial administration both in Africa and in the island colonies. Léon Goutran Damas (b. 1912) of French Guiana was particularly strongly opposed to attempts to form "black Frenchmen" by suppressing the Negro cultural heritage and by emphasizing French traditions. Damas' collection of poems *Pigments* (1937) was an indignant reaction to the white man's outrageous attitudes and a passionate defence of the black man.

Even more impressive verse was produced by Aimé Césaire (b. 1913) of the island of Martinique. In his *Cahiers d'un retour au pays natal* (Comments on a Return to One's Native Country, 1939) he lauded *négritude* as a philosophical concept. Césaire's neologism *négritude* was at times used by the entire Negro literary movement, particularly in francophone Africa. Césaire's book of poetry denied the formerly widespread assertions concerning the black man's alleged inferiority. In it, he condemns Europe for the injustices committed in the days of slavery and colonization. Like the early works of Damas and Senghor, Césaire's *Cahiers* was influenced by symbolism and surrealism.

Césaire's underlying outlook is the black intellectual's embitterment resulting from the white man's arrogance in his treatment of equally well-educated Africans. The artist's nostalgic feelings, due to his sojourn in an alien milieu, give way to his exaltation after his return to his native country where he can identify himself with the suffering masses. The white man's rationalism is bitterly attacked; Césaire likes to use provocative statements, giving a different meaning to the expressions repeated by the colonialists.

The principles of *négritude* were elaborated by Léopold Sédar Senghor (b. 1906) of Senegal, who became acquainted with Damas and Césaire in Paris. World War II accelerated the development of the Negro literary movement. While the Africans' stands varied considerably during World War I, in the late 1930's most Negro intellectuals adopted a decisively anti-fascist viewpoint. They despised many of the political views of their "mother countries", but correctly saw that the main danger lay in Nazism. In practice, however, the various blocs of colonies had differing fates. French West Africa, whose administrative centre was Dakar, remained loyal to the Vichy government, whereas French Equatorial Africa (with its capital Brazzaville) supported De Gaulle's wing of the resistance movement. The Atlantic Charter also bore some traces of more modern general views concerning racial problems.

After World War II, *la Société Africaine de Culture* (SAC), headed by Jean Price-Mars, originated in Paris. Black artists and thinkers met at two important congresses—in Paris

(1956) and in Rome (1959). In December 1947, the review *Présence Africaine* was founded by Alioune Diop (b. 1910), who later became one of the leaders of SAC. The black literary movement was then becoming more powerful, thanks to increasing numbers of young writers. When in 1947 Césaire's *Cahiers* appeared with André Breton's foreword, *négritude* was considered an offspring of surrealism. Simultaneously, there have been attempts to approach *négritude* as a major concept of francophone Africa.

The Nigerian writer Onuora Nzekwu understood it as "a philosophical concept of the Negro contribution to world civilization" and agreed that "it urged the recognition, acceptance and promotion of a rich and historical Negro civilization" (*Nigeria Magazine,* June 1966, p. 80). He was interested mainly in the programme of *négritude*. Martin Tucker correctly interpreted *négritude* as a historically determined phenomenon and characterized its role in poetry as follows: "It is both an attitude and a style: the assumption of an African personality. Its subject matter roots itself in the history of Africa—in colonial injustice, in slavery and in the slave trade, in exile and in alienation, in the forced assimilation into a dominant European culture... In poetry it is an expression of the Negro rhythm, tone and color" (1967, p. 17). Tucker's interpretation suits the purposes of literary criticism and is—like J. I. Gleason's—concerned with the aesthetic qualities of *négritude* poetry rather than with philosophy. In Gleason's opinion, "the poetry of *négritude* is based on the double assumption that there is such a thing as a black man's style, and that the language of poetry is evocative in a quasi-magical sense" (1965, p. 62).

An interpretation of *négritude* is, however, facilitated if we suggest that *négritude* should be regarded as an actually existing phenomenon, not a myth, a dream, etc. Particularly in the field of criticism, a "mythology" of *négritude* has become widespread. Those who hold to it usually neglect artistic forms. M. S. Dipoko's idea of *négritude* was that of "a sublimation of a social dream" (*The Writer in Modern Africa*, 1968, p. 68). This idea may be applied to Senghor's early verse, but it avoids all essential questions. Clive Wake (1969, p. 50) seems to confirm this by observing that *négritude* "remained, even in Senghor's poetry (except on the level of nostalgia) an intellectual notion". Wake separates the political appeal of *négritude,* resulting from the rise of Pan-Africanism, from its role in the field of modern African writing. Thus he eliminates various "myths" but does not explain why *négritude,* conceived as an intellectual notion, should fail in the search for its African cultural roots.

A symbiosis of real and mystical elements in the traditional art of Black Africa has always been recognized. It might have resulted from Africa's long intimate contact with surrounding nature. But highly sophisticated poets find their inspiration not only here, and it would be rather ironical to ensure world-wide recognition of black cultures through the well-known romantic idea of "the noble savage". Léopold Senghor uses too many poetic images in his philosophical essays. In *Négritude et Humanisme,* he characterizes *négritude* as one's presence in the world, the participation of the human being in the cosmic forces, the communion of individuals among themselves and with everything that exists, from a stone to God. But a number of misunderstandings have resulted from discussing the philosophical basis of *négritude* in vague terms.

Is *négritude,* as Clive Wake believes, a "temporary political myth" or does it possess a more permanent value? In his foreword entitled "L'Orphée noir" (XL—XLI) to the post-war edition of Césaire's *Cahiers,* Jean-Paul Sartre stresses the black man's suffering under colonialism and other negative aspects of *négritude* and concludes that "this negative stage will not satisfy the Negroes who are using it... *négritude* is destined to destroy itself; it is the path and not the goal, the means and not the end". This opinion was criticized by Lilyan Kesteloot in the following passage: "Sartre forgets—and this is serious—that *négritude* is not only the result of racial conflict and colonial problems but that it is based on the common civilization of all black Africans" (1967, p. 134). Sartre then asks what will happen after the destruction of *négritude:* Will the source of the Negro's poetry run dry? Or will the great black river colour the sea into which it flows? Kesteloot believes in the permanent value of *négritude:* "But for the African, *négritude* has none of the qualities of a myth. It is a reality in which he is constantly soaked, which has deeply determined, modelled, shaped him, which makes him unable to be assimilated into a different civilization" (*ibid.*).

Négritude is just as temporary as other literary movements but Miss Kesteloot appears to treat it as a popular and fairly widespread trend, involving the masses of the African population. Actually, as an intellectual notion it has always been limited to black intellectuals and has never become the concern of the African man-in-the-street. This point of view was reiterated by Ulli Beier as follows: "Those African poets who most strongly assert their *négritude* are often the most sophisticated and—on the surface, at least—the most assimilated Africans. One might ask oneself, therefore, whether this new proclamation of *négritude* is a genuine rediscovery of African attitudes and values in the poet's soul, or whether it is merely a deliberate self-conscious intention, a kind of cultural manifesto" (1967, p. 95).

The fair amount of scepticism on the part of writers and critics of anglophone Africa may be due to the lack of practical improvements which could be expected to result from *négritude.* Ezekiel Mphahlele, who experienced difficult times in South Africa, expressed his doubts in the following lines: "To us in multiracial communities, then, *négritude* is just so much intellectual talk, a cult. Of course, we have not had the misfortune of being educated like our French-speaking friends. But *Présence Africaine* would do better, while preserving African culture where something of value still exists, to help the African artist in his present predicament..." (1962, p. 40). One would expect the black man's self-assertion to be particularly useful in a society ruled by racists. It was not by chance that the ideological predecessors of *négritude* came from a North American and Caribbean milieu. But in South Africa, according to Mphahlele, the African has already been completely assimilated by European culture, which to some extent explains his opposition to *négritude. Négritude* was a reaction to the French policy of cultural assimilation, which never existed in countries dominated by Britain.

Gerald Moore in *Seven African Writers* (1962) explained in detail why *négritude* was so much ingnored in anglophone Africa (the linguistic barrier, a poor knowledge of French, no counterparts to French-speaking poet-politicians, the preference given to realistic or introspective writing, an aversion to generalizations, the influence of British thinking, etc.). English "indirect rule" conserved the traditional social patterns and maintained the existing "gap" between the white man and the well-educated African. One more reason could be added to Moore's: the relationship between modern writing and urgent political problems. We have seen that *négritude*, as a search for cultural roots, necessarily meant looking back. Claude Wauthier, analyzing Mphahlele's opinions, observes that "Mphahlele thinks that the pilgrimage back to traditional African origins... is negative because it excludes enrichment from external sources; it is ineffective because it has taken refuge in memories, when African writers should be tackling first and foremost the situation of the colonial subject" (1966, p. 178).

English-speaking intellectuals in Black Africa have had political objections to *négritude* as a French-African concept, and possibly to some of its representatives. "It would be ironic if the English-speaking Africans really base their objections to *négritude* on its Frenchified approach. The question of African personality and culture would again become a matter of Western spheres of influence... *Négritude* has more and more confined itself to French-African culture and thus, while claiming African universality—which by its very nature can merely exist as an abstraction—represents only one part of African culture" (M. Tucker, 1967, p. 21).

What is the nature of a typical *négritude* work? Even those who accept the principles enumerated by Alexis Kagame (1958) and Janheinz Jahn (1961)—living and dead persons are the same category of beings, things are parts of a universal cosmic force, the world possesses magic power, etc.—as essential characteristics find it difficult, for example, to tell an early *négritude* poem from a European surrealist one. According to Jahn, "while the surrealist poet abandons himself to the power of words, which he hopes to take control of him in a state of almost subconscious trance, the African poet remains master of the word, which in turn gives him authority over the material world" (1961, p. 146). But can we discover facts concerning the poet's creative process with any degree of reliability? How is this difference reflected in the text of the poem? We shall probably have to depend on another distinctive feature, on the function of a literary work. Jahn says that the African concept of art is communal, socially functional and utilitarian, while the Western concept is individualistic, egoistic—that it seeks after pure beauty, it is art for art's sake, etc. This sort of generalization may have been based on a relatively small number of early *négritude* poems but how can we speak of *négritude* as a French-African concept, representing and combining all these sharply contrasting qualities? One can hardly believe that European surrealism was stolen by the black poet and directed against Europe (Sartre's idea). It is true that surrealism has exerted some influence on some African poets (including Senghor), but also on non-African artists such as Aimé Césaire. Moreover, we must bear in mind that not all works coming from post-war francophone Africa can be labelled as the products *of négritude*.

J. I. Gleason writes as follows: "*Négritude* as a poetic objectifying process, therefore, is a re-creation of the absent and as such is closely linked to the methodology of the symbolist poet, Mallarmé... This is *négritude's* romantic, passive side. The active aspect is an attack on colonialism" (1965, p. 63). Is it really a two-sided question or is it a question of content and form? Claude Wauthier mentions that "Léon G. Damas... points out in his *Poètes d'expression française* (French-writing Poets)the political significance of the break between the black surrealist poets of the present generation and the Parnassian tradition of their elders" (1966, p. 21). At any rate, *négritude* should not be identified with "African surrealist writing". The newness of this cultural phenomenon has caused some confusion in the field of literary criticism. *Négritude* (or so-called neo-African literature, in general) has been treated by critics using terms which are very helpful in discussing European literatures. What else could they do, if they wished to avoid coining new terms? But because of these old terms, African phenomena have been too easily identified with their presumed counterparts in Europe, and though such labels did not fit very well, analogies had to be discovered at all costs. However, artificial analogies, arrived at by comparative methods, might well obscure vital differences resulting from historical conditions.

To give one example, we may quote J. I. Gleason's study "The African Novel in French" (*African Forum*, 4, 1966, p. 76): "... *Négritude* can be seen as traditional French humanism in the savanna, with visible strata including the *élan vital*, Baudelairian correspondences, cubist and then surrealist theory, essential self-consciousness, neo-Thomism, and pheno-menological animism. Because Europe has had these intellectual experiences, Europe is able to understand Senghor." Does Europe really understand Senghor? And if it does, could it understand him even without these intellectual experiences? So many analogies are used in analyzing *négritude* just because its very forefathers defined it primarily in the negative sense, as a reaction to 'white' culture. *Négritude* has borne its basic contradiction since its origin.

"Senghor, in particular, convinced as he is of the need to return to Negro roots, is all the same a keen advocate of a mixture of cultures" (Claude Wauthier, 1966, p. 105).

Wauthier also mentions that Senghor's idea of *négritude* as "the crossroads of give and take" was opposed by Thomas Mélone, who thinks that in the life of the African black man there was never any "sense of giving" that had been systematically inhibited by the activities of the colonial powers (Thomas Mélone, 1962, p. 129). Mélone obviously disregards the true meaning of Senghor's "giving" which probably implies the Africans' contribution to the treasury of world culture.

Frantz Fanon in *The Wretched of the Earth* (1965) sees *négritude* as a necessary stage for a colonial intellectual who does not wish to become stateless and rootless. But he acknowledges as one of the main dangers the resulting "banal quest for the exotic". Most opponents of *négritude* do not understand it aesthetically so much as ideologically, and they stress its uselessness in contemporary efforts to solve the main problems of Africa. The racial element of *négritude* was emphasized by Daniel Boukman who, in an interview (*L'Afrique littéraire et artistique*, 1969, 7, p. 26), remarks that *négritude* was a crystallization of the African personality on aesthetic, emotional and racial bases.

Critics of *négritude* often cross the boundaries of literature—and even those of culture—in order to find arguments against it. Their first task is to show *négritude* as something more vague and more general than a literary movement and only then do they attack it more vigorously. But should a literary movement be judged by its ability to solve non-literary problems? Has there ever been any literary movement which was really capable of solving them? And if *négritude* is not condemned as a whole, there nevertheless remains an obvious tendency to condemn at least its "second phase". This phase, however, is viewed differently by different critics. Wauthier believes that we are now at the end of the first phase and he regards the second phase as a matter of the future. Similarly, Kesteloot's next phase of *négritude* is in the sphere of predictions. This approach is characteristic of those critics who do not consider the first phase a positive one, in order that they may be able to condemn the second phase. But if *négritude* is thought of as a developing phenomenon, then there could be more than two periods or phases. The most effective criticism is directed against its basic contradiction. Wole Soyinka wrote: "The movement which began with the war-cry of cultural separatism and modified itself with an acknowledgement of the historical expediency of the revolt... has found a latter-day succession in a call to be the bridge, to bring about the salvation of the world by a marriage of abstractions" (*The Writer in Modern Africa*, 1968, p. 20). Paradoxically enough, linguistic unity, which was considered one of the advantages of *négritude*, is later interpreted as an advantage of an *anti-négritude* group.

How can we explain the "quest for the exotic" so often mentioned by opponents of *négritude*? *Négritude* implies *inter alia* a re-creation of the past. African authors realize very well that they could hardly succeed in imitating foreign models. They feel that in stressing specific African qualities they can increase the originality of their works and thus be successful in international competition. This standpoint logically results from their approach to their cultural heritage. Traditional material, which is used only as a source of inspiration, should, however, be fused in the process of creation, permitting a higher stage of self-expression.

It is probably for this reason that Janheinz Jahn believes that the greater is the writer's talent, the more African elements may be found in his work. The so-called Africanness of a poem or short story is, of course, more closely associated with its originality than with the author's talent. Some very African works have been produced by authors obviously lacking in talent; on the other hand, there are gifted writers who introduce few African elements into their works. V. V. Ivasheva arrives at a conclusion diametrically opposite to that of Jahn's: "The more accomplished a particular African writer is, the less is folklore stressed in his method and system of images. The greater the author, the more independent are his creative standards, and the more are folklore *motifs* relegated in his books, if not to the background, then definitely to a secondary place in his system of images" (1969, p. 66). The question remains whether these general considerations are really useful for the future development of African writing. It seems that critics expressing generalizations devote relatively little attention to the true essence of creative writing, and sometimes one can see that one generalization is simply replaced by another.

Having condemned *négritude*, some critics begin discussing the so-called oneness of African authors.

The ideological unification of the black literary movement, as characterized in this chapter, was an inevitable step in the process of emancipation. It need not be divided into two separately discussed phases, as it is too early to describe its individual periods. It is too real and too much alive to reduce it to a mere dream, myth or cult. Moreover, its significance for the development of modern African writing consists precisely in the fact that it is an intellectual notion, rather than a mere French-African concept.

V. THE FRENCH-WRITTEN LITERATURE
OF WEST AFRICA

0. Introduction

The consequences of the French assimilationist policies have been very strongly felt in former French West Africa. In educating Africans, the French were consistent in suppressing everything that could recall the famous African past. On the other hand, they tried to bring the black educated élite closer to French culture. Thus, the Africans were to have coalesced with the inhabitants of France, differing from them only in their colour of skin and in the fact that they lived in the overseas territories. This policy in the sphere of culture undoubtedly led to an easier domination of the colonies and to a strengthened attachment to the "mother country" on the part of the Africans under its domination.

It is natural that the literary renascence of the African countries should have been accompanied by an ostentatious emphasis on genuine African elements and on the specific qualities of the black man. Since the French implemented their cultural policies long and consistently in Senegal, the most notable rise of the Negro literary movement could be observed precisely there. Although literary activities started to develop in the period between the two world wars, no national literature in the proper sense of the word existed at that time. It originated only after World War II and has matured since the 1950's, i.e. since the climax of the national liberation movement. This direct dependence of literature on political developments is no exclusive characteristic of Senegal; it exists in all the countries of Black Africa.

The development of *négritude* in Senegal has continued, but its character of a relatively unified trend has disappeared and certain divergencies have occurred (according to the political views of the main representatives of the literary movement). As one part of Senegal's literary production has lost its explicitly anti-French orientation, this process of the splitting up of *négritude* is sometimes understood in an oversimplified manner as a struggle between "radicals" and "chauvinists". Variations of *négritude* may, however, have resulted from the complicated and successful political career of Léopold Sédar Senghor, the President of Senegal, who has exerted a significant influence on both Senegal's political and cultural life.

As Senghor has always played this double role, it is advisable to distinguish between that statesman's speeches and his verses. Certain contradictions have resulted from the fact that this originally anti-colonialist intellectual has come to adopt a pro-French political orientation (especially during the period of French Presidents De Gaulle and Pompidou). A number of literary works have originated under Senghor's ideological influence, or as polemics directed against it.

An interest in folklore is characteristic of Senegalese (and also other West African) writing. For generations, myths, legends, eposes, fairy-tales, fables, proverbs and sayings have been handed down and preserved through oral traditions. They appeared in the form of written records relatively late, enriching the basis of the national literature. Even experienced writers and collectors have found the compiling of folklore and its adaptation for literary purposes a difficult task. Folklore possesses some characteristic advantages, as well, but these cannot be utilized in written works. Direct contact between the narrator and the listener enables the latter to react on the spot. Folk-tales are usually anonymous, and are often the result of some sort of collective co-operation. Details are added or omitted by different narrators and approaches to them must obviously have varied from one generation to another. Unlike written creative writing, which rejects and condemns imitation and literary "pilferage", folklore thrives on its lack of originality and repetitiveness, which is very much appreciated by its listeners. Far from inventing fresh, original stories of their own, the narrators remain faithful to the traditional, strictly limited range of themes. During personal contact between their listeners and themselves, non-literary components of their performances—e.g. singing, drumming or mimicry—can be used to enhance their presentation. Unfortunately, all this is practically lost, once the story is recorded and adapted. A writer must therefore endeavour to find at least some corresponding substitutes for the narrator's specific ways of presentation. If he succeeds, as Birago Diop has, his literary adaptation becomes successful thanks to his application of the specific advantages of the written form of a language to traditional folk subjects. Moreover, the ancient themes chosen by Birago Diop gave him an opportunity of celebrating African folklore in the contemporary politico-cultural context. Folklore has become a source of inspiration for young poets. The degree of transformation of original folklore elements varies widely in individual cases.

Senegal has heard the sharpest voices of the anti-colonialist vanguard (for example, David Diop) and is the native country of one of the first proletarian authors—Sembène Ousmane. The national literature of Senegal is rich in prose and poetry, while its share of drama is still modest. The linguistic standard of Senegalese works is comparatively high, which may be due to the fact that children are used to learning French from the first day of their educational careers (English in the British colonies, on the other hand, was usually taught only to older schoolboys).

Another significant centre of French-language literature in Africa is Cameroon, where the various genres are equalized quantitatively, rather than qualitatively. The leading form has been the novel whose development constitutes a positive contribution to the rise of the modern literatures of sub-Saharan Africa. The novelists of Cameroon, whose works will be discussed later, have applied the method of critical realism, giving their works a strong sarcastic, ironical or satirical flavour. The philosophical basis of most Cameroonian works is rationalism.

In other countries of former French Africa, there have been gifted individuals rather than groups of writers. We can hardly speak of national literatures there. Generally speaking, most advanced from the literary viewpoint are Guinea and the Ivory Coast.

For practical purposes, the writing of these two countries, like that of Upper Volta, Niger, Togoland, Mali, Dahomey, etc., will be briefly mentioned in one summarizing chapter. The less developed literatures of Black Africa have much in common, and the limited number of writers discussed here does not mean that many more authors in those countries could not be found. Our summarizing approach, which will also be used in the chapter dealing with certain literatures of East and Central Africa may enable us to concentrate more attention on the most important writers whose work deserves more space. It is, of course, necessary to indicate from which country a particular writer comes. But at the same time, it should be noted that the author's nationality or place of birth need not be relevant at all. As long as there are no really national literatures, these authors may be regarded as French-writing West Africans. Owing to the above-mentioned political reasons, they do not usually emphasize their tribal appurtenance. Many writers who studied in Paris intermingled with their colleagues from neighbouring countries. In some cases, African graduates did not return to their native countries, but went to other African countries, which was a further consequence of the European "melting-pot". Tribal differences have been overshadowed by the process of the formation of nations. Due to various circumstances, they moved from one country to another, especially during the dramatic 1960's. All these facts might also partly justify our summarizing chapter, which presents not only various types of creativity but also a broad range of opinions and creative methods. None of these writers can be thought of as adhering to one particular trend. Nevertheless, they share certain common ideological ground in terms of their anti-colonialism, which links them to the writers of other countries of Black Africa.

1. Senegal

The exceptional position of Senegalese writing derives from the above-mentioned historical causes. The educated *evolués* could vote—alongside the whites—as French citizens in four privileged cities: Dakar, Gorée, Rufisque and St. Louis. As early as the 1880's the main preconditions for gaining citizenship were an acceptance of Christianity and a mastery of French. As a result of this official position, the country became more closely related to France with respect to its political, economic and cultural life. This tendency was endorsed by the so-called black Frenchmen, those inhabitants of Senegal who, following their visit to France, adopted a European way of living. The label is often used in a pejorative sense, but the fact was that gifted young people could obtain a higher education only in France; they had no other choice. The role of the Senegalese intelligentsia in later emancipation activities and social developments can hardly be overestimated.

Modern Senegalese writing, however, does not date from any intellectual work, but from the time of the publication of *Force-Beauté* (Force-Beauty, 1926). Bakary Diallo, an ordinary villager, wrote this naïve autobiography in a politically pro-French spirit. His work possesses historical, rather than artistic, value. It is to be noted that such "schoolboys' exercises", as they were sometimes called with some contempt, existed also in other West

African countries. Although they cannot satisfy present-day critical criteria, they still bear witness to the late colonial period.

Ousmane-Socé Diop (b. 1911) studied veterinary medicine and then devoted much time to collecting folklore material at the source. He travelled widely and discovered a number of interesting oral traditions. His *Contes et légendes de l'Afrique Noire* (Tales and Legends of Black Africa, 1942) revived the realm of animals and plants, recalling the wisdom of dead but influential ancestors. His first novel *Karim* (1935) surprised the critics by its numerous impressive details depicting in picturesque images the life of a Senegalese city. Saint Louis attracts both Karim, the young hero of the novel, and Marième who comes from a wealthy family. Longing for all accessible pleasures, Karim gradually abandons his Wolof tribal customs, but his expensive courtship soon empties his pockets. Thinking that Marième will marry a richer suitor, Karim leaves for Dakar to live at his uncle's house.

There he can enjoy all the advantages of modern city life; he wears a European suit and, thanks to his "French manners", gets a job in a department store. But again he runs short of money, because a charming widow from Rufisque wants too much. Then he meets Marie, a Roman Catholic girl, but the difference in religions proves important. Finally, Karim returns home to find out that Marième is still unmarried. Their wedding ceremony is arranged according to traditional customs.

The writer's mild criticism is directed against the new "morality" penetrating Senegalese cities. This early *roman de moeurs* is, however, charged with realistic thinking and the author himself realizes that the invasion of new elements cannot be stopped. He criticizes mainly the ridiculous outward adaptation to the white man's way of living, as it appeared in the so-called "hybrid civilization". He shows the many contradictions leading to uncertainty and unsteadiness in Karim's way of thinking and behaviour.

The writer obviously expects his book to be read chiefly by foreigners, and so he presents long descriptions of Senegalese city and village life. Karim is a literary type of *évolué*, a product of the specific French-imposed assimilationist policies. He has the special Wolof pride, which is best shown when he feels offended by his boss, who blames him for coming late to work. Rather than bearing such reprimands, he leaves his good job and looks for another.

The novel *Mirages de Paris* (Mirages of Paris, 1937) contrasts Fara, a villager, with the splendour of a European city. During the colonial exhibition (in 1931), Fara meets Jacqueline, falls in love with this French woman, and marries her, despite the disapproval of her parents. The young married couple has no financial support and lacks any means of subsistance, though Fara earns some money working as a hawker. Jacqueline dies during childbirth and her desperate husband commits suicide. The central idea: "If you abandon me, you will die", would sound more convincing if there were not so many naïve and sentimental passages. His first novel *Karim* is written more effectively. Ousmane-Socé Diop also produced *Les rythmes du khalam* (The Rhythms of Khalam, 1956), a collection of lyrical poetry inspired by folk motifs. In 1960, the author was appointed Ambassador to the United States.

Birago Diop (born in 1906 in Dakar) also studied veterinary medicine (in Toulouse). He was also attracted by folklore, which inspired his first poems. As a member of the *négritude* movement he became well-known thanks to his inclusion in Damas' anthology *Poètes noirs d'expression française* (French-writing Negro Poets, 1947) and in *Nouvelle Anthologie de la Poésie nègre et malgache* (New Anthology of Negro and Malagasy Poetry, 1948). Birago Diop loves the narratives of travelling bards, called *griots,* who recounted throughout the land ancient tales, legends, fables, etc. He used the stories of one of these *griots,* adapting them in *Les contes d'Amadou Koumba* (The Tales of Amadou Koumba, 1947) and *Les nouveaux contes d'Amadou Koumba* (The New Tales of Amadou Koumba, 1958). These witty narratives are often satirical or socially critical. The writer's selection of expressions and his refinement of formulations makes these collections clearly different from their popular models. The same stylistic qualities can be found in his *Contes et lavanes* (Tales and "Lavanes", 1963). Birago Diop also published a collection of poems called *Leurres et lueurs* (Lures and Glimmers, 1960), in which he utilized his knowledge of folk poetry and his ability to describe the beauty of Nature. As a poet, Birago Diop was strongly influenced by Mallarmé.

Another representative of the old generation of Senegalese authors is Léopold Sédar Senghor (born in 1906 in Joal-la-Portugaise). Coming from a merchant's family, he was originally destined to become a Roman Catholic priest. In 1928, he left Dakar for Paris, where he successfully finished his university studies and met many other black intellectuals. His friendship with Aimé Césaire and Léon Damas was particularly important as regards the origin and formulation of the concept of *négritude.*

After finishing his studies, Senghor taught French literature in Tours. During World War II, he served in the French army and was taken prisoner by the Germans. Two years later, he worked in the anti-Nazi resistance movement in France.

Although he lived more or less away from his country, which he visited rarely staying there only for a short time, he took an interest in the social situation of Senegal. Together with Lamine Guèye, he represented Senegal in the First Constituent Assembly of France (elected on October 21, 1945). Nine deputies from Black Africa formed the *Bloc Africain,* which was affiliated to the Socialist Party of France (SFIO). But relatively soon—at the beginning of 1946—most of them began to co-operate with the Communist Party of France (PCF). Senghor, Guèye and Diallo of Guinea, however, kept their close links with the Socialists. As General Councillor of Senegal and a member of the *Grand Conseil* of French West Africa (AOF), Senghor assisted in preparing a comparatively liberal draft constitution, which was passed by the Constituent Assembly in April 1946 but rejected in the referendum of May 1946. He was also elected to the Second Constituent Assembly (on June 2, 1946) which produced another draft constitution (that was accepted by the Assembly in September 1946 and in the referendum of October 1946).

Until May 7, 1946, the population of Senegal had been divided into "subjects" and much less numerous "citizens". It was only then that all the inhabitants began to be officially considered as "citizens". Like other colonies, Senegal had—on the basis of the constitution—its own General Council, which was renamed Territorial Assembly in 1952). But in most respects, the idea of the French Union was completely unsatisfactory to West Africans, as well as to other overseas "citizens". The year 1946, therefore, saw a rise of radicalism and a favourable consideration of Marxism among the leading politicians of Black Africa. The main idea was to achieve a greater degree of decentralization, as the influence of the Assembly of the French Union, in which Black African and other colonial nations were relatively well represented, remained small.

Among the radicals of Black Africa, Félix Houphouet-Boigny of the Ivory Coast, who himself belonged to the *Union Républicaine de la Résistance,* sympathized with the French Communists. As most West African Deputies shared this attitude, they organized a conference in Bamako at which a new party—the *Rassemblement Démocratique Africain* (RDA)—was founded with Houphouet as its first President (October 1946). Following the policies of the Socialist Party, Senghor and Guèye decided not to attend the conference.

However, the SFIO could not satisfy the African aspirations for long, since the Socialist Party, supporting various reforms, in fact aimed at the assimilation of black Africans. At the end of 1946, Senghor, who had been re-elected to the French Parliament in November of that year, probably intended to leave sooner or later the pattern of French political parties. He was neither a Socialist nor a Communist, and despite his popularity in Senegal he became rather isolated from the main trends in French West Africa, particularly from the RDA. In his journal *La Condition Humaine* he criticized his own party, the *Bloc Africain.* He strongly opposed the French colonial policy of assimilation both in politics and culture. In March 1947, the French Communists left the French Government and became a leading opposition force. They remained the strongest ally of the RDA, whose position was, however, becoming more difficult, due to the increasingly hostile attitudes of the government.

In October 1948, Senghor formed his own party, the *Bloc Démocratique Sénégalais* (BDS) and joined the *Indépendents d'Outre Mer* (IOM). After this split with the SFIO there were three significant political groups in Senegal: Senghor's *Bloc Démocratique Sénégalais,* Guèye's party, and the *Union Démocratique Sénégalaise* (UDS)—a section of the RDA in Senegal. Under the pressure exerted by the French administration (the activities of the RDA had been prohibited on February 1, 1950), the UDS became less important and by 1951 Guèye also lost his position. Senghor's party became the leading political group in Senegal and Senghor himself the leading politician of the IOM. After a number of dramatic events, the RDA led by Houphouet-Boigny, decided to leave the alliance with the Communist Party of France. Its Senegalese section, the UDS, was against this decision and was expelled from the RDA in July 1955. Houphouet's line was supported by a minor part of the UDS renamed the *Mouvement Populaire Sénégalais* (MPS).

Senghor's political programme during that period was federalism, while Houphouet-Boigny started to co-operate with the French Government. The RDA under his leadership formed an alliance with the French *Union Démocratique et Socialiste de la Résistance* (the party of Pleven and Mitterand). During the 1950's, Houphouet succeeded in strengthening the influence of the RDA, and in 1956 he became Mayor of Abidjan and joined the French Cabinet. For tactical purposes, he rejected Senghor's federalism: he wished to keep the favour of France and was afraid that prosperous businessmen of the Ivory Coast would have to sacrifice some of their profits if a West African Federation were formed.

Senghor, on the contrary, believed in the concept of a French Euro-African community. He expressed this belief in his speech at the Council of Europe in 1953 and elsewhere. In 1954, Senghor suggested that two federations be formed, with their capitals in Dakar and Abidjan. But Houphouet's particularism won out, since the RDA was stronger than the IOM. The so-called *loi cadre* ("framework law") finally defeated Senghor's conception.

Even before the decisive struggle for independence, France had decided to grant universal suffrage and an Executive Council to each territory. Senghor was bitterly opposed to this "Balkanization". In July 1955, he still hoped to gain more effective autonomy and more influence for African Deputies. The *loi cadre* established Government Councils having limited executive competency. The local administration replaced the former concentration of power in the capitals of French West Africa (Dakar) and French Equatorial Africa (Brazzaville). The Government Councils were subordinated to the High Commissioner, which was probably what provoked Senghor to call the reforms "toys". Senghor's own idea of a confederation of French West Africa and French Equatorial Africa was now out of the question, but he tried at least to strengthen the unity of Senegal, forming a coalition between his own BDS and the smaller parties. Thus, his own *Bloc Progressiste Sénégalais* (BPS) came into being and soon became a part of the new interterritorial party formed by the IOM's Deputies—the *Convention Africaine* (CA) on January 1, 1957. Hoping to obtain political autonomy, the *Convention Africaine* merged with Lamine Guèye's *Mouvement Socialist Africain* (MSA). Senghor's BPS won the elections in March 1957, obtaining 47 seats out of 60 and formed a government. Senghor then tried to unite all the political groups outside the RDA, and this gave rise to the *Parti du Regroupement Africain* (PRA) which was established on March 26, 1958. At the same time, however, he wished to achieve a reasonable degree of unity, agreement and co-ordination with the RDA which was by no means a complete, unified whole. The unity of action proposed by the *Convention Africaine* was accepted by the RDA on November 2, 1957. In 1958, Senghor and Guèye formed the *Union Progressiste Sénégalaise* (UPS) within the Senegal section of the *Parti du Regroupement Africain,* and voted "Yes" in De Gaulle's referendum of September 28, 1958. Most politicians of the *Union Progressiste Sénégalaise* voted "Yes", but there was also a Leftist opposition that voted "No". The latter left the UPS and formed a new party, the *Parti du Regroupement Africain* (Sénégal), which, together with the *Parti Africain de l'Indépendence,* had voted "No".

Guinea voted "No" and became independent. Sekou Touré led a strong opposition against Houphouet-Boigny. Sekou Touré, a Guinean trade-unionist, became the chairman of the *Confédération Générale des Travailleurs de l'Afrique Noire* (CGTA) in 1956, and in 1957 he founded the *Union Générale des Travailleurs d'Afrique Noire* (UGTAN). The RDA continued to reject Marxist groups: e.g. the Senegalese *Parti Africain de l'Indépendence* (PAI) was not admitted to the conference in Paris (in February 1958).

Under these conditions, Senghor's gradualist approach, resulting probably from his wish to form a federation, prevailed completely over the idea of asking for immediate independence. Senghor joined the RDA leaders in July 1958 and asked Charles de Gaulle, the new President of France, for the Africans' right to self-determination. But neither De Gaulle nor Houphouet-Boigny agreed to establish the federation of Senghor's dreams. While the former did not want to see a strong, formerly French-controlled political bloc formed in Africa, the latter obviously disliked a possible excessive concentration of power in Dakar. But Senghor still refused to give up his plans. He attempted to form a smaller federation of four West African French-speaking countries: Senegal, French Sudan (now Mali), Dahomey and Upper Volta. The chances of the plan were not very promising. There were personal difficulties, problems with the scattered territories and especially economic handicaps. Senegal's economy was more advanced and the question remained of how to level out the existing differences without any detriment to it. Moreover, Senegal, which became an independent republic in January 1959, was still dependent on France, owing to its monoculture of ground-nuts. "It is difficult to see how Senegal, in particular, can manage without a French subsidy for her ground-nuts, and President Senghor has already called attention to the serious economic position into which this puts his country", Kwame Nkrumah pointed out. (Kwame Nkrumah, *Neo-Colonialism,* London 1969, pp. 18—19). The same author cited Senghor's idea that "the French union is a marriage, rather than an association" and added: "It was mass pressure for independence which forced these leaders (Senghor and Houphouet-Boigny — V. K.) to reverse their previous positions and to declare themselves in favour of national sovereignty. At the end of 1958, the congress at Bamako discussed the federation of the four states, but Houphouet-Boigny soon succeeded in destroying Senghor's plan. Dahomey and Upper Volta, together with Niger and the Ivory Coast, formed the *Conseil de l'Entente* (in May 1959).

The Federation of Mali (former French Sudan and Senegal) suffered from a serious crisis in September 1960. The Senegalese leaders preferred conciliation with France and a capitalist economic system, and were afraid that their country would be handicapped by the economic support given to poorer Sudan (now Mali). They left the Federation, and two independent republics (Mali and Senegal) came into being. As the President of Senegal, Senghor often had to solve difficult problems (e.g. his conflict with Prime Minister Mamadou Dia, undergraduate opposition, etc.). But now let us turn to his literary activities, which are just as significant as his political ones.

Senghor's first collection of poems *Chants d'ombre* (Songs of Shadow, 1945) resulted from the Expressionist assumption that logic is less important in poetry than fascination. Most Western critics praised the verses conveying a mere stream of emotions (i.e. love poems, childhood reminiscences and the lauding of ancestors). Senghor was considered to be an African poet using the French language in order to express his African mind. This ideological dualism characterizes his poems of reconciliation—such as "Prière de Paix" (Prayer of Peace). In fact, a survey of Senghor's political evolution shows that after World War II, the poet's period of radicalism came to an end. In his opinion, Africa's economic and social problems would have to be solved in co-operation with Western capitalists. The more significant Senghor's political position became, the less he was able to express any criticism of colonialism or neo-colonialism.

This basic contradiction can also be seen in the form and imagery of his poetry. In it, dynamic symbols are gradually replaced by static ones. The poet believes that Africa may make a significant contribution to the treasury of world culture, and that it will be *"le levain qui est nécessaire à la farine blanche"* (the leaven that is necessary for the white flour). This contribution is often symbolized by rhythm. Senghor, one of the disciples of the Jesuit philosopher, Teilhard de Chardin, believes that the universal civilization of the future will be a synthesis of European reason and African emotion.

Apart from nostalgia, alienation, the cult of one's ancestors and other *négritude* ideas, we can find in his poetry a remarkable celebration of blackness. After the "shadow" in the title of his first collection there followed *Hosties noires* (Black Victims, 1948). The same idea is recalled in the title of his latest collection *Nocturnes* (1961) and in many verses in *Chants pour Naëtt* (1949) and *Ethiopiques* (1956). The black woman, night and shadows symbolize life and beauty, in contradiction with the white colour of Europe: snow in his poem "Neige sur Paris" (Snow over Paris), written during the Spanish Civil War, white death, flags and the hands of the colonialists represent coldness and disaster. While beauty and innocence are traditionally associated with whiteness in Europe, they are black in this African aesthetic conception. Black Roman Catholics imagine white devils and black angels.

But Senghor can utilize other colours as well. We come across expressions like "purple" or "burning voice", "green scent", etc. In *Chants pour Naëtt*, containing mostly love poetry, and in *Ethiopiques* he introduces more vernacular words. To his *Nocturnes* he even added a small dictionary. His verse is long, melodious, rich in sounds onomatopoeia, alliteration, characteristic rhythm, etc. African poetry should be combined with singing and accompanied by African musical instruments. The poet stresses that he does not seek originality at any cost, however his poems become increasingly complicated. Some of them are filled with the names of African rulers, deities and mythological concepts, while others are sometimes inspired by European philosophy and French classical poetry. The critics have mentioned his affinity with Valéry, Claudel and Saint-John Perse, on the one hand, and with Whitman, Hughes, Brown and Wright, on the other, while Senghor himself confesses his devotion to Barrès, Proust, Gide, Baudelaire and Rimbaud.

His dramatic poem "Chaka" (1964) describes the famous Zulu ruler at the end of his life, showing him not as a tyrant, but as a martyr. The poet certainly fails to justify Chaka's cruelty, but gives an impressive mental picture of his hero obsessed with the idea of freedom. This Miltonian approach is well characterized by J. I. Gleason, who remarked: "Senghor, like the English romantics who later made Satan the hero of the piece, has temporarily abrogated the moral framework in which Mofolo wrote" (J. I. Gleason, 1965, p. 65). The Basuto writer, whose presentation will be discussed in the chapter dealing with the literature of South Africa, regarded Chaka from the standpoint of Christian morality. Senghor's attitude was probably influenced by topical aspects of African political life, requiring the poet's increased social commitment.

Together with Abdoulaye Sadji, Senghor wrote *La belle histoire de Leuk - Le Lièvre* (The Charming Story of Leuk the Hare, 1953), a book for children. Many of Senghor's essays, reports and public speeches are included in *Négritude et Humanisme*, 1964. The "ambassador of black nations" expressed his opinions concerning literary criticism at numerous meetings and conferences. In 1937, he took part in the Congress for Cultural Development of the Colonial Nations. After World War II, he contributed to the newly-founded review *Présence Africaine*.

The same generation of Senegalese authors is represented by Abdoulaye Sadji (1910 to 1961). He was born in Rufisque and graduated from the William Ponty School in Gorée in 1929. After teaching in various towns of Senegal, he worked as a headmaster and inspector of schools in Dakar. Apart from studies dealing with educational problems, he wrote the short story "Maimouna, petite fille noire" (Maimouna, a Little Black Girl, 1953) and two novels, *Nini, mulâtresse de Sénégal* (Nini, Mulatto of Senegal, 1954) and *Maimouna* (1958).

In the latter novel he portrays life in a small bush village. Maimouna lives there together with her mother who keeps her household. The girl is invited to Dakar by her older sister, Rihanna, who had come to the city after her marriage. The naïve girl, lacking experience and bearing in mind her ideals, is not aware of the danger of the city. A young *évolué*, who has made her pregnant, refuses to marry her. Driven away by her sister, Maimouna returns to her native village.

Sadji uses this sharp contrast between youthful illusions and the harsh reality of the city in order to show the contemporary decay of traditional social norms. The bush village way of living gradually gives way to modern influences. The author does not idealize village life, which he judges from the viewpoint of social realism. The presentation of the story involves a synthesis of European and African elements. Sadji's book *Tounka* (1965) appeared after his death. It is a collection of legends and ancient narratives about tribal migrations and the cultural characteristics of Mali.

The William Ponty School, where Sadji studied, has an important position in the history of drama in Senegal. Many plays were staged there in the 1930's: *La dernière entrevue de Behanzin et de Bayol* (The Last Meeting of Behanzin and Bayol, 1933), the three-act comedy *Un mariage au Dahomey* (A Marriage in Dahomey, 1934), *L'élection d'un roi au Dahomey* (The Election of a King in Dahomey, 1935), *Le triomphe du griote* (The Griot's Triumph, 1935) and the adaptation *Sokamé* (1937).

The writer Lamine Diakhaté (born in 1928, in Saint Louis) adapted Birago Diop's tale *Sarzan* (1955), continuing in the tradition of Senegalese drama. His lyrical poems appeared in the following collections: *La joie d'un continent* (The Joy of a Continent, 1954), *Fils du Soleil* (Son of the Sun, 1953), *Primordiale du Sixième jour* (The Sixth Day's Primordial, 1963) and *Temps de mémoire* (Time of Memory, 1967). Lyrical verses were also written by Ibrahima Sourang, including *Auréoles* (1961) and *Chants du crépuscule* (Songs of Dusk, 1964), as well as by Malick Fall, who lauds in his *Relièfs* (1964) the peaceful coexistence of different races and the ideas of national liberation. Malick Fall also wrote the symbolical novel *La plaie* (The Disaster, 1967).

No survey of Senegalese poetry can omit the poet whose work was characterized by Gerald Moore (*Seven African Writers*, p. 21) as follows: "What softens his poetry is a certain sensuality and tenderness towards his own people, but there is no forgiveness for their oppressors. Tenderness, love, joy, fidelity—these are found only among his black brethren... The poet is thus never alone; always there is his inward appeal to brothers, friends, comrades, to the warmth of a companionship, which will sooner or later triumph. He is the Mayakovsky of the African Revolution."

This best-known representative of the younger poetic generation was David Diop (1927—1960), whose promising activities were cut off by an air-crash. He spent his childhood partly in West Africa, partly in France. Born in Bordeaux, his European experience probably made his early attitudes closer to those of other *négritude* poets. His early verses were included in *Anthologie de la nouvelle poésie nègre et malgache de langue française* (1948).

While the literary movement was gradually losing its original radicalism in the 1950's, David Diop went precisely in the opposite direction. In his poetry, he expresses a sharp criticism of colonialism and indentifies himself with the aims of the national liberation movement. His collection *Coups de pilon* (Sounds of the Pestle, 1956) is directed against racial oppression. Some poems call for the solidarity of black people living on both sides of the Atlantic and a revolutionary struggle for a better world. Diop exposes the inhumanity and hypocrisy of the colonial regimes, contrasting them with the famous historical empires established by the Africans themselves. Speaking about his compatriots, he mentions solely their positive qualities and is sharply critical of the white masters. His idealizing vision is revolutionary-romantic.

Just as categorical is his view of missions, whose activities he repudiates. His poetic diction is also sometimes "blasphemous" and pathetic, which reminds one of the bold generalizations of the Caribbean lyricists. Diop's verse is, however, less refined and less melodious. The poet's forte lies evidently in his impressive rhythm. It would have been most exciting to follow his further artistic development, especially after the heyday of Negro nationalism.

The greatest novelists of the same generation in Senegal are Cheikh Hamidou Kane (b. 1928) and Sembène Ousmane (b. 1923). Kane's *L'aventure ambiguë* (The Ambiguous Adventure, 1961) is to some extent the author's autobiography describing the psychological crisis of Samba Diallo, who was educated in the Islamic faith but later suffered from doubts brought about by European philosophy. The author shows the nostalgic feelings of this black intellectual during his studies in Paris and his general disappointment resulting from the fact that he loses his old faith without finding any substitute for it. After his return to his native country, he is restless and unsatisfied. His nihilism and sense of alienation lead to his personal tragedy.

The analysis of the mental processes, individual psychology and mystical flavour of Kane's novel differ sharply from the descriptive presentation of Sembène Ousmane, the first proletarian writer of Senegal. Coming from a Wolof fisherman's family, he worked as a bricklayer and mechanic. He served in the French army during World War II and then became a dockworker in Marseilles. Quickly becoming active as a trade-unionist, he simultaneously tried to improve his education.

His first autobiographical novel *Le dockeur noir* (The Black Dock-worker, 1956) is technically weaker than the following books *O pays, mon beau peuple* (Oh, Country, My

Beautiful People! 1957) and *Les bouts de bois de Dieu* (God's Bits of Wood, 1960). The hero of the novel *O pays, mon beau peuple* is Oumar Faye, who uses modern, pioneering forms of agricultural cooperation. His French wife, Isabelle, finds it difficult to adapt herself to living conditions in Africa. The novel recommends the introduction of new technology and the progressive organization of work. The author feels that retarding traditions must be abandoned and all kinds of prejudice should be eliminated forever.

The novel *Les bouts de bois de Dieu* was written during the writer's stay in a hospital. It describes one of the great social conflicts in post-war West Africa, the five months' strike of African railwaymen employed on the Dakar—Bamako railway, during the winter of 1947—1948. In it, Sembène Ousmane leaves aside the racial aspects, so important in his first novel, to concentrate totally on the class nature of the social struggle described. The life and attitudes of African workers had never been discussed in such detail before this novel was published.

A collection of short stories, *Voltaïque* (1962) contains works of different standards and with different settings. The best-known of them "La noire de..." (The Black Woman from...) was filmed by the author, who is also a film-producer. The main conflict here is the suicide of a black servant girl who had been distraught over the continual injustice she suffered in the employ of a French family.

The political novel *L'Harmattan* (1964) illustrates the disappointment of Tangara, the African physician and head of a hospital. Tangara is concerned with medicine and refuses to enter the restless arena of political struggle. The action of the novel shows the atmosphere in which De Gaulle's referendum of 1958 took place. Devoting much attention to general political problems, Sembène Ousmane has failed here to create convincing true-to-life characters, comparable to those in his following novelettes *Vehi ciosane* and *Le mandat* (The Money Order). The volume containing them appeared in 1966 and was awarded the first prize in the literary contest of the World Festival of Negro Arts in Dakar. The former novelette tells of an incestuous scandal in a magistrate's family, while the latter describes the difficulties of an old man, who blindly believes that he will receive a large amount of money from his nephew. The money is stolen while the old man falls into debt because of the parasitic, greedy behaviour of his relatives and friends. This satirical work is obviously a fresh attack on backward traditions.

2. Cameroon

Cameroonian poets are mostly young or middle-aged. Folklore and politics are their principal sources of inspiration. Elolongué Epanya Yondo (born in 1930 in Douala) wrote chiefly patriotic poetry in French (Cameroun! Cameroun! 1960) and in Duala. Jean-Paul Nyuanai born in 1935 in Yaoundé published his collections *La nuit de ma vie* (The Night-time of My Life, 1961), *Pigments sang* (Blood Pigments, 1963), *Salut à la nation camerounaise* (Greeting to the Cameroonian Nation) and *Chansons pour Ngo-lima* (Songs for Ngo-lima, 1964) in a similarly nationalistic spirit. The lyrical collections *Les Heures souhaitées* (The Desired Hours) and *La harpe ailée* (The Winged Harp) were written by James Oto (b. 1928), while Louis-Maria Pouka was the author of *Les rêveries tumultueuses* (Tumultuous Reveries, 1954).

Francis Bebey (born in 1929 in Douala) is the author of *Le fils d'Agatha Moudio* (The Son of Agatha Moudio, 1967), the novel awarded the *Grand Prix Littéraire de l'Afrique Noire* in 1968. Mbenda, the hero of the novel, is a man torn between two women. He is more attracted by Agatha from a neighbouring village than by his wife. But he does not know that Agatha still maintains erotic relations with some wealthy whites. After Agatha has become his second wife, she bears a Mulatto baby, which, despite the colour, is accepted by Mbenda as his own. The banal story represents only the average standard of Cameroonian prose writing, as does *Embarras et Cie; nouvelles et poèmes* (Distress and Co.: Short Stories and Poems, 1968), which, as the title suggests, is an interesting combination of short stories and verses. The most typical quality of his poetry is rhythm, which naturally follows from the fact that the writer is a successful composer as well.

René Philombé (b. 1930), who has worked as the General Secretary of the Association of Cameroonian Poets and Writers since 1960, wrote the collection of stories *Lettres de ma cambuse* (Letters from My Room, 1965) and two novels: *Sola ma chérie* (Sola, My Darling, 1966) and *Un sorcier blanc à Zangali* (A White Sorcerer in Zangali, 1967). The latter is his best published work so far. The white sorcerer is Père Marius, a German missionary, sent to Christianize the pagan tribes. His predecessor had been killed by the natives and the missionary's task is very hard. He succeeds in curing several diseased people who help him in the most dramatic situation, when he is threatened by the "savages". But just at the moment when he gains a moral victory, the German commander arrives to punish his enemies. The missionary tries to persuade him that peaceful means are more suitable than executions, but in vain. Harsh, psychologically incorrect methods were used by the Germans in Africa at the beginning of World War I.

Joseph Owono (b. 1921) in *Tante Bella* (Aunt Bella), Jacques Kuoh Moukori in his autobiography *Doigts noirs* (Black Fingers, 1963) and the novelist Jean Ikella Matiba (b. 1936) in *Cette Afrique-là* (That Africa, 1963) and *La solitude* (Solitude) achieved an average standard. The satirist Daniel Ewandé in his novelette *Vive le président!* (Long Live the President! 1967), Jacques-Muriel Nzouankeu (b. 1938) in his long short stories *Le souffle des ancêtres* (Breath of the Ancestors) and in the play *L'agent spécial* (Special Agent, 1964) and Guillaume Oyono-Mbia in his comedies *Trois prétendants, un mari* (Three Suitors, One Husband, 1964) and *Jusqu'à nouvel avis* (Until Further Notice, 1970) have all introduced fresh qualities into Cameroonian writing: Ewandé, wittiness; Nzouankeu, a successful combination of folk and modern elements, and Oyono-Mbia, a sense of humour. All of them possess a fine feeling for style.

Benjamin Matip (born in 1932 in Eséka) studied law and economics. He started his career by writing a number of articles discussing the cultural and economic interrelations of Europe and Africa. He also dealt with the contemporary writer's tasks in his essay "Le rôle et responsabilité de l'écrivain en Afrique Noire aujourd'hui" (The Role and Responsibility of the Writer in Black Africa Today, 1958). Much attention was attracted by his essay "Heurts et malheurs des rapports Europe-Afrique avant la colonisation" (Clashes and Calamities in European-African Relations before Colonization).

Matip's first novel *Afrique, nous t'ignorons* (Africa, We do not Know You, 1956) tells of a Cameroonian village at the time that its inhabitants learned of the outbreak of World War II. Relations between Africans and Europeans are well characterized. Both are criticized: the former for their conservative adherence to traditions, the latter for their cruel cynicism and defeatism. With his sense of humour, the author ridicules the old Negroes and exposes their servility. Matip proves his ability to create convincing types, but provides little action for a full-length novel. His work has not been completed.

His collection of short stories *A la belle étoile* (Under the Open Skies, 1962) is more successful. The writer applied certain characteristic narrative techniques used by the folk narrators of fables, and combined them with his entirely modern approach. He is not satisfied with the traditional attributes and characteristics of his animal heroes and inserts a number of topical allusions.

Ferdinand Oyono (born in 1929 in Ngoulemakong) has gone even further in psychological analysis. He studied law and became a diplomat. After independence, he represented his country in the United Nations and became an ambassador.

His first novel *Une vie de boy* (The Life of a "Boy", 1956) although technically immature, nevertheless comprises a series of keenly observed episodes. The corruption of the late phase of colonialism is described by a young African working as a servant to the commander's wife. Through this naïve narrator, Oyono succeeds in giving his story a great deal of irony. The vices of the white characters are exposed in a satirical manner. One of the most impressive scenes shows the boy discovering the secrets of his mistress' amours, which makes her hate him. Accused of robbery, he is imprisoned and flogged. He succeeds in fleeing from his tyrants, but he cannot enjoy his freedom long. He dies near the frontier of his native country, where he has suffered so much.

Le vieux nègre et la médaille (The Old Negro and the Medal, 1956), Oyono's most popular novel, is based on a more interesting subject. Meka, an old Negro, whose two sons fell in the war as French soldiers, is invited by the French Commander to a decoration ceremony. Meka lives with his family in a poor hut, as his lands have been taken by the Roman Catholic mission. He still maintains some illusions concerning the possibility of better relations between blacks and whites in the future. Misled by sweet-sounding phrases pronounced during the ceremony, he wrongly thinks that he can treat the French officials of the colonial administration as equals. Getting drunk, he loses his medal as well as his way, and so comes to the European quarter of the town where he is imprisoned. The authorities do not allow Negroes to wander in the "white" part of the town at night. Released from jail, he returns home and realizes that he cannot become the white man's friend. He is disappointed and disillusioned.

Chemin de l'Europe (The Path of Europe, 1960) is also satirical. Aki Barnabas is a young African who wishes to visit Europe, or rather France. He is expelled from the seminary and cannot find a suitable job. His application for a scholarship is refused and so he decides to join a Christian sect, hoping to realize his dream with the missionaries' assistance.

The young man suffers from his inner conflicts, although his intellectual capacity is considerable. He tries to avoid the African's usual fate—an inferior kind of work. He hopes for a better career, but when he discovers that his longings are unrealistic, he becomes confused. The creative method used in this novel reminds one of modern French novel writing. Oyono devotes, in this work, too much attention to individuals and too little attention to the general social situation.

Alexandre Biyidi (born in 1932 in Mbalmayo) used for his first novel *Ville cruelle* (Cruel City, 1955), the pseudonym "Eza Boto". But his later, more successful novels were signed "Mongo Beti". He studied in France at Aix-en-Provence and at the Sorbonne, taught literature and married a Frenchwoman.

Ville cruelle deals with the adventures of Banda, a young black man. He comes to a city to sell his cocoa crops, but fails to earn the expected sum of money that he needs for his wedding. Moreover, he is imprisoned and after his release goes through a series of unbelievable experiences. The real hero of the book is better characterized than the motivation of the main figures. In fact, the action, though illustrated by inner dialogues and numerous details, is presented—to some degree at least—with artificial, naïve sentimentality. Nevertheless, *Ville cruelle* has a definite place in the history of Cameroonian novel-writing, as it analyzes the contemporary situation from the social, rather than racial, point of view.

Le pauvre Christ de Bomba (The Poor Christ of Bomba, 1956) is similar in form to Oyono's *Une vie de boy,* but the utilization of a naïve boy's diary is much more effective here. Denis is an acolyte serving the French missionary, Drumont, nicknamed "the Poor Christ". Much of what is recorded by Denis is meant seriously by the boy, but ironically by the author.

Drumont's portrait of "the good white man", who is convinced of the fruitfulness of his twenty years' activities in Africa, is very intriguing. Only at the end of the novel does the missionary realize that the acceptance of Christianity by the Africans living in his district has been only superficial. During his inspection trips, Drumont discovers many vices. Right in his own mission, in fact, his catechist is misusing his position and is sleeping with young African girls, who are being educated there to become true Christian wives. The scandal reaches its climax when the girls prove to be suffering from syphilis. Viewed from the African standpoint, the missionary's efforts appear to be in vain and even unjustified. But Mongo Beti criticizes not only the missionaries. He exposes the very nature of the colonial system and repudiates the white man's civilizing "burden". Finally, Drumont closes his mission and leaves for Europe.

Beti chose the pre-World War II period in order to express certain topical opinions. He was criticized for his excessive identification of Christianity with colonialism. Although his dialogues sometimes sound unnatural, he succeeded in creating several excellent literary types.

Similarly successful was his following novel *Mission terminée* (Mission Accomplished, 1957), which was awarded the Sainte-Beuve Prize. After having failed in his examinations, the young student Medza returns to his native village to spend his holidays there. He enjoys very high prestige among the villagers, who greatly respect this "intellectual".

They send him to a distant village to bring back the unfaithful wife of his cousin, who has fled from her husband. Medza increasingly feels his own isolation and alienation resulting, probably, from his studies. Unlike the other village boys, he is no longer able to enjoy a spontaneous life without inhibitions. His knowledge is more than fully offset by the other boys' strength and joy of living. At last, Medza accomplishes his mission, brings back his cousin's wife. Avoiding the feared banality of married life, he decides to wander on. Medza exemplifies the process of the deterioration of ancient social norms in the African villages, and in particular the significant role played in this process by education. Medza is forced to rely solely on himself, as he no longer understands the world he came from.

More burlesque elements can be found in Beti's next novel *Le roi miraculé* (King Lazarus, 1958), which is freely linked with *Le pauvre Christ de Bomba*. Drumont's former subordinate, Le Guen, tries to convert the king of the Essazam tribe to Christianity. When the king falls seriously ill, his aunt baptizes him by pouring a jug of water on his head. Suddenly the king recovers, and is persuaded by Le Guen that this miracle was caused by Jesus. God did not allow him to die as a pagan ruler. The king begins a perfect Christian's life. He decides to give up all his wives but one, and the women contend for his decision as to which of them should be his only legitimate wife. Le Guen expects praise and promotion from the French administration, but he is criticized instead, and has to move on to another region where he creates confusion among the Africans, without achieving any personal satisfaction. Surprisingly enough, the colonial administrator, together with the Roman Catholic clergy, play, in this work, the hypocritical roles of "the defenders" of African traditions, obviously feeling that these traditions make colonial domination easier. Beti does not hesitate to point out that the ancient way of living also possesses negative qualities. After Le Guen's departure, the king takes all of his former wives back again.

After *Le roi miraculé*, Beti stopped writing novels and devoted himself to other tasks. Perhaps he believes that creative writing cannot solve certain problems as effectively as journalism. He has pointed out the topical conflict between "political propaganda" and "aesthetically impressive writing" and is aware of the desirable difference between journalism and creative writing, both in content and in form. Opposing a one-sided emphasis on racial "particularities", Beti and Oyono stress the social aspects und understand their realism as "a child of common sense". In the 1950's, Cameroonian realistic prose revolted thus against stale stereotypes and struggled for more creative freedom.

One of the best novels in the 1960's was *Sur la terre en passant* (On Earth Temporarily, 1966) by François-Borgia Marie Ewembe. Young Iyoni suffers from a serious disease. He knows that he must die very soon, but does not want to feel sorry for himself. He behaves proudly and nobly, though his unfortunate condition invariably brings him into conflict with his surroundings. Through Iyoni, the author expresses an extraordinarily strong moral message, a piece of his personal philosophy dealing with the meaning of human life and relationships, and with the conflict between mind and body. Thanks to this basis, Ewembe succeeds in blending the genuine tragic essence of the novel with a certain amount of irony, or rather, Iyoni's self-irony. This anti-melodramatic approach could hardly be realized without the author's remarkable stylistic abilities.

One of the most important literary centres in Cameroon is the Abbia Magazine and Publishing-house which produced many worthwhile works under its director, Bernard Fonlon, the well-known literary critic. Remy Medou-Mvomo (b. 1938) published there his novel, *Afrika Ba'a* (1969). This technically weak novel has, nevertheless, an admirable hero, Kambara. Kambara looks for a job in a city, but after a number of bad experiences comes back to his village, in order to unite its inhabitants in a common struggle against famine by cultivating larger plots of land. This basically good idea would deserve a better presentation and probably some useful omissions of naïve passages which spoil the overall impression.

3. The French-written Literature of Other West African Countries]

3.1 *Mali*

Few West African politicians understand the social significance of creative writing as well as the ruling circles of Mali. After independence, urgent economic and political problems overshadowed cultural ones almost everywhere. But this was not the case of Mali, which was trying to use literature as much as possible for ideological purposes. This not only implied governmental control and supervision, but large investments in literary ventures as well. Modern creative writing began to develop at that time, side by side with folkloristic, ethnographic, linguistic, archaeological and historical investigation, and frequently it found fresh impetuses in these branches of research. Moreover, the politicians themselves sometimes entered the realm of literature as writers, while creative authors often became politically committed, which resulted in a part of modern writing acquiring a propagandist character. As in other West]African countries, these poems conveyed messages of patriotism while most prose works were didactic or moralizing. The plot itself might well have been less important than the instruction concerning various social questions and the virtues and vices of individuals.

A synthesis of political tendency and lyrical musicality is typical of the poems of Fily-Dabo Sissoko (1900—1964), who had a splendid political career, first as a chief, later as a deputy and government minister. Finally, he was imprisoned and killed in jail. His collections *Crayons et portraits* (Pencil and Portraits, 1953), *Harmakhis* (1955) and *Poèmes de l'Afrique Noire* (Poems of Black Africa, 1953) repudiate all types of racism. The form of his verse is based on folklore sources. Sissoko is particularly skilful in portraying the beauty of nature and its lyrical atmosphere, which can be seen also in his prose works, *La passion de Djimé* (The Passion of Djimé, 1956) and *La savane rouge* (The Red Savanna, 1962).

Other poets of Mali, e.g. Albakaye Ousmane, Mamadou Lamine Sisse and Bouna Boukary Dioura, have produced chiefly patriotic poetry. They praise traditions, diligence, the river Niger and other natural beauties, as well as folk wisdom and African solidarity.

Proverbs and sayings were collected by Fily-Dabo Sissoko in *Sagesse noire; sentences et proverbes malinkes* (Black Wisdom and Malinke Maxims and Proverbs, 1955). The collection of poems *Mon coeur est un volcan* (My Heart is a Volcano, 1962) was written by Mamadou Gologo (b. 1924), Minister of Information in Modibo Keita's cabinet. His most successful work is his novel *Le rescapé de l'Ethylos* (The Survivor of Ethylos, 1963). This confession describes the slow, gradual recovery of an alcoholic; drinking is interpreted here as an evil brought to Africa by the white colonizers. The novel describes a series of dramatic experiences in various towns of West Africa.

Seydou Badian Kouyaté (b. 1918), another Minister of Mali, wrote many political and sociological essays and the historical drama *La mort de Chaka* (The Death of Shaka, 1961), which adds little to the presentations of Mofolo and Senghor. The drama ends with Shaka's death. He is killed after a battle, by his own brothers, who are disgusted by his cruelty. Drama has acquired more significance in the general context of Mali cultural life. Its staging is especially inventive and lively. The subject-matter is, however, purely traditional in most cases. The development of drama is partly enhanced by literary criticism.

Seydou Badian wrote also the novel *Sous l'orage* (Under the Storm, 1963), which deals with the recent reality of Mali villages. The writer examines the vestiges of traditional customs in the countryside and chooses for this purpose a banal story of two young people who fall in love and want to get married in order to start their independent life. The girl's father interferes, however, as he wishes her to marry an older, richer man. The old require traditional obedience, while the young remain faithful to their mutual love. The author suggests solving this conflict with a compromise: the young should continue to respect the ancient traditions after their wedding. The novel contains a number of picturesque scenes from village life, describing ceremonies, customs, costumes, dances etc.

Djibril Tamsir Niane (b. 1932) successfully adapts in *Soundjata ou l'épopée mandingue* (Sundiata, or An Epic of Old Mali, 1960) the old griot's tale about the founder of the medieval Mandingo Empire. The story ends with Sundiata's assuming power. The author, who comes from Guinea, is more concerned with hero's portrait than with historical events. It should be noted that the present-day Republic of Mali should not be considered as covering exactly the same territory as the old empire. This mention serves only to inform those who were attracted by Niane's well-written work.

Yambo Ouologuem (b. 1938) attracted much attention with his *Lettre à la France Nègre* (Letter to Black France, 1968) and even more by his novel *Le devoir de violence* (Bound to Violence, 1968) which was awarded the Prix Renaudot in Paris (1968). The vivid, dramatic action of this novel covers seven centuries of African history. With the characteristic scepticism of the young generation, this author presents his conception of the philosophy of African history. It is well-known that in the colonial era it was often thought in Europe that a barbarous part of the black continent lay south of the Sahara. That area allegedly lacked true culture and civilization. In the present era of political independence, however, the African past has been glorified and lauded and the dark, infamous or unpleasant episodes of history have scarcely been mentioned.

Ouologuem studied at the Sorbonne and was acquainted with African history. His novel constitutes his personal reaction to both above-mentioned extremes: His fictitious Nakem Empire survived seven centuries of violence perpetrated by wealthy foreigners, slave-traders and colonisers of different nationalities, races and religions. All its rulers were greedy oppressors. There is too much bloodshed, crime and vice in this novel, but Ouologuem's lingustic skill somehow manages to hold the reader's attention. He uses archaic French expressions, contrived formulations and colourful sayings in order to more closely approach the narrative methods of the popular story-tellers.

The novel was much praised by the critics, but several experts found its originality controversial. This was partly provoked by the author himself, as he stressed mainly authenticity, the stylistic qualities of the text, the preserving of African rhythms, etc. Moreover, it was wrongly denoted as the first truly African novel. Eric Sellin compared its text with André Schwarz-Bart's *Le dernier des justes* (The Last of the Just) published by Editions du Seuil, 1959 to discover some surprisingly striking analogies in some passages. But even if this analogy were deliberate and the publisher wished to obtain an imitation of the successful earlier work, the question would remain: how far does this very fact affect the artistic value of Ouologuem's novel. As the whole atmosphere of the most recent African products is rather similar, we may quote Sellin's comments in his article, "Ouologuem's Blueprint for *Le devoir de violence*" (Research in African Literatures, vol. 2, No. 2, 1971, pp. 119—120):

"The supreme irony in the blurb on Ouologuem's book lies in the publisher' declaration that '*Dès maintenant, Ouologuem montre tout ce que l'imaginaire africain peut apporter au roman français*'. (As of now, Ouologuem displays everything that the African imagination can contribute to the French novel.) This is, of course, an equivocal statement and can, as it were, work both ways. Ouologuem has not, to my knowledge, admitted that he used *Le Dernier des Justes* as a blueprint for his novel, but once the fact is obvious, there are many oblique references in the same spirit as that just quoted which one could interpret as veiled confessions or spoofs... Furthermore, many of the passages of Ouologuem's follow-up *Lettre à la France Nègre*, which an uninitiated reader would admire as sheer vitriol and righteous indignation, can now, in the light of Ouologuem's extensive debt, only be considered persiflage or pathetic irony. (The footnote: The essay entitled "Lettre aux pisse-copie nègres d'écrivains celèbres" [Letter to Negro imitators of famous writers: pp. 163—179)] with its formula for literary brain-picking, now emerges not as the satire it appears to be, but rather as an all-too-real modus operandi.) *Le devoir de violence* is not, after all, the first real African novel! It is as deeply set in European literary tradition as, say, Ferdinand Oyono's *Une Vie de boy* or Camara Laye's *L'Enfant noir* (The Black Child)."

Ouologuem's novel is certainly very exceptional in modern African writing and despite the controversial problem of its originality, it nevertheless must assume a significant place in the series of recent efforts.

3.2 Upper Volta

Anoumou Pedro Santos wrote a five-act play, *Fasi, Moussa Sawadogo*. He produced his play *Fille de la Volta* (Daughter of Volta, 1961) on the occasion of the country's independence celebrations, and also the historical drama *L'oracle* (The Oracle, 1961). Ouamdégré Ouedraogo's *L'avare moaga* (The Miser Moaga, 1961) is a typical *comédie de moeurs*.

Nazi Boni, the politician of the illegal Republican Party of Liberty, is the only novelist of Upper Volta. Born in 1912, he followed the development of the Negro literary movement and was particularly influenced by the writings of René Maran of the island of Martinique. Maran, whose *Batouala* was awarded the Goncourt Prize in 1921, also wrote *Le livre de la brousse* (The Book of the Bush, 1934), which inspired Nazi Boni's *Le crépuscule des temps anciens* (The Dusk of Ancient Times, 1962). It records the history of the Bwamu region, dwelling on details describing village life, with its ceremonies and customs as well as battles.

3.3 Guinea

The famous poet and organizer of *Ballet Africain,* Keita Fodéba (b. 1921), worked as a teacher. He produced the following collections: *Poèmes africains* (African Poems, 1950) and *l'Aube africaine* (African Dawn, 1965). He uses the traditional poetic garb for his modern subjects, but has achieved only an average standard; the same is true of his plays *Le maître d'école* (The Schoolmaster) and *Minuit* (Midnight, 1952). All his works are based on folklore.

Condotto Nené Khali Camara (b. 1930) also wrote poetry influenced by popular motifs. Emile Cissé wrote the novels *Faralando* (1958) and *Assiatou de septembre* (Assiatou of September, 1959), describing a love story taking place in the period of the national liberation struggle. The naïve children's book *Moussa, enfant de Guinée* (Moussa, Child of Guinea, 1964) was written by Nabi Youla.

Camara Laye (born in 1924 in Kouroussa) acquired renown after the publication of *L'enfant noir* (The black Child, 1953), his autobiography, telling of his childhood in an African village where his father worked as a blacksmith and goldsmith. He describes his native house, his comrades, the other villagers, the harvest, circumcision rites and other passages, he tends to idealize the vanishing ways of life. The characteristic nostalgia of the book results, probably, from the fact that it was written during the author's stay in Paris. Having finished his primary schooling, Camara Laye continued his education first in Conakry; then he went to France, where he was employed in the Citroen Works. After his return to Guinea, he held several significant posts but finally left for Senegal, as he was not in agreement with Sékou Touré's regime.

Camara Laye proved to be a very gifted writer, even in his first book, which was awarded the Charles Veillon Prize. Left-wing critics were not very enthusiastic about

L'enfant noir, as they felt these reminiscences and descriptions of tribal traditions were turning attention away from the most topical problems. The work was translated into many foreign languages, as its fresh style and simple but graceful narrative presentation were generally appreciated.

Readers found more difficult to understand his second novel *Le regard du roi* (The Radiance of the King, 1954). Many symbols and mystical allusions make the text much more obtuse than *L'enfant noir.* The second book, however, reveals some new qualities of the writer.

This work has a European hero named Clarence who has lost all his money at cards. He comes to some unknown part of Africa, gets into trouble and does not know what to do. So he decides to look for a mysterious African king, in order to find some protection. But this is by no means easy, as the king is rarely seen in public. A beggar advises Clarence to go south to seek the king. His journey is full of difficulties, but finally he succeeds in meeting him.

The novel was regarded as man's search for God, but certain critics viewed it differently. Janheinz Jahn saw in Clarence the white man affected by African traditions. Clarence is treated in Africa as badly as the Negroes used to be. Clarence's bitter experiences do not seem to show the validity of Christian attitudes. It is significant, in our opinion, that Clarence constantly learns new things in Africa, thus increasing his wisdom. Camara Laye probably tried to reverse the old-fashioned "European teacher—African pupil" concept, in order to show that the whites could be taught by the blacks as well. This would undoubtedly be in accordance with his belief in the equality of peoples and races.

"Quite as much as a search for God, Clarence's pilgrimage seems to be a search for identification. He becomes more and more like his human companions, plunging far deeper into sensuality than they, only in order to purge away his separation and superiority. The beggar not only bosses and tricks him, but teaches him a lesson in humility. For, as he says, ,,begging is not an easy life" (G. Moore, 1962, p. 37).

Camara Laye's short story *Les yeux de la statue* (The Eyes of the Statue, 1959) poses even more problems for its interpreters. It narrates the story of a woman who comes to the ruins of a palace, where, under the thick grass, lies a statue with penetrating eyes. The lonely heroine flees upstairs as the grass mysteriously grows up and the statue rises as well. The woman cannot escape; she must die. The palace may symbolize the ancient historical glory of African empires, while the persecuting eyes represent an eternal vague element, which provoked some critics to refer to Camara Laye's specifically African manner of thinking. But it is probable that this fantastic story cannot be satisfactorily interpreted in rationalistic terms, as the author, unlike in *Le regard du roi,* never departs from his mysteries, to give the reader some solid ground.

His latest novel *Dramouss* (A Dream of Africa, 1966) describes a man who has spent six years in Paris. He comes back to his native country, which is about to become independent. During numerous meetings, which give him opportunities to observe the new life in his homeland, he gradually arrives at a bitter criticism of the behaviour of politicians, increasing violence in human relations and the deterioration of good traditions. It is evident that Camara Laye intended to show the present-day regime in Guinea in black colours. But in comparison with his previous works, it only shows the decline of the author's creative abilities. Even those who might agree with Camara Laye's critical comments would certainly admit that the effect of this criticism—and, of course, the general artistic impression—suffers much from the inaccuracy of some passages.

3.4 The Ivory Coast

Poetry is a well-developed sector of Ivory Coast writing. Joseph Miezan Bognini (b. 1936) offered his melodious verses in his collection *Ce dur appel de l'espoir* (This Harsh Appeal of Hope, 1960). Maurice Koné wrote *La guirlande des verbes* (The Garland of Words, 1961), *Au bout du petit matin* (At the End of Early Morning, 1962) and *Au seuil du crépuscule* (On the Threshold of Dusk, 1965). He also produced the novel *Le jeune homme de Bouaké* (The Young Man of Bouaké, 1963). Charles Nokan (b. 1937), in his novel *Le soleil noir point* (The Black Sun Rises, 1962), speaks of a young African student's sojourn in Paris. After his return home, he organizes the economic and cultural life of his village. Despite the sentimentality and banality of the subject, the novel is impressive, thanks to its style and composition.

The most famous writer of the Ivory Coast is Bernard Boua Dadié (born in 1916 in Assini). He studied first in his own country and then in Senegal, at the William Ponty School. He continued his work in Senegal at the well-known *Institut Français d'Afrique Noire* (IFAN), spending eleven years there (1936—1947). His early historical play *Assémien Déhylé, roi du Sanwi* (Assémien Déhylé, King of Sanwi) is based on a legend. Dadié also wrote the collection of poems *Afrique debout!* (Africa Arise! 1950), *La ronde des jours* (The Cycle of the Days, 1956) and *Hommes de tous les continents* (People of All Continents, 1967), the novels *Climbié* (1953), *Un nègre à Paris* (A Negro in Paris, 1959), *Patron de New York* (New York Boss, 1964), *La ville où nul ne meurt* (The City Where No One Dies, 1969), collections of folk-tales *Le pagne noir* (The Black Loin-Cloth, 1955), *Légendes africaines* (African Legends, 1954) and the plays *Sidi Maître Escroc* (Sidi, Master Swindler), *Situation difficile* (Difficult Situation), *Serment d'amour* (Oath of Love, 1969) and *Monsieur Thogo-Ghini* (1970). He also published numerous essays and articles, e.g. "Le rôle de la légende dans la culture populaire des noirs d'Afrique" (The Role of the Legend in the Popular Culture of Black Africans) in *Présence africaine*, XIV—XV, 1957) and "Le conte-élément de solidarité et d'universalité" (The Tale—An Element of Solidarity and Universality), his paper at the Second Congress of Negro Writers and Artists.

With regard to his literary works, Dadié's ideological development after World War II was of decisive importance. He came back to the Ivory Coast in 1947, where numerous inhabitants were taking part in protest actions against the colonial system. He became one of the leaders of the Ivory Coast section of the *Rassemblement Démocratique Africain* (RDA), the political organization referred to in the section of this book dealing with Senghor's political activities. In 1948, it was still an ally of the Communist Party of

France, but the liberation struggle was also waged by other Left-wing forces and by the liberal intelligentsia.

The second congress of the RDA met at Treichville (the suburban district of Abidjan, capital of the Ivory Coast) to elect its committee headed by Houphouet-Boigny, the present-day president of the Ivory Coast. The activities of the organization conflicted with the colonial administration which was trying to frighten its opponents. On February 6, 1949, disturbances were provoked in which the police force interfered and arrested many people, including Dadié. In March 1950, Dadié was sentenced to three years' imprisonment (he was released after sixteen months in jail). During this relatively short period, profound changes took place in the country. After consultations with the French, its political leaders, headed by Houphouet-Boigny, decided to abandon the revolutionary line of action and adopt a new political orientation, which was proclaimed on October 19, 1950. The basis of this orientation was the belief that liberation efforts do not imply anti-French policies or any alliance with the French Communists. Thus, future cooperation with France was ensured and the colonial administration halted its political persecution of the "loyalists".

In this critical phase of the Ivory Coast's national liberation struggle, Dadié came out of prison. He observed the behaviour of his companions and no longer took part in political life. Rather, he concentrated his attention on research and creative writing, in which we can find his answers to a number of topical questions. He continued compiling folklore, mainly legends and fables, and created his literary adaptations. His collections of poetry are contrasting: while *Afrique debout* is full of radicalism, *La ronde des jours* betrays a Senghorian tendency toward introspection and reconciliation. The influence of lyrical spirituals can be seen in the second collection as well. Both of them, however, present the poet's humanistic message and express his belief in the equality of nations and people.

His first novel *Climbié* is autobiographical, though it is not written in the European tradition can be perceived in the novel's content, and African tradition in its form. While the first part (written probably as early as 1953) deals with the hero's childhood, the second part touches—in some passages—on the crisis of the national liberation struggle. Climbié, like Dadié himself, studies at the William Ponty School. During his studies, he goes through some dramatic experiences and makes a series of philosophical considerations. Dadié is particularly successful in revealing how the white man's prestige was being lost at the beginning of World War II. He is very familiar with the colonial service and describes vividly the strike of its employees, following which Climbié is arrested. But despite the author's interest in the topical aspects of political reality, the novel is written in a moderate spirit, with humour and satire softening the sharp edges of his criticism.

Dadié's following novels could be considered as travel books about the great cities of the West: Paris, New York and Rome. *Le nègre à Paris* is notable for the satirical form of the letters sent from Paris to someone living in a developing country. This method used by Montesquieu in his *Lettres persanes* gives the writer an excellent chance to view life in the capital of France from a new and different angle. Similarly philosophical are *Patron de New York* and *La ville où nul ne meurt*. The former traces the immense differences between the highly advanced technological civilization of the USA and the author's own under-developed country, but it considers as the main problem the search for genuine human values.

Légendes africaines and *Le pagne noir* adopted the form of folktales and fables, in order to portray the African of our times. Their modern content appears in the ancient fable form to such an advantage because these collections of stories—like the author's novels—are written in excellent French, full of impressive images and sophisticated similes. Dadié's works are among the highlights of the French-written literature of the Ivory Coast and find many admirers abroad. Together with André Terrisse, Dadié published a collection of fables for children, *Les belles histoires de Kacou Annansé, l'araignée* (The Charming Stories of Kacou Ananse, the Spider, 1963).

Aké Loba (born in 1927 in Abobo Baoule) came from a large family. His father had twelve children and could send his son to study in France only after World War II. Aké Loba was then already eighteen years old. Although the young man wished to study agriculture, he first had to earn his living as a farm worker in Bretagne and Beauce. After his father's death, he worked in a factory in Paris, devoting evenings to his studies. He spent fifteen years in France and in 1960 returned to the Ivory Coast, like many other Africans.

The autobiographical elements in his novel *Kocoumbo, l'étudiant noir* (Kocoumbo, the Black Student, 1960) are rather limited, though the analogies between Kocoumbo's and the author's fates are evident. Kocoumbo also leaves his village to study at a secondary school where his fellow students are much younger than he. He often meets with racial prejudice and suffers from the misunderstandings resulting from it. His nostalgia and char-acteristic depressions are very convincingly shown by the writer. But it is in the Latin Quarter of Paris that he experiences the real conflict of two different worlds. This part is portrayed vividly and in great detail. Loba succeeds in presenting convincing psychological analyses of Kocoumbo's companions and companions espousing different political trends. He describes the black student's troubles, and his determination to finish his studies successfully. After doing so, Kocoumbo leaves Paris for his native country, where he is to become a judge. Loba obviously tries to show the process of emancipation as embodied in the young hero of his novel. But in concentrating his attention on the ideological and psycho-logical aspects of his writing, he sometimes neglects its artistic form. For this reason, some passages are not adequately elaborated, are naïve or else are carelessly written.

A struggle for the chieftaincy in a village is the basis of Ahmadou Kourouma's novel *Les soleils des indépendances* (The Suns of Independence, 1968).

Sidiki Dembele, in his novel *Les inutiles* (The Useless Ones), deals with Africans who stay in Europe rather than return to Africa, though they can only earn a very humble living abroad. The novel's hero rejects the African tradition which obliges him to financially support his relatives. He thinks he can solve all his problems by leaving for Paris, where he finds, however, only more discouraging factors. He decides that he is wasting his life in foreign surroundings and can never realize his aspirations. Why does the author denote him as a useless man? Because he is not courageous enough to face the difficulties in his na-tive country, which primarily requires the hard work of its inhabitants. The developing countries cannot attain a higher standard of living without such systematic efforts, for the wealth and prestige of any country have always been based on the diligence of its population, the author has us understand. Dembele's hero returns home to observe the great progress that the Ivory Coast has made during his long absence.

3.5 Togoland

Toussaint Viderot Mensah is the author of the collection of poems *Courage, si tu veux vivre et t'épanouir* (Courage, if you Want to Live and Flourish, 1957) and *Pour toi, nègre, mon frère* (For You, Negro, My Brother, 1960), which hails the country's independence.

David Ananou in *Le Fils du fétiche* (Son of the Fetish, 1955) introduces a young hero emerging from traditional thinking into Christianity. The work, the action of which takes place before World War II, is marked by excessive gratitude for the white man's civilization. The author is aware of the complications resulting from a compromise between tribal and modern ways of living.

3.6 Dahomey

Even before World War II, Paul Hazoumé (born in 1890 in Porto-Novo) gained a reputation for his anti-racist essays. His historical novel *Doguicimi* (1938) was awarded several prizes, including that of the French Academy. Hazoumé, who studied history and ethnography, describes the rule of King Ghezo (1818—1858), i.e. the period following Britain's abolition of the slave trade. Although the king follows his advisers' ideas too closely, he nevertheless succeeds in expanding his empire. Despite the brutality of his rule, the book is intended as a celebration of the heroic struggles for one's homeland. One interesting episode mentions the visit of a group from Portugal to the royal court. The European visitors admire the king's wealth, but still consider Negroes as barbarians. From the psychological point of view, the most detailed portrait is that of the heroine, who is finally killed by her husband's enemies. Mutual relationships between Africa and Europe are regarded as profitable by the author. Hazoumé's advanced style and vivid similes are worth mentioning.

Jean Pliya adapted several traditional legends in *L'arbre fétiche* (The Fetish Tree, 1963) and *Kondo le requin* (Kondo, the Shark, 1965). Maxmilian B. Quénum published *Trois légendes africaines* (Three African Legends, 1947.) Felix Couchoro wrote *Drame d'amour à Anecho* (A Drama of Love in Anecho, 1950), *L'héritage, cette peste* (Heritage, This Plague, 1963) and *L'esclave* (The Slave).

The best-known prose writer of Dahomey is Olympe Bhêly-Quénum (b. 1928), who spent his childhood in Cotonou and then studied in France. He has written two novels *Un piège sans fin* (An Unending Snare, 1960) and *Le chant du lac* (Song of the Lake, 1965). The herdsman Ahounna, hero of *Un piège sans fin*, is satisfied with his married life. But one day his wife becomes jealous as she has seen her husband, in her dream, with another woman. When the woman appears in reality, Ahounna's wife becomes very angry and Ahounna has to flee from his house, as he is afraid of his father-in law. His story nov becomes nearly tragic, because he must live in the forest, like an animal. Unintentionally, he kills a woman and is arrested by the police. Remarkable passages are devoted to descriptions of prison life. Ahounna is first sentenced to lifetime imprisonment, and then to death, after an unsuccessful attempt to flee from jail. He becomes a victim of the provocation planned by another prisoner, the murdered woman's son, who advises him to run away and at the same time discloses the plan to the prison guards. Ahounna's tragedy is now complete, for the chain of snares inevitably leads him to his death.

Le chant du lac analyzes the villagers' attitude to the powerful God of the Lake. In this work, Bhêly-Quénum confirms the positive qualities of his first novel, his excellent handling of linguistic means, and his good knowledge of African traditions. In both novels he devotes much space to descriptions of customs, the villagers' behaviour, and the psychological development of different characters of contrasting educational levels and both sexes. Moreover, the composition of his novels is comparatively satisfactory, with episodes effectively supporting the main lines of action.

Richard Dogbeh presented his impressions of his trip to the USSR in *Voyage au pays de Lénine* (Trip to the Country of Lenin, 1967) and produced the following books of poetry: *Les eaux du Mono* (The Waters of Mono, 1963), *Rives mortelles* (Mortal Banks, 1964) and *Cap Liberté* (Cape Liberty, 1969). Bazou Gibirila published his verses in *Rencontres et passions* (Meetings and Passions, 1961). The most prolific poet of Dahomey is Paulin Joachim (born in 1931 in Cotonou), who studied law in Lyon and then worked as a journalist in Paris. His best-known poem is probably "Pour saluer l'Afrique à l'envol rendu libre" (To Hail Africa in Flight Rendered Free), while his most significant collection of poems is *Anti-grâce* (1967). He is also the author of *Un nègre raconte* (A Negro Narrates, 1954).

3.7 Chad

Joseph Brahim Seid (born in 1927 in Fort-Lamy) has found his inspiration in folklore. His poetical patriotic narratives are called *Au Tchad sous les étoiles* (To Chad, Under the Stars, 1962) and *Un enfant du Tchad* (A Child of Chad, 1967).

3.8 The Central African Republic

Pierre Makombo Bamboté (b. 1932) is a poet with a keen social feeling, who attempts to write committed verses; they have been published in various journals. Although his work is not extensive, it is well written.

3.9 Niger

This country has not yet greatly developed its French-written literature. Ibrahim Issa's *Grandes eaux noires* (The Great Black Waters, 1959) is partly based on folk myths and legends interlaced with the author's personal treatment of the history of one tribe. The writer's approach to historical subject-matter (insofar as it is used in his heterogeneous type of book) is essentially idealistic. He undoubtedly overestimates the spiritual values of the vanishing world of traditions and does not see clearly the importance of scientific progress. However, his efforts to conserve oral traditions are commendable.

VI. WEST AFRICAN LITERATURES IN STANDARD ENGLISH

1. Nigerian English-written Literature

1.0 Introduction

Nigeria plays in anglophone West Africa just as prominent a role as Senegal does in the francophone zone. Before discussing individual modern authors, it should be noted that a number of gifted men came from that country, even at the time of the slave trade. One of them was Olaudah Equiano (b. 1745), a forefather of the sub-Saharan writers, who represented the abolitionist spirit of his period. He came from Iboland, the East Nigerian region that also has given the country the majority of outstanding authors of the present time. At the age of eleven, Olaudah Equiano was transported to America on a slave ship. Later, he went to Britain where he married an English girl and became a Christian. Thanks to his education and literary abilities, he took an active part in abolitionist efforts.

This purpose was served by his exciting autobiography *The Interesting Narrative of Olaudah Equiano or Gustavus Vassa, the African, Written by Himself* (1789). The author sold his book himself at 4 shillings a copy. He was very successful and by 1793 had |already seen seven editions of his work. Much attention was attracted by its most recent edition (in 1967), but Equiano's ideas had been quoted in literature much earlier. Olaudah Equiano's work is most remarkable in its passages relating to historical records. His book is written in a plain, expressive style, like other English abolitionist books.

The rise of modern Nigerian creative writing in English dates from the period following World War II. The dissatisfaction of the masses was demonstrated in the big strike of June 1945, but political activities were carried out mainly by the national bourgeoisie and students. The Richard Constitution, approved in 1946, divided Nigeria into three regions, each with its separate House of Assembly and House of Chiefs. Consequently, the political activities of the most radical party—the National Council of Nigeria and the Cameroons (NCNC)—were essentially restricted to the Eastern Region. It was by no means an easy matter for the Ibos and Ibibios to rise above existing tribal and local interests and seek the path towards Nigeria's independence. The NCNC party, led by Dr. Nnamdi Azikiwe from 1946 on, was probably the only political force capable of realizing this task throughout the country. The Action Group (AG) could influence only the Western Region. It had a more conservative programme corresponding to the outlooks of the authoritarian Yoruba chiefs. Logically enough, the Action Group did not request centralization—as the NC did—since the economic security of the Western Region seemed to be excellently ensured.

Azikiwe's party was never able to exert much influence in the Northern Region, which differed from the remaining parts of Nigeria both culturally and economically. It could rely on the petty bourgeoisie and intelligentsia and profited also from the increasing political activities of the working class. It was the eastern coal-miners and dockers, organized in their trade unions, who constituted a real political force. The NCNC refused to be a one-tribe organization and tried to unite all the anti-colonialist elements. This was particularly difficult, because of the increasing contradictions within the party. There were too many different social groups within it, with contrasting interests. The proletariat was obviously very radical and after a cruel lesson (the big strike of 1949) it demanded immediate political independence. At that time, the political leaders recommended peaceful means. A split in the party became inevitable.

The Macpherson Constitution of 1951 resulted from long and difficult negotiations. New British concessions did not seem to satisfy the Nigerians, who nevertheless achieved a better representation in the most important organs. The principle of parity suggested the solution of a new balance of power within the federal structure: the Northern Region had the same number of seats (68) in the House of Representatives as the two remaining regions put together. In addition to the basic contradiction (Britain-Nigeria), there was another (North-South). But this was to play an important part only in an independent country.

The Northern Region, influenced by the Northern People's Congress (the NPC—founded in 1951), was economically lagging behind. It could be satisfied by the Macpherson Constitution and did not try to ask for independence at once. On the contrary, the departure of the British colonialists, it was thought, might bring many troubles to the traditional rulers of the North. Finally (in 1957), however, the NPC also had to revise its attitude toward the colonial administration. Its position in the Northern Region remained unshaken after the Lyttleton Constitution had been declared in 1954. The party was represented in the newly-elected Federal Legislative Council most satisfactorily. The NCNC and the AG had to wait until December 1959, when they obtained a more adequate number of seats in the Parliament. The NCNC was able to retain a comparatively large number of voters in the Western Region, but it was not yet sufficient. Independent Nigeria (as of October 1, 1960) had to seek a compromise, as none of the parties could govern the Federation without the assistance of the others.

The first six years of independent Nigeria saw a deterioration of the existing federal system. The period ended with the two well-known military coups d'état in 1966, which took place on the eve of the Civil War that crippled both Nigeria's economy and its culture.

The Nigerian writers tried to find suitable criteria for defining their literature. Chinua Achebe thought that African literature was created by every writing African; Christopher Okigbo rejected both the chosen theme of the work and race of the author as criteria: Cyprian Ekwensi believed that African literature reflected African philosophy, culture and especially psychology.

Nigerian writers do not often attempt to entertain their readers, though some intentionally entertaining passages can be found in the works of Cyprian Ekwensi and Vincent Ike. On the whole, Nigerian reality is full of serious problems and the reminiscences of the colonial past are usually connected with some kind of bitterness. Irony occurs only very rarely in modern Nigerian novels; most authors are perhaps afraid of being misunderstood. The Nigerian novelists seem to realize their responsibility in the process of political, economic and cultural emancipation.

But pathetic writing, which is often encountered in African works written in French, can hardly be discovered in Nigeria. Instead of violent passions, pragmatic attitudes seem to prevail, resulting perhaps from the British rationalistic tradition. Chinua Achebe, for example, presents quite unbiased views, adopting a typically detached position in all his early novels. Nigerian novelists are undoubtedly less radical in their anti-colonialist statements than their Cameroonian colleagues, but their sober, matter-of-fact judgements are no less effective in a discussion of essential questions.

A balance between rationalistic and emotional elements is appreciated by Nigerians. The degree of radicalism partly depends on the author's social position. High officials, professors, diplomats, civil engineers, etc. employed by the government do not usually express their criticism as openly as political rebels. Most Nigerian writers served the political leadership of independent Nigeria. Only at the dawn of the Nigerian Civil War did their Ibo origin or liberal opinions make most of them more critical of the existing regime. The most perceptive authors, however, devoted attention to the ideological and economic contradictions several years before the outbreak of the conflict.

The conflict did not break out unexpectedly, but it came rapidly indeed. One must not forget that the young generation of Nigerian intellectuals taking part in the construction of their independent country lived in an atmosphere of enthusiasm and optimism. It was not easy to discern the depth of the incipient contradictions. Intellectuals in West Africa generally enjoy a much higher standard of living than the masses of the people. If they endeavour to depict the situation of the lower classes, they encounter certain difficulties. They seldom come into contact with small farmers and workers, as the existing gap in the present-day social structure has been maintained or even widened. The independent states of West Africa, having no sizeable European minorities, have great need for their own intelligentsia. There are no racial conflicts and the interests of the rising intelligentsia are sometimes similar to those of the national bourgeoisie, which is naturally much wealthier. The higher these new West African intellectuals rise on the social scale, the more remote they become from the masses of the population. Therefore educated persons, who are no longer able to understand the inhabitants of their native villages, are often portrayed in Nigerian literature.

The process of Africanization was successfully shown by Timothy Aluko in *One Man, One Matchet* and in *Kinsman and Foreman,* by Chinua Achebe in *No Longer at Ease,* and by some other writers, Nigerian novelists have naturally devoted much attention to the life of the upper middle class. Some Nigerian novels are devoted mainly to the intellectual milieu, e.g. Vincent Ike's *Toads for Supper* and Wole Soyinka's *The Interpreters.* Neither Achebe nor Ekwensi have dealt exclusively with the poorest sections of the Lagos population. On the contrary, such characters—e.g. Aina and her family in Ekwensi's *People of the City*—play only marginal parts in their novels. Moreover, the existence of the proletariat is hardly mentioned in modern Nigerian novels. Typical village novels (John

Munonye's *The Only Son*, Onuora Nzekwu's *Blade Among the Boys*, Flora Nwapa's *Efuru*, Chinua Achebe's *Things Fall Apart* and *Arrow of God*, Elechi Amadi's *The Concubine*, Cyprian Ekwensi's *Burning Grass*, etc.) only occasionally show the poverty of the villagers. Instead, they describe religious rites, folklore, customs and traditions, psychological problems, spreading literacy, etc. One of their aims is to illustrate the transformation of the social structure, but the sociological aspect is frequently overshadowed by the psychological one.

Although the white man is regularly portrayed with some criticism, he is never shown with hatred. We may recall Chinua Achebe's ironical characterization of the District Commissioner in *Things Fall Apart*, of Mr. Green in *No Longer at Ease* (Mr. Green is a minor character) and of Captain Winterbottom in *Arrow of God*, Aluko's interesting study of Stanfield in *One Man, One Matchet* and of the British director in *Kinsman and Foreman*. The conflicts of the black and white characters in modern Nigerian novels result from different social positions and possibilities rather than from racial differences.

The situation in Nigeria is seen through the eyes of a well-educated South African as follows: "...the main concern of the average educated African in Nigeria is to get into government service, which affords him civil servants' quarters, a car, at least two servants and a comfortable living. There is a mad rush to pass examinations as a gateway to this El Dorado. Anything offered that does not ensure a certificate in the end is avoided. Cultural activity becomes the business mainly of those in the lower strata who find their lives empty without some ritual or another. Extra-mural lectures and week-end schools organized by the university college have a bias for studies in government and economics" (Mphahlele, 1962).

The difference between the Yorubas and the Ibos results from the different degree of urbanization, as well. This important process started in Yorubaland in pre-colonial times, when the Ibos lived exclusively in their villages. The principal urban communities of Iboland are very young indeed and only a very small fragment of the Ibo population can be found in the towns. This is not due to the Nigerian Civil War alone. It results from their traditional way of living. Practically every second Yoruba is a town dweller.

"The superficial delights and real terrors of the city have been known ever since Aesop, who was in all probability an African, too. Expanding African cities like Lagos, Accra and Dakar impress those who visit them with their vivacity and their incongruities—fine public buildings and sprawling, corrugated slum dwellings, elegant discourse and incredible journalese, ambitious, intelligent economic planning and egregious personal self-improvement schemes. As in all cities, the appearances govern the realities." (J. I. Gleason, *This Africa*, Evanston, 1965).

This comment of J. I. Gleason enables the reader to understand why the idea of "city life" is always used by Nigerians in a very narrow sense. We know that most modern Nigerian writers came from Iboland and we might expect that the Eastern towns (Calabar, Enugu, Port Harcourt) would be portrayed in their works. But these towns are considered neither attractive nor interesting. In fact, city life means in modern Nigerian novels Lagos life, though Lagos has neither the greatest number of inhabitants nor the most valuable cultural monuments. Lagos is, however, not only the capital of the Federation, but also an important centre of intellectual life.

There are many newcomers in West African cities, and the heroes of Nigerian novels are often linked with their village backgrounds. Many of Ekwensi's characters, for instance, come from villages (Filia, in Iska) or leave their towns (Jagua Nana). Some larger communities in the provinces are often denoted as "towns" although they are actually still villages. The typical distribution to be found in the industrialized countries—towns inhabited chiefly by factory workers and villages by farmers—has not yet become valid for certain West African towns. The small towns still remain the agricultural centres, since industry is not developed. Busy market relations, immigration resulting from the relative lack of jobs, the backwardness of provincial life and other factors create a number of problems. Traditional family ties, tribal and economic prejudices and economic difficulties prevent the people of the cities from achieving real emancipation.

Despite the requirements of modern life, a group of outcasts exists. The very serious problem of the osù was touched on by Chinua Achebe in *No Longer at Ease*. It is now the task of the political leadership to find suitable means for eliminating the surviving ideas of religious cults and superstitions and to implement the social integration of all citizens. The modern Nigerian novelists can be compared to people who have come to a crossroad. Some of them reflect on the choice of the right direction. At the same time, relatively small financial means, the proper utilization of which in the peaceful development of Nigeria would have been most desirable, have been squandered. This cannot be undone. For this reason, precisely at this critical time the writer's work may acquire an exceptional importance, appealing to the collective conscience of the whole world.

Nigerian novelists are generally regarded as progressive individuals. They are also expected to attack all kinds of vestiges of the past. However, the best Nigerian novelists really defend those aspects of the old life that are worth preserving. Cyprian Ekwensi wishes to help preserve the old moral code in the general scramble for money. Few modern writers have exposed bribery so vigorously as he, Achebe and Aluko.

Our interpretation of Nigerian novels would have been easier if their authors had stuck to a certain theory (the African personality, négritude, etc.). But the Nigerian authors are mostly very sceptical in this respect. Such theories do not stand high in their favour and cannot be considered as ideological bases for their works. Moreover, hardly any Nigerian novelists will accepta "generalization": this aversion, however, does not result from the fact that such theories usually come from the French-writing countries.

Twenty-five years ago, Nigerian and other West African writers were almost entirely dependent on journals, magazines and reviews. Some of them (e. g. *The West African Review* and *The Atlantic Monthly*) enjoyed a high reputation. Each contributor could consider it a personal success if his short stories or poems weer published therein. This one-sided orientation, it should be pointed out, resulted from the lack of opportunities. The very limited number of non-periodical publications was in contradiction with the post-war abundance of short stories. Most of these could not be published in collections or anthologies and had to find their way to the editorial boards of periodicals. In the Fifties, many literary competitions were organized to enable beginners to gain both experience and their first laurels. The most important competitions were launched by the British Council in Nigeria and by the new publishing house and literary club, Mbari, in Ibadan (founded in 1961). The main journal *Black Orpheus* originated in 1957 and has played an important role ever since.

This journal has published not only Nigerian poems and short stories, but also works by other English-writing Africans. Language has not been regarded as a limitation, for translations from French and Portuguese, etc. have also been included. But the journal has centred mainly on English writing, publishing contributions by West Indian and North American writers as well. Preference has been given to non-white artists, though criticism has been accepted from white authors and editors. The racial criterion has always been felt, as it corresponds to the title of the journal. Another characteristic quality of the journal has been its interest in various kinds of art, chiefly painting. The relationships between painting and literature have not been analyzed in much detail, but they may be interesting and useful in some cases, as a few sub-Saharan authors express their ideas also in their pictures. Another inspiring source of aesthetic information may result from comparative studies of folk sculpture and traditional oral art; although we cannot expect from this approach conclusions having general validity, nevertheless they could enable us to better understand the specific means of artistic expression chosen by the different tribes. Ulli Beier has done a good deal to discern the main aesthetic principles of traditional Africa, in his comments published in *Black Orpheus*.

Criticizing the direction chosen by the editors, V. N. Vavilov (in his Russian-written essay "Zhurnal Chornyy Orfey" in *Literatura stran Afriki,* Moscow, 1964) observes that the publicist poetry of Nigeria and Ghana is not appreciated, while modernist, stream-of-consciousness poems are praised, despite their vague and unclear meaning. He shows that the principles of English and American "new criticism" are applied with the intention of creating "typically African" writing and turning away from contemporary problems. Hence, V. N. Vavilov demonstrates the fact that the critics prefer formalist, rather eccentric, experiments to the realistic method, which is considered too European and too much bound up with 19th century artistic expression. For this reason, true-to-life painting has been neglected by the journal. Vavilov also dislikes Beier's favourite criterion used in determining the "typically African" qualities of a work of art: i.e. the African does not draw a demarcation line between the living and the dead.

If modern Nigerian novelists had found suitable examples to follow in Europe and in America, they might have started their activities sooner. But one of the reasons why modern Nigerian novels are worth reading and studying is that they originated only in response to internal changes appearing in the country's historical development. This should be stressed, chiefly because the masses of the population were still illiterate and therefore relevant numbers of readers had to be found abroad and particularly outside Africa.

Another factor contributing to the rise of Nigerian literature lies in the sphere of material prerequisites. Eldred Jones wrote on this subject: "One of the most striking things to me in Nigeria is the large number of small printing presses in the whole of southern Nigeria. So it is no surprise that Nigeria as a whole produces more creative literature than the rest of English-speaking West Africa put together. Mere size does not quite explain it, for Nigerian literature comes from a comparatively small area of the country." (Eldred Jones, "Jungle Drums and Wailing Piano" in *African Forum*, Vol. 1, No. 4, 1966).

In 1958, when the golden age of the modern Nigerian novel began, a new series was launched in London: Heinemann's *African Writers Series*. It is not by mere chance that many Nigerian novels have been published since that time. After all, Chinua Achebe himself works as an editorial adviser with that enterprise.

Heinemann's series is certainly not the only important collection of African writings, but it has done some pioneering work in this field. Despite some commercial risk, which is inevitable in publishing beginners' work, the series has popularized many gifted writers in the early stage of their artistic development. These systematic paper-back editions have helped to make the most notable works constantly accessible to all serious students of African writing, at relatively low prices.

1.1 Cyprian Ekwensi

Like most major novelists of Nigeria, Cyprian Ekwensi (b. 1921) is an Ibo. He does not come from the east, however; his birthplace was Minna in the Northern Region. He studied at Achimota College (Ghana), at Ibadan and in England. Although his subjects were pharmacy and forestry, writing became his main occupation very early. As a writer, he proceeded from magazine sketches to sophisticated novels, from modest beginnings to international renown. After World War II, he produced fables and reproductions of folk-tales. His short stories and novelettes, written in the manner of Onitsha market literature, are still rather naïve.

One of these, *When Love Whispers* (Onitsha 1947), is strikingly didactic, and, as F. R. Kuti remarks in the preface, the heroine's experience should be a lesson to all young women. The positive characters helping the young girl are strictly separated from the "villains", while the heroine stands in the very centre of this simple structure. This basic pattern, with more complications, appears even in Ekwensi's first novel *People of the City* (London 1954).

In 1958, Ekwensi was appointed head of a department in the Nigerian Broadcasting Corporation and in 1961 he became director of the Federal Ministry of Information. Apart from folk-tales, popular tales and thrillers: *Ikolo the Wrestler* (1947), *The Leopard's Claw* (1947), *Yara Roundabout Murder* (1962), *The Rainmaker* (1964), *The Great Elephant-Bird* (1965), and *Trouble in Form Six* (1966) — he has published a few children's books: *The Drummer Boy* (1960), *Passport to Mallam Ilia* (1960) and *An African Night's Entertainment* (1962). Such books are still rare in West Africa.

Ekwensi's first novel—*People the of City* (1954)—was a pioneering work, both as a bold representation of Lagos life and as an attempt at novel-writing in West Africa. In contrast to a great number of post-war short stories, novels had been neglected, probably because they were considered too demanding. Ekwensi himself regarded short stories as a preparation for a higher stage, i.e. novels. There are two protagonists in *People of the City;* an ambitious journalist who comes to Lagos from the east, and the city itself. Although Ekwensi mentions the name of the city only once, it is quite clear that he is portraying the splendour and vices of Lagos, the capital of the Federation. He was well aware of its complexity and variety and succeeded in showing different aspects of Lagos life, though unfortunately in doing so he partly sacrificed the structure of the novel. Lacking experience, he turned it into a series of episodes suffering from technical shortcomings and an overloose composition.

From the professional viewpoint, *Jagua Nana* (1960) constituted an improvement. It is the study of the heroine, a Lagos prostitute who grows old while trying to achieve the tranquility and comfort of middle-class respectability through a marriage with a young man needing her financial support during his studies in England. Jagua Nana, whose name is derived partly from a fashionable make of automobile, partly from the name of Zola's memorable character, has to contend with her disappointment when her lover finally marries a younger and more attractive girl. Ekwensi's narrative power increases particularly in the second part of the novel, in which he contrasts Jagua with the squalor of the corruption and criminality of her surroundings. Thus he succeeds in making his heroine fairly sympathetic, though he never conceals her faults. He seems to abandon, in this novel at least, the descriptive realism of *People of the City,* and introduces a more "scientific" approach in the naturalistic manner. His choice of details and expressions is more careful and more sophisticated than heretofore.

Pidgin English is used, chiefly in some dialogues and regularly by Jagua, most effectively for increasing the vividness and authenticity of his story. It is rather ironical that Ekwensi, a great admirer of Lagos, was criticized for "blackening" reality. Some Nigerian intellectuals felt that he ought to have chosen more pleasant aspects of their urban milieu; they did not realize that Ekwensi's intention was to expose the vices of Lagos in order to bring some benefit to his beloved city. He has spent there almost three decades of his life and, in his literary rediscoveries of the changing dimensions of Lagos, he endeavoured to preserve the African moral code that was being lost in the era of vulgar materialism.

More objections could be raised to his linguistic habits, as different elements of argot and pidgin usually served the purpose of stylistic diversity and appeared rather inconsistently. In *Jagua Nana* and his subsequent city novels, Ekwensi tried to produce politically committed literature, though he must have known that his primary interest lying in intimacy would suffer. The character of Jagua is more successful than that of Wilson Iyari in *Beautiful Feathers* (1963), because Ekwensi failed to combine scenes of Lagos public life naturally and spontaneously with his description of Wilson's troublesome married life. Moreover, Ekwensi seems here to be interested more in general considerations.

In *Beautiful Feathers,* one of the most significant problems is that of woman's emancipation. The name of the novel comes from an Ibo proverb and shows the contrast between Wilson's two roles: a brilliant politician and, at the same time, an unsuccessful husband. This contrast is illustrated in the novel several times, e.g. during the hero's public speech, an inserted text in italics shows what he says to himself: "*I talk about solidarity. There it is! My own family, split. But how can Africa be united when such a small unit as my family is not united?*" Like his following city novel—*Iska* (1966)—*Beautiful Feathers* contains a number of satirical allusions to contemporary practices in Nigeria. Both novels show the author's ability to present highly dramatic situations (usually in a couple of powerful sentences maintaining the suspense in the episode). Iska, an Ibo girl from the north, is one of Ekwensi's best female characters, for the dynamics of her actions are conveyed in equally dynamic diction.

The criticism contained in *Iska* in a way summarizes the critical points scattered throughout the writer's preceding works—cynical journalists, corrupt politicians, irresponsible adventurers, religious fanatics, selfish public servants—all these are bitterly exposed. Ekwensi proves in practice that—unlike so many francophone artists—he can do without any traditional background, that the African author need not write primarily about circumcision and ritual murders.

But he did not avoid the traditional subject-matter completely: his *Burning Grass* (1962), praised by some critics and condemned by others, is a surprisingly compact portrayal of the life of Fulani herdsmen living in the Northern Region. Most readers will appreciate the large amount of folklore included, but some of them will be interested in the writer's philosophy and symbols. The fantastic bird followed by the herdsmen has a symbolical function, though the Fulanis follow him also because they must move, continually seeking fresh pastures. Of course, it should be noted that the idyllic traditional picture was found attractive and "genuinely African" by overseas readers, and that Ekwensi could not afford to neglect his non-African audience. Despite the obvious success of *Burning Grass*, he came back to his "city topics", realizing where his forte lay. The linguistic quality of *Burning Grass* is generally praised; Gerald Moore even contrasts its precise descriptions with the low style of *Jagua Nana* and other novels by the same author, the action of which takes place in the city (see *Présence africaine* No. 54, 1965).

Ulli Beier, on the other hand, does not object to the style of *Jagua Nana*, but rather to its "contrived ending": "Jagua, having lost her rival lovers in tragic deaths, returns home, a broken woman. More misfortune befalls her—until a happy ending is fabricated with the help of 50,000 francs that come to her like a *deus ex machina*." (*Black Orpheus*, No. 10). This is not the first case of Ekwensi's yielding to the bad taste of the reader, and one can hardly account for it. The writer was perhaps eager to achieve a commercial success and at the same time he found the handling of the artistic problem very difficult. To tell the truth, he solves similar tasks more skilfully in his later novels than in the earlier ones.

It would be only too easy to enumerate passages in which he "obviously revels in lush descriptions of feminine attractions" to quote Elizabeth Bevan (*Black Orpheus*, No. 4), who discovers a note of sentimentality in *People of the City*. Even those who speak about the "blatant sexual values" accepted by Ekwensi in his descriptions of his charming females could admit that at least some of them serve a higher purpose than teasing the reader. The passionate love-affairs and erotic adventures so frequently occurring in his novels are made more believable and comprehensible in this latter work, and this certainly entitles the writer to run the risk of being criticized for "sensationalism and a station bookstall manner of writing".

On the whole, Ekwensi's "sensationalism" penetrates into other spheres as well. Basing his creative writing on his previous experience in the realm of journalism, thrillers and romantic didactic tales, he presents even his most serious subject-matter in his novels lightly and elegantly. There is an element of superficiality in them, too; but it obviously becomes less apparent in his later fiction. Too much ethnography is found in certain Nigerian novels by some critics, too much sociology in others (including Ekwensi's), but this would not be a major weakness in itself. The principal shortcoming in Ekwensi's case is probably his insufficient ability to integrate these matter-of-fact elements into the structure of some of his novels and his difficulties in combining descriptions of political events with the personality traits of his characters.

Unlike Achebe, Ekwensi usually describes individualities, not literary types, and is more successful in his psychological analyses of women than Achebe is. His novels are less abstracted from reality and represent more immediate accounts of real events. They are more journalistic, more in line with the orientation of Nigerian descriptive realism. Their true-to-life nature is strictly preserved and the characters' way of speaking is carefully presented as authentically as possible.

Nancy Jeanne Schmidt in *An Anthropological Analysis of Nigerian Fiction* quoted by Martin Tucker (1965) wrote as follows: "The descriptions of Lagos and Nigerian feeling in his (Ekwensi's) fiction are indistinguishable from those in factual articles he has written, and his portrayal of employment problems in fiction are identical with those he ascribed to two Nigerian students who asked him for advice about getting a job upon their return to Nigeria." To sum up, one can say that Ekwensi more often presents a registration of social facts than their artistic transformation, which is perhaps a criterion distinguishing his narrative realism from social or critical realism, whose elements are occasionally seen in his novels but which are very typical of those written by Achebe.

Special attention should be paid to Ekwensi's long efforts to convey his ideas in English as effectively as possible. Being a pioneer of Nigerian fiction, he naturally set examples for his West African anglophone followers, but he was handicapped by the fact that the English language was foreign both to him and to his surroundings. The above-mentioned introduction of pidgin into dialogues in *Jagua Nana* and some other books was an attempt to "Africanize" Nigerian fiction in English to a generally acceptable extent. It was a compromise in practice and hardly any theoretical conclusions can be drawn from it, because pidgin is not standardized. It is definitely less understandable than Standard English to readers overseas and, after all, its application will always depend on the writer's desires and tastes.

It is clear, however, that the number of linguistic experiments in modern Nigerian fiction (including Ekwensi's fiction) is not accidental but symptomatic. This is due to the urgent need (felt not only by Nigerian writers) to look for a more genuine expression within a foreign language. Ekwensi's efforts are to be seen in the context of post-war

Nigerian writing, where different approaches have existed. There have been writers who have used their own vernacular only (e.g. the Yoruba author, Fagunwa), authors who have moulded their English on the vernacular structure (Amos Tutuola, in his books, and Gabriel Okara in his novel *The Voice*), novelists using Standard English mixed with frequent elements translated from the vernacular (Nwankwo, in *Danda* et al.) and many others who have either "Africanized" their English very mildly, or used Standard English in its purest form.

While a certain compromise can be found in Ekwensi's language, none exists in the content of his novels. He was asked, of course, why he was so critical of his compatriots living in Lagos and why he wrote so little criticism of the colonialists. This question is answered by his fiction, which shows little interest in the problem of racial oppression in Africa—a problem so intensely discussed in multi-racial communities and countries still dominated by the whites. But the situation in Nigeria is different and Ekwensi deals with other issues. Unlike most of his Nigerian colleagues, he rarely portrays the disintegration of the old tribal society in a direct way (*Burning Grass* pursues a different purpose and constitutes an exception among his novels). While many other Nigerian writers describe villagers in the countryside, Ekwensi is interested chiefly in the fates of these villagers after their arrival in the city and during the process of their urbanization.

1.2   Chinua Achebe

Chinua Achebe (b. 1930) is among those Nigerian authors writing in Standard English who have created a new tradition of West African prose and novel-writing in particular, which reflects the whole complex social and cultural coexistence of the two parallel, mutually interpenetrating worlds in contemporary West Africa, and in Nigeria in particular. Although Achebe should by no means be considered merely a "Nigerian" author—since his literary work is appreciated throughout the English-speaking world, and even outside it—definite links clearly exist between his creative activity, especially during its first decade, and the attempts to create a parliamentary democracy in the area where both Uthman dan Fodio's flag-bearers and the Yoruba Alafin's power were crushed by the early bucaneers and Lugard's troops in the not too remote past. Achebe belongs to that generation of Nigerian realistic intellectuals who—though deeply aware of their African cultural roots—refuse both to simply idealize and glorify the traditional African past and to flatly reject all aspects of the European impact.

After having received his early education in a missionary school and later at a gramar-school in Umuahia, the city from which his main hero comes, he graduated from one of the first English-speaking West African universities (Ibadan University College). In the early years of his literary activity he worked as a journalist, and subsequently devoted much time to broadcasting and TV activity. During the second half of the 1960's, he became the director of the foreign service of the Nigerian Broadcasting, so that he might symbolically be virtually identified with the Voice of Nigeria of that time. Although having risen to such a relatively high post during the Nigerian "first republic", he nevertheless has never shut his eyes to the inherent vices of the system and its deep internal crisis. However, when reading his literary work carefully, one cannot escape the feeling that his deep criticism of and shock over any corrupt hand falsifying the voter's ballot (whether the skin of the hand was white or black has always been of little importance to Achebe) never entirely shook his belief in the value of the principle in question.

Achebe's four main novels (*Things Fall Apart*, 1958; *No Longer at Ease*, 1960; *Arrow of God*, 1964; *A Man of the People*, 1966) undoubtedly reflect in a literary way the deep roots of the present Nigerian situation (and much of them is valid for the whole of West Africa, especially its English-speaking part). Nigerian society and, in a way, the whole of sub-Saharan Africa is to be seen as "a people at the crossroads". The tribal societies and great African empires belong to the past; nobody today carries the banners of the great African chiefs of the past, nobody collects taxes for them, nobody is executed on their behalf, nor is anybody praised or promoted in their name. The pride and terror, the happy days and sorrow connected with them in the daily lives of millions of Nigerians and Africans are gone for ever. But the social habits, moral codes and ideological, religious and cultural values remain; they not merely survive, as some sociologists frequently say, but really live, deeply rooted in the thinking, beliefs and hopes of the present—and perhaps even coming—generations of millions of simple Africans. The ordinary African has learned to use the white man's technical commodities; he has been forced to respect the superficial aspects of his moral code, at least in the cities, but the world of the past lives on in his thinking, regardless of how heavily influenced by the impact of Europe and the technological world of the 20th century it may be. Political independence has, in fact, changed very little in this respect; only the years, decades and generations to come may bring about gradual changes in this sphere as well. It is perhaps no exaggeration to say that no other African author has succeeded better than Achebe in illustrating this process in such a fascinating literary way.

The main story of his first novel (*Things Fall Apart*) is focused on the life and death of a representative of traditional African (Ibo) life, old Okonkwo. A proud chief and warrior, identified with the life-style of tribal, pre-colonial Africa, he must confront situations in which the representatives of the European impact—the missionaries and colonial administrators—have penetrated into the world of his realities and dreams. The resulting conflict comes to a dramatic end and solution: he kills a colonial clerk and prefers suicide to shameful imprisonment and humiliation. Arriving to arrest him, the police find only his corpse to bury, as Okonkwo's fellow countrymen refuse to bury him themselves: by his suicide he has committed an offense against his own tribe's customs. The District Commissioner who has witnessed this final scene contemplates—when leaving the village—the idea of writing a book on his field experience in Africa, to be entitled: *The Pacification of the Primitive Tribes of Lower Niger*. Cruel irony, combined with moderation and restraint, have become—even at this early stage—the main weapon of Achebe's arguments. After reading Achebe's first novel, one must conclude—to paraphrase Oscar Wilde—that real strength is not expressed in strong words. Facts are not stressed through radical slogans, nor through an extremist's words. In the test of literary survival they prove clearly to be strong enough in themselves to survive.

If the generation of grandfathers wanted—in vain—to struggle with the white man's church or colonial messengers, the generation of their sons, as illustrated in the life of Obi Okonkwo's father, was wiser, as illustrated in *No Longer at Ease*. It has been converted—at least superficially—to the white man's belief, morals and codes. If Obi's father had lived in a town, he would certainly have belonged to that category of people, characterized by Achebe on another occasion, as "those who are ashamed not to use a fork and a knife in eating their meals", merely in order not to be considered "uncivilized". The attentive reader must, however, very soon realize that this influence of Christianity and Europe affects Okonkwo's father only superficially. A minor crisis or excitement are enough to provoke the whole psychical and cultural essence of Obi's father's deeply traditional emotions back to the surface in all their complexity, originality, and even cruel determination. This becomes perfectly clear when Obi Okonkwo, the main hero of his second novel, wants to marry a girl-friend of Ibo origin whom he has met in England but who is an *osù:* at this point, the whole Christian and Europe-influenced superficial veneer collapses and Obi faces insurmountable obstacles to his original intention, both from his parents and from the whole tribal and village community. Obi's story is, however, not a mere love-story. It expresses the much deeper conflict of a young student returning from his overseas studies in England to post-independence Nigeria, full of progressive ideals, youthful energy and zeal. For the corruption found so frequently in the Nigerian "first" republic's state apparatus, he has only sincere words of contempt; in fact he has returned home with a firm determination to struggle it in all its forms. Here we have a hero who is confronting not only the traditional customs, opposing them with sincere love, but also the disastrous side-effects of Afro-European contact and all the social vices of his society. He is relatively well-situated, having started his career after his university studies in England, in the senior service; his salary is many times higher than the wages of his simple fellow countrymen who helped him to get to England. He enjoys all the privileges and rights of the senior service inherited from the period of the colonial administration: the loan of a car, a luxurious flat in Ikoyi and an opportunity to live in the world of the "privileged". He soon discovers, however, that life is not as easy as it might have appeared before the ship bringing him back from England docked in Lagos harbour. Loans and his scholarship—financed by funds raised by his simple fellow countrymen—must be repaid. Debts increase all around him, resulting from the duties connected with the style of life necessary for his post. Simultaneously, the animosity of his tribal union and community increases with respect to his unpopular choice in love.

The great ideals of Obi's youth, his love for Clara, and his whole personality and outlook come under the fire of cruel reality.

One of the high points of Achebe's mastery of literary composition lies undoubtedly in the fact that he discloses Obi's ultimate fate even on the first page of his story. The trial of Obi, who is found guilty of taking bribes, creates the framework of Achebe's entire second novel, so that the reader is left in no doubt as to the destiny of the main hero. But what is important is his description and analysis of the process of the step-by-step break-down of Obi's character. It is quite clear that Obi is unwilling to surrender to circumstances; however, he is pushed by them, inch by inch, to ultimately betray all that he has loved, that he has believed in, and that he has stood for. True, the novel's entire story makes it quite clear that whereas Obi has lost his case, Africa and its society cannot lose—at least in the long run, providing it does not commit the main fault committed by Obi. But it is difficult not to entirely surrender to circumstances, especially when life confronts us with one obstacle and problem after another. When committing the first wrong step, when betraying our own youthful soul for the first time, we are not fully aware of what will follow and that is the main problem.

In reading the story of Obi Okonkwo, we realize how right Réné Clair was many years ago when, depicting the eternal dilemma of Dr. Faust in a film scene in which his main hero is enabled to perceive his own future, he shows him gradually betraying himself and all his ideals, in a mirror—doing all those things that are generally attributed to the work of the devil... From the standpoint of such an analysis of the whole, complex psychological process of self-betrayal, Achebe's second novel undoubtedly exceeds the mere limits of the African context, constituting a major contribution to the world-wide development of the psychological novel.

While his third novel (*Arrow of God*) is also principally concentrated on the conflict of the traditional African affected by the impact of modernity, the fourth one (*A Man of the People*) further develops the sphere of Achebe's inspiration. All the negative aspects of corrupt Nigerian politics at that time about which he writes are taken into consideration and Achebe's entire richness of style and mastery of composition are utilized in his criticism of the system and its representatives. It is not merely by chance that the novel ends with a military coup; we feel, in fact, that both for the author and for the attentive reader this was one of the few possible alternatives left. It had to come, and so it came. Achebe also published several short stories ("The Sacrificial Egg", 1959), and even attempted to write poems, but his main literary strength lies in his novels. He has become popular especially owing to them. Gerald Moore qualified his first novel, for instance, as "the first West African novel in English which could be applauded without reserve... (1962, p. 58). He received the Margaret Wrong Memorial Prize in 1959, the Nigerian National Trophy for Literature in 1960 and many other awards, honorary degrees and prizes. His novels have been translated into many languages (German and Czech in Central Europe, where readers responded particularly positively). In the years of the Nigerian Civil War and the Ibo rebellion he chose—with some hesitation— the losing side, but this may have been just one period of his life. The early period of that Civil War was once referred to by the weekly *West Africa* under a heading which was the title of Achebe's first novel *Things Fall Apart*. Nigeria, however, survived the hour of its trial and crisis and did not fall apart; it is to be hoped that the same will be true of Achebe's literary work and human courage, which may well render Nigeria and West Africa its best results in the years ahead. His literary abilities, so persuasive in their moderation, restraint and self-control and so courageous in their sober approach to facts, will no doubt present us with new surprises.

1.3   *Other Nigerian Authors*

Onuora Nzekwu (born in 1928 in Kafanchan) is a well-known specialist in the field of East Nigerian customs and superstitions. He worked first as a teacher and then as the editor of *Nigeria Magazine*. His novel *Wand of Noble Wood* (1961) deals with the conflict between modern and traditional ways of living. Its main character, Pete Obiesie, is a young Ibo journalist who works for a magazine in Lagos. Like many other Ibo men and other people who have recently come to the city, he is strongly tied to his native village, its inhabitants and traditions. He reaches the age when he is able to marry his girl-friend. But, following the custom, he does not marry his pregnant mistress, as she does not belong to his tribe. On the other hand, marrying a tribeswoman usually requires buying her and Pete's income is not sufficient to enable him to pay a comparatively high price. According to traditions, he must wait till his elder brothers get married. Refusing to become an old bachelor, he finally finds a girl who satisfies all his requirements—the school-teacher, Nneka. However, Pete does not know that a mysterious curse makes Nneka, as well, an unsuitable bride. She can magically bring certain death to her husband. Although Pete and Nneka try to break the dreadful curse through complicated rites, their love affair ends tragically. Nneka commits suicide in order to save Pete.

The traditional framework is equally solid in Nzekwu's second novel *Blade among the Boys* (1962): Patrick Ikenga was brought up in the traditional faith, but he accepts Christianity in order to find his path toward a higher education. The religious conflict increases when he decides to become a Roman Catholic priest. His mother opposes this decision, because she believes that her son's celibacy conflicts with their traditional faith and harms the family. She says that the ancestors wish Patrick to get married and have children. The role of sexuality in the two different doctrines is well illustrated in the novel. The hero's tragic fall is due to a lack of realistic thinking in the two opposing camps.

Highlife for Lizards (1965), Nzekwu's third novel, discusses the problems of traditional marriages. The author shows woman's social handicaps, hard work and difficulties in family life. He is particularly successful in revealing the psychic tension between two wives of the same husband. Like the preceding novel, *Highlife for Lizards* owes much of its linguistic interest to folk sayings and other colourful details concerning tribal life.

Together with Michael Crowder, the well-known historian, Nzekwu wrote one short story for children—"Eze Goes to School" (1963). The hero is a little boy who wants to obtain an education but who has to face a number of obstacles. His father died a heroic death while protecting his village from a leopard. The boy's relatives refuse to finance Eze's educational career, though the school fee is not too high (32 shillings per year). Fortunately, the boy is helped by an old uncle and his teacher who prepares him for his studies at Onitsha. Although Eze is insulted by the town boys, he becomes accustomed to his new surroundings.

Nkem Nwankwo (born in 1936 in Nawfia) studied English in Lagos. After graduating from the University of Ibadan in 1962, he taught at a grammar school in Ibadan and then worked as a manager of the broadcasting company in Lagos. He was awarded second prize in the literary contest organized on the occasion of the celebration of Nigerian independence.

Apart from a number of short stories and poems, Nwankwo wrote the novel *Danda* (1964). Danda is a jolly good-for-nothing embodying the freedom and gaiety of the common people. He walks from one village to another, singing, dancing and playing his flute. The elders are mostly indignant, but the women are enchanted. According to traditional laws, Danda should be punished for his arrogance and pleasure-seeking, but he is forgiven by the chief. The easy-going subject seems to correspond to the evident looseness of the novel's composition, whose structure is elaborated rather carelessly. It consists of a series of more or less amusing episodes. Nwankwo does not endeavour to form a compact whole. For this reason, Danda reminds one of the European picturesque novels which were sometimes also based on folk narratives. The author uses relatively many Ibo expressions and adds a brief dictionary to his work, in order to make its reading easier. Adapted for the stage, *Danda* was very successful at the First World Festival of Negro Arts in Dakar. Nwankwo also wrote the stories "The Gambler" and "Broken Images" and the play *Two Sisters*.

Timothy Mofolorunso Aluko (born in 1918 in Ilesha) comes from Yorubaland (unlike most Nigerian prominent writers who, as we have said, come from Iboland). He studied in his native town and then in Ibadan, Lagos and London. In 1960, he started working as a director of the West Nigerian public works. Some of his early short stories were adapted for broadcasting. Aluko became famous chiefly as a novelist.

His first novel *One Man, One Wife* (1959) describes living conditions during the process of social modernization. He shows the penetration of Christianity into the villages where many conservatives are still living. The novel contains a satirical criticism of missionaries who sometimes use wrong and harmful methods. The dramatic climax of the novel is a smallpox epidemic, which is interpreted as the pagan god's wrath. The villagers are, therefore, ready to return to their old faith but they are afraid of the whites. However, there are also other conflicting opinions. The author is concerned with the character of Royasin, the village teacher, who wants to satisfy his own ambitions in this disturbing period. In a way, the study of Royasin is the writer's preparation for another, even more impressive portrait—that of Benjamin Benjamin, the black demagogue in his following novel *One Man One Matchet* (1964).

This novel is certainly better from the standpoint of literary presentation. While in *One Man, One Wife* he injects himself personally into a number of comments and speculations, in *One Man, One Matchet* he gives his characters more freedom and more scope to show the evolution of their attitudes. Thus, the reader can easily follow their behaviour and deduce the "ideology" of the novel himself. Its action takes place in a dramatic period (1949). The British District Officer orders that the diseased cocoa trees be cut down, in order to save the rest of them. The peasants refuse and start their resistance movement under the slogan: "One man, one matchet—one wife, one stick—one child, one stone".

"The new African District Officer, Udo Akpan, who speaks of tackling problems in an essentially African way and yet talks and acts like any white expatriate, is soon described as 'the black white man' by his opponents. He is a graduate of Cambridge with an upper second in Classics, and, of course, a Cambridge cricket blue. He is a perfect example of the African élite whose self-appointed task is to make colonialism—lock, stock and barrel—work.

"But the man who gets the biggest lashing is a rabble-rousing politician who exploits the ignorance of the illiterate masses to line his own pockets. Mr. Benjamin Benjamin urges people to resist paying taxes, to resist cutting down trees, and persuades them to undertake a law-suit for the recovery of the land which they claim to be theirs, but which obviously belongs to a neighbouring tribe. His love of long words and fine flourishes, his use of public platforms and public issues to gain personal power, his hypocrisy in whatever he does are the main object of Aluko's harmless satire... The duel between Benjamin Benjamin and Akpan, 'the black white man', is really the story of Aluko's novel. But Aluko's satire is ponderous. It lacks that bite which can expose a social miasma mainly because he does not really know what he wants" (James Ngugi, "Satire in Nigeria", in *Protest and Conflict in African Literature,* 1969).

The role of the press, Yoruba traditions and the Church is also revealed. Aluko analyses deeply the basic problems of Nigerian democracy, which were becoming particularly topical in the days preceding independence. The author appears to share the doubts concerning the mechanical applications of the British parliamentary system to the tropical countries of English-speaking Africa. At the same time, he is very critical of the violent methods used by the colonizers, which led to occasional bloodshed.

The novel *One Man, One Matchet* shows the period of transition in an interesting way. Colonialism had already decayed and could not ensure public order or effective organization in tropical Africa, while the prerequisites for the establishment of an independent state had not yet developed. Akpan expresses this author's idea at the end of the novel in the following way: "Benjamin Benjamin's three-and-half-years' operations in Ipaja have shown conclusively that whatever brand of democracy we import into this country, we must make sure that we sift out the seed of the disease that will otherwise choke to death the new freedom from imperialism which we hope to achieve soon."

Aluko's third novel, *Kinsman and Foreman* (1966), develops certain ideas touched on in *One Man, One Matchet.* While Udo Akpan, the African District Officer, the first native to reach this post, finally resigns as his reputation among his compatriots has been lost in the "cocoa-nut tree dispute", Titus Oti, the main character of *Kinsman and Foreman,* succeeds, after a dramatic struggle. In about 1950, he comes back from Britain as a graduate from an English college.

It is characteristic of Aluko that he pays increasing attention to the psychological analysis of his heroes. At the same time, he tends to identify himself, to a certain degree at least, with the educated African standing in the centre of the whole action and bravely facing his opponents.

The hero of this work—the engineer, Titus Oti—is evidently very close to the author. After his studies in England, he returns to the Western Region of the Federation of Nigeria to take a post there, which had previously been held by the English only. Roughly at the same time—in 1950—he gets involved in a typical conflict resulting from contemporary technical progress. The solidarity of the tribes and clans is disrupted, as the organization of work requires entirely different relationships. This conflict is illustrated in the relationship between Titus Oti and Simeon, his kinsman and foreman. Simeon is a shameless person who, through unfair tricks, has amassed much money as well as the favour of his too credulous fellow citizens. Although Simeon and Titus are kinsmen, they cannot stand each other. Their moral ideas are different. Titus Oti's position is very difficult because the revealing of a hidden immorality under the mask of conventions is generally understood as a provocation. He fails to gain the support of the pastor who has been blinded by the splendid gifts of the shrewd foreman, Simeon. Titus is driven still further into isolation and his situation remains unchanged, even at the moment Simeon is persecuted and forced to flee from the community that has long put up with him. The gap between the intellectual and the masses is now unbridgeable, chiefly for two reasons. Expensive studies and a relatively low salary do not enable Titus to display unlimited generosity. Furthermore, the fact that he is employed in the colonial service decreases the confidence of his compatriots. Simeon is cleared by the court, but Titus is still convinced that his kinsman is guilty. Simeon's sins would never have become known, if there had not been a stroke of luck—a public confession of believers on the day denoted as the Day of Judgement by a certain religious sect. Simeon confesses his sins in order to avoid his eternal damnation. Titus Oti was right, but his victory has a bitter flavour. It is really remarkable to see how Aluko started a vigorous re-evaluation of the traditional norms of social life in Western Nigeria.

Kinsman and Foreman, containing an unusual portion of humour and irony, is at the same time a psychological study of the new African intellectual who adapts himself to the requirements and peculiarities of his original milieu with many difficulties resulting also from his own inhibitions. As in French-writing Africa, we can also find here an answer to the basic question: to what extent can a man become alienated from his native community during several years' studies abroad?

Aluko's third novel is a significant point in the author's artistic development. From the schematic pattern of his first novel, Aluko has arrived at a comparatively advanced expression and a real balance between artistic method and socially-oriented thinking. Only one thing may be regretted: in a monotonous way, he returns to the same area and period, trying to deepen his insight and to present us specimens of Nigerian reality. Despite his giftedness, Aluko is less ambitious than Achebe in that he does not attempt to create large canvases from different places and times.

Kinsman and Foreman is Aluko's critical portrayal of the surviving social structures. His words concerning tribal traditions have sometimes been considered too strict and bitter, but the author is evidently aware of the relative slowness of contemporary modernization. He exposes false interpretations of family and commercial traditions as effectively as he condemns corruption in political life in his fourth novel, *Chief, the Honourable Minister* (1970).

Like Achebe in *A Man of the People,* Aluko presents a satirical portrait of the contemporary politician who must take into account all vicious and puzzling facts existing in the strange climate of public affairs. Aluko appears to believe that there has been too much violence and absurdity in public life. He depicts the transition from traditional rule to modern administration in the novel *His Worshipful Majesty* (1973).

Isidore Okpewho deals in his novel *The Victims* (1970) with family life, in particular with its polygamous character. Polygamy is discussed also in Obi B. Egbuna's *Wind versus Polygamy* (1964), with its amusing character, Chief Ozuomba, who does not believe in the equality of the sexes.

Polygamy remains one of the serious social problems in modern Africa, but Egbuna decided to treat it in a humorous manner. Chief Ozuomba, the novel's main character, is to judge the dispute between two wooers trying to win a young, pretty girl. The first half of the novel itself proves that Egbuna chose quite an inadequate form for his subject. Ozuomba's long speeches at the court confirm our assumption that these ideas on polygamy would have been put to better use in a comedy. The novel can hardly sustain such rhetoric passages. Ideas dominate this whole work; moreover, Egbuna's presentation is imperfect. In a word, the book is as disputable as the problem of polygamy itself. In Ozuomba's opinion, a man's tendency to change women is ancient and quite natural. It results from man's potential superiority and numerical inferiority, while woman's situation is the reverse. Monogamy is denoted as an experiment that failed in Europe and in America and to attempt to introduce it into Africa is to make this mistake "an accepted canon in Africa". We may ask whether the defence of polygamy implies a glorification of African culture after the victory of the national liberation movement. Egbuna does not appear to be making an original contribution, for he adopts some ideas of the European adversaries of monogamy: e.g. Ozuomba's argument that monogamous marriage leads in fact to the encouragement of prostitution. But the author must not be identified with his hero, for he was completely aware of the complicated nature of the problem and, therefore, avoided cheap happy endings. Few Nigerian novelists, however, have succeeded in analyzing the economic and social roots of polygamy, though they observe clearly the advantages of the first wives and the role of marriage in the process of women's emancipation. Generally speaking, they are mostly satisfied with a description of the present-day situation and its comparison with that in the Western capitalist countries.

Egbuna also wrote the play *Anthill* (1965), which deals with an African student in England and his experiences there.

Vincent Chukwuemeka Ike writes in his first novel *Toads for Supper* (1965) about Amobi, a student of a Nigerian University, who meets different girls there—his bright fellow student, a village girl strongly recommended by Amobi's father, and Sweetie, who is rather frivolous. As Sweetie asserts that Amobi is the father of her child, Amobi must leave the University. He finally marries the village girl from his own tribe.

Ike's second novel—*The Naked Gods* (1970)—is another vivid picture of university life in West Africa. Ike displays again his sense of humour, but his new story is satirical as well. The portrait of a young African professor who is trying to become Vice-Chancellor of the university is excellent. Moreover, Ike observes certain broad and general tendencies in public life, though he centres his action on the academic setting. The novel's social and individual aspects are well balanced.

Mbella Sonne Dipoko (born in 1936 in Douala) is a Cameroonian author, whose name was omitted from the chapter concerning French-written literatures of West Africa because he uses English. He may be mentioned here—among the Nigerian writers— as he grew up in Nigeria and worked for the Nigerian Broadcasting Corporation. His poetry was broadcast by the BBC African service and all his works clearly differ from the rest of Cameroonian writing, though he is partly influenced by the French literary tradition (he has lived in France since 1960), especially in his novels.

A Few Nights and Days (1966) deals with the experience of an African student in Paris. He loves a French girl, but her father dislikes the idea of his daughter marrying a Negro. The student thinks over the possibility of taking the girl to Africa, but finally he leaves her. The main reason for his departure is the fact that parents on both sides insist on the couple iving in their own native countries respectively, after the young people get married. These stubborn attitudes lead to the girl's suicide. Dipoko's almost complete concentration on the emotional sphere is rare in modern West African literature. But the book contains a few generalizing comments on the roots of racial prejudice, mixed marriages, etc. Even though the Paris milieu is described very vividly, the descriptive part is not the most decisive positive quality of Dipoko's work, which was intended as the first part of a trilogy. The author was interested mainly in an analysis of certain moral and sexual aspects, which are regarded differently by Africans and Europeans. We cannot say that this quite limited observation of various intimate problems was entirely successful. Dipoko has introduced himself as an undoubtedly gifted author who is able to write easily but has not been able to avoid a certain superficiality and lengthiness, which decrease the artistic effect of the novel. Some of Dipoko's inspiring thoughts relating to relationships between blacks and whites appeared later in his verses *Black and White in Love* (1972) and in his play, *Overseas* (1970).

Dipoko's second novel *Because of Women* (1969) is a close examination of traditional and modern social structures in Cameroon. In it, Dipoko elaborates a deep psychological analysis of women in love, and their satisfaction in sexual life.

The African woman's life is the central theme of Flora Nwapa's novels. Flora Nwapa (born in 1931 in Oguta) studied at the girls' school in Lagos and later at the University of Ibadan. She continued her studies in Edinburgh, where she graduated in 1958. After her return to her native country, she taught at the East Nigerian schools of Calabar and Enugu. Her educational career reached its climax when she lectured at the University of Lagos. Miss Nwapa has devoted much attention chiefly to the education of African girls.

Her novel *Efuru* is concentrated on questions of women's emancipation. The action does not take place in intellectual surroundings, but in a village. There, the heroine—Efuru— lives. She is a pretty woman, but her life is full of tragic experiences. Unlike the other women of her neighbourhood, she has a sense of business management and activity that enables her to compete with the men in spheres that are not typically feminine. This is perhaps why she cannot enjoy the pleasures of family life for which the majority of women are destined. She is unfortunate to lose her child, and her two marriages prove failures. According to traditional African wisdom, her strange fate is ascribed to the supernatural influence of the goddess of the river. Unknown powers have decided that Efuru must live her life in relative isolation, misunderstood by those nearest to her. The novel is a notable though lengthy portrayal of a vanishing way of life and an indirect tribute to the joys and sorrows of motherhood, the presence or absence of which respectively affect the heroine most. The author shows the European reader what barrenness means in African circumstances and how strictly the main function of an African village woman is still defined. The idea of the contradiction between the woman's desire to carry out other functions in her society and her instincts is presented as extremely debatable in this work. The reason may be that the writer realized that the problem is an old one. Numerous women in Europe and in America have had to solve it in some way or other, and to find a compromise between their social activities and family life under changing conditions. To flee to one's father cannot be a solution, even in the case of Efuru.

Miss Nwapa's second novel *Idu* (1969) essentially repeats the basic problem of Efuru. Once again, the heroine suffers from her unsatisfied desire to have a child, a theme so frequently expressed in African countryside milieux. She finally bears a child, but her happiness does not last very long and she commits suicide after the death of her husband whom she loved very much. The authoress describes well the social isolation and handicaps of a widow in traditional surroundings. Although there is no goddess of the lake in her second novel, Idu's fate is also directed by mysterious unknown forces. Miss Nwapa's language is mostly based on folklore imagery, which makes their reading attractive, though the two novels are rather too long for the little action contained in them.

Another woman writer—Adaora Lily Ulasi—has set her novel, *Many Thing You No Understand* (1970) in the mid-Thirties. She develops the question of a ritual murder in an ironical manner. She shows the different attitudes of the colonial officers toward African traditions.

John Munonye shows in *The Only Son* (1966) the conflict between Christianity and animism in an Ibo village. Chiaku, a widow, has an only son, Nnanna, who is attracted by the missionaries' activities. Although Chiaku would like to have her son educated in the traditional way, Nnanna becomes the servant of a white priest and attends a Christian mission school. He no longer understands his mother's faith. His desperate mother loses her son forever. Munonye's second novel *Obi* (1969) describes the situation of a young married couple who come back from the city to their native village. It continues discussing the main problems of *The Only Son*—education, faith, tradition—as a conflict in the mind of the central character. While Nwapa presents the psychology of a Nigerian woman, Munonye reveals that of a Nigerian man.

Elechi Amadi (b. 1934) in *The Concubine* (1966) tells about an independent widow whose beauty attracts several men. She is very honest but mysteriously brings misfortune to all her lovers. She is concerned both about her children and about public opinion. Her mystery is like that of Efuru—her fate is governed by a sea god. East Nigerian village life is portrayed successfully thanks to the vivid descriptions of tradional customs.

Amadi was primarily interested in portraying the relationships between his characters and illustrating the general atmosphere in the village. He concentrated upon his simple love-story to such an extent that he made no digressions. His narrative is mixed with abundant dialogues which are true-to-life, and his descriptions never lack that necessary amount of monumentality that raises a commonplace story to the level of a gloomy legend. *The Concubine* is an excessively instructive explanation of the ancient moral code, which is gradually being eliminated in this period of modernizing social relations.

Amadi's second novel *The Great Ponds* (1970) deals with the sharp conflict between two villages which try to gain control over a pond with plenty of fish. Custom requires a representative of a village to swear that the pond belongs to his village. If he survives the following half-year period, his village is generally regarded as the owner of the pond. The story can be understood as a picture of vanishing life, but also as a parable on the recent conflict in Nigeria.

The Civil War is the centre of interest of the young author, Kole Omotoso (born in 1943 in Akure), who presents his impressions in his novels, *The Edifice* (1971) and *The Combat* (1972). Omotoso also produced the play *Pitched Against the Gods*.

Rems Nna Umeasiegbu (b. 1943, Aba) studied in Enugu, Prague and Philadelphia. His main subjects are English and folklore. *The Way We Lived* (1969) is a collection of Ibo folk customs and animal fables. He also deals with interesting cases of magic, secret societies, etc.

The poet Gabriel Imomotimi Gbaingbaing Okara (b. 1921) comes from the Ijaw country. He started his career as a translator of folklore and became well-known at the Nigerian Arts Festival in 1953. He worked at the East Nigerian Ministry of Information and has contributed to the literary journal *Black Orpheus*. His only novel *The Voice* (1964) is a commendable attempt to convey African thought in adapted English. The hero of the novel—Okolo—is a young, well-educated man who returns to his native village. He comes into conflict with the chief and elders as he represents a potential treat to their authority. Unfortunately, the other tribesmen no longer understand him and he becomes completely isolated. He is forced at first to leave the village; then his enemies decide to get rid of him at all costs. The only human being ready to share his tragic fate is Tuere, a young girl generally considered to be a witch. Okara links his rich philosophical content with an exceptional form, a linguistic experiment aimed at translating Ijaw speech into somewhat distorted English. These efforts, though highly controversial, show one possibility of Africanizing a European language. Okara says as follows:

"In order to capture the vivid images of African speech, I had to eschew the habit of expressing my thoughts first in English. It was difficult at first, but I had to learn. I had to study each Ijaw expression I used and to bring out the nearest meaning in English. I found it a fascinating exercise." (*African Speech... English Words*, Transition, Vol. 3, No. 3, 1963).

Wole Soyinka (born in 1934 in Ijebu Isara) studied in Ibadan and Leeds and worked for the British Royal Theatre. After his return to Nigeria, he dealt with the history and structure of the Yoruba traditional drama. He started his research at the University of

Ibadan and then lectured at the Universities of Ife and Lagos. The beginning of the Civil War found him in jail, as he opposed the official policies. This period is reflected in his *Poems from Prison* (1969), the collection that followed *Idanre* and other poems (1967), inspired by Yoruba myths.

Soyinka's only novel *The Interpreters* (1965) is an amazing piece of fiction, very different from the rest of Nigerian prose writing. The author chose intellectual life in Lagos with a clear satirical intention. He observes the obvious lack of communication and understanding among his characters and expresses this idea also in the form of his novel which is basically comprised of a series of episodes. He exposes snobbery, corruption, bureaucracy, immorality, hypocrisy and other vices of modern urban life and presents a number of excellent portraits of intellectuals, artists and other professional people. In the characteristic atmosphere of offices, night-clubs and private flats, they carry on their witty dialogues with comments on public affairs as well as psychologically convincing observations. The complex structure of *The Interpreters* might be due to the influence of the American modernists, whom Soyinka knows very well.

S. P. Kartuzov in "Some Problems of Modern Prose in the Republic of South Africa" (*Essays on African Culture*, pp. 162—163) expresses this opinion in the following words: "This is seen in the composition of the novel, its delicate abruptness, its numerous digressions into the past which are not immediately understood and are given in the form of the hero's recollections, without any noticeable transition from the past to present. The novel does not have a very definite plot and its chapters are mainly connected by the same characters, whose images (especially the heroine's) are reminiscent of those in modern American literature, especially in novels by Caldwell and Faulkner. But the affected complication of the book does not diminish its criticism and satire."

Nigerian poetry has not been greatly popularized. Its poets never formed a school and never professed a unifying doctrine. From the very beginning, the Nigerian poets were very independent and highly individualistic. The only unifying idea was perhaps that of nationalism, but even this was not quite generally accepted. The simple patriotic verse of pupils emerging from missionary schools could hardly attract many overseas readers. These poets have described their native country in charming personifications, comparing it to a beloved mother or sweetheart. The beauties of nature are appreciated as are its famous historical epochs. The aim of these poems has been to throw a new light on the "barbaric past". This tendency can be seen in the works of Mortu Yusufu Giva and Raymond Tong, the latter of whom became popular thanks to his love poems. Kay Epelle's works appear to be more traditional in form, while the poetry of Dennis Chukude Osadebay is traditional in content. Some of Osadebay's poems, published in the collection *Africa Sings* (1952), are typical pieces of journalism.

Much more elaborate are the works of Gabriel Imomotimi Gbaingbaing Okara, whose only novel has already been discussed. Okara started his career by translating Ijaw folk-songs and was very successful at the Nigerian Arts Festival in 1953. He is not radical, though he sometimes chooses as his themes certain serious social and moral problems of his times. All his poems seem to be written in honour of the black African living in very close contact with his native country. Most of his verses are distinctly sensory. Okara never tries to present a hierarchy of values; he simply wishes to jot down his volatile impressions and feelings. He would have been more radical if he had lived in South Africa. As it is, he only longs for the black man's real participation in creating the future world.

Wole Soyinka worked for some time as an editor of the literary journal *Black Orpheus* and helped to promote modern poetry in Nigeria. His own verse is rather sophisticated, indulging in a great number of complicated symbols. He could even be regarded as a counterpart of the Senegalese poet, Léopold Sédar Senghor, if he possessed such a definite programme. But Soyinka hates oversimplifications and generalizations of all kinds and does not want to be dependent on any dogma. Ezekiel Mphahlele wrote the following lines about Soyinka's poem, "The Immigrant":

"Again, against a white background, the black stands out in bold outline in Wole Soyinka's poem 'The Immigrant' which shows his incisive sophistication, born no doubt of his long stay in Britain as a teacher. A black immigrant asks for a dance in Mammersmith Palace. He subconsciously wants to assert his dignity. A white girl refuses. At the suggestion of 'You? Not at any price!' in her eyes, he feels hurt.

He felt the wound grow septic
(Hard though he tried to close it)
His fingers twitched
And toyed with the idea,
The knife that waited on the slight,
On the sudden nerve that would join her face
To scars identical
With what he felt inside.
The blade remained
In the sweat-filled pocket.

He knows the 'fatality of his black flattened nose'. He wants a chance to have his revenge, to degrade her sex and race." The poem was published in *Black Orpheus*, No. 5.

Soyinka is among the first West African poets to scourge renegades and snobbish compatriots, even at the time when most writers were finding it sufficient to express their anti-colonialist attitudes. In his critiques, he rejected "narcissism", which he ascribed not only to the *négritude* poets, but also to his fellow-countrymen.

John Pepper Clark is another gifted poet and playwright. Clark seems to write quite spontaneously and very easily. He tries to modernize the form of his poems that sometimes lack both rhyme and regular rhythm. Clark (born in 1935 in Kiagbodu) studied at the University of Ibadan from which he graduated in 1960. He worked at the Ministry of Information in Ibadan and then went to Lagos. In 1962—1963, he studied at the University of Princeton, USA. His criticism of the Americans' snobbish attitudes, racism and rearmament policies appeared in the collection of essays, *America, Their America* (1964). After his return to Nigeria, Clark carried out research at the Institute for African Studies, in Ibadan and subsequently became a lecturer in English at the University of Lagos.

Clark's original poetry disclosed his profound interest in the construction of verse. This quality is clearly visible in *Poems* (1962), *A Reed in the Tide* (1965) and *Casualties* (1970), all of which is concentrated on the Nigerian Civil War.

Clark very often uses the so-called double adjective, so that his verse is usually overloaded with meaning. He works like a painter trying to give his picture a third dimension by putting an additional thick layer of paint directly on the canvas. This "heavy" verse is not very suitable for recitation; it must be seen, owing to its graphic pecularities. Mention might be made of foreign influences on modern Nigerian poetry. In Clark's case, it was perhaps T. S. Eliot who played the role of "a foreign instructor". He appears to look for his objective correlative as the only means of expressing human emotions in an artistic form. And like Eliot, Clark sometimes fails in these ambitious efforts.

Christopher Okigbo (1932—1967, Ojoto) studied in Ibadan and London. He was the editor of *Transition* and also worked for the Mbari Publishing House and Literary Club in Ibadan as a representative of the Cambridge University Press. He was killed fighting for Biafra in the Civil War in 1967.

His personal tragedy and artistic greatness were analyzed in Ali A. Mazrui's novel *The Trial of Christopher Okigbo* (1971). Mazrui (born 1933 in Mombasa), a Kenyan professor of political science who teaches at Makerere College and edits *Transition*, considers the central question the relationship between Okigbo's poetry and his political commitment (serving the Ibo cause).

Okigbo's most important collections of poems are *Heavensgate* (1962), *Limits and Other Poems* (1964) and *Labyrinths with Paths of Thunder* (1971). Okigbo was a bold innovator looking for new ways of expression. His poetry is very pleasant to hear, for it invariably creates an unexpected, refined acoustic impression. Moreover, it is very musical, even when no profound thoughts can be discerned. The recitation should—according to the author's notes—be accompanied by drums, flutes, etc.

Okigbo won high recognition at the World Festival of Negro Art in Dakar 1966. His poems—like Clark's—seem to illustrate the idea of the New Criticism, speaking as they do, of the special, independent life of words within a poem as an independent structure. Okigbo was influenced by imaginist views, by the idea of the simultaneous existence of several meanings in a single metaphor, and primarily by his aesthetic doctrine. Okigbo's poems are not intended for the masses but rather for a limited number of well-educated persons. Okigbo did not desire to play the role of a cultural worker; he tried to maintain the high standard of his verse at all costs. His poetry is therefore highly appreciated.

To give one example, we may quote Gerald Moore's words: "What Okigbo learnt from Eliot, and thus brought into the tradition of African poetry in English, was the art of handling complex ideas in simple language by the constant re-arrangement of a selected group of words and symbols. Okigbo rehandles such words as laughter, dream, light, presence, voice, blood, exactly as Eliot teases out all the possible meanings of beginning, middle and end in 'East Coker'. Both poets use fragments of Catholic liturgy mixed with others from the classical world, paganism and magic." (G. Moore, 1970, p. 176.)

The situation in modern Nigerian drama is even more complicated than in poetry. One part of it continues along traditional lines (e.g. the Yoruba Folk Opera), while the other sets itself a difficult task: to establish a really modern drama in the European sense of the word. It is hardly paradoxical that the more traditional type is much more closely related to the stage than the other type, which was strongly influenced by European drama. Consequently, some of these modern plays are not suitable for staging and are denoted by some critics as "literary drama". Existing in a written or printed form, it may be used as a dramatic text on which a theatrical performance may be based. On the other hand, fiction may be used for the purposes of Nigerian theatres. Tutuola's *Palm-wine Drinkard* and Nwankwo's *Danda* have provided good opportunities for dramatizations, which were more successful among African spectators than certain original plays.

One of the essential problems for Nigerian dramatists is the choice of subject-matter. The linguistic difficulties may partly account for the fact that there have been few realistic plays dealing with everyday life. Modern Nigerian drama is characterized by a variety of genres: classical types of comedies and farces exist side by side with tales or mythological scenes and tragedies. This probably results from the fact that the most outstanding playwrights have found their inspiration in both folk traditions and foreign subject-matter. Certain specific qualities have been acquired from religious rites and traditional entertainment using masks, drums, dances, etc. The synthetic character of the Yoruba folk opera, created by Hubert Ogunde, Duro Ladipo (b. 1931) and Kola Ogunmola (b. 1925) is generally recognized. This traditional branch is not, however, completely free of European influences. Duro Ladipo staged Shakespeare's *As You Like It* in 1957, though he later dealt exclusively with Yoruba history and mythology. J. P. Clark's first two plays were staged by the Eastern Nigeria Theatre Group, whose repertory has been a mixture of traditional and modern plays.

Like Soyinka, J. P. Clark not only produces original plays, but also deals with drama in his theoretical and critical comments. In his study "Aspects of Nigerian Drama" published in *Nigeria Magazine* (No. 89, June, pp. 118—126), he presents an instructive classification of traditional secular drama: 1. "magic" or trick plays; 2. pastoral or puppet plays; 3. the civic type; 4. dance or song dramas; 5. narrative or epic dramas.

Eschewing the idea of art for art's sake, he enumerates the essential functions of traditional Nigerian drama, which, in his opinion, is strongly related to social life. He mentions that "the very myths upon which many of these dramas are based... serve to record the origins and *raison d'être* of the institutions and people who own them" (p. 124). He goes on to show that dramas are representations of a special religion, of the gods and spirits, that they educate and initiate the young into the ways and duties of the community. Masquerade dramas foster good relations between members of one village and another and thus become the best means of promotion of a community. Dramas bring home native sons and daughters resident abroad, free the spirit of its flesh shackles and are a vehicle for social comment, satire, gossip and entertainment.

Both great playwrights are convinced that the stage can give man significant experience and instruction. They are never satisfied with the recording of reality; rather, they try to present philosophical content in a more or less timeless sphere, thus increasing the general validity of their observations. Soyinka seems to be more romantic in his plays and also more sophisticated in his attitudes. His favourite weapons are humour, satire, irony, paradox and allegory. He usually uses prose in a rather stylized form, sometimes loose blank verse and occasionally a dialect in the dialogues of such famous plays as *The Trial of Brother Jero* and *The Road*. Clark's favourite free verse is highly stylized and rich in rhythmic qualities. Martin Esslin characterizes his language as noteworthy for its highly sophisticated simplicity. In his essay "Two Nigerian Playwrights" (*Introduction to African Literature*, 1967, pp. 255—262), he observes:

"How enviable, for any European, is the African playwright's ability to refer to any aspects of the physical side of the human condition without shame or self-consciousness. In a European play, the line about the running nose would have been hopelessly sentimentalized into something like: *Forgive me, grief has overcome me quite...*
or *Tears, bitter tears prevent my going on...*
— clichés that drown the immediacy of physical sensation in empty phrase-making" (p. 259).

It is sufficient to add Clark's version:

...With a bound
She was running, kneeling, presenting the baby
As a shield although clutching it back
From harm and all this in one motion—
Do forgive my running nose. (From *The Masquerade*)

Wole Soyinka is undoubtedly the country's greatest playwright and drama expert. In 1958, he started working with the Royal Court Theatre in England. After his return to Nigeria, he dealt with the Yoruba drama. Well acquainted with traditional plays, he attempted to create a new synthetic kind of modern drama. He combines dialogues with music and dance, but the text has already acquired the dominant position in his plays. His plays *The Lion and the Jewel* and *The Swamp Dwellers* were performed by the students of University College, Ibadan, as early as 1959. The former was performed in London in the same year. It is based on an ironical contrast of modern manners and traditions in the life of a Nigerian village. Soyinka obviously fought against the idealization of old tribal customs. The same pragmatic attitude can be seen in *The Swamp Dwellers*, which show the inevitability of progressive changes in traditional communities. Although life in town is hard, the playwright seems to suggest, it is free of ancient prejudice and superstition. The symbols used in this play are relatively simpler than those of *A Dance of the Forests*.

The Swamp Dwellers is too rich in ideas for a comparatively short play: Igwezu, a young peasant, has spent eight months in the city looking for his brother, who has deceived him and taken away his wife. Suffering from his failure, he returns home to continue his farming, but is disappointed to see that the fertile soils have been turned into swamps as a result of the floods. At home, he meets only his powerless parents, a blind beggar and Kadiye, a very influential priest, whose task has been to defend the lands. As Kadiye has failed to ensure the god's protection, he is regarded by Igwezu as the man responsible for the economic disaster. While in his preceding plays, Soyinka seemed to favour traditions, here he shows Kadiye as the embodiment of obscurantist, backward thinking. The priest has led a profitable life, causing the suffering of the other villagers. Alienated from both the city and the land, Igwezu could attempt to solve his problem by killing the priest. Actually, he seems to be about to cut Kadiye's throat while shaving him, but at the last moment changes his mind and releases the clean-shaven priest. Igwezu finds no solution other than to leave home.

A Dance of the Forests is based on a strange paradox. Soyinka obviously does not share any illusions concerning the ancient African empires. Opposing the contemporary idealization of the past, he introduces a group of village people who have numerous vices and shortcomings but who believe that they can find positive qualities in their ancestors. They therefore call on their forefathers, in accordance with the African traditional belief in the ancestors' assistance. Two spirits actually do come back from "the other world", pushing their unattractive bones up through thick layers of funeral soil. But they do not help the embarassed villagers; on the contrary, they voice a number of accusations which give no rosy picture of the ancient empires. Soyinka shows that the present-day villagers possess the same vices as their ancestors, who, moreover, lived under hard conditions of slavery.

One of the specific qualities of *The Trials of Brother Jero* is that the main character is simultaneously the commentator. The play is an attack on false religion which is exemplified in the cunning practices of Brother Jero, the founder of a religious sect, who systematically cheats the all too credulous people. The play is a pure farce written in a clear style.

The Strong Breed, on the other hand, is a philosophical tragedy describing the teacher Eman's love for a chief's daughter. Being a stranger to the chief's village, Eman gradually comes to acknowledge its traditions. One of these is the New Year's ritual of purification, which calls for a human sacrifice. Eman does not want to let the village idiot to be sacrificed and voluntarily offers himself. Thus, he continues in the tradition of his ancestors and becomes another member of "the strong breed", which is, however, defeated. The irony of the tragedy consists in the fact that only the weak survive. The playwright criticizes superstitions, but at the same time he believes that the positive elements of tribal life should be preserved. The play can be understood as a profound discussion of the individual's responsibility and satisfaction.

The first performance of *The Road* took place at Stratford-on-Avon in October 1965. It is rather static, constituting philosophy, rather than drama in the proper sense. The basic idea is a metaphor: a road connects the spiritual world with the material one. The only uniting element between them might be "the Word". In order to express his philosophy in theatrical terms, Soyinka chooses clear symbols: a rainbow for the spiritual world and a palm-tree and palm wine for the material world. He shows that "the Word" is dominated and misused by the Professor, a rogue of a character who adopts Westernized ways of living. He meets his opponents in a young driver who refuses to believe in his propaganda, and in a cruel, sadistic gangster. In a way, *The Road* continues the cynical, pessimistic line begun by *A Dance of the Forests*. Thus viewed, Kongi's *Harvest* is a logical component in this creative sequence.

Kongi is the president of an African state. He comes into conflict with Oba Danlola, who represents traditional thinking and conservative opposition. Having assumed practically total political power in his country, Kongi wants to triumph during the New Yam Festival celebrating the harvest season. On this occasion, he wants Danlola to hand over the yam bowl to himself in public. Thus, Kongi hopes to gain both personal prestige and general respect. He does not hesitate to use various intrigues in order to achieve his aim. At last, he seems to be satisfied, as Danlola agrees to do what the President asks. But when Kongi opens the bowl, he discovers to his utmost surprise and dismay that it contains the head of one of the President's victims. Soyinka's sinister humour and sense of satire appear once again to strengthen the criticism of African methods of ruling. The subject-matter chosen by the playwright gives him many opportunities to comment on the basic problems of political life: the relations between progress and traditions, violence and freedom, dictatorship and democracy. As in his earlier plays, Soyinka tries to make his play function on the individual, as well as on the social level.

J. P. Clark's main concern lies in philosophical and sociological problems, while the requirements of the stage are somewhat relegated to the background. In writing his four plays—*Song of a Goat* (1961), *The Masquerade* (1964), *The Raft* (1964) and *Ozidi* (1966)—Clark acquired sufficient experience. The first play is a well-constructed drama, reminding us of the ancient Greek tragedies. The basic conflict is, however, derived from the still-persisting view of the present-day African: if he has no child, he feels unhappy. This is exactly the case of the hero—Zifa—who blames his wife. In reality, however, it is Zifa's impotence that is responsible. The tragic climax comes when Zifa discovers the love affair of his younger brother and his wife. The two brothers commit suicide.

Clark's plays are notable for their poetical atmosphere which are created chiefly by means of well-chosen expressions. In this way, an everyday event can be raised to the level of myths, which is particularly true of *The Masquerade*. It develops the central theme of romantic love. Man's life is, in this case, even more the toy of fate. People suffer from the lack of communication; their misunderstanding cannot be removed. This playwright does not believe in causality, but stresses, rather, that his characters are extraordinarily complicated. *The Masquerade* is linked with *The Song of a Goat*, since the young hero is the son of Zifa's wife and Zifa's younger brother. The play suggests that the tragic curse does not end with the death of the two brothers. When the father of Titi, the young girl who is in love with the hero, learns of the young man's origin, he refuses to give his consent to the marriage of the young couple. As Titi insists on marrying the boy, the furious father shoots both her and the hero.

Readers, spectators and critics have discussed the convincingness of this tragedy, especially the question of whether the conflict is in keeping with its almost classical treatment. Clark obviously could have presented his subject in another form, but the basic moral "masquerade", which gives rise to his dramatic crisis, seems to correspond to the masquerade of the modern realistic tragedy in its technical and aesthetic qualities, which dates back to the times of antiquity. *The Raft* is a genuine existentialist play. It describes the life of four men who spend some time together on the raft. Clark must know the river Niger very well, but he is not so interested in the scenery as in human psychology. Each of the men must die, none can reach his goal. All of them seem to be predestined to meet their tragic fate.

Both *The Raft* and *Ozidi* are based on epical narrations. But in *The Raft*, philosophical elements prevail to a great extent, which tends to decrease the dramatic effect of the play. The author must have worked very hard to elaborate a number of its details. The whole construction, however, appears to lack sufficient scope for the development of the plot. The dramatist's method can best be studied precisely here, although this play is perhaps a very difficult problem for a stage-manager. Clark's plays become more comprehensible if the playwright's political and aesthetic opinions are taken into account. It is not sufficient to study his text, but it is essential to note his attitudes toward such important questions as literature, politics and the social functions of drama, to which we have already referred. The following is his opinion concerning the writer's role in society:

"I think that the writer—whether African, European or American—is just like a lawyer, a doctor, a carpenter, a janitor, one type of citizen within society. He has his work, as has everyone with a job to do. I don't think that any role—not even that of the highest elective political office of the land—is so special that it should subsume the others. This is where I find it personally disturbing that some of my friends—some of my own kind—do not seem to be satisfied with their own role of writing and would rather become soldiers and politicians, preferring to play roles other than the one that they are good at and recognized for. If you are a poet and write songs for soldiers to march to, to fight to, I suppose you would be well within your field of militancy. If you write a play, like any of Brecht's, to propound and push an ideology, a way of life, you would be well within your field. But to be an artist while doing all this, you must at the same time create a work of art, carve a a figure which, when all capital has been made of it in the interest of whatever ideology that is attached to it, retains its hold upon us principally as an object of beauty.

"Another thing: the artist, we accept, is a social person. What he is creating is for consumption by a living group of people, and if it is anything valid, it will have as long a tenure as the collective life of the people into the future. He may create his work for worship, he may direct it to an audience that is political, and he may direct it to audiences that are not political or religious-minded. It depends on where his talents really lie; he tries to create a work that is of interest to his public, and this may or may not address itself to any kind of topical issue. To that extent of his being a communicating citizen, I feel he is engaged and committed. But when as a writer he puts pen aside to take up sword, gun and hand-grenade, or when he mounts a soap-box to spit slogans chosen for him by others, then I think he had left one role for another." (*Palaver*, 1972, p. 19).

In 1956, three comedies were published: *This Is Our Chance, The Jewel of the Shrine* and *A Man of Character*. Their author—James Ene Henshaw—tried to show human faults and weaknesses. His works are less original that Soyinka's and Clark's plays; they seem to continue in the English classical tradition. *A Man of Character,* for instance, reminds us of Sheridan, while *The Jewel of the Shrine* goes back to Ben Jonson's times.

This Is Our Chance is, however, up-to-date. It describes two rival villages (Uduru and Koloro), exposing chiefly the negative features of their life. An Uduru boy finally marries a Koloro girl, thanks to the great diplomat, Bambulu, headmaster at Koloro, the only person who rises above the narrow-mindedness of his countrymen. On the whole, Henshaw seldom attempts more than providing some entertainment. This can be seen in *Children of the Goddess and Other Plays from West Africa* (1964). In *Companion for a Chief*, he criticizes the practices of native doctors. Like *This Is Our Chance*, this play also expresses an ironical attitude toward the so-called cultural heritage, or rather, its modern misuse. The wittiest comedy by Henshaw is *Medicine for Love* (1964), which describes the intrigues in an election campaign. A committee trying to ensure Mr. Ekunyah's victory uses various tricks in order to influence public opinion. *Medicine for Love* is to be produced by a certain charlatan (an idea similar to that of *Companion for a Chief*), who is supposed to guarantee everybody's love for Mr. Ekunyah. But all this does not end very satisfactorily for the candidate: the campaign costs him a great deal of money and is not successful. The satirical comedy *Dinner for Promotion* (1967) is an amusing study of an African *nouveau-riche*. The comedies by Henshaw are not profound, but they are amusing; they may be labelled "traditional", but, in fact, they are nearer to the European tradition. The African traditional theatre is represented by such plays as Obotunde Ijimere's *The Imprisonment of Obatala* and other plays of his, and by Frank Aig-Imoukhuede's *Ikeke* (1966).

The future development of modern Nigerian drama will be influenced by the production of films. Nigerian writers have written film scripts (e.g. Gabriel Okara), and others have been interested in their production. Like Sembène Ousmane, the well-known Senegalese novelist and film-producer, John Pepper Clark has become involved in this attractive business. He utilized the Ijaw epical narrative (which forms the basis of his play (*Ozidi*) shooting in a 16 mm film (1963).

2. Ghana

As numerous Ghanaian soldiers fought in World War II, they became aware of the rising national liberation movement in foreign colonies, e.g. in Southern Asia. Nkrumah himself was strongly influenced by Gandhi's doctrine of non-violence and his philosophy.

The liberation movement in the country was led in the post-war period by Dr. J. B. Danquah who formed the United Gold Coast Convention (UGCC). The radical programme of that political party was enriched under Dr. Kwame Nkrumah by Pan-Africanist ideas, which were important because they encouraged the protesting masses who felt that they were not alone. The British Colonial Office rejected the idea of immediate self-government and tried to realize gradual, rather slow reforms. As Danquah was willing to talk with the British in order to achieve some compromise, he came into conflict with Nkrumah who chose more forceful methods such as strikes and boycotts of English goods. Nkrumah founded the Convention People's Party (CPP) and was persecuted by the colonial authorities. The new constitution in 1951 granted only minor concessions. The subsequent elections were very successful for the CPP.

Nkrumah was released from prison and in March 1952 became the Prime Minister of the Gold Coast. In two years, he succeeded in strengthening his position, though he had to overcome numerous economic difficulties and solve the specific problems of the influential tribal chiefs. In 1959, a popular referendum in British Togoland led that country to merge with the Gold Coast, constituting another success of Nkrumah's policies.

English-language writing in Ghana, the first country to gain independence (in 1957) in the vigorous wave of sub-Saharan emancipation, has developed under the strong influence of nationalism. Ancient African civilizations were eulogized in poetry, while folk subjects were introduced into prose writing. Different types of nationalism have emerged there. Only a few authors, however, shared the Leftist orientation of its former President, Kwame Nkrumah, whose autobiography (published in 1957) was one of the most widely-read books from Ghana. The impact of politics has been felt not only in literature, but also in other spheres of art, such as painting.

The rise of Ghanaian writing was partly due to literacy campaigns which helped the uneducated people to take part in cultural life. The Ghana Drama Studio in Accra and broadcasting stations also played an important role in this respect. Ghanaian drama developed at a pace with the increasing number of original plays and translations from English into the vernacular languages. Precisely this democratic character of the new literary production accounts for the fact that mainly short pieces were written, and that Ghana has not had so many or such famous novelists as Nigeria.

Raphael Ernest Grail Armattoe (1913—1953) was concerned with literature as well as with philology, anthropology, medicine and biology. He influenced the country's post-war political life in a significant manner. Although born in south-eastern Ghana, his parents came from Togoland, formerly a German colony. In 1930, Armattoe left his country for Germany. He studied in Hamburg, but after Hitler's assumption of power he continued his studies at the Universities of Besançon and Lille, where he took degrees in philosophy and education. In 1937, he came to Great Britain to study medicine at the Universities of Edinburgh and Glasgow. He worked in the field of anthropology in London.

In 1949, Armattoe was proposed for the Nobel Prize for medicine. He worked in Londonderry at a research institute on anthropology and racial biology, married a Swiss woman and had two children. During his stay in Europe, he came into contact with Huxley, Gide, Heidegger and Du Bois. As a nationalist, he took a stand in opposition to Nkrumah. As a writer, he was strongly influenced by Yeats, Brooke and probably by Tennyson. Armattoe regarded the Negro as a subject of his scientific examination. His rationalistic poetry is highly precise and bears some characteristic signs of bookish inspiration. But the poet tried to make up for this quality by inserting his personal observations gathered during his travels.

His collection *Between the Forest and the Sea* (1952) is Armattoe's typical view of African reality. Although he tends to romanticize it as a result of his devotion to his native country, he sometimes becomes satirical or sarcastic, as in his following collection of poems *Deep Down the Blackman's Mind* (1954). These tones, which were rather unusual in the pre-independence era, result from the fact that Armattoe disagreed with the cutting of the diseased cocoa-trees, declaring that he had discovered his own medicine for the diseased trees. This treatment would have been preferred by the peasants, who disliked the idea of chopping them down. Armattoe had a different opinion from Nkrumah with regard to the question of whether British Togoland should join Ghana; Armattoe believed that it should be independent, which conflicted, of course, with the Pan-Africanists' efforts to form large political entities in Africa.

Armattoe often criticized the unjustified optimism of those who were so enthusiastic about African independence that they neglected the difficulties complicating the trend of complete economic and cultural liberation. Armattoe disliked the hasty generalizations and rhetoric clichés of *négritude,* but he espoused some aspects of its aesthetic programme. Like certain *négritude* poets, he used rich rhymed verses, which were very effective from the acoustic standpoint. He also considered poetry as an opportunity for disseminating his opinions and firmly believed in the social commitment of art. But the most substantial part of Armattoe's philosophy differed sharply from that of *négritude*. He never ceased to emphasize the power of common sense and to appreciate man as a thinking creature. He also wrote two ethnographic studies Ewes in Eweland and Dawn Over Africa. His long short story *The Happy Bride* was not published.

Gladys May Casely-Hayford (1904—1950) devoted her life to the propagation of African culture. She studied in Wales and had a long sustained interest in folk-art (she also performed her dances in Berlin). In Sierra Leone, Miss Casely-Hayford taught and wrote under the pseudonym of Aqua Laluah. Her verses appeared in journals and anthologies. She died in Freetown.

Michael Francis Dei-Anang (born in 1909, in Mampong) studied at Achimota College. His specializations are history, education and literary criticism but he is famous chiefly as a poet and playwright. His collections of poems include *Wayward Lines from Africa* (1946), *Africa Speaks* (1959), *Ghana Semi-tones* (1962), *Ghana Glory* (1965) and *Two Faces of Africa* (1965, in cooperation with his son). Attractive lyrical passages can be found in his *Cocoa Comes to Mampong* (1949), containing dramatic scenes from history, while his best play *Okomfo Anokye's Golden Stool* (1963) describes the heroic deeds of an Akan hero at the court of the Ashanti king, Osei Tutu. The golden stool, given to the hero by the gods, symbolizes the unity of the Ashanti people. Dei-Anang considers it his task to explain the African cultural heritage. His poetry is deeply emotional and patriotic.

Dei-Anang sometimes mentions the well-known linguistic handicaps, for example, the necessity of using English for the popularization of African culture. But this language is no real handicap for him personally, as he has mastered it with much success. He inserts into his collections echoes of ancient epical songs and frequent historical reminiscences, but does not succumb to pessimism, even when meditating on the ruins of ancient civilizations.

Dei-Anang considers that the Africans do not suffer from inhibitions in expressing their emotions and he points out that they use songs as an accompaniment for all their events. He highly appreciates poetry and the poet's social function. This opinion is not only based on his studies of folklore, but also on an analysis of the topical meaning of poetry in the African renascence. He considers poetry to be particularly suitable for propagating Negro culture because the poet can use widely understandable means of expression. This poet sees the most serious obstacles as local limitations and the lack of financial means. Discussing the situation of French-writing representatives of *négritude*, he observes that they have not been able to achieve complete spiritual satisfaction, even though they have mastered the colonizers' language (i.e. French) better than their own. Dei-Anang seeks analogies in the history of English literature and mentions the cases of Geoffrey Chaucer and John Langland, who preferred English to Latin. His appeal for a linguistic renascence of the vernacular languages remains wholly in the sphere of theory; in practice, he uses his refined English. As a representative of the older generation of Ghanaian poets, he tends to stress the African's racial and national exclusivity, unlike the younger writers.

Geormbeeyi Adali-Mortty (born in 1916 in Gbledee, Togoland) worked as a teacher and social worker. He has published many articles dealing with educational problems, and especially with adult education. These works are of extraordinary importance in Africa, as in 1960 only one fifth of the population knew English and the lack of educated people has had a detrimental effect on their national economies. Adali-Mortty travelled widely abroad spending some time in Great Britain, Brazil, the USA and Ceylon.

In his studies, he analyzed Ewe poetry and its characteristics: melancholy, rich allegories, fantastic metaphors and peculiarities of rhythm and melody. The favourite Ewe themes are work, love, hunting and supernatural phenomena. Many of its nursery rhymes and lullabies are without meaning. Adali-Mortty discovered Ewe folk opetry, just as J. H. Kwabena Nketia (b. 1921) discovered Akan folk poetry in *The Poetry of Drums*.

Adali-Mortty published his own verses in *Voices of Ghana* and in the literary journal, *Okyeame*. He also produced several radio plays.

Israel Kafu Hoh (b. 1912) has written a part of his poetry in English. He completed his pedagogical studies at Akropong and has also written drama. Refusing to imitate European models, he decided to simplify his expression as much as possible. He likes to depict natural beauties, moods and states of mind but has also produced militant anti-colonialist poetry.

Albert Kayper Mensah (b. 1923) is the author of sophisticated, refined verses. His scientific approach can be seen in the careful, elaborated construction of his theatrical plays. Mensah came from Sekondi and studied at Achimota and later in London and Cambridge. In 1950, he started lecturing in Kumasi. His theatrical and radio plays became very popular. For his plays, Mensah was awarded a prize in 1956.

Kwesi Brew (b. 1928) wrote the collection of poems *The Shadow of Laughter* (1969) and a number of individual works. Francis Ernest Kobina Parkes (b. 1932) studied at Adisadele and then became a journalist. In 1955, he started working for the broadcasting company. His *Songs from the Wilderness* (1965) is a collection of nationalist poetry expressing the poet's attitude toward the social changes that had been brought about during the preceding decade.

George Awoonor-Williams (born in 1935, in Wheta) is an artist with manysided interests. He has worked as a teacher and researcher, but has also dealt with stage-acting and managed a film company. Today, he lectures on African literatures in New York.

His collection *Rediscovery and Other Poems* (1964) and his novel *This Earth, My Brother* (1971) made him well-known. Together with Adali-Mortty, he edited *Messages: Poems from Ghana* (1971) from which we quote as follows:

"What may be described as the second phase of his (Awoonor-Williams') development is marked by the poetry of *Night of My Blood,* and the poems which are included in this volume. He says of this phase: 'I have gone through the trauma of growth, anger, love, and the innocence and nostalgia of my personal dreams. These are beyond me now. Not anger, or love, but the sensibility that shaped and saw them as communal acts of which I am only the articulator. Now I write out my renewed anguish about the crippling distresses of my country and my people, of death by guns, of death by disease and malnutrition, of the death of friends whose lives held so much promise, of the chicanery of politics and the men who indulge in them, of the misery of the poor in the midst of plenty'" (*Messages,* 1971, p. 183).

Ellis Ayitey Komey (b. 1927) published his early verses in *West African Review* and in the anthology *Modern Poetry from Africa*. Together with Mphahlele, he edited the anthology of short stories entitled *Modern African Stories* (1964). His own stories are amusing, with occasional satirical lashes.

Christina Ama Ata Aidoo (b. 1942) works as a research fellow of the Institute for African Studies at the University of Ghana. Her verses and short stories possess a considerable degree of social feeling and show an interest in the life of the villagers. In 1962, still as an undergraduate of the University of Legon, she was awarded the third prize in the contest organized by the Mbari literary club in Ibadan. Her subject-matter is mostly tragic, the same is true of her plays *The Dilemma of a Ghost* (1965) and *Anowa* (1969). Both of them deal with the relationship between a man and a woman from the psychological viewpoint. At the same time, they represent the typical conflict of cultures: traditional Africa versus modern comportment. The characteristic contribution of this woman writer can be found in her short stories devoted to the problem of women's emancipation.

The Dilemma of a Ghost has been much appreciated for its dramatic conflict and exciting action. The contrast between America and Africa has been experienced by many black intellectuals and is, therefore, an intriguing theme in itself. But few critics have observed the linguistic qualities of the play. They are worth noting, as John Nagenda remarks in his essay "Generations in Conflict" (in *Protest and Conflict in African Literature,* London 1969, p. 107):

"Indeed the whole play is obviously much influenced by Greek drama. The plot is about Ato Yawson, who returns with his Afro-American wife, Eulalie, to Ghana. I like the way the language here represents Eulalie speaking as if she was on the American campus. If overdone, it might become a cliché on how Americans speak, but it is not overdone. When the plot refers back to Ghana, there is a change of dialogue—those women who form what is a kind of chorus, speaking in verse, the mother speaking not in verse but in African translations, and so on. Miss Aidoo is very sensitive to language, and employs it cunningly to suggest the nature of her characters.

„Ato comes back with his wife, and there is immediate tension between her and his family. Clearly this is not so much because of the difference in generations as the insensivity of the woman who has been brought back, plus the weakness of her husband who is at the same time unable to bridge for her the vast chasm which lies between her own experience and life in Ghana. So when a reconciliation comes about, it is the uneducated mother of a previous generation who brings it about with her compassion. Unfortunately, the reconciliation when it happens, does so contrary to everything that's gone before and is therefore artificial and unconvincing.''

Kojo Gyinaye Kyei (b. 1932) studied in America and became well-known as a painter and architect. *The Lone Voice* (1969) is a collection combining his personal philosophy with his sense of humour.

Radio plays are being written by many Ghanaian authors, including Henry Ofori (b. 1924), the author of the satire *Literary Society* (1957), Joyce Addo (b. 1932) who wrote *Mother in-law* (1957) and Efua Theodora Sutherland (b. 1924). It was she who founded the Ghana Drama Studio. Mrs. Sutherland studied at Mampong and then Cambridge and at the London School of Oriental and African Studies. She produced the plays *Foriwa* (1967), *Edufa* (1969) and *Vulture! Vulture!* (1968), as well as folk plays about Ananse, the traditional spider-fable hero. For children, she wrote the stories *Playtime in Africa* (1960) and *The Pineapple Child* (1962).

Mrs. Sutherland has tried to develop theatrical life in the Ghanaian villages and for this reason founded an experimental theatre in the Central Region. Her best prose works are *New Life in Kyerefoso* and *The Road-makers*. One of the characteristics of her books is an effective utilization of the rhythmic qualities of the English language. Her modified word order reminds one of Okara's experimental novel *The Voice*, though Mrs. Sutherland's efforts are less consistent.

One of her fellow workers in the Drama Studio was J.C. de Graft Johnson (b. 1920), the author of the historical book *African Glory* (1954), several children's stories and the theatrical plays, *Sons and Daughters* (1964), *The Secret of Opokuwa* (1967) and *Through a Film Darkly* (1970).

Sons and Daughters is rather carelessly written, but the subject chosen by the author is noteworthy. It might have been more successful in a short-story form. As it is, it lacks the real dramatic development of the individual characters in James Ofosu's family. Differences of opinion arise between the parents and their children. The mother understands better than the father the needs of her children; she realizes that they wish to have more freedom in choosing their partners. The most positive feature of this "family drama" is that it avoids a schematic, boring stereotyped division into wise children and stupid parents.

J. C. de Graft Johnson does not hesitate—either here or in his following plays—to enter the realm of complications and difficulties, in order to save his artistic truth.

Children's books have also been written by authors Anifeng, Lindsay, Apraku, Lartey and others. Humorous stories are the specialization of Peter Kwame Buahin.

Cameron Duodu (born in 1937 in Akyem Abuakwa) became well-known after the publication of his novel *The Gab Boys* (1967), though his poetry is also well worth reading. A large part of his work is satirical. Directed against the late colonial myths, they reveal picturesque details of contemporary African life.

Descriptive realism in modern Ghanaian prose-writing is the forte of Akosua Abbs—whose plain narrative *Ashanti Boy* (1959) is rather naïve—as well as of Ato Bedwei, Kwabena Annan and Bentil. These writers describe the migration of the peasants to the cities, hard work in the fields, and the introduction of new technology into the villages.

The poet and playwright Andrew Ananka Opoku (b. 1912) comes from a clergyman's family. He studied at Akropong, then taught for some time and devoted himself to studies in Twi, as well as to sculpture and broadcasting activities. He is the author of a number of journalistic and travel sketches.

J. Benibengor Blay wrote several popular stories: "Dr. Bengia Wants a Wife" (1953, "Stubborn Girl" (1958), "Thoughts of Youth" (1961) and "Emilia's Promise". His collection of stories bears the title *Here and There Stories* (1959). Gilbert A. Sam has published detective stories, including "A Christmastide Tragedy" (1956) and "Who Killed Inspector Kwasi Minta?" (1956), and the novel *Love in the Grave* (1959). This popular line of fiction was continued in Kwabena Asare Bediako's novels *Don't Leave Me Mercy* (1966) and *A Husband for Esi Ellua* (1968).

Psychological realism can be traced in J. W. Abruquah's novels *The Catechist* (1965) and *The Torrent* (1968), dealing with a young man's enthusiasm for European education. Francis Selormey, from the Ghanaian part of Togoland, presented his autobiographical narratives in *The Narrow Path* (1964) and *The Path Widens*. The first novel describes the young days of Kofi, an African teacher's son, in the 1920's. The relationships between the members of his family and the school life of those times are well described.

Samuel Asare Konadu (b. 1932), a journalist working for the Ghanaian Press Agency, received his education in his native country and at the University of Strasbourg. Apart from short stories, he has published a number of novels: *The Player Who Bungled His Life* (1965), *Come Back, Dora* (1966), *Shadow of Wealth* (1966), *Night Watchers of Korlebu* (1967). *Night Watchers of Korlebu* is an exciting account of the activities of traditional medicine-men. *A Woman in Her Prime* deals with an unhappy woman who cannot bear a child, though she is married for the third time. Her mother, firmly believing in old superstitions, thinks that it is necessary to offer sacrifices to the gods, whose magic power may help her daughter. This conflict between ancient faith and modern scepticism is, however, fully developed in *Ordained by the Oracle,* whose hero—Boateng—after becoming a widower, undergoes forty days' rites during which both he and the reader have an opportunity to think over the social and psychological implications of religion. The composition and dialogue in his latest novel reveal the author's constantly improving skill.

Konadu's straight-forward manner contrasts with Asare Bediako's novel *Rebel* (1969). He has worked as a journalist, first in Ghana and then in Dar-es-Salaam, the capital in Tanzania. He is concerned with the present-day need for more progressive methods in agricultural production. Consequently, he sends the main character of his novel to fight against a dangerous rival, a conservative priest who is about to commit a crime in order to preserve his traditional authority. The conflict between progressive and reactionary forces assumes an allegorical character in this novel.

The Beautiful Ones Are Not Yet Born (1969) and *Fragments* (1970) are novels written by Ayi Kwei Armah (b. 1939), one of the most promising novelists of Ghana. With unusually penetrating insight, this author reveals numerous moral problems of contemporary Africans.

Armah seems to be interested in the social decadence caused by corruption, and particularly bribery. It would be only too simple to denote his work as a criticism of the last period of Nkrumah's rule in Ghana. The vices exposed by the writer cannot be completely eliminated by the new regime that has existed since the military coup (which is well characterized by Armah). This novel attacks features that can be seen in other countries, as well. Armah is concerned not only with broad social problems, but he also presents occasional analyses of human nature, again dwelling principally on the negative qualities of his contemporaries, since it is obvious that—the beautiful ones are not yet born.

3. Sierra Leone

Adelaide Casely-Hayford (1868—1959) came from a Fante family. She spent a long time in Europe. Together with her sister, she founded a school in Freetown in 1897, then married a Ghanaian lawyer and spent two years with him in the USA. Her autobiography and short stories are still worth reading. She often dealt with the contrast of cultures and generations, keenly observing the paradoxical development in the late colonial era: the old devote their efforts to appearing "civilized" and readily accept European manners, while the young, affected by the emancipation movement, return to the ancient tribal traditions, stressing African elements.

The educational standard of Sierra Leone is similar to that of the neighbouring countries. Freetown, the country's capital, has a very old university, judged by African standards: Fourah Bay College was founded back in 1827. Many prominent writers graduated from this college or from some English university. As a result, most of the writing from Sierra Leone has a typically intellectual, rationalistic, matter-of-fact style. Generally speaking, technically advanced short stories prevail there, while the realistic method is mostly employed for the purpose of psychological analysis. Few novels are being written and poetry is certainly less important than in Ghana. Prose-writers frequently choose insignificant subjects, but they are able to develop them with some success. What a difference from other sub-Saharan countries, where even the "big" topics are sometimes spoiled by inadequate artistic treatment!

One may generalize even more by saying that the favourite subject of Sierra Leonean short-story writers is the so-called colonial mentality, i.e. the complex of attitudes surviving from the colonial period. For generations, Negroes had to be satisfied with inferior kinds of work. Since the liberation, they have had to face more responsible tasks requiring greater initiative. But people who have become used to obeying orders blindly and fulfilling them almost mechanically find it difficult to adopt more independent, decisive attitudes.

Another characteristic of some Sierra Leonean writers is their sense of humour, which is very rare in West African writing. Its occurrence might be ascribed to the above-mentioned fact: namely, the Sierra Leoneans often choose unimportant subjects, turning them into "literary trifles", which evidently call for light, amusing approaches.

R. Sarif Easmon builds his work on the basis of numerous keen perceptions whose meanings become apparent only when seen in a larger context. Although the author does not seem to strive for this, a picture of class differences and social contradictions often emerges from his work. Thus Koya, the little girl heroine of the short story of the same name, represents the almost aristocratic pride of her family, though she is only nine years old. Her mother is a beautiful woman, but a bad cook. Koya attends her cooking classes at the house of a poorer woman, who prepares excellent food. But Koya has been ordered by her mother not to eat anything during her visits. The unfortunate girl can hardly resist, and once she is seen pilfering delicacies in secret and is laughed at by the other girls. Koya suffers much from the deforming effects of her education, which are exposed by the writer. R. Sarif Easmon was awarded first prize for his play *Dear Parent and Ogre* (1961) in 1962. His following plays *The New Patriots* (1965) and *The Burnt-out Marriage* (1967) were equally successful, though they never surpassed their rather conservative ideological framework.

Dear Parent and Ogre deals with the problems of the trade-unionist Sawameh who wants to marry a girl from a bourgeois family. The playwright contrasts the attitudes of different generations and social strata and provides a mild criticism of snobbery. Similarly moderate but amusing is *The New Patriots,* which follows the relations between two contemporary politicians who are also rivals in their love for a widow. *The Burnt-out Marriage* studies the crisis of a tribal chief's married life, brought about by the conflicting effects of the couple's milieu, as well as their differing opinions.

Eldred Durosimi Jones is probably better known as a literary critic and professor of literature (he taught in Freetown, Leeds and in the USA) than as a creative writer. In his short story "One Can Try" he introduces a young, ambitious African into Sierra Leonean writing. The well-tested subject of love between a black man and a white woman is summed up here and modified in the typical colonial dilemma of Tullock. As he wants to continue his career and get a profitable job in England, he leaves his nice but illiterate black mistress, who has borne his child, and decides to marry a well-educated Englishwoman who refuses to live in Africa. Jones' subject has two different planes: the moral conflict of a man torn between two women, and the symbolic meaning of Africa's decision… which path to choose in the future? The story is more satisfactory on the former level, as the complex problem of modernization would require more space to be properly developed.

Abioseh Nicol (b. 1924), whose real name is Dr. Davidson Nicol, is one of the most gifted authors of Sierra Leone. He studied in Freetown, Cambridge and London and obtained several degrees (medicine, philosophy, science). Following his collaboration with the University of Ibadan, he became Sierra Leone's Ambassador to the United Nations. Dr. Nicol edited the works written by Africanus Horton, the nationalist who was active more than one hundred years ago (Africanus Horton: *The Dawn of Nationalism in Modern Africa,* 1970). Apart from poetry, he wrote short stories which were published in the collections *The Truly Married Woman and Other Stories* (1965) and *Two African Tales; The Leopard Hunt and The Devil at Yolahun Bridge* (1965). His detached style, lacking pathos, is surprisingly effective in conveying his humanistic message. In 1952, Nicol was awarded the Margaret Wrong Prize and Medal for Literature in Africa. His stories "As the Night, the Day" and "The Judge's Son" well exemplify his creative method. The former, bearing a Shakespearean title, is set in an African school: The characters long for mutual understanding, but their efforts lead to the opposite results. Thus, the whole story is based on a series of paradoxes in the characters' thinking and behaviour. The teacher fails to gain the confidence of his class; the boy who broke a thermometer fears to confess his guilt and lets his innocent comrade be punished in his place. When he finally decides to confess, nobody believes him, because the matter is generally regarded as settled. This banal episode is profitably used to characterize certain moral attitudes and criticize prejudice.

"The Judge's Son" is a clever analysis of an upper-class family in which the boy is brought up. He should be happy to be wealthy, but he is not, as he suffers from spiritual isolation. His father takes an important post in the colonial service and does not devote his valuable time to his son. The servant belongs to a different class and therefore cannot be in close contact with the boy, who imitates his father's behaviour towards the servants, thus depriving himself of all the positive values surrounding him. His psychic tension reaches its climax when he shoots his faithful dog, his best companion, but this sacrifice is as useless as his life.

Abioseh Nicol has always considered his writing as his specific contribution to African culture, whose relationship to overseas writing he understands well. In his foreword to *Two African Tales,* he writes as follows:

"These stories were written some years ago, and have now been modified for my young friends to give them an impression of what happened when we were under the rule of the Europeans. They owe something to European writers like E. M. Forster, Joyce Cary, Graham Greene and Evelyn Waugh, all of whom I admire and who, themselves, wrote about similar situations. However, being both black and African, I was then on the other side of the fence and perhaps saw things somewhat differently."

William Farquar Conton (born in 1925 in Bathurst) tried to express his many-sided scientific interests in his novel *The African* (1960). After becoming a teacher, he continued his studies in history, ethnography and sociology. He was a headmaster at Bo, and then started his work at the Ministry of Education in Freetown. The novel *The African* contains many autobiographical elements. The first half especially is written in a realistic manner.

It describes the career of Kisimi Kamara, a Hausa boy, who at first helps his parents, tilling the fields in a primitive way. He attends a mission school and continues his studies in a town, which greatly pleases the village people. Conton succeeds in describing the school milieu that he knows so well, and in convincingly characterizing the individual students. The passages describing the hero's experience in England are also dramatic. There, Kisimi Kamara meets Greta, a white South African girl, and their initial sympathies grow into a wonderful love affair, which, however, subsequently collapses in the face of deep-rooted racial prejudice. Kisimi Kamara suffers from a bitter affront and gives up his love. He realizes that an individual's resistance to the long mutual mistrust between blacks and whites is ineffective. He therefore embarks upon a political career and tries to do away with prejudice forever, organizing powerful united tribes and nationalities. In describing his political career, Conton sometimes sacrifices his story's probability. The true-to-life basis of the novel dissolves in the second half into a refined system of ideas and dreams. Kamara becomes one of his country's foremost politicians and, during the active struggle for independence, even assumes the post of Prime Minister of a free state.

But Kamara cannot forget Greta who lost her life due to her love for a black man. The hero, therefore, goes incognito to the Republic of South Africa, in order to avenge the girl's death. There, he meets his bloodthirsty rival, but does not carry out the intended revenge in the end. He shows mercy to his defeated rival, as—in Conton's opinion—liberated Black Africa should bring the world the message of humanism. The exclusivity of the hero's fate was much objected to by the critics, but Conton did not base his novel on a psychological analysis of the relationship between Kisimi Kamara and Greta. Rather, he centred the second part of it on political considerations. One is sometimes surprised by the carelessness with which he sketches his characters and the insensitive way he interrupts the plot's continuity in order to insert his comments on the Pan-African movement, nationalism, the problems of tribal life, etc. He asks more questions than he can answer and often oversimplifies. In the middle of the novel, it seems that everything can easily be solved. This error results from the fact that scenes from political life are lightly sketched and that many fictitious protagonists of the author's speculations replace realistic characters.

Conton has been more successful with his short stories, in which he analyzes the African mentality. His short story "Blood in the Basin" shows the feelings of a black captain who commands his ship for the first time in his life. He travels from Liverpool to Freetown, where he is awaited by his parents, and his pride is mixed with a feeling of heavy responsibility. A dramatic episode, which takes place on board, destroys the captain's hopes for a happy landing in his native country.

Owing to its content, Conton's work belongs to the first phase of development of the modern literature of Sierra Leone, when the main task was to reveal the essential qualities of the African's thinking to Europeans and Americans. The author does not address himself to his readers in his native country, since they know him well enough. The African literary audience also seems to dislike Conton's strong individualism and his emphasis upon those aspects in which black people differ from other racial groups. Conton never shows the

African's qualities with any intention of so-called inverse racism. He appears to be inclined toward the theory of the African personality, which, as it developed at the end of the Fifties, emphasized mainly a recognition of the specific character of African culture.

Gaston Bart-Williams is an author, who tends toward satirical writing. Bart-Williams dislikes pure theories and scorns even those theroretical terms which—until recently—were quite seriously discussed in Africa. His short story "The Bed-sitter", which was awarded the second prize of the Mbari Literary Club of Ibadan in 1962, attacks ironically the theory of the African personality. He rightly rejects the idealization of tribal life and its traditions and customs.

In this story, he speaks of an African who has lived in London for years, but who still sticks to the ancient customs. His brother in Africa choses a girl for him, and this Londoner is ready to marry her, without ever seeing her. Awaiting her at London Airport, he mistakes his future wife for an unknown pretty girl and kisses her. A policeman arriving to deal with the scandal observes that the African's future wife is old, fat and the mother of four children. The astonished man had decided to marry her on the basis of a photo which was thirty years old...

Robert Wellesley Cole described, in a simple but effective manner, his life's story in his book *Kossoh Town Boy* (1960), whose structure is relatively remote from contemporary attempts at novel-writing. Cole's work is an autobiographical narrative of the type that is fairly popular in Africa.

Unlike fiction, the poetry and drama of Sierra Leone are less well represented and seem to imitate English models more. This is true to a certain extent of the collection of poems *Dreams of Twilight* (1962) by Delphine King which contain sensitive but not too original verses. It is even truer of John Akar's play *The Valley without Echo*, in which the events taking place in an African village are described in an essentially unoriginal manner. The play deals with a young man born in a village who later, upon returning home, is killed in a railway accident.

George Crispin is the author of the collection of poems *Precious Gems Unearthed by an African* (1952). Syl Cheyney-Coker, a Sierra Leonean poet and critic living in the USA, has published a number of outstanding poems in various magazines. He took his degree in radio and TV journalism at the University of Oregon and soon became interested in African art. His poems have been published in the collection *Exile* (1971).

4. Gambia

Lenrie Peters (born in 1932 in Bathurst), who studied in his native town and later in Freetown, graduated from Trinity College, Cambridge, in 1959. This surgeon and writer has produced one novel—*The Second Round* (1964)—and three collections of poems, *Poems* (published in Ibadan, 1964), *Satellites*, (1967), and *Katchikali* (1971).

The main character in *The Second Round* is Dr. Kawa, graduate of a British university. He returns to Freetown and discovers that he cannot adapt himself satisfactorily to the life of his native country. The situation in Africa is described in a critical way.

Peters has also written theatrical plays, but his foremost achievements are in poetry. The fifty-five poems in his *Satellites* contain mostly modern imagery, tending toward philosophical lyrics and a scientific precision of poetical expression. His most sophisticated verse is filled with learned allusions. The most concentrated situations, such as "The Parachute Men", turn in the end into figuratively conceived ideas, which confirm his conviction that the world can be improved. Peters as an optimistic "believer" repeats "I believe" three times at the end of his "Skyflood of Locusts", insisting on his profoundly felt desire: "Leave me the colour of truth". Peters is pleased to be able to witness the progress of our times, including technology and cosmic flights ("Wider Excursions"). But the poet is also aware of the horrors of the civilized world ("Remember they say the dead"). Peters often mentions the painful problems of the contemporary world. He finds the international political arena exciting. His genuine humanistic fervour makes itself felt in "The Room is Ten Foot Square", where ten balding men are unable to understand a young writer's plans (for survival) and his special interests (life), and so the young man applies for a job in vain.

The sharp attack on the corruption, demagogy and dishonesty existing in some new African states in the poem "In the Beginning" combines irony (We shall abolish the tsetse fly) and direct statements:

"The taxes rose."

"The common income fell."

"The death rate stayed alive."

He shows that the common people in Africa are disillusioned by the fact that they lack food, clothing and education, while the leading politicians, enjoying luxury with their houses and cars, etc., talk about gigantic schemes. But some of Peters' longest poems are too descriptive.

"On Exploding the Chinese Bomb" is full of fine imagery, expressing mainly the central idea that "the prestige and chaos of world vandalism ignites primitive fears".

5. Liberia

The best-known authors of Liberia are Bai T. Moore, who wrote the collection of poems *Ebony Dust* (1965) and the detective story *Murder in the Cassava Patch* (1968), and Roland Tombekai Dempster whose *Mystic Reformation of Gondola* (1953) attracted the critics' attention. Dempster's poetry, published in his collections *To Monrovia, Old and New* (1958) and *A Song out of Midnight* (1968), is essentially patriotic.

VII. LITERATURES IN WEST AFRICAN LANGUAGES

1. Roots and Origins of Literacy and Literature in West African Languages

1.0 As suggested in Chapter 1, the choice of a script has always been somehow linked with the broader problems of cultural, ideological and religious affinities in Black Africa, as elsewhere. It appears, however, highly probable that these affinities operate to some extent in one direction only; whereas the choice of the script is always linked to the above-mentioned factors, the importance of these factors in the sphere of literacy and literature is by no means limited to the texts written in the script connected with the respective culture or ideology. One might find sufficient evidence of a certain interaction between the cultural and ideological systems, which extend their influence far beyond the formal (and always superficial) limits of the graphical form of the particular literacy. The more a particular literacy develops towards literature in the true sense, the less is it apparently culturally restricted by its respective origin and the limits of the script connected with it. From this standpoint, the relationship between literacy and literature in the various languages of West Africa provides a certain paradox. Though graphically unimportant or certainly less important, the local, pre-Islamic and pre-colonial cultural traditions appear to have influenced all types of literacies and literatures in that area. The other two types of literacy (i.e. those in the Arabic and Latin scripts), though culturally and ideologically heavily influenced by their original, external roots, have actually been transformed through a gradual process of adaptation towards West African "oral civilizations" (the term is used in this sense by M. Houis, 1967, p. 279).

1.1 A sort of exclusive, dichotomic coexistence of pre-Islamic traditions with Islamic traditions and values may be presumed in some areas of West Africa for certain historical periods between the introduction of Islam and prior to the massive European ideological and cultural penetration. The scattered European presence on the West African coast or individual expeditions into the interior of the Savannah Belt throughout the 17th and 18th centuries do not appear to have influenced such a dichotomic co-existence in the sphere of literacy in any substantial way. Consequently, the literacy and literature deriving from Islamic sources have the advantage of a longer historical co-existence with traditional African cultures, whether oral or written. As a result, they are much more deeply connected with them and at the moment of the first contacts with European culture, power and religion, they may well enjoy the prestige of "an accepted" phenomenon. Occasionally they even function in a defensive manner, providing a sort of resistance against them.

The 19th and 20th century exploration, conquest and ultimate partition of West Africa gradually abolished the exclusivity of this dichotomic co-existence of Islamic culture with the traditional cultures of West Africa. The dichotomy that had existed until then in several areas of that region was being gradually transformed into a religious and cultural, but also graphical and linguistic trichotomy. Christianity arrived to challenge both the traditional religions and Islam.

Islam was no longer alone in its co-existence or challenge to them. Nineteenth and early 20th-century Europe started to challenge and influence both the local elements of the traditional African cultures and the elements of the Middle Eastern cultures and civilizations existing in the area already for a longer period. As literacy based upon the traditonal graphical systems of Africa is restricted (concerning the concept of "restricted" literacy, see Goody, 1968, p. 11), two types of literacy entered into large-scale competition for the writing of West African languages. The Roman and Arabic scripts were their external symbols, but deep roots in the cultures and religions of either the Middle East or Europe inherently accompanied these external graphical symbols. Although surviving in the literacies using "local" scripts, elements of the traditional cultures were gradually implanted into the two graphically foreign literacies. In our opinion, it may well have been this implementation of traditional, African cultural phenomena into the graphically "foreign" literacies which laid the foundations for their development from mere literacies towards real African literatures. This does not mean that all these basic factors have been competing and co-existing in every West African region. The opposite is true: only certain regions display such a fascinating process of interference and interaction. Certain forms of literacy are mostly limited to particular regions, either due to historical or even accidental factors, and some areas manifest no literacy at all.

1.2   The origins of most extended types of literacy in the West African languages can perhaps be reduced to three main sources—the Islamic religion and its culture as manifested by various organizational or ideological groups, the Christian missions and their activities, and certain types of colonial administration and their institutions. This triadic schema seems to have been valid for substantial parts of West Africa, as far as the historical roots of the situation until the late Fifties or early Sixties of this century are concerned. New factors entered the scene at this period: the independent African states, although inheriting many of the literacy policies introduced by the previous colonial administrations, began expressing their own will with increasing, accentuated determination. They are continuing to be assisted in their literacy efforts and policies by various international cultural and pedagogical institutions (such as U N E S C O), which support their African member states, both in their short-term and perspective efforts.

From this standpoint, the origins of literacy in certain West African languages may be analyzed as a sort of by-product or secondary consequence of the different intellectual, ideological, cultural and religious penetrations into Africa as confronted recently with Africa's own self-determination. Islamic morals, Christian Bible translations and decrees or laws of the colonial administration represent only typical examples of such origins of literacy and can be by no means classified as a literature. They were merely the first evidence of the tendency to write a particular West African language and to use it for certain precisely defined and limited social or cultural functions. Moreover, such texts in the West African languages were usually merely parallel to the more important and prestigious originals in the particular languages of the given cultures or powers. Already at that stage, a certain difference in the style of approach appeared, even within the concrete cultural or religious groups. Whereas the pre-Jihadi attitude toward using the Arabic script for Hausa is not yet clear, Uthman dan Fodio and his followers did not hide their intention of using the language of the majority of the population in order to be able to influence their thinking and feelings with their ideas and arguments. Similarly, most Christian missions attempted to use the major African languages of their respective areas of activities, although important differences existed in the form, extent and respective styles of their approach to the language question, and to the idea of creating literacy in the African languages (more details on this problem can be found in Welmers, 1971, pp. 559—69).

Such differences existing among the colonial administrations had, however, deeper roots: whereas the French administration in West Africa (as almost everywhere) refused to accept the vernacular languages in any official function, the British "indirect rule" permitted a relatively rich range of functions for their written and oral usage. As a result, vernacular literatures in the French-speaking areas of West Africa were limited in the past to missionary publications only, whereas in the English-speaking area certain languages and areas may well have displayed not only a relatively flourishing literacy, but perhaps also the initial stages of a literary development.

As the initial phases of such literacies or literatures are characterized by efforts to reach the thinking and feelings of the African populations, they can hardly be separated from certain pedagogical and educational aims. We cannot overlook the fact that these are, in fact, the first attempts to write particular languages and consequently that they must imply the process of teaching people how to read or rewrite the texts in question. Although certain pedagogical features may be observed even with Arabic script-based literacy, with the different cases of Roman script-based literacies they definitely come to the fore. Most missionary literacy drives, as well as administratively-based attempts originating from various so-called Vernacular Literatures and/or Language Bureaux in the British zone of influence, offer, during their initial stages, a rich choice of readers, textbooks and reading material for initial and advanced pupils, as well for adults. These publications have preceded, in fact, even most functional publications of such institutions, whether they are of a religious or administrative character; readers and textbooks logically precede both the religious and administrative texts, as both missionaries and administrators feel, usually correctly, that if anyone is to be expected to read their respective religious hymns or administrative decrees and regulations, a certain basic, important group of literate people must be established. This is perhaps why particular links between the development of a literature and large-scale literacy campaigns have developed. Such literacy campaigns have also served the broader purposes of popular education and enlightenment; various aspects of modern science and technology, hygiene and prophylaxis, progressive agriculture, etc. find their rightful places in the pages of such usually anynomous booklets serving such literacy drives and thereby establishing a valid platform for the initial phases of literacy. Moreover, in many cases the authors of such initial literacy booklets, in particular those in the West African languages, are not Africans whose mother tongues are the languages in question, but expatriate missionaries or colonial administrators. It should be stressed in this context that at least in our opinion this fact does not invalidate the value of their initial efforts: the linguistic, literary or pedagogical efforts of such authors as J. G. Christaller, D. Westermann or R. M. East have undoubtedly contributed to the establishment of the bases of literacy as a precondition for the creation of any literature in such languages as Twi, Ewe, Hausa and others.

Apart from some really exceptional cases (and such seems to be the case of R. M. East in the context of Hausa) they should not, however, be considered real authors in the strictly literary sense.

1.3 The process of a possible transition from literacy to the inital stages of a developing literature in a particular case may be characterized by many features. The West African regions offer a very rich picture of possible transitional stages and the modifications of such a process.

1.3.1 The quantitative growth of the reading community, as well as the simultaneous qualitative shift in the range of topics, genres and styles of the written or printed texts produced, seems to be a characteristic in most cases. The gradually expanding African public of either an active missionary centre or an active Literature Bureau requires more than highly specialized, strictly uni-functional texts of a religious, administrative or pedagogical character. Initial attempts to write or translate short stories, novels, plays or poems appear with unequal style or quality, and obviously also with unequal success. Such a quantitative and qualitative growth of any literature in a West Africa language also discloses attempts to draw on material from other literatures, and especially from the finest treasuries of the world's literatures. Both translations and adaptations of the best examples of the world's literatures are used to fill the gaps in the developing literature. This has occurred in other areas of the world when a particular literature has had to bridge the gap between the unequal stages of its development, and the West African scene does not represent any exception from this standpoint. Owing to the strong influence of the literature in the English language, (including obviously, English, American and Commonwealth literatures), the classical works of this literature are frequently translated or adapted. The works of the classical authors of other world literature are also translated or adapted; such is the case of French-language works and also Russian classical authors (for example, Lev Tolstoy), although English translations might have served as an intermediary basis. Such attempts to fill the gaps or broaden the inventories of the developing literatures in the West African languages have more or less systematically paralleled a certain Africanization in style, the topics selected, and the personalities of the authors. First and second-generation Africans writing in their own mother tongues started to work in the missionary centres and, later, also in the Literature Bureaux. Unquestionably this at least partial Africanization with respect to topic, style, genre and the personalities of the authors offered an opportunity to the first vernacular authors, in the true sense of the word, the works of whom can stand comparison with real literary phenomena. The Ewe plays by Fiawoo, as well as the Hausa novels of the early Thirties, can testify to this process.

This phase also represented the stage when literatures in the West African languages surpassed the phase of a mere passive acceptance of the values of other literatures and started to actively influence other literatures as well. The first works of West African literatures have been translated into English (and occasionally other languages). The frequent bilingualism of the authors and their active interest in publishing their works in the "prestige" languages as well may, however, also play an important role in this frequent bilingualism of the authors and their active interest in publishing their works in the "prestige" languages as well may, however, also play an important role in this development.

1.3.2 Factors connected with the quantitative growth of the reading and writing community appear to be closely related to those connected with the qualitative growth of the reading materials produced. This, in turn, has been clearly related to the expansion of the community of writers and authors. The interdependence of these factors in the process of development from literacy to literature is obvious, and it is hardly possible to abstract one of the factors from the other. The role of those organizations which are actively supporting and propagating literacy in the West African languages has been important throughout this entire process, although it has been most intensive in the first stages of such development. In this connection it is not without interest to compare certain similarities and differences in the work of the missionary and administrative literacy centres.

1.3.2.1 The activity of the missions is obviously historically older and chronologically longer. Most missions started their activities long before the establishment of the colonial administrative entities and the activities of certain of them may have been related to the "buccaneer" period of European activity on the West African coast. On the other hand, the activities of the various Language and Literature Bureaux were more or less directly linked to the establishment of 19th and 20th-century colonial administrative territories.

This difference was not a mere chronological one, as the field of activity of these different literacy institutions was closely connected with it. Missionary literacy activities have been usually oriented, especially in the early periods, towards concrete African language com-munities. Their activities were never entirely identified with particular administrative entities, nor did they respect altogether their arbitrary barriers. However, the language and literacy institutions of the colonial administration oriented their activity mainly toward the newly-created administrative entities and the colonial territories, for the organizational needs of which they were practically created. Therefore, from the earliest periods of their activities they served multilingual territories in the West African area. Although certain relations between the geographical and national bases of the missionary societies and that of the territories of the respective colonial powers clearly existed, a simple correlation of this type never developed. As the Language and Literacy Bureaux were, in fact, an integral part of the administration of the given territories, they had to cope primarily with their territorial problems. Thus, the Translation Bureau in Nigeria (and various other institutions which inherited its activities in the different regions later on) served to advance literacy only in Nigeria (and in some periods also in those parts of Cameroon which were administratively attached to it); the Vernacular Languages Bureau in the Gold Coast (and later the Bureau of Ghana Languages) served only this territory, while comparable one-to-one correlations appear elsewhere. A curious situation arose in those cases where the major languages spoken in the respective colonial territories were also spoken outside their administrative frontiers. In such a situation, the limitations imposed upon the activities of these administrative literacy institutions through their subordination to the administration of the respective territory within its arbitrary frontiers never permitted them to take great notice of the needs of those members of the African language communities who lived outside their administratively allotted zone: neither Ewe outside the Gold Coast, nor Hausa or Yoruba outside Nigeria, were taken very much into consideration by them. Similarly, the activity of certain Gambian institutions in the sphere of the literacy of Mandinka has never been practically profitable to the Manding areas of Senegal and other French-speaking territories. (Concerning the problems of the division of Hausa in Nigeria and Niger, see details in Zima, 1968.) It is to the credit of the missions that at least occasional attempts have been made on their part to fill such gaps. Moreover, the official character of the administrative institutions imposed certain restrictions upon them in the sphere of the social stratification of the language, especially if the "prestige" language were concerned. So while the Sierra Leonian institutions have devoted particular attention to literacy in the various vernaculars, they paid little or no attention to Krio (cf. Berry, 1962, p. 220).

The activities of these two main sponsors of literacy in West Africa (i.e. the missionary and administrative institutions) were sometimes separated, but sometimes also parallel. In rare cases were they in mutual contradiction. There is no doubt that in the cases of such important West African Language communities as the Akans, Ewes and Yorubas, the missions contributed mainly to the initial stages of the transition from literacy to literature, whereas the merits of the administrative sponsors of literacy lay in the latter stages of this transition. The latter institutions contributed especially to a certain broadening of both genres and forms of these and other literatures in West Africa, as the limitations imposed upon missionary-inspired literacy by its main function were apparently much more strict and gave any future development a relatively narrower margin of choice.

1.3.2.2 In the Islamic areas of West Africa, however, this parallelism also existed, although in the strongly Islamic-influenced regions literacy based upon the Arabic script competed with the Roman-script-based literacy originating from the administrative sources in the British zones of influence. Such a dual competition of the Islamic literacy and Europe-influenced literacy was expressed even in the form of the script (digraphia, cf.

section 3.1). Sometimes, however, the missionary-inspired literacy also penetrated into the marginal areal of language communities which had otherwise been strongly influenced by Islam. A classical example of such a situation is the case of the Hausa language community. Influenced as it was mainly by Islam in its central areas (Kano-Sokoto), it produced there an Arabic-script-based literacy with a relatively long historical tradition. This type of literacy has been challenged in recent periods by the Roman-script-based administratively sponsored literacy (Translation Bureau, NORLA, Hausa Language Board etc.). Modest Roman-script-based missionary literacy attempts also exist, but their influence is limited to certain marginal Hausa areas or to those non-Islamic areas where Hausa is used as a lingua franca (e.g. the Middle Belt of Nigeria, or at least some parts of it).

1.4   The whole process of the transition from "oral civilizations" towards literacy, and from literacy towards a developing literature has been, therefore, a very complex one. A number of factors must have ultimately influenced this process, some of them positively, some others negatively. Convinced as we are that this process also took place in other areas of the world and in other cultures (though this happened under different conditions and in different historical periods), we think that West Africa—and perhaps the whole remaining part of Black Africa—may offer one of the few contemporary pictures of this process. While in other areas of the world we can observe or analyze merely the results or consequences of this process or only the vestiges of its transitional stages, West Africa offers a unique opportunity to observe this process in all its dynamism. Both positive and negative factors have influenced this process in such a way that some subjectively well-based literacy efforts have been replaced by a full-scale transition towards a developing literature, while in other cases similar literacy efforts have produced meager or no results. We think that it was this contradiction between subjectively well-founded efforts and objectively existing negative factors preventing the transition from literacy towards a developing literature, which may well have been the real reason why literacy campaigns have resulted in a developing literature in some cases, while similar campaigns in other areas left their traces only in a number of bibliographic items, readers and text-books, which were never fully materialized.

Apart from two such extremes, West Africa also offers a rich transitional scale of literacy-to-literature transitions. Some of them may die out sooner or later, while others may still reach the literature phase some time in the future.

As a result of this, we believe that the West African vernacular literature is to some extent a valuable and rewarding subject for both linguistic and literary analysis. While the aesthetic and literary values of its products do not always reach top quality, in comparison to works from other areas it may ultimately be seen as one of the best sources of evidence for the study and analysis of the formation of standard literary languages and the transition from a mere literacy to a genuine developing literature.

The aim of the following lines and remarks is by no means to present an extensive literary analysis of all the most important literatures in this area; it is merely to draw attention to certain opportunities which may arise for analyses of standard literary languages and developing literatures, on the basis of materials from this thus-far almost neglected region.

Although this author does not feel competent to undertake an exhaustive analysis of all types of literacy-to-literature transitions and development in West Africa, and although the extensive range of such phenomena in that area will undoubtedly require further and deeper analysis and sub-classification in the future, it may be assumed that two more general types of literary development there can be distinguished: the West African coastal type and the West Sudanic (Islamic-influenced) type.

2. The West African Coastal Area

2.0 The creation of literacies and the perspectives and possibilities of a literacy-to-literature transition and development share, at least in some major areas of the West African coast, certain common features. These features, which are inherent in the social, economic, ideological (religious) and last but not least even political factors, have brought about a situation in which this creation of literacy and the further transition from literacy towards literature and the development of this literature may be analyzed with respect to these similarities. One may wonder, in this connection, whether a sort of "coastal type" of literature could not—at least for methodological purposes—be presumed to exist. Both for methodological nad practical reasons it has been impossible to analyze all the types of literacy-to-literature transitions and literary developments in that area. But three major cases of such a transition, and hence of a developing literature, are to differing degrees accessible, at least for preliminary analysis. Although the author had to rely heavily—even in these cases—upon the materials and information supplied by friends and from local sources (and partly also on those obtained during his field research and academic activity in this area)*, the existence of these three major literatures which are developing at an unequal rate and with unequal intensity is obvious. Developing from similar or comparable bases, they offer the most extensive examples of the literary development of

---

*) With respect to the three main "coastal areas" the assistance and help of the following friends and colleagues is to be especially acknowledged:

In Ghana: Prof. J. H. Kwabena Nketia, Director, Institute of African Studies, University of Ghana and Mr. A. C. Denteh, from the same Institute; Mr. S. K. Otoo, Manager, Bureau of Ghana Languages and practically the whole staff of this Bureau, especially the following editors: Mr. A. A. Amartey, Mr. F. S. Konu, Mr. J. E. Longdon, Mr. I. E. Boama and many others; Mr. J. A. Annobil of the Methodist Book Dept, Capecoast.

In Togo: Prof. Gabriel Kwaovi-Johnson, who was serving as the Head of the local IFAN-base in Lomé in the early times of my field reseach (later Institut Togolais de Recherches); he is now the rector of Lomé University.

In Nigeria: Prof. Ayọ Bamgboṣe of the University of Ibadan and Prof. A. Babalọla of the University of Lagos supplied me with certain valuable information on Yoruba literacy and literature.

My thanks are also to be extended to numerous West African students of mine, both at Charles University and November 17th University in Prague, and at the University of Ghana, who helped occasionally to clarify many points in this "pioneer" field.

a West African language in that region: These are Yoruba, Ewe and the Akan languages. One may wonder whether a further analysis should include other languages and literary communities in the same category, or whether these three communities really represent the major literary achievements of that area, as far as literature in the West African languages is concerned. This question however, should be still further investigated.

2.1 Yoruba

2.1 For both objective and subjective reasons, literacy in Yoruba developed under particularly favourable conditions from the time of its early stages. The roots of the transition from Yoruba literacy to Yoruba literature, and of the development of Yoruba as a standard literary language, are relatively clear, and if compared with a similar development in the other two language communities which will be treated in this same respect, i.e. with the Ewe and Akan languages, it can be seen that there were relatively less obstacles to such transformations.

In spite of certain problems connected with graphization and dialect integration (cf. Bamgboṣe, 1965), a clear tendency to develop a sort of standard form exists in the case of this language community. Bamgboṣe (1966, p. 2) defines such a standard Yoruba as a koinē based on the Oyo dialect, but not co-extensive with it.

Yoruba is in a particularly favourable position culturally, as well, as its oral literature traditions are long and intensive.

Moreover, Yoruba is one of those rare exceptions among West African language communities, as powerful African personalities had been active in Yoruba missionary literacy work from its early stages. Although S. A. Crowther (1807—1891) cannot be labelled a classical author in the strictly literary sense, he was undoubtedly the most outstanding personality in the initial stages of development of Yoruba missionary literacy, and perhaps in the initial stages of Yoruba literature in general. Attempting to teach the Christian religion to his fellow countrymen, he contributed considerably to the spreading of literacy in the Latin script through the major parts of the Yoruba language community. Moreover, he laid the foundations for a description of the Yoruba language, thus facilitating its application in writing and printing respectively. He took an active part in the preparation and editing of the first description of its lexicon (*A Vocabulary of the Yoruba language*, 1843) and later published a joint edition of the lexicon and grammar (*A Grammar and a Vocabulary of the Yoruba Language*, 1852). Innumerable religious texts in Yoruba must be considered either his own translations and/or adaptations, or it may be supposed that he was very active in their editing. Starting from a Yoruba book of common prayer (*Iwe adua Yoruba*, 1850) and culminating with a whole translation of the Bible into that language which appeared only after his death (*Bibeli Mimọ*, London, 1900), he can be said to have virtually originated the written usage of the Yoruba language (a detailed bibliography of large religious publications in Yoruba, produced by Crowther and other missionaries, may be found in Hair, 1967, pp. 20—30; for an interesting comparison with Luther see Herms, 1973, 583).

The whole initial stage of the development of literacy in Yoruba was obviously deeply influenced by factors having to do with its oral culture and literature. Starting from the early periods of missionary literacy, collections of songs, proverbs, riddles, sayings and prosaic folk-tales manifested not only the inherent interdependence of the two forms of culture, but were also in many cases the first examples of an oral literature recorded in script and print; items from the folklore of other areas and their translations were occasionally added. Thus, a collection of proverbs appeared in 1885 (*Iwe Owe*) prepared by S. W. Allen; riddles collected by D. B. Vincent appeared in the same year (*Iwe alọ*). One year later, a collection of songs amassed by E. M. Lijadu was published under the title *Kekere Iwe Orin Aribiloṣo*, (A Small Book of Aribiloso's songs, 1886). Lijadu, formerly a teacher at the CMS seminar in Lagos, later also published a collection of Yoruba sayings *Ifa; imọlẹ rẹ ti iṣe ipilẹ isin ni ilẹ Yoruba*, 1901. The activity of a bilingual news-sheet in Yoruba and English entitled *Iwe Irohin* (The Newspaper), started by H. Townsend, an Abeokuta missionary, in 1859, is reported by Babalọla and Gérard (1971, p. 189). Some 190 issues of this periodical appeared between 1859—1867, according to these authors.

The emphasis on the pedagogical and teaching purposes of literacy and its dissemination was particularly strong during the initial dacades of this century. Readers, textbooks and educational booklets published by missionary or administrative and pedagogical sources appeared very frequently. An initial series of Yoruba readers was published between 1909—1915 (*Iwe Kika*). An important representative section of such documents was oriented towards the vulgarization of the aspects of Yoruba history and geography. J. D. Losi published *Iwe Itan Abeokuta*, (A History of Abeokuta, 1921) and *Iwe Itan Eko*, (A History of Lagos, 1931). A similar publication about Ibadan (*Iwe Itan Ibadan*) appeared in 1935, published by I. Babalọla Akinyele.

All these publications testified to the complicated transition from literacy to literature. This transitional character is particularly clear in the work of such authors as A. Kolawola Ajisafẹ (1877—1940) and E. Akintunde Akintan (1890—1957). Both of them devoted much of their efforts to writing or editing either translations or adaptations of oral literature, but a considerable part of their activity was also devoted to original fiction and literature in Yoruba. Ajisafẹ wrote a collection of original poems under the title *Ayié Akamara* (Human Life Full of Pitfalls, 1921). In addition to contributing various textbooks, Akintan also edited an important bilingual weekly *Eleti Ofe* (Clever Listener). On the other hand, the poetry and other texts written by J. Osoyemi Ajibọla (b. 1988) is much closer to the pattern of oral traditions; his *Owe Yoruba* (Yoruba Proverbs) and *Orin Yoruba* (Yoruba Sings) both appeared in 1947.

As far as Yoruba literary prose is concerned, two authors are responsible for starting its tradition and popularity: D. O. Fagunwa and I. O. Delanọ. The former drew heavily from Yoruba mythology and folklore, while never limiting his literary activity to their mere recording. Chief Delanọ, on the other hand, never restricted his literary activity to the traditional world; his books also reflect the impact of modernity and the newly-arriving European influence in Yorubaland.

With a few exceptions, D. O. Fagunwa's (1900 or 1903—1963) books are practically monothematic. *Ogboju Ọdẹ Ninu Igbo Irunmalẹ,* (Brave Hunter in the Bush of the Spirits, 1938) as well his following works, such as *Igbo Olodumare* (The Jungle of the Almighty, 1949), the story *Ireke Onibudo* (1950) and *Irinkerindo ninu igbo Elegbeje* (Wanderings in the Forest of E. 1954) are all frame-stories. This is a history of a brave hunter who is sent by royal orders into the dark forests and bush where he encounters not only wild animals and birds, but probably the whole world or real or invented Yoruba mythology and traditional narrations. The boundary-line between real life, mythology, tradition and adventure is never clear, although one senses that the author tends to keep the reader as much as possible on the fantasy side. When reading Fagunwa's books, one realizes how difficult it is to analyze them according to any "classical" European literary criteria. They are neither novels, nor real frame-stories, nor folk narratives. They are stories, which when narrated in the evening in a village far off in the bush would seem realistic, especially when night and darkness surround both the narrator and his audience, and man's uncertainty and fear of the unknown is felt by everyone. The popularity of this genre, confirmed by the success of Fagunwa's books, may have served as a basis of inspiration for various of his successors, some of whom used Yoruba (Ogunsina Ogundele) but others of whom also used various sorts of local English (Amos Tutuola).

Although Fagunwa's last novel *Adiitu Olodumare* (The Secret of the Almighty), as well as various short stories of his e.g. *Ajala ati Ajade* (Ajale and Ajade), published in a collection of short stories in cooperation with I. O. Delano, Amos Akyniemi and E. A. Akinlade in 1959 under the title *Aṣayan Itan* (Short Stories), never succeeded in achieving the popularity of the *Brave Hunter* series, their literary value must also not be underestimated.

Joseph Ogunsina Ogundele (b. 1926) follows Fagunwa's style and genres, but he has succeeded in finding his own place in the elaboration of what might be called Yoruba fairy-tale novels. Both his *Ibu Olokun* (Shrine of the Olokun, 1956) and *Ejigbede l'Ọna isalu-orun* (Ejigbede on the Way to Heaven, 1956) incorporate the basic motifs of Fagunwa's stories: their heroes travel not only between this and the other world, but the reader is guided by the author along a complicated road between fantasy and reality.

On the other hand, the personality and literary position of Chief I. O. Delano is in some respects closer to literacy, due to its unquestionable theoretical and applied attention to the cultivation and development of Yoruba as a standard literary language. Apart from recording traditional proverbs in *Owe l'ẹṣin ọrọ* (The Proverb Rides a Horse), he has published a book on Yoruba phraseology (*Agbeka Ọrọ Yoruba,* 1960) and a monolingual Yoruba dictionary (*Atumọ Ede Yoruba,* 1958)—one of the first attempts to draw up an inventory of the lexicon of a West African language, using the same language for explanation and notes and eliminating other languages as far as possible.

Apart from this literacy and linguistic activity, Chief Delano has also produced two interesting books and several short stories dealing with a very important, serious topic: the impact of Europe and Europeans on Yorubaland and West Africa in general. *Ayie d'aiyé Oyinbo,* (The European is Coming to Us, 1955), *L'Ọjọ Ojọun* (In the Days of the Past, 1963) Delano's prose is therefore much closer to a realistic analysis of certain grave problems confronting African society in particular periods of its historical past. The style of his narration, which is rich in proverbs and idioms (one recognizes in them the author of the collection of Yoruba proverbs and idioms), is not too different from that of Fagunwa's fairy-tales; both authors contributed considerably to the basic inventory of the Yoruba prosaic genre with respect to both style and language.

The same trend of penetrating form the traditional world of Yoruba fantasy into reality can also be seen in the novel *Kuye*, the story of a mute boy, written by J. Folahan Odunjo (b. 1904). Similar topics—i.e. the fate of unhappy children, concluding with a happy ending, is dealt with by the same author in another short novel which appeared under the title *Omo oku Orun* (The Deceased Woman's Daughter, 1964). Odunjo also contributed to the establishment of a Yoruba drama.

The importance of the drama in the development of Yoruba literature cannot, however, be underestimated. Although we might not entirely share the opinion of Babalola and Gérard, who appear to draw direct links between early Yoruba religious plays in the late 19th century, the classical period of the Yoruba drama, as represented by Babalola himself and Faleti—and the modern wave, originating in the Mbari Club and culminating, thus far, in Wole Soyinka's dramas, the importance of drama both in traditional Yoruba culture and in modern Yoruba literature is unquestionable. Thus, a possibility of some correspondence between the traditional, oral drama and the written form of this genre cannot be altogether excluded. If this is correct, then Babalola himself, as a dramatic author, probably served as an active link between these two forms of drama in Yoruba. Born in 1926, he was originally active as a teacher, and one may presume that the pedagogical requirements of his activity enabled him to realize the importance of the drama in teaching, and especially in developing a healthy attitude on the part of his pupils towards their own cultural and language heritage. He enriched the Yoruba drama both by translating Shakespeare's *Merchant of Venice* (published in an adapted version under the Yoruba title *Ika k'Onika*, 1954), and also published his own play *Pasan Sina* (The Whip Descends on the Wrong Person, 1958). Babalola also wrote prose stories: *Itan Sanusini Dendekori* (The Story of Sanusini Dendekori, 1958) and poems, which were often published in *Odu*, a magazine of Yoruba culture, and elsewhere. He devoted particular attention to poetic traditions of the oral past and to hunters' songs, the so-called *Ijàlá*. Not only was his PhD thesis in English devoted to them, but also a small booklet published in Ibadan under the title *Ijala Atenudenu*. Today he is one of the outstanding specialists at the School of African and Asiatic Studies at the University of Lagos.

While Babalola started with dramatic works and later oriented his efforts towards broader fields, Adebayo Faleti's career followed a different pattern. His long, moralistic poem "Eda ko l'aropin" (Do not Provoke Destiny, 1956) as well as a frame-narrative published under the title *Ogun Awitele* (A War Well-Publicized in Advance, 1965) are on the boundary-line between reality and fantasy, though his attitude towards traditional folklore appears to be to some extent even critical. His main literary work is, however the tragi-comedy *Nwon Ro pe were ni* (They Thought That She Was Mad, 1965). The world of traditional customs, as represented by drummers and palm-wine drunkards, co-exists here with a world of fact and stark modern realism. In this sense, Falẹti clearly represents the beginning of a new, rather realistic Yoruba drama and there are undoubtedly links between him and several other authors writing in Yoruba or English. Wole Soyinka, who became popular through his English-written works, is obviously the best-known of the playwrights of modern Yoruba drama. Such authors who either started their careers in the Mbari Club or in the company of those who contributed in the recent past to the literary magazine *Black Orpheus*, or who cooperated with one of the many dramatic groups, producing plays and operas in Yorubaland and in the Yoruba language (such as Duro Ladipo and many others), are clearly the instigators of the new wave of Yoruba drama.

Some links between the early, purely Yoruba form of the drama (or opera) and recent forms appear clearly to have emerged; in some cases, works in Yoruba are being translated to English (thus, Soyinka translated Fagunwa's first book into English), but the reverse also occurs: Tutuola's *Palm-wine Drinkard* was retranslated into Yoruba and performed as a Yoruba folk-opera with drums. What form and which language this deeply Yoruba literature will choose in the near future remains so far a matter of conjecture and hypothesis. The final choice of the language for education may well be decisive for the solution of this question in the coming generations (cf. Fafunwa, Ologunde, 1969).

2.2 Ewe

2.2 Although following in general a pattern comparable to that of Yoruba, the transition of Ewe literacy towards Ewe literature and the formation of a literary standard of this language involved certain problems which differed in scope and relative importance from those confronting Yoruba.

Ewe literacy also started with a missionary period, as far as literacy in the Latin script is concerned. The beginnings of a missionary literacy in the case of Ewe was not, however, marked by the activity of any personality of Ewe origin comparable to Crowther in the Yoruba area. Although the more or less anonymous activity of various African pupils and missionaries or teachers educated by the first generation of expatriate missionaries probably contributed considerably to the development of literacy in this field as well, the main initiative in Ewe missionary literacy work throughout the last decades of the 19th century came from expatriate and mainly German missionaries. The North German Mission from Bremen carried on intensive activity in the Ewe field from the mid-19th century on. The names of two German missionaries are linked directly or indirectly with the development of Ewe literacy. The first of them, Bernard Schlegel, laid the bases for the developing of literacy in Ewe and although his activity in the sphere of Ewe was relatively short, he came to Keta in 1854 and died there only a few years later, in 1859), he must be considered one of the first pioneers of Ewe literacy, as well one of those who took a particular interest in analyzing the structure of that language. He was the author of what is probably the first published grammar of the Ewe language, *Schlüssel zur Ewe-Sprache, dargeboten in den*

Gramatischen Grundzügen des Aṅlo dialekts derselben mit Wörter-sammlung nebst einer Sammlung von Sprüchwörtern und einigen Fablen der Eingeborenen (Key to the Ewe Language, Presented on the Grammatical Basis of the Aŋlɔ Dialect of This Same Language, together with a Collection of Proverbs and Some Fairy-Tales of the Aborigines, 1857). His translation of four evangelic texts into Ewe were published only posthumously, as one of the first printed Ewe texts.

While Schlegel's life and activity in Eweland finished tragically so soon after he had started his work in Africa and his name is passed over almost unnoticed today, the name of one of his followers and younger colleagues, Diedrich Westermann (1876—1957), who devoted more than two-thirds of his long, fruitful life to Ewe and West Africa, is known today as that of a classic of linguistic and literary studies in that area. The Ewe language, which became synonymous to Westermann with both his youthful and mature research, undoubtedly profited from such personal ties between a particular language and its literacy, on the one hand, and the contributions of such an outstanding scholar, on the other. The main importance of Westermann's work for Ewe literacy and literature is obviously not to be found in his various booklets in Ewe, but rather in his theoretical and applied research into the complex process of literarization and growing literacy in that language. Apart from producing a monumentary Ewe dictionary (1954), an Ewe grammar and various textbooks, he also contributed much to the reduction of Ewe to writing.

Schlegel and Westermann are obviously not the only outstanding instigators of this missionary literacy drive in Ewe. Several other authors of expatriate origin (such as Spieth, Härter, etc.) as well as many of their unknown Ewe assistants would undoubtedly also deserve attention, since the entire process must have relied upon them.

Another offshoot of missionary literacy work in Ewe were the activities of the Catholic missions which, however, were concentrated in the central and eastern parts of Eweland. The earliest written text in Ewe, the so-called *Doctrina Christiana* (a Spanish-Ewe catechism in the Gɛ̃ dialect) is reported by Labouret and Rivet (1929) to have been written as early as in the 17th century (see Westermann, 1954, p. XXII); it can be attributed to the work of the initial stages of this missonary centre.

As a result of this territorial distribution of literacy activity, both types of Ewe literacy were based mainly upon two (if not three) distinct Ewe dialects. This produced the problems of a choice of dialect, so frequent in the initial stages of language standardization. The case of Ewe, as dealt with in detail by Ansre (1971, pp. 684—88) was solved practically by the choice of Aŋlɔ, the western dialect, as the basis of the standard, although objections against it from the Ewe-speaking community have appeared even recently (see G. Kuawovi Johnson, 1947).

The need to create a wider reading community was felt by both missionary literacy movements; the creation of Ewe periodicals in both sections of the literacy movement represented one of the attempts to solve these problems. Protestant missoinaries started their periodical *Ṇutifafa na mi* (The Messenger of Peace) as early as 1903. In the first period of its publication, it was printed in Bremen and imported into Togoland for distribution and reading. Transport became increasingly difficult, however, especially with the outbreak of World War I, the consequences of which in no way facilitated this costly, arduous foreign production and the journal's transport. As a result, its production and publication were shifted definitely to Lomé in 1925. Meanwhile, the Catholic missions had started a competing Ewe periodical called *Mia Xɔlɔ* (Our Friend) in 1919. Although primarily functional religious publications, both early missionary periodicals in Ewe also served as a basis for the first attempts to write at all in Ewe. Apart from publishing pedagogically-oriented articles, studies devoted to the teaching and learning of literacy in Ewe, articles on hygiene and prophylaxis, as well as on modern technology and ways of living, these periodicals also provided the first forum for initial attempts to translate short stories, excerpts from world literature and for the writing of short original stories in Ewe. Oral poetry and other forms of oral literature, collected by expatriate or Ewe teachers and missionaries, were also recorded and published. In the 1920's, a discussion on problems of language norms, correctness, codification and the pitfalls of laguage assimilation appeared in these periodicals. The youngest literacy sponsors among the German missionaries were active in this field, together with the first generation of Ewe writers—I. K. Hoh (b. 1912) E. T. Adiku (b. 1908), E. M. Amegashie (d. 1949) and the Rev. F. K. Fiawoo (b. 1891) the last-mentioned being the most prominent. Moreover, their activity is linked not only with the previously-mentioned missionary literacy centres in Togoland, but also with increasing attempts to use Ewe as a written language for certain educational and social functions in what was then known as the Gold Coast.

F. K. Fiawoo's name became very closely connected with Ewe drama. As in the case of Babalọla and Faleti in Yoruba, he too attempted to bridge the gap between the oral traditions of Ewe and the impact of Europe and its literature. Although drawing the attention of spectators and readers to the problems deriving from the confrontation of these very different life styles an systems of values, his main attention was nevertheless focused on the traditional way of life. Together with his colleagues and assistants at the so-called Zion College in Aŋloga he staged several dramatic sketches and dramas. Some of these were original plays, other adaptations of foreign dramatic works. One of his best-known original plays known in Ewe as *Tɔkɔ Atɔ̃lia* (The Fifth Landing Stage, 1937) was not only published, but was also translated into English and German. It deals with the partly-romantic, partly-realistic story of two suitors of an Ewe girl in the period of the slave raids and tribal wars of the past. Although even "The Fifth Landing Stage" is not free of foreign inspiration (Shakespeare) nor is the moralizing tone so characteristic of most booklets of the initial stages of the developing literacies altogether absent from it, it undoubtedly laid the foundations for the classical Ewe drama and represented a major achievement of Ewe literature before World War II. The play won not only a certain popularity in Eweland, but also the prize of the International African Institute in London for 1937. None of Fiawoo's other works written either in Ewe (*Fia yi Dziehe*—Fia's Upland Journey) or in English (Peace-gloria, Africa Awakes to Glory) attracted so much attention.

Fiawoo's one-time assistant and, it might be said, follower, Bidi H. K. Setsoafia (b. cca 1926), not only helped him to adapt and translate various plays, but soon embarked upon dramatic activity himself with several translations of Shakespeare's plays (*Julius Caesar, King Lear, Richard II*). In 1945, he published a Ewe play *Fia Agokoli* (Chief Agokoli) followed by another three years later (*Kato Fiayidzi*). In the 1950's, he wrote bilingually for the needs of the then Gold Coast Broadcasting Corporation. His comedy *Meɖe Ablotsidela alo Asinam kple Dadzi*, (I married a Been to..., 1956) became very popular, winning him a prize in the Ghana Broadcasting Corporation competition of 1957.

The 1940's saw increasing attention being devoted to educational and cultural literacy in Ewe, oriented toward the needs of the Ewe-speaking community of the Gold Coast, where Ewe was beginning to be incorporated into educational syllabuses, and hence a certain amount of Ewe reading material and textbooks was badly needed. A London publisher (Longmans, Green, Co.) produced a whole series of Ewe textbooks under the title *Xlem kpɔ̃* (Read Me!); various other reading materials for the newly literate, such as translations of Lamb's *Tales from Shakespeare* and *Grimms' Fairy-Tales,* were also published in Ewe. Some of these booklets described various oral traditions of the Ewe people (see further details in Wiegräbe, 1960, pp. 133—134). During that same period, A.M.K. Amegashie presented his collection of fables and short stories entitled *Vovoyi* (Leisure Time); a booklet of traditions of the coastal Ewes was published under the title *Eweɖukɔ siwo le futa* (Ewe People on the Coast, 1947), and P.M. Ɖesewu published his volume of narratives *Le nye aɖaba te* (As I Saw It, 1941).

As in the initial stages of the development of drama, a comparison with Yoruba is possible with respect to the relative importance of historical works which were also prepared largely for school and broader pedagogical purposes. In this case, too, they represent a further transitional stage of the development from literacy to a real literature. I. K. Hoh, the Ewe author of the pioneer generation, published the biography of Jacob Vomawo (*Yacobo Võmawɔ*, 1948), an interesting story of an African missionary who was sometimes called "the St. Paul of the Ewe Church". Even more interesting was *Famfamtɔ,* 1948, the biography of Joseph Kwaku Famfamto, who was taken prisoner during the Asanti war in 1869—1870. The latter work was written by G. K. Tsekpo, one-time Ewe editor of the Languages and Literatures Bureau in Accra. In that capacity this same author published various pedagogically-oriented booklets, including a collection of stories in Ewe entitled *Ketonase* (Open Your Ears, 1953). In 1956, after having left his official position in the Bureau, he started an Ewe weekly known as *Mia Denyigba* (Our Country). From purely literary topics the focus of that weekly's interest developed gradually towards social and political issues; during the period of strained relations between Ghana and Togoland, its publication was shifted to Lomé in Togoland. An official monthly, published by the Bureau in Accra under the title *Mɔtabiala* (He Who Asks the Way) then took over most of the pedagogical and cultural functions of an Ewe periodical in Ghana.

During the 1950's and early 1960's, it became increasingly evident that in spite of certain difficulties produced partly by the administrative division of the Ewe-speaking territory, the transition of an Ewe literacy towards the initial stages of an Ewe literature had reached a decisive point. Frank K. Nyaku (b. 1924), the author of an Ewe adaptation of Dr. Aggrey's biography, published his first short novel *Kofi Nyamako Nutinya* (The

Story of Kofi Nyamako), as well as a collection of six short stories entitled *Modzakadegbale* (A Book for Leisure Time, 1955). Another author, S. J. Obianim (b. 1920), also contributed overwhelmingly to this period of development of Ewe literature. After having studied both at Achimota College and in India, he served for several years as a teacher and then embarked upon a diplomatic career (becoming Ghana's Ambassador to various countries). His novel *Amegbetɔa alo Agbezuge fe ŋutinya* (The Story of Agbezuge, 1949) and his poetic reflexions on his country's oral traditions, published under the title *Ewekɔnuwo* (Ewe Customs, 1953) undoubtedly constitute a major achievement.

At the beginning of the 1960's, a whole new group of Ewe authors publishing their works mainly through the newly-reorganized Bureau of Ghana Languages in Accra, began to formulate their contribution to the growing Ewe literature: C. K. Nyomi, M. K. Agbodza, E.Y. Dogoe and many others wrote books and booklets of unequal value and size. Simultaneously, the works of the previously-mentioned authors were reprinted.

2.3   The Akan Languages of Ghana

2.3.0   The historical factors dictating the creation of the arbitrary frontiers of the colonial territories and states of West Africa were particularly favourable to the Akan languages. The arbitrary administrative frontiers which divided the Ewe language community into three unequal sectors by chance conserved the main bulk of the Akan-speaking territory within the confines of one single territorial unit having a relatively favourable language and literacy policy. Apart from those Akans who became incorporated into former French West Africa (and who now are comprised in the Republic of the Ivory Coast), the entire bulk of the people speaking relatively closely related Akan languages was conserved as one of the main ethnical and social factors of the Gold Coast (now Ghana). Within these newly-established frontiers, they were the object of a missionary and administrative language and literacy policy aimed at introducing or at least tolerating them in certain rather important social functions. A good, effective, economic literacy was therefore one of the perspective aims of such a language policy. However, not all historical factors have been equally propitious for the rapid spreading of literacy in the Akan languages, or for the possible creation of literary standards and subsequent modern literatures. The problem of a choice of dialect, which is important in all processes of standardization, became particularly crucial in the Akan area. The division of the Fante-Twi language cluster obviously has its ancient roots in the pre-colonial period. The European presence on the Coast and early contacts with the Fantes, but not with the Twis, apparently only deepened this existing difference. The close relationship between the Fante and Twi dialects and the relatively high level of mutual intelligibility prompted both expatriate experts and local language-users to attempt some sort of unitary solution aimed at standardization, while disregarding to a certain extent social, cultural and even psychological differences between the respective language communities. However, later in this century the flourishing literacy centres based in Cape Coast (Fante) and Akropong (Akuapem-Twi) did little to facilitate such a unitary Fante-Twi solution, as spoken differences were being congealed in the written norm.

Even the choice of the Twi dialect as the basis of its standard literary form was not an easy one. Literacy attempts in the Twi-speaking community were started early by the Presbyterian mission in Akropong (Akuapem area). While the choice of Cape Coast as the seat of the Methodists' Fante literacy campaign was particularly fortunate, the choice of the Akuapem dialect for Twi was different. In our opinion, one of the reasons for a substantial part of the Twi-speaking community's refusal to accept Akuapem-Twi as a basis for its literary standard was the fact that this Akuapem dialect, though spoken in an area which was much more accessible to literacy efforts of that time, was marginal from the standpoint of the Twi-speaking community as a whole. Certain Asante-Twi speakers were especially opposed to such a choice; one may well wonder whether the pre-colonial life and existence of the so-called Asante Empire did not create a tendency to use a sort of local "oral standard" based on the prestige dialect of the Asante areas, as the core of that social and ethnical unit. If this hypothesis is correct and if pre-colonial communication in the Twi areas had an oral standard based upon the Asante-Twi dialect, then early efforts toward establishing a missionary literacy in the Akuapem dialect would have created an artificial contradiction between the spontaneously developed basis of an "oral standard" and an arbitrarily imposed, and hence dialectally different, written standard. From this standpoint, the late creation of another type of literacy, based upon the Asante-Twi dialect, would be perfectly explicable, not only in the light of personal, missionary and local differences which obviously also played their role, but also and primarily as an objective sociolinguistic reaction of this community. Orthographical, pedagogical and occasionally even religious differences obviously did little to facilitate the solution of such a sociolinguistically complex situation.

The literacies and literatures of the Akan languages of the Gold Coast (today Ghana) which developed in Fante and in the two Twi branches therefore confront both missionary and administrative literacy and language experts with an academically fascinating but culturally and even politically difficult situation. The way towards a unitary solution, or even at least towards some modest form of a Fante-Twi dualism, is by no means simple.

2.3.1 Fante

Early attempts to create a literacy in Fante were based in the missionary and also administrative centre of the Gold Coast in Cape Coast. These early missionary efforts were carried out mainly by certain expatriate experts among whom the personality of J. G. Christaller—although oriented towards the Twi dialect cluster—undoubtedly played a considerable role, even in the Fante area. Energetic African participation in the literacy efforts of the Wesleyan (later Methodist) mission based in Cape Coast began to develop relatively soon, its intensive influence being felt as early as 1860 when one of the first

Fante primers (*Fante Akenkan Ahyesie*) was published by the Rev. Timothy Laing and his assistant, Mr. W. A. Hanson. According to S. K. Otoo (1962, p. 164), both these authors were natives of the then Gold Coast. The trend toward the establishment of a large literate community in Fante continued throughout the second half of the 19th century, and especially during its last decades when it was marked by the active participation of such authors and missionaries as J. B. Anaman, who not only contributed in the field of textbooks, religious translations and primers, but also edited the first secular texts in Fante. The influence of the Methodist mission was also connected with the existence in Cape Coast of various centres of learning and education, the famous Mfantsipim school being the most notable. Several generations of missionaries and teachers in Ghana were, in fact, directly or indirectly associated with it. The beginning of this century brought a turning-point with the incipient literary activity of R. G. Acquaah (cca. 1884—1954).

As both a former Mfantsipim boy and later a Mfantsipim teacher and headmaster, Acquaah naturally focused the initial stages of his literacy efforts on providing Fante with religious texts. As a Methodist missionary, he devoted much of his attention and energies to such texts: *J. W. Welsley, methodist asɔr ne farbaa* (J. Welsley, the Founder of Methodism, 1938), *Basia Monica, Afrikanyi ɔbaatan pa* (Monica, the Good African Mother). He also contributed considerably to the work of translating the Bible into Fante.

However, Acquaah was also deeply influenced by Fante oral traditions. Apart from recording and re-writing such poems in English (*Fante Classical Poems*, 1920), he was also interested in folk-tales and proverbs: *Ababaawa na atwer* (The Maid and the Toad, 1932), *Mfantse mbɛbusɛm* (Fante Proverbs, 1940) and *Mfantse amambra* (Fante Traditional Customs, 1947). A book of his original poetry was published under the title *Akyekyewerɛ ndwom* (Songs of Comfort). Apart from these and other publications, Acquaah also helped to edit various school manuals for the Fante community (readers, textbooks and grammars), in which field he was active almost until his death.

Two other Fante authors are associated with the younger generation: J. A. Annobil (b. 1910) and Joseph Ghartey (b. 1911). Annobil's life and activity has been closely associated with the fate of the Methodists' Book Depôt in Cape Coast. A teacher and graduate of the School of Oriental and African studies of the University of London, he was in charge of the literary centre for some time. Even his literary work was deeply linked with Fante oral traditions. Some of his books recorded and reflected these traditions either directly or indirectly for example *Mbɛbusɛm nkyerɛkyerɛmu* (Proverbs Explained, 1935), *Ebususɛm* (The Akan Family System, 1958). His other works, such as *Mfantse ebirɛmpɔn* (The Fante Chief, 1955) and *Abotar* (Patience) describe the strong influence of traditional cultural factors, while mixing traditional features with either historical or even contemporary motifs.

Joseph Ghartey also began his activity as a teacher and editor, but joined the newly-established Gold Coast Broadcasting Company—later the Ghana Broadcasting Company—which started its activity in Kumasi in 1937. Ghartey became one of its regular contributors writing short stories and plays especially for its needs. Although performed for broadcasting and becoming well-known among radio audiences, most of his plays were not published.

Twer Nyame (The Flower-Basket, 1960) was an exception in this sense and a great success. Younger authors such as D. K. Abbiw (b. 1915) and E. A. Winful (b. 1922), though also deeply influenced by oral traditions and folklore, have contributed unequally toward narrowing the gap between the developing literature in Fante and other literatures. While Abbiw's merit lies in his translations from world literatures into Fante, he has even published translations from Lev Tolstoy's classical short stories, though probably translated through English *Kodzi eduonu ebiasa* (Twenty-three Short Stories, 1961). However, Winful is one of those Fante authors who wishes to make the values achieved by the newly-developing Fante literature known to outside readers, and who therefore publishes his works both in Fante and in English. His *Akan Awensem* (Akan Poems, 1964) include lyrical, sentimental and patriotic poem-songs. One of his English-written poems—about a young mulatto boy ("The Harmless Boy") was published in the anthology *Voices of Ghana* in 1958.

A welcome forum for the newly-developing Fante literature were obviously also periodicals, especially in the later period. The Cape Coast-based unofficial weekly *Amansum* (Seven States), which became an important cultural and literary vehicle, was published from 1943 until the 1960's, when its role was partly taken over by the official monthly *Nkwantabisa* (The Teacher), published by the Bureau of Ghana Languages in Accra. This Bureau became a new, administratively-backed centre of Fante literacy in the late 1950's and early 1960's. Although edited in Accra, it developed a very active Fante section, to which several Fante authors belonging to both the younger and older generations made important contributions. The senior representative of the Bureau's Fante production was S. K. Otoo (b. 1908), its one-time editor and manager. He started his career as a teacher, later becoming a headmaster; this pedagogical activity made him particularly receptive to the problems and needs of school text-books and books generally. Moreover, coming from a small fishing community on the Coast (Otiam), his roots are deeply embedded in the traditional style of life of his native community, and especially in fishing, which is far more than a mere profession or job, but rather a part of the entire context of the life of the Fante fishermen. His first book, published by the Cape Coast editors, was devoted to this aspect of life on the coast: *Apɔkɔ ho nyimdzee* (Hints on Traditional Fishing, 1946). His *Mbrɛ wosi sen hɛmba* (The Art of Making a Canoe, 1956) and especially his *Nworaba na apoko* (Star Lore and Fishing, 1963) provide deep insight into the world of the Fante fishermen. His novel *Nyame bɛkyerɛ* (God Will Provide, 1967) and his play—an imaginary dispute— *Nana Asaase ɛfuwa* (The Earth's Goodness, 1960) are linked with various other aspects of traditional life.

The pedagogical aspect of his activity is also reflected in his publications which comprise important textbooks, readers and information booklets, as well as various short articles on languages and literacy in Ghana.

A group of younger Fante authors has also been active in the same Bureau. J. E. Longdon (b. 1925) writes scientific and popularization books dealing with various social, political and scientific questions. However, he does not neglect poetry, which he publishes mainly in English (in the review *Ɔkyeamɛ* and elsewhere). His books on scientific farming (*Ekuayɛ pa*

1963) and his booklet on the impact of traditional customs in the sphere of law-*Samansew,* (A Will, 1962) illustrate the former type of literature in Fante. Other authors, such as A. B. Ayansu-Mensah, I. B. Dadze and many others, have also appeared on the scene, contributing considerably to this newly-developing Fante literature.

2.3.2 Akuapem Twi

As in the case of Fante, Akuapem-Twi literacy also originated from two main centres, one in Akropong and the other in Accra—the former being a missionary centre, while the latter is both a mission and the Akuapem-Twi seciton of the Bureau of Ghana Languages.

In the Presbytarian mission, J. G. Christaller, an eminent expatriate missionary, played a role comparable to those of Schlegel or Westermann in the Ewe area or S. A. Crowther and H. Townsend in the Yoruba region. A Twi author who helped to implement the rules and theoretical principles established by Christaller and other expatriots was the Rev. C. A. Akrofi (1901—1967), a missionary teacher and pioneer editor of Akuapem-Twi publications. He was the author of a Twi grammar published in Twi (comparable, perhaps, to Delano's Yoruba-Yoruba dictionary and book of idioms): *Twi Kasa Mmara,* 1937. Akrofi intensively cooperated in editing various Akuapem-Twi textbooks, readers and last but not least religious texts. He also contributed to solving the vexatious problems of the graphization and orthographization of Twi (*Twi Spelling Book,* 1938) and was actively interested in collecting and recording the wealth of Twi oral traditions—*Twi mmebusɛm* (Twi Proverbs, 1958). The literary importance of Akrofi's activity derives, however, not only from the value of his own original texts, but perhaps even more from his editorial activity. This is particularly clear in the case of the literary work of an older Akuapem-Twi author, J. J. Addaye. Although details about Addaye's life and work are not quite clear, he was apparently of modest origin, having had an average education and social position, but certainly no modest talent. Perhaps future Ghanaian literary criticism will one day clarify not only the particular details of Addaye's life (he apparently worked as a minor clerk and was a veteran soldier), but will also throw light on the nature and duration of Akrofi's cooperation in editing Addaye's books. Addaye published a collection of twenty-five short stories in Twi, even before World War I, as one of the first prose works in this sphere, entitled *Bere adu* (The Hour Has Struck, 1913). One cannot exclude the possibility that Addaye may have produced further prose works, whose manuscripts have disappeared but which may have influenced other Twi authors. With the editorial assistance of Akrofi, Addaye's selection of Twi proverbs was published in Akropong *Twi mmebusɛm ahanum mmoaano* (A Collection of Five Hundred Twi Proverbs, 1934). Addaye's participation— together with Akrofi—in the writing or editing of another collection of short stories *Mmodenbɔ bu mmusu abasa so* (Perseverance Overcomes Difficulties, 1948) is also possible.

The other Akuapem Twi author E. J. Osew (b. 1900) became known for his Twi plays. *Nana Agyeman hwehwɛ* (The Search of Nana Agyeman, 1935), written in blank verse, provides an allegorical solution—the greatest wealth is a treasury of wisdom and knowledge, the seat of which at that time was Achimota College. On the other hand, his *Asantehene Osee Tutu* (1956) is a historical drama based on the days of the Asante Empire. Other plays by this same author were performed, but did not appear in print.

Two other early Akuapem-Twi authors Fianko Safori (b. 1895) and B. S. Akuffo (b. 1902) contributed by publishing records or reflections on the various aspects of Twi oral traditions, customs and folklore.

Koranteg E. Owusu (b. 1915) and A. A. Opoku (b. 1919) represent the younger generation of Twi authors. Although writing in Akuapem-Twi, neither author was born in the Akuapem area and their written literary standard was therefore acquired through education. In his books, Koranteg Owusu draws heavily from oral traditions and folklore, as in *Mpuaasa Ntiamoa* (A Man with Three Tufts of Hair, 1950). His major novel *Guasohantan* (Vain Glory, 1963) is the story of a man who, intending to marry a girl, must play the role of a fabulously rich man. His drama *Ɔsabarima* (The Hero, 1961) depicts the tribal wars and feuds of pre-colonial periods. A. A. Opoku rose from a teaching post to that of an editor in the Bureau of Ghana Languages; later he joined the Ghana Broadcasting Company. Apart from a highly traditional drama *Ɔdehuro* (The Yam Festival, 1956), he has published various excellent poems, some about the beauties of nature in his home-land—for instance, the Afram River—in various magazines and journals. A selection of his poems was also published in the representative anthology *Voices of Ghana*.

Whereas some other Akuapem authors should be mentioned here, at least by name (Edwin Effa, L. D. Apraku, I. Yeboah-Dankwah, S. N. Safo and others), the cases of V. A. Amarteifio and Daniel Offei Darko are most interesting, as they too, like some Fante authors, produced literary works bilingually, at least during some periods of their creative work. Offei Darko started his literary activity with a successful story in Fante *Obra yɛ bɔna* (Life is a Battle, 1940) and subsequently switched his literary activity to English. The dividing-line between his Twi literary activity and his literary activity in English is relatively clear. The case of V. A. Amarteifio is, however, different. His novel *Bediako* (1962) was only later published (1965) in a direct English translation under the title *The African Adventurer*.

2.3.3 Asante Twi

Although the Asante-Twi branch of Twi literacy is comparatively younger and more restricted in a quantity, it has produced worthwhile achievements within a relatively short time. Its peak is centred around three main "classical" Twi authors: J. H. K. Nketia (b. 1921), R. A. Tabi (died in 1958 at the age of cca. 40) and A. C. Denteh (b. 1913).

Both Tabi and Denteh were more or less closely associated with the activity of the Bureau of Ghana Languages (and its colonial predecessor); Nketia soon specialized in the fields of science and art. Tabi served as an Asante-Twi editor of the Bureau from around 1951 to 1956; Denteh assumed the same post between 1960 and 1964. J. H. Kwabena Nketia is one of the first Asantes to have graduated with honours both at home and from foreign universities and he has been awarded degrees from various European and American educational institutions. He is deeply interested in the study of traditional customs and oral art, but does not neglect the study of languages and linguistics. He later became a professor at the University of Ghana and the first Ghanaian director of its Institute of African Studies. Although he approaches the problems of literature and literacy increasingly from the standpoint of an academician, his contribution to the creation of Asante-Twi literature cannot be overlooked. Nketia has published two short selections of folklore: *Akanfoɔ anansesɛm* (Folk-tales of the Akans, 1949) and *Akanfoɔ nnwom bi* (Akan Songs, 1949). His play *Ananwoma* (1951), his short story "Kwabena Amoa" (1951) and especially his original poems *Anwonsɛm* (1952) are a part of the classical foundations of Asante-Twi literature. In addition to these, Nketia has written and published several books of an educational nature (readers and textbooks), but he has also been very active in the field of graphization, helping to establish the Twi orthography (*The Writing of Twi*, 1955).

Denteh's literary activity is profoundly influenced both by oral traditions and his religious feelings. He has translated and adapted various religious texts as well as texts of a pedagogical and administrative nature. His main works are focused, however, on traditional customs, oral folklore and the great past of the Asantes: *Agyaa Ananse* (Father Spider, 1964), *Akwasi Mahuw* (1964). Especially the latter provides a particularly interesting biography of a legendary Asante character.

Tabi also does not neglect traditional customs: *Odwiratwa* (1953). His plays *Aka m'ani* (I Would Just Watch, 1953) and *Me nko me yam* (My Own Stomach Only, 1960) as well as his historical novel dealing with 19th-century Gold Coast questions *Ohia nhyɛ da* (Poverty Comes Unexpectedly, 1962) are also oriented toward several more general problems. In addition, Tabi has also contributed pedagogical materials for schools, including the translations of short stories by various famous authors of the world's classical literatures (including those of Lev Tolstoy). Various other authors have also contributed to the development of literacy in Asante-Twi: R. M. Opong and Boateng Amafo could be cited as examples to illustrate the fact that modern Asante-Twi literature is by no means restricted to the activity of the three above-mentioned "classical" authors. Other authors follow, and one may well speculate as to what the final outcome of the Akuapem-Asanti literary split will be. Will this split continue, with two literary standards co-existing, or will some way for the unification of literacy and language be found, despite all the difficulties? Only time will provide the solution to one of the most sociolinquistically fascinating, but socially, educationally and even economically difficult problems of West Africa, and of Ghana, in particular.

2.4 Not all cases of literary development of the West African coastal communities have followed the same path as the three major examples analyzed thus far. In some cases, this development may have started off in the same direction and also produced notable results; however, numerical, economic and even historical factors may have been a more substantial obstacle. In this connection, it should be mentioned that the literature written and published in Gã (the language of the coastal area of Ghana, around the capital Accra) although serving a numerically much less important linguistic community (less than 100,000) has nevertheless achieved—in such a narrow context—notable results. Its authors, including the Rev. Augustus Wiedekund Engmann, Emmanuel Lamte-Lawson, E. J. K. Klufio and Albert Amah Amartey, have produced literary (predominantly prose) works which are fully comparable to the most outstanding literary achievements in Ewe or the Akan languages of the same country. Literacy and literature in some major Nigerian languages of the Southern zone (such as Bini or Efik) have also manifested outstanding results and only their future development will show whether a complete transition from literacy towards a developing literature in the true sense of the word will really take place in their cases, as well, or whether such literacy will remain a purely functional, practical phenomenon. It should be stressed, however, that West African missionary and administrative bibliographies present evidence of many such "still-born" literatures, which—despite the best efforts of individuals or particular centres—did not proceed further toward becoming real literatures. On the other hand, the temporary success and flourishing of a literacy does not guarantee its final establishment as a real literature which is accepted both by its readers and by its authors. From this standpoint, the dynamic situation of the rapidly developing West African countries during the second half of the 20th century presents problems even for certain well-established literacies and developing literatures. According to Ansre (1968, p. 7): "Our colonial masters seem to have appreciated the necessity for us to know and use our linguistic heritage far more than we ourselves do. There has been more neglect of our responsibilities for these languages since we became independent...". Efua Sutherland puts it in plain words, expressing her opinion at the same time (1968, p. 29): "Why has there been such little creative writing in the Ghanaian languages? Isn't the survival of the creative well-springs of the whole society at stake?"

Even from this standpoint, the dynamic picture of the developing and decreasing of literacies and literatures in the languages of the West African coastal area may well be subject to further modifications. The phenomena of literary birth, as well as literary death, may be observed in this context. Even in this respect, however, the picture of this area does not differ from comparable pictures of other areas. Once more, we may stress the fact that processes which have occurred elsewhere in past centuries may be taking place in this area under our very eyes, within a single lifetime, or at least within the lifetimes of a couple of generations.

3. The Islamic Area

3.0 While vernacular literature on the coast developed under the impact of the two competing and mutually interfering cultural and ideological systems, the vernacular literatures in some areas of the West African savannah developed under three such mutually competing and historically or geographically interfering impacts. Original African traditions came into contact with the Islamic culture and literature, and automatically also with the Arabic languages and its script, long before the arrival of the first European. This obviously created a background which was substantially different from that of the "coastal" area.

Two major literacies have developed within this context, both of them being transformed gradually into literatures in the true sense, and both of them constituting today major contributions to African literatures: Hausa and Fula. The case of Hausa is analyzed in detail within the context of this section, both for objective and subjective reasons, and the particular features of the literacy-literature transition and literary development of this area are substantiated on the basis of it. Our remarks about Fula (and marginally about certain other minor literatures) are intended only for the sake of comparison, as a comprehensive analysis will undoubtedly appear sooner or later from a more competent pen.

3.1 *Hausa*

3.1.0 Contact with the Islamic culture and religion and with the Arabic language and its script apparently brought the first type of literacy to Hausaland, as far as we know today. The duration and origin of this contact have been studied whithin the historical context (cf. Hiskett, 1968, p. 275). From the standpoint of the possible origins of a Hausa literacy based upon the Arabic script, it is important to stress that the intensity of such contacts with Islam might have varied considerably, both with respect to the given historical period and to the particular region. Thus, while this contact reached one of its peaks probably during the period of the Fulani Holy War (*Djihadi*), in other periods it may have proved to be considerably weaker. Similarly, the intensity of such contact with Islam must have been much stronger in the central areas of Hausaland (Kano-Sokoto), while the much weaker intensity of Islamization in certain marginal areas is still manifested today be the existence of "pagan" Hausa tribes (see Piault, 1970).

3.1.0.1 Although the connection between literacy in the Arabic script and the Islamic influence in Hausaland is clear, the period and roots of such literacy in the Hausa language itself and not in the Arabic language still remain to some extent open to discussion. We should stress in this context the difference between the existence of a literacy in the Arabic language, written in Hausaland and in Western Sudan for an apparently much longer period, and the literacy which—while still using the Arabic script—was already using the Hausa language (no matter how much influenced by written interference with the Arabic language it may have been at such initial stages). Oral traditions, as well as certain scholars, have supposed the existence of such a literacy in Hausa for a relatively long historical period, although little documentary evidence of this has been available so far. As for concerning pre-Djihadi literacy in Hausa, the situation remains almost unchanged (no one, however, can exclude the possibility of further surprises). Recent scholars are more inclined to accept the thesis that it was precisely this very Djihadi period, with its emphasis on reaching the broad masses of Hausa-speaking or Hausa-understanding people with the Shehu's philosophical and religious ideas that should be considered as the main incentive for the introduction of writing in the Hausa language, presumably as an instrument for reaching those who were unable to communicate in Arabic (Hiskett 1965, p. 25).

Although present documentary evidence speaks greatly in favour of such a hypothesis, one may wonder whether during the whole historical period between the establishment of the first Islamic contacts in Hausaland (cca. between the 14th and 15th centuries A.D.) and the Djihadi period at the end of the 17th century A.D. Ajami literacy in Hausa was really completely absent from that area. Moreover, it is doubtful whether such an important process as the creation of a literacy in Hausa was really an instantaneous consequence of a rapid social and ideological change occurring during the Djihadi period. It should be stressed that the roots of such an important phenomenon as writing in the main language of Hausaland might perhaps also be found in the long drawn-out process of the interference of Hausa and Arabic into the written texts produced in that area, in a situation in which neither the majority of scribes nor the majority of perspective readers were Arabs, but mostly Hausas or Hausa-speaking persons. Thus, the revolutionary situation during the Djihadi period might have represented only the final incentive and an impetus towards a shift in the written form of the languages, the roots of which had already objectively existed in the Hausa language community for a relatively long period.

3.1.0.2   The position of the Roman script at the moment of its introduction into Hausaland was different from various points of view. Although it penetrated into Hausaland also as a consequence of cultural and linguistic contacts with an external area, it appeared in a different situation and at a different historical period, i.e. in the second half of the 19th century. Sociolinguistically and even psychologically, it is important to stress that while the Arabic script penetrated into a presumably script-less language community, the Roman script penetrated into a language community with a certain knowledge and usage of script. From the very beginning, it co-existed in competition with a script which, at the period of the early penetration of European cultural influence and linguistic contacts, was clearly currently being used for the writing of Hausa.

While the ties between the Arabic script, language and the Islamic religion at particular moments facilitated the penetration of this script, similar though not identical links between the Roman script and the Christian misions did little to propagate the script and even occasionally discouraged the Hausa people, who were oriented towards the Islamic culture, from using it. Nevertheless, the strong administrative backing (see Skinner, 1968, p. XII ff.) and assistance of certain mass communications media in subsequent periods contributed to the relative dissemination of the usage of the Roman script for Hausa, as well.

3.1.0.3   As a consequence, today's Hausa language community uses two different scripts and therefore it is to be considered to some extent digraphic. Moreover, digraphia, at least in the case of Hausa, cannot be viewed as a mere formal phenomenon. The difference in script must be considered an external symptom of a much deeper stratification of the entire community of those who write in a different way, using what must be considered as one and the same language in a given historical period. The reasons for such a situation may have to do with the existence of particular correlations between the script itself and certain other factors determining the language of written texts. This may enable us to characterize the difference between texts written in different scripts as a profound difference between two types of a written form of a single language. In the case of the Hausa language community, we meet with at least two types of such correlations: a correlation between the script and particular language contacts, with the consequent language interference, and a correlation between the script and a particular literary function or particular functions of written texts in differing cultural contexts. These two correlations seem to determine the basic patterns of the development of literacies in Hausa and the creation, or rather integration, of a single Hausa literature.

While the linguistic consequences of such a complex situation have been analyzed elsewhere (Zima, 1974), the literary results of such a division and of the reintegration of Hausa literacy and literature are of primary concern within the context of this section, especially as the choice of a script should be seen as an external symptom of the entire cultural, ideological and even formal orientation of particular Hausa literary texts.

3.1.0 As the origins of Hausa literacy are closely linked with literacy in the Arabic language, and this in turn is very close to Islam, the basis of such literacy and literature deals primarily with religious topics. The most obvious and most frequent form of such a religious Hausa text is the poem.

3.1.1 According to popular traditions, Shehu Uthman dan Fodio himself, as well as perhaps other close relatives and pupils of his (e.g. his son Isa, his daughter Nana, his brother Abdullahi), contributed personally to the creation of such a Hausa tradition of religious poetry. The name of Shehu's son, Isa, is given some prominence in oral traditions, and we cannot exclude the possibility that he translated into Hausa the autobiography which Uthman dan Fodio himself composed in Fula. If the hypothesis about the Djihadi origin of Hausa literacy in the Arabic script is correct, then this long poem, generally known by the Hausa name *Siffofin Shehu* (the Attributes of the Shehu), may well represent one of the first literary monuments of Hausa. The aim of the poem, which is preserved in the form of 67 double verses in conformity with the Arabic metre known as *al-wāfir*, is to publicize the favours Allah has bestowed upon the Shehu. This poetic autobiography may also have been written by the author, perhaps with the additional aim of giving much information about himself, particularly in the forms of similarities between himself and the Mahdi. His intentions seems to be to demonstrate the extent to which he has followed in the paths of the Prophet and the Mahdi and how closely his life's work approximates the ideals of Islam. As analyzed by El-Masri and Adeley (1966, p. 4), the Hausa version is highly Arabicized: 44 out of the 67 rhyming words at the end of the lines are of Arabic origin. "Even when allowance has been made for the heavy borrowing of Hausa vocabulary from Arabic, this still represents a high proportion. One gets the impression that many

166

of the rhyming words, which hang rather loosely at the end of the lines and obscure rather than elicit understanding, are introduced for conformity with the metrical pattern. The language of the Hausa version is therefore difficult and rather stilted" (*ibid*).

The whole poem is divided into two parts, the first part (lines 2—23) comparing the Shehu's attributes with those of the Prophet, the second part drawing parallels between his attributes and those of the anticipated Mahdi.

The traditions of Islamic religious poetry in Hausa were based—apart from the immediate contributions of the Shehu's relatives and friends—upon the poetic creations of many of his followers. Muhammadu na Birnin Gwari, who lived in the 19th century, was prominent among them. Educated probably in Timbuktu (cf. Aliyu-Don Scharfe, 1967, p. 34), he offered his learned services to the Shehu's successors and contributed a great deal to the further development of the tradition of Hausa religious Islamic poetry written in the Ajami variant of the Arabic script.

One such meditative poem of his, composed in 175 verses, consists of an introduction, the necessary prayer for assistance in writing, and an exhortation to follow Mohammed (verse 15—21). The problems of choice between this world and the next world (verse 22—31) are analyzed together with the difficulties connected with service to Allah (verse 35—43). The reader is requested to reject this world, in view of the possibility of living in the next one (verse 47—52) and the example of our ancestors, who preceded us along this path, is used as a sort of warning (verse 81—90). This world is described as old and untrustworthy (verse 91—112). The need to prepare for the future is mentioned and the nature of the preparations required is indicated (verse 113—29); moreover, the pilgrimage to Mecca and the nature of the rites to be performed there are described (verse 162—175 — cf. Robinson, 1896, pp. 15—35).

M. Hiskett attempts to classify all Hausa poems of this genre in four main categories:

1. *begen Annabi*—eulogies of the Prophet Mohammed;
2. *Wa'azi*—the threat of eternal punishment and the promise of divine reward;
3. *tauhidi*—Muslim theology, the science of unity;
4. *Fikihu*—Muslim law.

He thinks that while the first category of Hausa poems is primarily devotional, the remaining three had either the intent of reaching the common people with the message of salvation or (in the post-Djihadi era) of upholding the Muslim hierarchy through the possible sanctions of Islam (1968, p. 281). Arabic obviously not only influenced the language of these Hausa poems, but coexistence with Islamic poetry in this language also heavily influenced their forms. They are metrical and their metres are close to the classical metres of Arabic poetry—*al-tawīl, al-wāfir, al-kāmil* (concerning Hausa verse prosody, see Greenberg, 1949).

Although in the early stages of such poetry, the focus was mainly on religious questions and meditations, other subjects and topics appeared, especially in the more recent periods of the development of this genre of poetry, by the end of the 19th and early decades of the

20th century. Such poets as Shehu na Salga, Ibrahim Nalado Katsina, Salihu Kwantagora and Aliyu ɗan Sidi were obviously mostly interested in religious meditation and the virtues of the traditional Islamic culture, but certain other aspects also appeared and such Hausa poetry—though still mainly religious—occasionally also dealt with the impact of Europe and the dangers threatening the traditional style of life from this European impact. This topic was particularly developed by Aliyu ɗan Sidi. That one-time ruling chief of Zaria was forced by Lugard's administration to retire from his function and live in exile in Lokoja. In a long poem, he enumerated the virtues of traditional rule and presented the picture of the peaceful, prosperous country flourishing before the establishment of Lugard's administration. However, the same author also praised the beauties of abundance and perfection in his lyrical poem *Mu sha Falala* (Let us Enjoy Abundance).

3.1.1.2 Although the Islamic religion and culture, together with the forms and metres of Arabic religious poetry, undoubtedly greatly influenced the initial stages of this similar poetry composed in Hausa, other factors which were local in character, must also have influenced its origin. As the term itself suggest, *waƙa* means both song and poem in Hausa (an old tradition of oral poetry exists in Hausa, as well). All Hausa poems, including those closely resembling their Arabic models, are primarily sung to a tune accompanied, if possible, by a *mailo* or another musical instrument. Popular singers and poets travel from town to town (or—in the past—from one chief's residence to another) and compose their songs or poems with considerable ability and skill, modifying them at will, as the need arises.

Such Hausa oral poetry is usually described in terms of three basic genres (Prietze, 1931): the *yabo* (the praise-song), *zambo* (a satirical poem deeply ironical in nature) and *bege* (this term is used in the context of popular poetry in the sense of a '*Sehnsuchtslied*'). Moreover, certain features of pro-Islamic Hausa culture and traditions are also manifested in this form of poetry. The selection of subjects and their treatment are often clearly uninfluenced by the Islamic code of morality, or at least it is influenced to a much lesser extent (songs about fertility, women, etc.). This is particularly clear in some *bege* songs (see Prietze, 1927 and 1931, especially p. 90 of the latter). The basically pre-Islamic *bori* cults also often found their way into such poetry (cf. King, 1966). Whereas the metres and verses of such popular oral poems differ greatly from the classical "learned" ones, certain basic features of their choice of topics, and even their genres and style, may perhaps have influenced the initial stages of such "learned" poetry, as well. Moreover, in the particular casa of Hausa (and perhaps in a comparable situation in some Fula areas) oral poetry cannot be labelled altogether oral only in form, as evidence exists that especially in the later periods some Hausa scribes started to use their writing skills to record such poems in the written form, using the Ajami variant of the Arabic script. It could be seen that most examples of such poetry, collected by various scholars (Rudolf Prietze, Julius Lippert and other German scholars, who were particularly active in this field) were recorded in the Arabic script. Although one cannot exclude the possibility that their informants used the script for recording the songs only to satisfy their requirements ad hoc, the readiness with the songs were recorded in this type of written form of Hausa is particularly interesting. The famous *Waƙar Bagauda* (Song of Bagauda) as published by Hiskett (1964) may also represent a type of poetry that has existed for a longer historical period both in its oral (sung) and written forms. Recorded, transcribed and published in a scholarly work recently, this poem presents a brief history of the rulers of Kano together with a religious homily incorporating the traditional admonitions and warnings so famous in religious Hausa poetry, "beware the end of your lives!" The whole poem is composed of three parts: an introduction with an invocation of the Prophet is followed by a brief history of Kano; lists of emirs are given with some essential comments on their rules. The religious homily concludes this poem, which is greatly influenced by Arabic metres (*al-wāfir*). Rhyming in -*wa* is used throughout the entire poem.

3.1.1.3 While the influence of oral poetic traditions seems to have been weaker in the early periods when religious meditation prevailed in content and Arabic metres prevailed in form, throughout the whole lengthy process of "Hausanization" of classical Hausa poetry, the influence of oral traditions seems to have increased. Some of the poems by the above-mentioned Aliyu ɗan Sidi could be quoted as evidence of this process (Song of Abundance), but poems about various aspects of contemporary life, the beauties of nature or human misery were also not rare among other authors.

Aliyu na Mangi (born at the end of the 19th century in Zaria) was one of those Hausa poets who recited and composed their poetry primarily in the oral form (he was blind). His poems, though also reflecting religious meditations and doubts repeating the usual theme of death and salvation, by far exceed the narrow limits of purely religious poetry. His *Waƙar Imfiraji* (Song of Praise) deals in eight volumes not only with religious subjects, but as Liman Muhammad says (1966, p. 47) "… he addressed all of us, not simply the prostitute, the trader or the butcher". His humour and realistic attitude toward life is partly reflected in certain shorter poems; one of which personifies the bicycle, newly-introduced into Hausaland; some of his poems deal with women and other topics.

Generally, Hausa poets continue to write (or recite) classical forms of poetry, using essentially the Ajami variant of the Arabic script. These poets include Malam ɗan Adamu, Malam Ali Akilu and many others. Some collections of their poetry have been published (the Gaskiya Corporation has published the poems of M. ɗan Adamu under the title *Waƙoƙin Malam dan Adamu* (The Poems of M. ɗan Adamu) in the Ajami variant of the Arabic script; other collections have been printed locally or circulate in hand-written copies.

The transition between traditional forms of oral songs and written printed poems has, however, by no means been accomplished even today.

A new wave of poets writing either in the Ajami variant of the Arabic script or in Roman characters, who have appeared in the relatively recent period, will be dealt with in Section 3.1.4. Before doing so, however, we should devote brief attention to the subject of prose texts.

3.1.2 In dealing with Hausa literacy utilizing the Ajami variant of the Arabic script, we have analyzed thus far almost exclusively poetry, since, in fact, most texts of any literary value which have been discovered or published in this form of Hausa literacy are poetic in nature and form. Prose texts in Ajami are altogether rare, mostly recent historically speaking, and—as in the case of certain poems—one may doubt whether their texts are primarily written at all. In fact, most of the texts recorded by G. A. Krause, R. Prietze, A. Mischlich, K. Krieger and several other critical editors appear to be texts, the original form of which was oral; the Ajami variant of the Arabic script has been used only for a secondary recording and is apparently a transcription used by Hausa scribes and narrators. Most of these texts, if in prose, are historic or ethnographic in character, dealing with particular aspects of Hausa history, culture, oral traditions, customs, the economy, etc. A thorough critical edition and commentary prepared by D. A. Olderogge and his pupils appeared in 1960.

It might be worth mentioning that many—although by no means all—of these texts come either directly or indirectly from Hausa settlements in the so-called Hausa diaspora, either in West Africa (Togoland and the former Gold Coast) or outside it (Tripoli, Cairo). A very representative collection of them was assembled and recorded in Kete-Krachie, and M. Umaru Krachie (who himself also composes "classical" poems) is probably one of their main sources and narrators (scribes).

Their style resembles mostly oral narratives, a false dialogue being used in some instances. The oral nature of these texts of autonomous written tradition may not be altogether excluded. A dramatic dialogue, resembling in some aspects almost a play, is presented in the report of a Hausa trader, who relates his impressions of his travels with camels and goods across the desert from Murzuk to Kano. This text was recorded by Rudolf Prietze and his assistant and friend in the Hansa colony of Tripoli (Prietze, 1924—25).

This type of Hausa literacy also indicates a relatively rich epistolary tradition as revealed by comprehensive collections of Hausa letters to and from traditional rulers in Hausaland and elsewhere, assembled by certain early British administrators (see e.g. specimens of Major Burdon's collection, published by Frank Edgar, 1911, I., Nos. 72—82 and elsewhere). Unfortunately, very little is known about the actual age and historical origins of this epistolary usage of Hausa in Ajami.

Apart from such highly specialized and marginal prose texts, which are mostly non-literary in character, few examples of prose in the Ajami variant of the Arabic script were written, as far as we know, at that time.

This lack of a prose tradition in the Ajami form of Hausa literacy obviously had serious consequence with respect to the process of developing a Hausa literature. While poetic literature was influenced by traditional Ajami literacy to the extent of being almost "swallowed up" by it in its initial stages, prose had very little to build upon in this sphere at the time that literacy in the Roman script was initiated. This might well be the factor that has favoured the oral tradition which—apart from minor exceptions—represents the only known local tradition of prose texts. Seen from this point of view, the fairy-tale character of certain modern Hausa novels of the 1930's (as shown by Skinner, 1971, p. 172) would not appear too surprising, but rather natural: these were, in fact, the prevailing Hausa traditions in the field of prose.

3.1.3.1 The initial phases of a Hausa literacy in the Roman script were also connected with missionary efforts. Although some of these early efforts in Hausa were based more or less upon miscalculations (cf. Hair, 1967, p. 40 ff.), one missionary pioneer—J. F. Schön—contributed not only the first linguistic studies of Hausa, but also translated various Christian religious texts as early as 1859 (*Letafi Musa na Biu*—The Second Book of Moses). Other Christian religious texts were translated and even published at a later date, including the Old and New Testaments (*Sabon Alkawali* and *Tsofon Alkawali,* 1925); even the entire Bible was translated into Hausa (*Littafi maitsarki,* 1932). But owing to strong Muslim opposition, the Christian missions (their literature in Hausa is recorded in some detail by Rowling-Wilson, 1923, pp. 114—115) never succeeded in influencing the central Hausa areas and their effects remained limited essentially to certain "pagan" Hausa areas and some areas in the Middle Belt. Because of this, Christian religious texts in Hausa written or printed in the Roman script never assumed an importance comparable to that of the Islamic texts in the Ajami variant of the Arabic script.

3.1.3.2 On the other hand, however, a considerable stimulus was given to literacy in the Roman script by administrative incentives originating, until fairly recently, mainly in Northern Nigeria. The language policies of most administrations in that region after Lugard's time favoured this type of written usage of Hausa and introduced it into public functions during the first decade of this century (cf. Kirk-Green 1964, p. 190). The Translation Bureau, the NORLA (Northern Region Literature Agency), the Gaskiya Corporation and the Hausa Language Board all of which were administratively-backed and at least partly subsidized institutions, produced a solid mass of Hausa texts, thereby creating a new type of Hausa literacy; the Roman script gave it its external form, while its links with European administration, secular education and European technology characterized its language and cultural orientation. The first printed Hausa booklets and pamphlets had—as everywhere—very little literary character: these were readers (Littafin Koyon Karatu, 1923), health prophylaxis (Littafi Kiwon Lafiya, 1914) and an introduction to history and culture (Littafi na da da na yanzu, 1931). The first reactions of Hausa readers were not altogether favourable. The Arabic script and and literacy in it had the advantage of being already in use; restricted though Ajami literacy may have been at that time, it was established. The Roman script, on the other hand, was automatically associated with foreign, "pagan" or unbelievers' ideas. The common name given to this Roman-script-based literacy—*boko*—might well have been associated both with the English word "book" and with the Hausa original sense, which means "deceit" or "fraud". However, throughout the 1930's a new wave of administrative, technological, agricultural and pedagogical literature arose, though—especially at first—most writers of these booklets were expatriate officers. R. M. East, who for years headed the Translation Bureau and then the Literature Bureau, was one of the most outstanding expatriates active in this field, perhaps in all of West Africa. His anthology *Labarun Hausawa da Makwabtansu* (The History of the Hausas and Their Neighbours, 1932) reflects not only his good knowledge of the language, but also a deep interest in its traditions and history. Moreover, he published, together with a Hausa co-author named Tafida, one of the first Hausa novels: *Jiki Magayi* (The Body Will Explain, 1934).

3.1.3.3.3 This together with the intensive training of the first generation of Hausa teachers, students and intellectuals, as well as a growing interest in literacy and literature on the part of the traditional rulers and their officers, created a growing Hausa community writing and reading in the Roman script. A whole group of Hausa prose novels (or novelettes) was produced in the 1930's by a new generation of Hausa authors: *Gandoki* (the name of a brave warrior, also the title of the novel) was published in 1934 by A. Bello Kagara (born around the end of the 19th century). *Idon Matambayi* (The Eye of the Questioner) 1934 was written by Muhammad Gwarzo (b. 1911). The name of the author of another novel entitled *Shaihu Umar* (1934) was originally listed as M. Abubakar Bauchi but its writer was actually none other than the one-time federal Prime Minister of Nigeria, Alhaji Abubakar Tafawa Balewa.

A few years later, these works were joined by the prose novels written by the greatest living contemporary Hausa prose—author, Alhaji Abubakar Imam (b. 1912): *Magana Jari Ce* (Speech is a Treasure, 1938) and *Ruwan Bagaja* (Unpure Water, 1935). The topics of these books cover widely differing fields. *Gandoki,* is the history of a courageous warrior of pre-colonial Africa who fights Lugard's soldiers but later moves into the world of fantasy, fighting with jinns and ogres, to return only at the end of the book to the reality of Northern Nigeria under indirect rule. *Shaihu Umar,* too, has biographical features, but the influence of Muslim customs and habits seems stronger in it. *Jiki Magayi, Ruwan Bagaja* and *Idon Matambayi* are all prose novels deeply influenced by traditional folk-tales, *tatsuniyoyi* and *labarai*. *Magana Jari Ce* is also a frame-story, the whole group of sub-plots being connected by a parrot who must invent stories, in order to prevent his young prince from rushing into mortal danger. The external influences of foreign folklore are here combined with Hausa traditions, and the author's debts to *Arabian Nights* is quite evident. Still, the language of this book is so rich in Hausa idioms and phrases that it has been used ever since its first publication as the best advanced Hausa reader.

Further attempts at prose literature appeared later with M. Aminu Kano's lively travel-book giving the impressions of a young Hausa in 20th-century Europe entitled *Motsi ya fi Zama* (It is Better to Travel Than to Stay at Home, 1955). An attempt at a fantastic sci-fi story by Umaru A. Dembo, *Tauraruwa Mai Wutsiya* (The Shooting Star, 1969) is reported by Skinner (1971, p. 176).

In spite of the continuing development of modern Hausa prose literature, the period of the 1930's was undoubtedly the most fruitful and perhaps also most "classical" stage of its formation. Its main form was the short novel, which was highly influenced by traditional forms of Hausa folk-tales. Initial attempts at a Hausa dramatic literature also appeared in *boko* (i.e. Roman characters). Some of the first plays published by NORLA for educational purposes and for the needs of the schools were clearly marked by their applied and pedagogical character. These included *Wasan Marafa* (A Play about Marafa, 1956) by Abubakar Tunau, *Malam Inkuntum* by Alhaji Dogondaji, etc. Similar pedagogical plays were not published but were performed by the pupils of various Hausa schools in Northern Nigeria throughout the late 1950's. On the other hand, the dramatic works of Shu'aibu Makarfi (b.cca. 1920), *Zamanin Nan Namu* (This Time of Ours, 1959) and *Jatau na Kyallu* (1960), are real, complete plays analyzing certain vices and problems of Hausa society and presenting a surprisingly realistic atmosphere of the Kano milieu. Skinner (1971, pp. 181—2) also reports on other plays which have appeared only recently and praises the comedy written by two authors, one Hausa and one American (Dan Gogo and Dauda Kano), entitled *Tabarmar Kunya* (The Mat of Shame).

The editing of several journals and magazines, either exclusively in Hausa or with an important Hausa section alongside the English one, have offered the opportunity of extending the scope of Hausa texts written in the Roman script to the field of journalism and modern politics. The official publication *Jaridar Nijeriya ta Arewa* (Journal of Northern Nigeria) was later replaced by the famous *Gaskiya ta fi Kwabo*, (Truth is Worth More Than a Penny), published as a weekly until today, while important Hausa journals or magazines have been or are being published either by literacy or by administrative institutions in Northern Nigeria. Such illustrated magazines as *Aboki* have been important, owing to their appeal to the broader public. In the field of journalism especially, a major contribution has been made in recent years in the Republic of Niger. A large literacy campaign was started there by the authorities, with the competent assistance of UNESCO; Hausa was one of the languages used as tools in that campaign. Within the context of the campaign, the local *Service d'Alphabétisation et d'Education des Adultes* published an official journal *Le Sahel* (also in Hausa) as well as instructive, lively locally roneotyped Hausa periodicals in the main Hausa centres of Niger: *Muryar Damagaram* (The Voice of Zinder), *Saabon Ra'ayii* (New Opinion, Magaria), *Kasar Albarka* (The Country of Prosperity, Maradi), *Kaakaakin Abzin* (The Trumpet of Abzin, Agades) and *Taurayar Adar* (The Star of Ader, Tahoua).

3.1.4 While most traditional poetic literature is written in the Ajami variant of the Arabic script and most modern prose is written in the Roman script, a new transitional feature has arisen, rooted in the inter-war period but flourishing especially after World War II. This was the new Hausa school of poetry, which used both Ajami and *boko* (i.e. Roman characters) or else one of these two scripts. Always deeply linked with the forms (and sometimes even subjects) of "classical" Hausa poetry, it nevertheless attempts to modernize Hausa poetry while introducing Hausa topics, form and content.

Four names characterize this new poetic wave in Hausa—those of Sa'adu Zungur, Mu'azu Hadeja, Mudi Sipikin, and Na'ibi Wali. Sa'adu Zungur (d. cca. 1959) was born in the Middle Belt and acquired a secular education at Yaba College in Lagos. Moving slowly away from original religious and traditional poems, he devoted increasing attention to contemporary topics and subjects. Focusing intensely on the evils of World War II, his 43—stanza poem "Maraba da Soja" (Welcome, Soldier) describes the horrors of war, including the first use of the atomic bomb, against Hiroshima. The atrocities of war and a critical attitude toward certain realities of Nigerian society even moved this poet to adopt some relatively radical opinions, so that before the end of his life he composed a political poem entitled "Arewa Jumhuriya ko Mullukiya?" (Should the North become a Republic or a Kingdom?)

Mu'azu Hadeja (1920—1955) published his poems in a small booklet *Wakokin Mu'azu Hadeja* (The Poems of Mu'azu Hedeja, 1958). A teacher, his pedagogical activity had undoubtedly a profound influence of his poetic skill. Such poems as "Ilmin Zamani" (Modern Education) or "Mu Yaki da Jahilci" (Let Us Fight Ignorance!) clearly manifest a highly pedagogical character. On the other hand, however, many of them reflect popular wisdom and wit: "Gaskiya be ta sake Gashi" (Truth Does not Change Its Hair). Moreover, some of them touch deeply the very roots of prevailing morality and its weakness: "Karuwa" (Prostitution) "Wakar Giya" (Song of Liquor), etc.

Mudi Sipikin, whose poems were also published in a summary form by Gaskiya (*Wakokin Mudi Sipikin*, no date) attracted attention to his activity, both artistically and politically, in the atmosphere of the 1950's. At that time, he helped to organize the so-called Askianist Movement—a cultural-historical society with particular interests in reviving the knowledge and popularity of certain aspects of the Hausa past and its history. Later, it became affiliated to the *Jami'ar Samarin Sawaba*—the so-called Northern Elements' Progressive Union—a liberal democratic group and moderate Leftist party of Northern Nigeria. An American author (Paden 1965, p. 35) thinks that… "British officials were shocked to read Mudi Sipikin's anti-colonial 'Song in Praise of Russia' in *The Daily Comet*" (Hausa).

Later, however, he abandoned his radical opinions and joined the NPC (Northern Peoples' Congress), the ruling conservative party of the North under the Nigerian "first republic". He became particularly interested in religious poetry, writing both in the Arabic script and in *boko*, preferring the latter, however, for Hausa usage.

Na'ibi Wali (b. 1929), the son of an older Hausa poet and literate, Wali Suleiman, had both a traditional, Koranic, as well as secular education. He entered the administration and climbed the ladder of its hierarchy, but throughout his pedagogical and administrative activity, he maintained an intense interest in literacy and the Hausa language. For some time, Na'ibi Wali served as Secretary of the Hausa Language Board attached to the then Northern Ministry of Education in Kaduna. He later became active as a UNESCO expert on Hausa literacy and represented Nigerian Hausas at various international meetings on literacy. He is now a high senior official at the Ministry of Education in his native Kano State. Though considerably influenced by the forms, topics and metres of traditional poetry, his poems reflect the beauties of nature; he sings of traditions and customs and his imagination plays upon nuances sometimes unknown among preceding generations of Hausa poets. Some of his poems were published in a collective anthology prepared by the Gaskiya editors entitled *Wakokin Hausa* (Hausa Poems). The most famous of them is a long poem-song on the coming of the rainy season—"*Wakar Damina*" (Song of the Rains) which eulogizes the coming rains giving new life to the dry savannah after the long hot period; it was analyzed in detail by Arnott (1968) and King (1968). Particular rhythmical and stylistic features, and especially differences from the classical patterns of Arabic poetry, were discerned by these scholars.

It would seem that stylistically, linguistically and even metrically the new wave of Hausa poetry is following a path which is also reflected in its literary development: though still heavily relying on the pattern of "classical" religious poetry, it seems to be opening itself ever more both to the influence of popular poetry and to the influence of the literary and social contexts of contemporary Hausaland inside Nigeria as well as outside it. Curiously enough, this situation seems to be—to some extent at least—also reflected in the sphere of script. Although *boko* (i.e. the Roman script) is officially preferred, and even if the restricted literacy in it is modified in time into a full-scale literacy—at present both types of graphical usage still persist in the field of poetry.

3.1.5.0 The present situation—that of the transition from literacy to the initial stages of a Hausa literature—is, therefore, considerably richer, but also more complicated than the situations of the language communities on the coast.

Instead of only one, two forms of literacy (though both are still restricted in usage) coexist in the present Hausa language community. While cultural, educational or political orientations and other individual factors may well dictate the choice of script in some cases, in certain areas this choice—especially among those who have mastered both types of literacy—is predictable by the literary or social function of the text. From this standpoint, the entire body of historical and contemporary written Hausa texts can be divided into three basic categories:

3.1.5.1 Hausa texts using essentially the Ajami variant of the Arabic script and influenced to some extent by the interference of Arabic and its classical senses in a primary way: almost the entire corpus of Hausa Islamic religious literature, which is mainly poetic in form, is included in this category. Certain historical texts and texts dealing with traditional administration or law might perhaps also be included.

3.1.5.2 Hausa texts using essentially the Roman script with all its respective language consequences: modern prose literature (including novels, short stories, frame-stories, dramatic efforts), administrative and pedagogical literature for secular schools, as well as journalistic, administrative and political texts.

3.1.5.3 Hausa texts using either the Ajami variant of the Arabic script or the Roman script with a subsequent difference in the written form of the language (sometimes in free alternation): poetry—especially modern poetry, letters and certain genres dealing with traditional business and administration or finance.

3.1.5.4 It seems, therefore, that the whole corpus of Hausa written and printed texts may be analyzed in terms of two unequal parts: as for the literary as well as non-literary texts mentioned under Sections 3.1.5.1 and 3.1.5.2, the choice of the script is still largely predictable by the literary character of the text. In this sense, Hausa literature may still be said to be to some extent a divided literature. In this context, however, the relative unity and homogeneity of the Hausa-speaking community plays an important role, compensating for the divisive effects of a difference in script. Together with the category of texts analyzed in Section 3.1.5.3, it may well serve as a bridge between the two graphically, formally and originally even culturally different branches of Hausa literature. From this point of view, this script difference may soon cease to be a barrier, becoming, rather, a feature of a possible functional differentiation or an important stylistic aspect of written Hausa. Functional complementation may even ultimately replace the former individual division. An expansion of the inventory of stylistic and formal patterns of Hausa could take place in future, although this might ultimately give way to the usage of a single script in the historical long-run.

3.2 Remarks on Fula and Other Languages of the Islamic Zone

3.2.0 While we have devoted particular attention to the question of literacy and literature in Hausa (both for objective and subjective reasons) in the context of the Islamic(Savannah) zone, this by no means implies that Hausa literacy and literature are the sole such phenomena in that area. Apart from certain less important literacies—such as Kanuri and the literacy of several languages of Northern Ghana—one major literacy and important literature exists alongside Hausa in this zone to such an extent that it should be considered within the same context, and certainly with the same amount of interest: that is, Fula literacy and literature. We are very much aware that a comprehensive analysis of Fula literature, which is comparable both in volume and importance to Hausa literature—should be presented within the context of this section; however, we must necessarily restrict our section on Fula literacy and literature to certain basic remarks of an essentially comparative character. Our lack of specialized competence is not the sole reason for such an approach, as, in contrast to Hausa, Fula literature—and especially its traditional part—has as yet by no means been so well described and analyzed, so that a comprehensive analysis of this literature still partly awaits a competent description of its relevant material by Fula specialists.

3.2.1 Both Fula and Hausa literacies and literatures offer certain parallels, the roots of which may be found in comparable aspects of their cultural, religious and even social development. Both the Fulanis and the Hausas are nations of the so-called Savannah Belt, and, as the two most important ethnic groups of that area, they were both subjected to relatively intensive Islamization. Both nations have, however, preserved—in some areas and to a different extent—certain pre-Islamic traditions and cultural features. As a consequence, both languages had to accept a sort of coexistence and language contact with Arabic, the prestige language of Islam; the early acceptance of the Arabic script first had, in this context, an almost more decisive role, as the presumable basis for any literacy or literary attempts. On the other hand, both the Fulanis and the Hausas entered at a later period into more or less intensive contact with Europeans, since most of the nations responsible for the European impact on Hausaland introduced the same influences in the Fulani-inhabited areas, as well.

3.2.2   However, two major factors appear to be at the basis of certain crucial differences in the early development of the two literacies and literatures.

So-called Hausaland (or rather, the more or less homogeneous territory inhabited by those who used Hausa as their mother tongue) was a relatively large, compact expanse of territory covering most parts of what are today Nigeria and the Republic of Niger. Hausa settlements also existed outside this homogeneous Hausa-speaking zone, but apart from a few exceptions these were primarily urban (or semi-urban) commercial agglomerations of itinerant petty traders and craftsmen, and not compact territories comprising Hausa villages or towns; it is in this context that we speak of a Hausa diaspora. Fula, on the other hand, also covered larger or smaller areas in West Africa, but none of these sometimes rather extensive and impressive zones of Fula speakers can be entirely presumed to have overshadowed the other zones. These Fula-speaking areas of unequal size and importance were scattered throughout a large section of the West African Savannah Belt, from Senegal to Lake Chad.

From this point of view, the main homogeneous Fula-speaking territories were by no means limited to what is now Nigeria and Niger (although they exist there, as well). This had—at least twice in the brief period of the last few centuries—a limiting effect upon Hausa which was not valid (or only partly valid) for Fula. Both Uthman dan Fodio's Islamic movement and the European-inspired literacy campaigns organized in that area later on affected only an important section of the Fula-speaking community and consequently—unlike the case of Hausa—they were not the sole cultural or ideological factors inciting literary and literacy movements. Conversely, we may say that their impact could never have been so strong as in the case of Hausa.

Another important difference has subsisted in the sphere of the sociolinguistic functions of the two languages, especially beyond the strict borders of their "mother tongue" zones. As the nature of Fula society is rather more introverted, few reports have reached us until now about any possible usage of that language in the function of a lingua franca. As we know from the preceding section, in Hausaland even the greatest Fulani thinkers and ideologists accepted the Hausa language in the function of a lingua franca.

3.2.2.2   On the other hand, however, the Islamic impact and influence appear stronger with respect to Fula; from this point of view, the fact that the Fulanis were at the origin of the Islamic renascence and reform in West Africa may not be altogether a historical chance. The position of the Islamic-based literacy branch within the whole inventory of Fula written texts seems incomparably stronger than that of the Latin script administrative branch, especially if a comparison with analogical conditions of Hausa is attempted. Thus, if Hausa literature were to be analyzed as having originated from three main sources: oral traditions, Islamic literacy and administratively-based literacy, then Fula would appear to be associated primarily with the two former sources, since the administrative branch of literacy, based mainly upon various literacy campaigns in Nigeria, has left few texts and met with only isolated or sporadic acceptance. In fact, apart from several missionary texts, some educational texts printed in Northern Nigeria and attempts connected with the work of the Translation Bureau and the NORLA or Gaskiya to initiate mass literacy in the Roman script, little remains to support the evidence that the Fula community—strong as its literary traditions are—may be shifting to the Roman script, after all.

One may wonder whether the recent literacy campaigns in the Roman script organized efficiently and with cautious linguistic guidance under the sponsorship of UNESCO in the Republic of Niger and in some other West African countries, will bring about a turning-point in this respect.

3.2.3   The tradition of writing Fula in the Arabic script is, however, at least as old as that of Hausa. If we accept the thesis that the origin of this sort of literacy in Hausa may be linked with the Djihadi period and its attempts to reach the broad masses of the population with the Prophet's words, then the origin of a comparable literacy in Fula might well be similar. It appears certain that Uthman dan Fodio himself contributed to its development. His own poem "Allah is the Supreme Master" (known in Fula under the title *Yimre Shehu Usman*) was recorded in Fula by Barth (1857—1858, t. IV, p. 544, and later by Mohamadou Eldridge, 1963). As already stated in the Hausa Section the original of "Siffofin Shehu" (The Attributes of the Shehu) must very probably have been written by the Prophet himself, in his mother tongue, i.e. in Fula. A few traces and verses of the Fula original have survived in the Hausa text, as well as in some texts in the Arabic language. Moreover, the whole family and most relatives, friends and pupils of the great reformer contributed to the development of his sort of religious poetry in Fula: Mohammed Bello, who took over the rule of the Fula empire, and Said dan Bello contributed to it. The latter is also known as the author of one of the first Fula grammars (*Nahawu Fulfulde*). One might wonder to what extent these literary attempts (like the attempts of other, mostly anonymous, authors in this same area) were related to Fula literary efforts originating in other parts of the Fula settlements in West Africa, particularly in the Western branches. Research into Fula literature, and especially such literature outside the Nigeria-Cameroon area, will perhaps explain this. But as such areas as Futa Djallon and Futa Toro have been recently identified (and rightly so) as bastions and bases of Fula literature (Christiane Seydou, 1966, 1967; A. I. Sow, 1965a, b, 1966), then possible links, or at least parallels, cannot be altogether excluded.

Fula literature, and especially poetry, also undoubtedly has deep links with oral traditional poetry. As in the case of Hausa, no exact, strict borderline between oral poetry (and, for Fula, prose must also be added) and the written form of these same genres can be established.

According to Pfeffer (1939, p. 290), the Fula *gimol* (pl. *yimre*) is usually composed of a *daande* (neck), which is, in fact, the introductory part of it, and a *mayo* river, its main part. These oral, and sometimes written, poem-songs manifest some links with pre-Islamic life and culture. There are also *yimre* about men (*gimol wor 'be*) and women (*gimol ro 'be*); most chiefs and heroes have their own *gimol* praise-song, and especially famous warriors of flag-bearers (*lamido*), Many such *yimre* from Adamawa have been recorded or transcribed by P. F. Lacroix (1965), the most famous being the *Gimol Lamido Yola* (The praise-song of the Lamido of Yola). There are also *yimre* about famines (*gimol tshi'e*) and other topics.

Prose exists, too, on the borderline between oral and written literature. While Fula legends (*gisa*) are greatly influenced by Islamic traditions, ist narratives (*habaru*) often reflect not only local history, traditions and culture, but also events of daily life. Other types of Fula narratives, such as *hala* (pl. *halaji*) and *yetshaul* (i.e. what is being told, narrated) are occasionally also recorded in script.

The transitional line between oral traditions and recorded, written literature are very fluid indeed, as most narrators are able to record their speech in the Arabic script, supposedly basing their narratives on more ancient, non-available manuscripts. There are whole groups, families and schools of Fula learned men and authors and the tradition of recording this sort of literature in writing in the Arabic script is still very much alive throughout the major Fula communities and areas of West Africa. As such tendencies prevail in other parts of the Fula diaspora as well, while little original writing in the Roman script exists apart from official administrative literature and textbooks, we might be inclined to believe that the Fula writing community—at least at the present stage of restricted literacy—prefers a literacy based on the Arabic script. Much research, however, needs to be done, not only in order to record, transcribe and publish such texts, but also to discern the personalities of the authors of this literature.

From this point of view, a substantial part of Fula literature still remains to be analyzed, especially since so few points of contact with the impact of Europe have developed. This was also one of the reasons why our remarks concerning it have been limited to only certain points of comparison with Hausa. Undoubtedly, the wealth of existing Fula literature would deserve such a complex analysis in future. The coexistence of the older generation of religiously-based Fula literates and the relatively younger generation of scholars which is maintaining the best Fula traditions, but not ignoring the positive features of the European impact (such as M. Hampate Ba, Amadou Seydou and many others), will undoubtedly facilitate such a task.

VIII. OLD BANTU LITERATURE

0. Introduction

From the linguistic viewpoint, the Bantu population comprises the blacks of Central, East and South Africa (approximately south of a dermacation line which would run from the Gulf of Guinea along the northern frontier of the Congo and the southern border of Somaliland). These peoples speak Bantu languages (the term is derived from the word *ba-ntu* meaning "people", the singular being *mu-ntu* "man"). Bantu is a linguistic term, not an ethnographical or anthropological one, and consequently we cannot speak of a Bantu race. From the anthropological standpoint, there are considerable differences between the various Bantu tribes. The Pokomo of Kenya, for instance, are short and strong, the Herero of Southwest Africa are tall and thin, the Zulu of Natal (Republic of South Africa), are equally tall, often even taller, but slimmer, etc. Furthermore, the skin colour differs, ranging from dark brown to bronze or copper tints. The expression "Red Kaffirs", i.e. the Xhosa Kaffirs of the Cape Province of the Republic of South Africa, is not related to skin colour, but to the painting of the skin with red ochre for the sake of hygiene. Apart from these, there are peoples who are intermixed with Europeans, Hamites, Arabs, Bushmen, Hottentots and Pygmies, which shows up both in their bodily construction (mainly, shape of the head) and in their skin colour.

The population speaking Bantu languages in almost one-half the total area of the African continent is composed of a large number of tribes, nationalities and nations. Most important among these are the Douala and Yaoundé in southern Cameroon; the Congo, Luba, Lunda, Mongo and Ngala in the Congo; the Ruanda and Rundi in Rwanda and Burundi; the Ganda, Nyoro and Toro in Uganda; the Kikuyu, Kamba and Pokomo in Kenya; the Sukuma, Zarama and Kondo in Tanzania; the Bemba, Lamba, Tonga, Ila (Mashukulumbwe) and Lozi in Zambia; the Yao, Muku, Chewa and Nyanja in Mozambique; the Shona and Ndebele (Matabele) in Rhodesia; the Mbunda, Chokwe and Lwena in Angola; the Kwanyama, Ndongo and Herero in Namibia; the Tswana in Botswana; the Venda, Basuto, Zulu and Xhosa in South Africa; the Basuto in Lesotho and the Swazi in Ngwane. About eight hundred languages and over two hundred dialects are spoken by these peoples.

The Bantu languages are harmonious and euphonic. All of them have the same grammatical structure, their differences being similar to those existing among the Slavonic languages. Each noun belongs to one of the twenty-five classes, according to the form of its class prefix which usually distinguishes the singular from the plural and its meaning.

The class of human beings has the class prefix *omu-, mu-, m-, n-*, and in the plural form *ova-, ba-, wa-, a-*. The class of things and languages has the class prefix *otyi-, isi-, chi-, ki-, se-*, or *lu-* in the singular.

It is strangely paradoxical that one Bantu-speaking person usually cannot understand another who speaks a different, perhaps even neighbouring, language, but he may learn two or three Bantu languages (e.g. a Kikuyu in Kenya may learn Kamba and Swahili). The oral tradition has been common to all Bantu (and, of course, other Black African) tribes, nationalities and nations. It is difficult to say which existed earlier—poetry or prose—as poetry was very frequently unrhymed. The only criterion might be derived from the distinction between that which was spoken and recited and that which was sung.

But even here we can ascertain that some folk-tales were both recited and sung. The following distinction may have general validity: prose includes folk-tales (i.e. fairy-tales, fables and myths, popular sayings, proverbs, sagas, chronicles, historical and biographical stories, novels, orations, etc.), while poetry comprises legends, eposes and eulogies, dynastic, warrior and pastoral poems, elegies, lyrical poems and songs, etc.

According to W. H. Whiteley, the Kamba in Kenya use special criterion, distinguishing between *mbano*—quite improbable stories—and *ngewa*—those containing at least some truth. In Cameroon, an "ordinary speech" is distinguished from a "deliberate speech" (i.e. oration) and from "artificial speech" (i.e. rhymed prose which is not sung).

James R. Sutherland (quoted by Whiteley) says that the evolution of prose almost always lags behind that of poetry. Even though we might object to this opinion, we must admit that Negro writing has had a longer tradition in poetry than in prose and that this is certainly no exceptional case.

It is interesting and characteristic that historical traditions, as frequently handed down in poetical forms (legends, eposes and eulogies, as well as dynastic, warrior and pastoral poems) occurred especially in those African regions where large, strong or well-organized states existed, e.g. in Rwanda, Uganda, Kenya-Tanganyika-Zanzibar (under Arab political, religious and cultural influences), and South Africa and, naturally, West Africa. Eulogies and dynastic poems existed particularly in Rwanda, some parts of Uganda, Bechuanaland, Zululand and elsewhere. Strangely enough, there has never been any mention of eulogies from the great medieval kingdom of Monomotapa, which was situated in Southeast Africa.

1. Rwanda

As society was divided into three groups, three analogical poetic genres originated: dynastic, warrior and pastoral. The dynastic poet *umusizi* composed eulogies (*bísigo*) on the ruler and his dynasty. According to common belief, the first poets appeared in the year 1400—these were the tribesmen of the Sing clan. Later poets came from other clans. The term *umusizi* does not distinguish between poet-composers and poet-reciters, i.e. those reciting a poet's poems from memory.

The kings of Rwanda formed (the date is unknown) the official Association of Dynastic Poets, *Umútwé w'Ábásizi*, i.e. "The Army of Dynastic Poets" to which only recognized amilies of poets were appointed. At first, the hereditary appointment was restricted to the Sing clan but later (about 1790) the most merited poets were admitted. Each family in the Association had a permanent representative at the royal court, who recited at least his own family's poems and was present in order to entertain the king, should he wish to listen. If any family were in a position to send a gifted poet-composer to the court, its reputation and material advantages increased. The composer's descendants, in attempting to immortalize their ancestor, passed his poems on from one generation to another. Concern for the family's prestige was important also because the common law of the court considered this function hereditary, which meant that it was exempt from the competence of the civil chief and free from the requirements of slave labour and taxation.

Under King Yuhi V. Musing (1897—1931), nine representatives "worked" in regular monthly turns at the court. Apart from these official poets, many unofficial reciters also appeared there.

The Association of Dynastic Poets was headed by Intébé y' Ábásizi, "the president of dynastic poets", a poet-composer whose duty was to obtain a particular poem for a certain ceremony, or in support of or in order to suppress a discussion on a traditional subject. If neither the president nor the poets were able to acquire the complete text in question within a particular month, they had to indicate a poet or reciter who was known to have the required poem and the latter was rapidly summoned and introduced to the king.

All poems were dedicated exclusively to the king who heard them as their first listener. Contests were organized and prizes awarded at special sessions in the presence of the king. Thus, the spirit of competition was enhanced; for one poem the composer was given one cow as an incentive for the "king's thinker" or *Intití z' Úmwami*. This "literary encouragement" might sometimes consist of as much as ten head of cattle. This was the case of the composer Nyakayonga, when he recited his poem "To Multiply through Children Pleases Parents" (*Úkwibyara guttera abábyeyi ineza*) at the inaugural ceremony of the new King, Mútara II Rwogera (1825—1853).

According to common law, reciters, both members of the poets' families and independent "amateurs", were exempt from the obligation of slave labour imposed by the civil authorities. It was often sufficient for a reciter to learn a few poems by heart to be declared "the crown's servant".

Schools of recitation. The patriarchal father ruled his family of poet-composers and was, in fact, a local deputy of the president of dynastic poets. The children in such families had to learn poems by heart from their earliest childhood. Together with their fathers they attended regularly, several times a month, sessions presided over by the patriarchal father. These recitation sessions took place in the open, either in the afternoon or as "poetic evenings". Those children who could successfully recite poems, standing before the invited visitors, were given a cow from their father's herd as a reward and encouragement.

The duty of this school of recitation was to preserve the word-by-word rendition of all poems and thereby prevent them from being forgotten. This was at that time the best indirect and most effective method of protecting these poems from text alterations, since written records were unknown.

The Association of Dynastic Poets, one of the most meritorious social organizations and oldest "literary" institutions maintaining the old traditions and supported by all of Rwanda's rulers, ceased to exist under Mútara III Rudahigwa more than forty years ago. The new generation of chiefs regarded poets as "narrators of old fables", which fact helped to eliminate the function of reciter. This process was also influenced by modern thought emanating from Europe. Another reason for this was that the youth were no longer interested in ancient poems and they refused to learn them by heart. The old poets and reciters had died off, particularly during the famine of 1940—1945. Twelve poets died at that time and the repertoires of three of them were never recorded. The last three poets died in 1945—1946, thus bringing to an end the famous era of dynastic poets. Segatwa, an old reciter from Rwanda's Bufundu Province, said melancholically in 1946 (according to Kagame) that no new poems would henceforth be composed.

In 1936, Mútara III Rudahigwa founded "The Treasury of Editions" and ordered all the remaining poets and reciters to dictate all the preserved poems to specially commissioned officials. In this way, one hundred-and-seventy-six complete and fragmentary poems by fifty-two known and fourteen unknown poets and reciters were recorded. But the King's order obviously came too late; about forty-two poems having great historical value had been irretrievably lost.

On that occasion all poems but one were recited before the king in the customary manner. Only one of these poems was missing, due to the fact that Mútara III was only informed about the existence of the poem (*Ndabukire Immana yunamuye u Rwands*) (I Congratulate God on Advancing Rwanda) much later. Its text was, however, recorded. The poet Sekaráma (c. middle of the 19th century) had at first refused to dictate the poem before it was recited to the king. Finally he agreed, after being assured that no one would know about it before his recitation at court. This advance recording was a stroke of good luck, for the old poet died before being able to visit the court.

Classification of Poems. The original dynastic poems were called *vinyeto:* their etymological meaning can no longer be explained. These short poems, which did not exceed ten verses, were dedicated by the poets to individual rulers. This was the practice until the 16th century. Under Ruganza II Ndoli (about 1580), a new type of dynastic poem originated which was preserved until recent times. Nyírarumága, an adoptive queen-mother of the Sing clan, established this new type by composing the first two poems. According to the Secret Code of the Rwanda Dynasty, an orphan king was not allowed to ascend the throne. As Ruganza II was an orphan—his mother, together with the whole royal family, had died—Nyírárumága was appointed his adoptive queen-mother.

The new type of dynastic poems, *bísigo* (sing. *gísigo*), contained 1) an introduction or explanation—*intéruro*, 2) a core, either *impakanizi, ibyânzu* or *ikobyo* according to its form, and 3) a conclusion incorporating the poet's traditional prayer, *umusayuko*. The introduction often mentions the recent or heroic deeds of some of the older kings.

Bísigo containing *impakanizi* (refrains) mention briefly the history of all members of the dynasty in chronological order. The last strophe is devoted to the king presently in power, who is lauded in the poem. Individual strophes are separated by an *impakanizi* refrain which is regularly repeated at the beginning of each strophe.

The *impakanizi* form also appears in pastoral poetry. In this case it comprises 1) a collective eulogy of a herd in all strophes, 2) the last line of the refrain closing all strophes of the poem and devoted to the same cow, the queen of the herd, 3) the second strophe of the poem extended by one verse.

In *bísigo* containing *ibyânzu* (refrains), the strophes are separated—as in the preceding type—by refrains called *ibyânzu*. The difference is that the history of the kings is not arranged chronologically. The poet mentions the history of one or several kings, according to his own choice.

Bísigo containing *ikobyo* have neither separate verses nor refrains. They were written continuously, which fact is implicit in the word *ikobyo* itself. These poetic works consist of congratulations to the king. This form of poems was frequently to be found in satires.

Among the most significant and prolific poets were Máguta (17th century), Bagorozi (beginning of the 18th century). Musare (middle of the 18th century), Semidorogo and Mutsinzi (end of the 18th century), Bamenya and Bikwakwanya (first quarter of the 19th century), Sekaráma and Munyanganzo (middle of the 19th century).

Semidorogo dedicated an intriguing poem to Míbambwe III Sentâby (about 1790—1795) entitled "A King is not a Man" (*Umwami si umuntu*). The work, with its one hundred and fourteen verses, is a categorical epic about the king, his rights, duties and privileges. In it, the poet summarizes all the known traditions and explains the traditional doctrine. Following the recitations of this poem. Semidorogo was sharply criticized for the name of the poem, which could be interpreted as "the King is inhuman" or "the King does not behave properly". In order to justify himself, the poet wrote a new work, an apology (its title is no longer known) in which he defends himself: "I said the King is not... if it is not so, let anyone persuade me and I shall risk my cattle... I stated that I could not be blamed for it: I can only be instructed by wiser people". In the second poem, a fragment of forty lines, Semidorogo defends and justifies the title of the first poem, which was considered ambiguous by some.

2. South Africa

In South Africa, eulogies (in Tswana, *mabôko*—sing. *lebôko*, from the verb *bôka* "to praise someone in poems"; in Zulu, *izibongo*—sing. *isibongo*) are a kind of traditional literature occurring among nearly all tribes, nationalities and nations, e.g. the Tswana, Zulu, Basuto and Xhosa. These eulogies are devoted to rulers (chiefs), famous warriors, ordinary men and women, tribes, clans, domestic animals—in particular cattle, beasts of prey, birds, insects, harvests, trees, rivers, mountains, augural bones, hunting, etc. There are also modern eulogies on schools, trains, railway stations, bicycles and other commonplace things.

The ancestors of the present-day Tswana migrated to South Africa from the north in about 1500 and settled in the south-western region of today's Transvaal. These were the Rolonga, Hurucha, Kwena and Kgatla, who were later split up into independent chiefdoms. In the 18th century, these tribes started migrating to new locations (which, with a few exceptions, were in the territory of present-day Botswana). The local Bantu tribes and Bushmen (Sarwos) who had lived there were either "peacefully" incorporated, or else defeated and dominated. The Tswana tribe of Kwenas—called "Sechele's Kwenas" from the name of their famous chief, Sechele—was split into three parts in the middle of the 18th century; the Kwena remained in their territory, the Ngwaketse migrated to the south and the Ngwata went north. The Kgatla—known as "Kgafela's Kgatlas" from the name of their great chief, Kgafela—migrated to the western Transvaal. During the first quarter of the 19th century, all four Tswana tribes were attacked in Bechuanaland by the looting Mantasi hordes (1822—1823) as well as by the Ndebele and Matabele, i.e. the Zulus who had fled from Zululand under the reign of Shaka. Led by Mzilikazi, they occupied the western Transvaal. For several years, the Ndebele ruled despotically carrying out plundering forays into Bechuanaland. In 1837, the Transvaal was invaded by the Boers who imposed slave labour on the population. In 1852, the Boers attacked Sechele's Kwenas under the pretext that the Kwena had refused to hand over a rebellious chief who had fled to them, asking for asylum. These attacks by the Zulus (under Shaka, who ruled from 1816 to 1828) and the Boers provoked the confused migrations of many tribes in South Africa. The Boers used the Kgatla as "allies" in their later battles (after 1854) and even compelled them to participate in the Boer War (1899—1902).

All these historical events can clearly be seen in the eulogies of all four Tswana tribes. Moreover, allusions are made to British interventions into tribal and intertribal disputes, as well as to European influence, the introduction of guns and horses in the army, etc. An increased usage of foreign—Afrikaans, rather than English—expressions may be observed as well.

The Tswana chiefs had their professional bards (poets and reciters at the same time) who composed eulogies to them and their herds and recited ancient traditional poems, as well. Such a bard—*mmôki*—served his chief not only out of feelings of loyalty or to further his personal reputation, but also—and mainly—to earn a reward—a cow, bull, sheep, gun or some other thing. He usually added a special request for such remuneration to his poem.

Formerly, "morning serenades" were organized at the chief's hut but today the eulogists attend public meetings—*kgotla*. Before or after the meeting, the poets present themselves successively to recite their eulogies as loudly and quickly as they can. They also appear at wedding parties to praise each participant and obtain the highest possible remuneration.

The most propitious occasions for them are celebrations of important events in the life of a tribe, such as a new chief's inauguration, the arrival of his significant European visitors, etc. The poems recited on such occasions are usually of ancient origin and laud either the chief or some of his ancestors. Apart from these, totally or partly new poems are presented celebrating some extraordinary event. Original eulogies are the property of the author; therefore no other person has the right to recite them at tribal gatherings Others may recite eulogies which they have learnt either directly or indirectly from composers now dead or who were long forgotten. Creative solidarity exists in this sphere as well: The reciter's rights are respected; therefore, no other reciter knowing those poems would think of reciting them in public. Usually only a few people can understand these works, but everybody listens carefully, applauds enthusiastically and calls *"pula!"* (meaning "rain"—an expression of the highest appreciation).

The former eulogists improvised their poems and repeated them till they could recite them perfectly by heart. Thus, the tradition of oral rendition, with poems being passed on from poets to reciters and listeners, has preserved for subsequent generations large numbers of ancient poems (often in abbreviated versions), although the composers' names usually have been forgotten. Today's poets, most of whom are literate, enjoy an advantage over their predecessors: they can write, adapt and refine their poems before learning them by heart. Incidentally, no *mmôki* reads his verse publicly from a manuscript. The eulogies of the Tswana rulers of the four above-mentioned tribes have been preserved from the beginning of the 18th century almost without interruption down to the 1930's.

The lower social groups of the Tswana (and Zulu, etc.) society usually composed their own eulogies—on the author himself, on his own cattle, etc. This was sometimes done by the chiefs themselves. In olden times, boys undergoing *bogwera* initiation ceremonies (before they were included in a group of their own age) had to compose *leina* (i.e. words, speeches, eulogies). Today, such initiation ceremonies are no longer practised and consequently also the boys' self-eulogies no longer exist. As intertribal disputes and conflicts have died out, there is no longer any major incentive for composing eulogies. Instead, a new type of eulogy connected with work in the South African mines has evolved. It provides a new opportunity for the expression of self-praise, mainly in pubs (though this is not a generally shared custom).

The themes of these modern eulogies deal with those events in which the ruler has played an important role. Other members of his family and the tribe's history are also referred to. In olden times, the main themes were intertribal wars and the praising of great chiefs (Khama, Bathwen, Lentswe, Chekedi, Sechele, et al.). Although these eulogies were usual, the ruler's behaviour was sometimes criticized overtly or covertly (e.g. Chekedi, Molefo, et al.). The events evoked in modern eulogies have to do with rebellious members of the tribe, intertribal border disputes, relations with the British administration or hunting expeditions.

If one compares these new poems with the older ones, one will see that the former are much lengthier. The longer ago the chief ruled, the shorter is the eulogy on him. Does this imply that the structure of such poems has changed, or that the ancient poets were sparing of laudatory words? Neither one nor the other. The reason is simple. The old poems gradually lost their length and content, as they could be retained only in people's memories, while the new poets can dictate or write their poems themselves.

The Bantu (including the Tswana) consider the eulogy to be "the highest product of their literary art". What is most significant in these poems—their content, language, poetry or style? The Tswana appreciate most their content and language. What is said, they feel, matters more than how it is said, which means that "poetical beauty" ranks only third. This is relevant, as the Tswana regard eulogies as a basic source of historical information.

Do eulogies possess a special poetic form? A certain Tswana teacher writes that there is no prosody, no rhyme, no metre, no strophe in the pure original form of Tswana poetry and that it should not be denoted as poetry. His judgement is not relevant, however, as this teacher of languages was strongly influenced by the English conception of poetry.

G. P. Lestrade (*Bantu Eulogies*, 1935) proves that Tswana (and Zulu) eulogies are clearly distinguishable from normal prose by their specific features: 1) dynamic stress (metrical rhythm), 2) parallelism, 3) chiasmus (cross parallelism), 4) "linking".

1) Each word has a dynamic stress on the next to the last syllable (this is where the normal stress falls in all South and East African Bantu languages); apart from it, the next to the last syllable of certain words (i.e. of the last word of the verse) has a special stress followed by a pause. Thus, the whole poem is divided into short phrases (verses recited in one breath). The listener perceives this as an imposing rhythm. Short phrases, later written as individual verses, mostly contained three or four words (and sometime more), so that poets were bound by the number of words (just as European poets are bound by the number of syllables in the pentameter or alexandrine).

2) Parallelism (mutual similarity) occurs in two successive verses, the first halves of which are identical, while their second halves are similar.

3) Chiasmus (cross parallelism) in two successive verses means that the first half (or first word) of the verse is identical with the second half (or last word) of the second verse.

4) So-called "linking" means that the second half of the first verse is identical with the first half of the second verse.

Another characteristic is the occurence of numerous metaphors, parables and similes, etc. with historical allusions and archaic expressions which have complicated translation and interpretation but allegedly confirm linguistic richness and inventiveness.

The themes and characteristics of Zulu, Bantu and Xhosa eulogies are similar to those of the Tswana. The only difference is that Zulu eulogies appeared as late as during the reign of Shaka, i.e. at the beginning of the 19th century. In addition to the eulogies, there are rich folk legends about Shaka, collected by the Basuto teacher and writer Thomas Mofolo. Legends were later replaced by historical novels.

3. East Africa

It is often asserted that the Swahili are the only Bantu-speaking people of East Africa having a long (approximately three-hundred-year) tradition in poetry. To confirm, deny or generalize this requires an explanation of the expression "Swahili". Who are these people?

Arabs (from Yemen, Hadhramaut and Oman) and Persians (from the vicinity of Shiraz) migrated to East Africa from the 7th century on, and gradually came to dominate nearly the whole East African coast. All the coastal inhabitants from Lamu to Lindi, who spoke their own Bantu language (or languages), were called by the Arabs *Sawáhilí* (i.e. "coastal inhabitants"). The denomination *Mswahili* (pl. *Waswahili*) originally had only a general caste of coastal Negroes (mostly intermixed with Arabs and Persians) who became Moslems and were allowed to participate in retail trade. They were called *Wastaarabu* ("Arabized", i.e. "civilized people") or *Waungwana* (i.e. "free") in contrast to the others, *Watumwa* ("slaves") or *Washenzi* ("barbarians", "savages", "infidels"), as the inhabitants of the interior were called by the coastal people, though the former were often better educated and nobler than the latter. (*Shenzi* is derived from the Persian word *Zandjee,* meaning "Negro" in general). The members of this Swahili caste even denied their Negro origin and called themselves *Waarabu* (Arabs), regarding themselves as Arabs and adopting the Arab way of living. Much later (perhaps in the 18th or 19th century), the name *"Swahili"* was used to denote the inhabitants of certain towns and villages scattered along the East African coast from Mogadiscio in Somaliland down to northern Mozambique. The same was true of the Negro inhabitants of coastal and insular towns and villages dominated by the Persians (from Shiraz, hence the Swahili name *Washirazi,* i.e. "people from Shiraz"). In an effort to show their nobler origin, the Negroes started to call themselves *Washirazi* and they still regard themselves as their descendants.

Little is known about the origin of the Swahili language, Kiswahili, or its date. All we know is that the coastal inhabitants spoke the so-called "coastal language", Kimrima, a few words of which have been preserved. This language, which became intermixed with the languages of other coastal Bantu tribes, later became the basis of Tanganyikan Swahili, which differs from the standard language by its lower percentage of Arabic words. The population of the coast, islands and interior belonged to various Bantu tribes and spoke different Bantu languages. Later (before the 16th century), a common language gradually evolved from several coastal Bantu languages and from Arabic. The Bantu grammatical structure was essentially preserved, but half the vocabulary was Arabic. In the 16th or 17th century, a few cultural centres originated, each of them dominated by a certain language (dialect). The dialect of Zanzibar, Kiunguja, most strongly influenced by Arabic, became the basis of a commercial language. The dialect of Lamu, Kiamu, and that of Pate, Kipate, became the basis of a poetic language. The dialect of Mombasa, Kimwita, became the basis of a prosaic language, etc. Originally, Swahili was written in the Arabic script, later in the Swahili-Arabic script. But the spreading of Swahili as a means of communication (lingua franca) for ignoble reasons—as frequently happens— began only in the 16th century, as the result of the activities of Arab and Arab-Swahili merchants and slave-traders who searched for slaves and ivory in the interior of East Africa. Arab culture and civilization was thus spread by the Koran, as well as by force. Merchants and slave-traders brought the Swahili dialect of Zanzibar to large territories of East Africa and to the eastern region of Congo-Kinshasa (now Zaire), where it later became an official language, Kingwana ("the language of a free people"), under Belgian rule.

The Arabs spread the language, but also simplified and deformed it. Swahili differs from most other Bantu languages in its prefixes, the number of classes and tenses, the superfluous usage of Arabic loanwords—which amount at present to about 25 %—incorrect accents, etc. New loanwords came from Persian, Hindi, Gudjarati, Portuguese, French, German, Turkish and, in the recent period, from English. The standard Swahili language was constituted in the second half of the 19th century, as an amalgamation of the dialects of Zanzibar, Mombasa and Lamu. It began to be written in Roman characters. This script was more suitable because Swahili has five vowels (a, e, i, o, u), while the Arabic script has only three (a, i, u), which made Swahili texts less comprehensible. Moreover, one Arabic character, for example, *b*, might denote in Swahili the consonant *b* or *p*, or a group of two consonants, *mb, mp, bw* or a group of three consonants, *mbw, mpw:* another example: the Arabic character *g* might mean in Swahili *j, nj, ng, ng', ny,* etc. The Swahili *ny* could be written in the Arabic script as *g, k, q* or *y*. The Swahili *ng* could be written as *g, ġ* (ghain), *k, q,* etc. The transliteration into modern Swahili of all legends, poems and chronicles originally in the Arabic script was very difficult and could not succeed without the assistance of local experts. There are still hundreds of Swahili poems in European libraries which cannot be interpreted. Their true meaning cannot be discerned from the context, and each poem relates to a certain historical situation which can hardly be reconstructed, even by East African experts.

Today, Swahili is a widespread language spoken by 30 to 50 million people in vast areas of East and Central Africa. It is the official language and the language of instruction in Tanzania, as well as the official language in the eastern part of Zaïre. Moreover, it serves as a means of communication in Kenya, Uganda, Rwanda, Burundi, Malawi, southern Mozambique, Zambia, Madagascar, the Comoro Islands and the southern coastal region of Somalia.

From earliest times, Arab seamen and merchants were in constant contact with the East African coast. Arabs from Yemen, Hadhramaut and Oman especially introduced religious poems and acquainted the East African inhabitants with them. Lyndon Harries stressed the role of the Saiyids—the religious leaders—who directed all education and established the tradition of Swahili versification.

The members of the Saiyid family, who moved from Hadhramaut to East Africa, were Arabs who wrote both in Arabic and Swahili. They introduced homiletic and didactic poems written in Arabic, which were later paraphrased into Swahili. These usually included the Arabic interlinear version, the meaning and content of which was not always identical with the Swahili version. Poems of this kind were complemented by a freer translation of popular Islamic tales describing events from the life of the prophet Mohammed and mystical legends which bordered on both fact and fiction.

"Although Swahili poetry derives from Arabic poetry, in many respects there are fundamental differences. It cannot properly be compared with Arabic poetry, for it is *sui generis*. The Arabists may recognize the obvious connexion between Swahili poetry and Arabic poetry, especially in much of its subject-matter, but Swahili poetry cannot be considered as an extension of Arabic poetry or even as a modification of it... From the amalgam of two traditions we find in Swahili poetry a positive contribution to literature. In early literature, epic poetry is of particular interest, not least because in this medium

the Swahili poet was able to move freely away from the imitation of Arabian models...
Although it was, and still is, possible for Swahili versification to degenerate into a clever
trick of easy rhyming, at its best it has qualities that are truly poetic" (Lyndon Harries,
1962, p. 3).

Harries overestimates the independence of the Swahili poetical tradition, since this is
based completely upon Arabic models and was influenced by Islam up to the end of the
19th century. He remarks that religion required the Swahili to use those means of
expression which originated in Islam. The Arab and Islamic sense and way of life have
always been a matter of prestige and pride for the orthodox coastal Swahili, who identified
himself with the Arabic. In many respects, there are no fundamental differences between
Swahili and Arabic poetry; there is only one difference—namely, that the Swahili poet
could handle Arabic subject-matter independently and freely. Otherwise, he was bound
by all the prosodic forms of Arabic poetry:

1) The form of the strophe: mostly quatrains, eight-verse strophes, five-verse strophes
called *tachmís,* or acrostichons—a poem whose first three verses of each strophe began with
the same letter (there were 28 letters in the alphabet), while the fourth verse was free.
This was a part of Moslem education which was aimed at teaching believers the Arabic
language and enabling them to read the Koran.

2) The number of syllables: as in Arabic, the length of the vowel did not matter. The
main accent in Swahili usually falls on the next to the last syllable, secondary accents
on the second, fourth, or sixth, etc. syllable, counting from the main accent, but there
was no unified or regular metric system.

3) The rhyme was monosyllabic (i.e. a vowel and a consonant) in a *aaab, xxxb,* quatrain
etc., or *ab ab ab bc* (if there was a caesura in the middle of the verse and rhyme preceding
the caesura).

4) According to the Old Arabian and Old Persian custom, the melody was called
maqámát. Ten types of this melody were used in Mombasa, Malindi and Lamu: Jirka,
Rasit, Rasidi, Bayat, Sika, Hijaz, Hijaz Kar, Nawandi, Duka and Swaba. Like Arabic
poems, Swahili poems were also usually sung.

Lyndon Harries writes about melody as follows: "No doubt, the modern popularity
of these Arabian tunes is partly due to modern Egyptian influence and is found only
among the Swahili élite, but it is generally held that poems with Arabian influence,
especially the epics, have always been sung to Arabian tunes" (Lyndon Harries, 1962,
p. 12). There is sufficient evidence to the effect that the subjects of Swahili poetry were
mostly taken over from Arabian religious history. One cannot speak of an extension of
Arabian poetry, but rather of a modification of it.

It would be incorrect to speak of a degeneration of Swahili poetry. It is true that its
climax was reached long ago; subsequently, its form deteriorated and stagnation followed.
Its poets lacked inventiveness, both with respect to subjects (they returned to the old ones)
and prosodic forms. But this decline was compensated for by the stereotype form of skilful
and facile rhyming. Until the end of the 19th century, Swahili literature was never

connected with the common people. It was written for a small stratum of the denationalized élite and was entirely incomprehensible to the illiterate majority of the population, who were treated as slaves. Consequently, it did not possess any inseminating influence and was not exposed to public criticism. Its prestige in its own cultural milieu was almost nil. Even though it expressed certain moral values, creating a sense of pride and increasing the prestige of Islamic culture, it was never concerned with folk culture or with the majority of the Bantu population. Swahili literature has acquired an official function, that of an adjunct to Arab politics, religion and education, helping to corroborate contemporary efforts to make East Africa Arabian and Islamic. As its influence has been restricted to a narrow caste of the population, it has developed into a purely provincial literature. Its crisis has resulted from the fact that it has never pursued a path toward truth and freedom any different from that determined for it originally in the spheres of politics, history and religion. Its indifference to humanism, to the fight against slavery, the struggle for justice, progress, truth, freedom and a better life for mankind has prevented it from becoming—and indeed it could not become—a national literature.

The oldest known and still preserved Swahili manuscript is *Utendi wa Tambuka* (Epos of Tambuka), an epic poem written in Pate, in 1728, for Sultan Laiti Nabhani. It is to be found in the Hamburg University Library. Another poem, *Al-Hamziyah*, written by Saiyid Aidarus in 1749, is an interlinear Swahili version of the Arabic poem *Umm al-Qura* (Mother of Cities), composed by Muhammad ibn Said Al-Busiri. It is to be found in the Library of the School of Oriental and African Studies, London. Other members of the Saiyid family included Saiyid Abdallah bin Ali bin Násir (1720—1820), the author of *The Epos of Self-discovery,* and Saiyid Abu Bakr bin Abd ar-Rahman, known as Saiyid Mansab, the author of many religious poems in Swahili. The latter was born in Lamu, probably in 1828, and studied law and theology in Mecca and Hadhramaut. Muhammad bin Abubakar bin Umar al-Bakari, known as Muhammad Kijuma, wrote, on the basis of oral traditions, *Utendi wa Liyongo Fumo* (The Epos of King Liyongo, 1913), describing legends and heroic deeds in East Africa.

As concerns Swahili prosodic forms, the most frequent form used is epos (in the north, it is called *utendi*—pl. *tendi*, in the south, *utenzi*—pl. *tenzi*) and sometimes also *hadithi*. The latter has four verses (*vipande*—sing. *kipande*), the first three of which are rhymed, while the fourth has a free rhyme which is repeated throughout the whole poem, e.g. *aaab, xxxb*, etc. This form of *tendi* is used in that country for poems preserved through oral tradition (*The Epos of King Liyongo*) or for those describing historical events, wars, riots (the Majimaji riot in 1905), etc.

Tendi can be compared to three kinds of Arabic legends. *Maghází* literature (*maghází* means raids) consists of narratives mostly in rhymed prose based partly on historical facts and describing the Prophet Mohammed's fight after his moving (hegira) from Mecca to Medina, particularly in the period of the forceful spreading of Islam. Shorter *tendi* can be compared to *maulidi* writing, dealing with Mohammed's birth and early childhood. *Futúh* writing (*futúh* means conquest) celebrates later Islamic aggressions under the first caliphs. Such *tendi* are not known in Swahili, but they may have existed.

As the *maghází* type of literature is well known, there is no doubt that long Swahili *tendi* (usually having over five thousand verses) originated directly from these Arabic legends, though the poetic presentation of the subject was purely Swahili. Long eposes were originally sung and accompanied by music in public, as a sort of entertainment as well as education of the illiterate masses. They also served the purpose of instructing young members of Islamic society on religion practices. They included frequent passages in which the narrator asked his listeners to join in reciting verses from the Koran.

Although there exist many Arabian versions of various eposes such as *The Epos of Ras al-Ghuli*, their tales differ and are also not identical in the Swahili adaptations. The Swahili *Epos of Ras al-Ghuli* presents a picturesque description of the adventurous (mostly military) experiences of the Prophet's companions who carry out revenge on behalf of Wafari, a desperate Moslem woman whose children were killed by an infidel (i.e. non-Moslem) sultan, the cursed Ras al-Ghuli.

One of the historical—or rather legendary—eposes dealing with African history is *The Epos of King Liyongo*, which originated probably between the 12th and 14th centuries in the territory of Kenya. But it was set down in writing on the basis of oral traditions only in 1913. It can be compared to the *Legend of King Arthur*, the *Saga of Siegfried* or the French *chansons de geste*. It is not without a mythical flavour. It is interesting that the hero's name does not occur in Swahili historical chronicles, but only in songs and poems on the basis of which historical short stories or short stories or short novels were written later. Although there is no historical evidence concerning Liyongo, numerous references to him in poems and prose works seem to suggest that he actually lived. Liyongo, a poet and excellent archer, was said to have come from a royal family which emigrated from Persia and settled at the former mouth of the river Tana less than thirty miles southwest of Lamu (in the present-day northern coastal region of Kenya, near Kipini). The Persian family founded a residence called Shaka (probably Shaaha) and a small estate of the same name, which, in addition to the coastal area, also comprised Pate. Although Liyongo was the oldest son, he could not ascend as ruler after his father, since his mother was not the ruler's first wife. The legitimate ascendant was Liyongo's step-brother, Daud Mringwari. Liyongo suffered from this injustice. He hated his brother and therefore became a robber.

The epos describes him as a man of gigantic stature, a courageous fighter who could put to flight one hundred warriors. No wonder his brother Mringwari, the Sultan of Pate, feared him as a possible usurper of the throne. He arranged Liyongo's marriage to a Galla woman, hoping that Liyongo would follow his wife to the Galla country. But Liyongo soon returned to Shaka. Several times, Mringwari bribed various tribes to kill him, but all his schemes failed. The Sultan organized a dancing party, a *gungu*, where Liyongo got drunk and was then imprisoned. However, he found a way to escape: His food was brought in by Saada, a slave girl. In a song he asked his mother to prepare good food and to bake a loaf of bread containing files for him. The good food was eaten by his guards and Liyongo was given the loaf of bread. The day before his execution, he was allowed to express his last wish. He wanted the musicians to play *gungu* songs in front of the prison. As the music grew louder, Liyongo broke his fetters, overcame the guards and walked out of the prison, causing general panic. Then the Sultan Mringwari prepared another scheme: He invited Liyongo's son, regaled him and promised to give him his own daughter, if Liyongo's son discovered where and how his father could be mortally injured. The son, blinded by the Sultan's promises, deceived his father and killed him, stabbing his navel with a copper dagger. The Sultan was delighted, but he did not keep his word and Liyongo's son—after being stoned—had to flee to his mother in the Galla country.

Swahili poetry belongs to East African history as it reflects the Saiyids' contribution to the cultural and religious life of Moslem society. It comprises a certain amount of oral traditions, which, while not based on historical events, nevertheless form a part of the cultural heritage. Old Swahili poetry never dealt with historical events in East Africa itself, which is most regrettable from the historical viewpoint. It made up for this during the 19th and 20th centuries, but obviously too late for the historians, who by that time had obtained their information from other, more reliable sources. The epos form was suitable for descriptions of historical events, but only in the 19th century did poets begin to use it for describing the East African events—either those experienced by themselves or those narrated to them by their fathers.

Another epos dealing with East African events is *Utendi wa al-Akida* (The Epos of Al-Akida) written by Abdallah bin Masud bin Salim al-Mazrui (1797—1894). This epos described the events of 1837—1875, when Muhammad bin Abdallah bin Mbarak Bakhash-weini (known as al-Akida) was commander (*akida*) of Mombasa, appointed by the Sultan of Zanzibar. In Mombasa he had many enemies, mainly Suud bin Said al-Maamiry, a poet and political party leader who had gone to Zanzibar and slandered Akida before the Sultan. Akida was summoned to justify himself and after his return to Mombasa he took revenge on the local population. The Sultan's vizier came to Mombasa and proclaimed Akida's dismissal. Akida went to Fort Jesus and expelled its garrison. In 1875, the Sultan sent three ships with Arab soldiers to Mombasa. Akida attacked the Sultan's army and ordered Mombasa burned to the ground. But Akida's soldiers were defeated and the commander himself had to take refuge in the fortress. Two British cruisers, the "Rifleman" and the "Nassau", were sent to Mombasa to drive Akida from the fortress. The cruisers began firing and caused great damage. Akida finally capitulated and was taken to the prison of Zanzibar.

Lyndon Harries quotes G.S.P. Freeman-Grenville (in *Swahili Literature and the History and Archeology of the East African Coast*, J.E. African Swahili Committee, No. 28/2, p. 19) as follows: "...the *Utenzi wa al-Akida* is without question a work of first-class historical importance, for it makes clear beyond all shadow of a doubt the connection between poetry and history. It is regrettable that it is out of print. We have not got nearly enough documents of this kind." Lyndon Harries adds: "It is an exaggeration to call the *Utendi wa al-Akida* a work of first-class historical importance. It presents no single fact that is not known from other sources, and, indeed, one must first know the history in order to understand what the poem is all about." (Lyndon Harries, 1962, pp. 128—129). One cannot disagree with this opinion of Harries.

The only genuine Bantu saga—if defined (according to A. Werner) as a collection of legends about the daily life and all the stories of presumably historical heroes—is *Habari za Wakilindi* (The Kilindi Chronicle, 1904), prepared in the Swahili transcription by Abdallah bin Hemedi and published in Magila. This saga deals with the chiefs and rulers of Usambara in the north-eastern region of Tanganyika, and mainly with Mbega, the national hero of Usambara, and his family. The characters are probably historical, but some stories ascribed to them are undoubtedly legendary.

Historical chronicles (or fragments of them), written either in Swahili or in Arabic, have been preserved from Kenya, Tanganyika and the adjoining islands (Pate, Lamu, Pemba, Zanzibar, Kilwa, Kisiwani, etc.). The basic shortcoming of most of these chronicles is that they were written too late—from the 16th to the 19th centuries—so that the majority of them are based on oral tradition. Today, most chronicles indicate only the rulers' genealogy, the length of their reign (which is often omitted) and a few details concerning their lives and rule. It should be noted that the Arab scribes who copied them shortened and adapted these chronicles and were particularly intent on, or commissioned—as in all Islamic countries—to add or invent new legends and odes on the rulers of Arabian or Persian origin, or on those African rulers who regarded themselves as Arabs or Persians. This was done, obviously, at the expense of the historical truth.

The Yao in southern Tanganyika still have a few professional reciters who until recently accepted pupils for training. Their listeners follow attentively the narration of traditional stories interlaced with songs, and join in the critical discussions after such recitations.

IX. BANTU TALES, FABLES AND SHORT STORIES

Negro tales, fables and short stories are remarkable genres in which the black people have achieved indisputable perfection. One cannot deny that this kind of literature, which has been mostly preserved by oral tradition, possesses considerable educative value, for both children and adults.

In addition to their language, all the Bantu peoples have many common, identical customs, manners, habits and also a belief in spirits. The vague idea of God is frequently identified with that of the sky, the Sun, a certain mountain or the forefather of the tribe. They believe in life after death, and think that the spirits of the dead can interfere with all matters of the living. They imagine that the dead depart for the underground world into which the living can penetrate through caves or animals' lairs, for instance, those of porcupines, wild boars, etc. The essential element of the Bantu religion is a belief in reincarnation. The spirits may appear among the living in the form of animals—lions, leopards, crocodiles, snakes, lizards or any other animal or bird—and they may help or harm the living. In their animal form, they are taboo, which means that they must not be molested or killed.

The Zarama (near Dar-es-Salaam) worship and make sacrifices to the family spirits (father, grandfather, mother's uncle) which are called *Makungu,* and also to collective spirits known as *Vinyamkela* (sing. *Kinyamkela*) or *Majini* (sing. *Jini*). *Kinyamkela,* the children's good spirit, is usually invisible, but if he appears, he has only one half of his body—one leg, one arm, one eye and one ear. *Jini* is the adults' evil spirit. Both of them reside in trees.

The Zarama narrate the following story: "A hollow tree, a *kinyamkela's* abode, stood near the village of Mkongole. Two boys from this village were running about the forest. Suddenly they came to the tree from which a bunch of bananas was hanging. They pulled down and ate the bananas and went home. At night, they were awakened by the wild voice of the one-armed, one-legged *Kinyamkela,* who was standing at the door of the hut, shouting: "You have eaten my bananas, so you shall die!" As soon as he said this, there was a downpour of stones, clay and human bones. The boys ran out of the hut to seek shelter, but the stones followed them everywhere. The same thing happened for four successive nights (The *Kinyamkela* probably intended to frighten, rather than to injure them). Then the medicine-man, Kikwilo, decided to settle the matter. He took a gourd, twice seven slices of bread, a hen, some rice, several bananas and went to the *Kinyamkela's* tree. He laid all these things down and said: "The boys are sorry for what they have done. Can you forgive them?" Next night the *Kinyamkela* visited the boys once again and said: "Now it is all right, but it must not happen any more!"

There are also various bloodthirsty monsters, cannibals, ogres, "all-swallowers", etc. in Bantu tales. The ogres are called *Zimwi* by the Swahili, *Amazinu* by the Zulu, *Irimu* by the Kikuyu, *Eimu* by the Kamba, *Edimo* by the Douala, *Madino* by the Basuto, *Esisi* by the Ndongo, *Nkishi* by the Kongo (it is often a monster with several heads), etc. Other monsters usually have the same names as ogres, or some imaginary names. Such a monster is the subject of the following Swahili fairy-tale, *Watoto na zimwi* (The Children and Zimwi): Several girls were gathering shells on a beach. One of them found a nice shell and placed it on a rock so as not to lose it. When returning home, she remembered the shell and asked her companions to go back with her. But they refused, and she had to return alone. Upon arriving at the rock, she saw a *Zimwi* sitting on it. He asked the girl: "What do you want?" "I have left a shell here," answered the girl. "I cannot hear you," said the *Zimwi*. "Come closer to me!" When the girl, came close to the *Zimwi*, she was seized and put into a drum.

Then the *Zimwi* travelled from one village to another, performing concerts at *barazas* (public places) to obtain food and drink. He beat the drum and the imprisoned girl sang to this rhythmic beat. The Zimwi got enough food and drink but he gave nothing to the girl. One day, he arrived at the village where the girl was born. He asked for *pombe* (native beer) in payment for his performance and was promised lots of it. When the girl started singing, her parents recognized her voice. After the concert, the *Zimwi* drank a great deal of beer until he fell asleep. Then the girl's parents opened the drum, freed their daughter and after filling the drum with a poisonous snake, a swarm of bees and biting termites, they closed up the drum again. After a while, they woke up the *Zimwi;* "Strangers have come to listen to your music!" they said. The cannibal raised his drum, but it was silent, although he beat it. So he ran away from the village and opened it. The snake crawled out and bit him, followed by the stinging bees and poisonous termites. And so the *Zimwi* died!

The Zulu, Xhosa and other tales also start with a similar opening scene, but in the Basuto and Xhosa versions the ogre does not become drunk. He is sent to fetch water from a river with a pot which is full of holes, and thus he loses much time. In the meantime, they put a dog, poisonous termites or snakes and toads into his drum. In other versions, the ogre comes home and asks his wife to prepare food. But his wife refuses, saying that "the drum is biting", and so do his daughter and son. The ogre therefore shuts himself in his hut and opens the drum (the bag, in some versions) with the same result. But before he dies, he runs away and plunges his head into a swamp. A tree grows up on that spot. The Basuto, Zulu and Xhosa versions end with a mention of this hollow tree which is equally harmful. If people take honey from it, their hands will stick fast. The same thing happens in a Ronga fairy-tale to women who offend the spirits by entering their sacred grove.

The Swahili tale continues: Where the *Zimwi* dies, a gourd shrub with gigantic fruit grows up. One day, a few boys pass along, admiring the gourds. One of them suggests that they cut them off. The biggest gourd becomes angry and starts attacking the boys. The boys run to a river and there they see a ferryman with a boat. "Be so kind and transport us across the river—we are running away from the gourd!" they shout. The old man awaits no further explanation and transports them across. The boys continue running and arrive at a village whose inhabitants are sitting at the *baraza*. "Hide us from the gourd! The *Zimwi* has transformed himself into it! When he comes rolling in here, cut him into pieces and burn him!"

The villagers comprehend the danger and hide the boys in a remote hut. They have just returned to the *baraza* when the gourd addresses them in a human voice: "Have you seen my fleeing slaves?" Taking their snuff the elders ask: "Who are you looking for? We have not seen anyone." But the gourd says: "I know you have shut them in a remote hut." Then three strong men cut it into pieces and burn it. The ashes are thrown about. Then they release the boys who go quickly home to their parents.

The tales of the Usambara also describe the gourd as an "all-swallowing monster". In one Nirambe tale, the ogre appears in the form of a porcupine. He is killed and buried near the camp-fire. The following day, a gourd grows up there and starts speaking and repeating everything that was said. Finally, he swallows all the inhabitants of the village. The favourite animal in the tales and fables of all Bantu tribes, nationalities and nations is the hare, who plays the role of the clever, shrewd hero. The Swahili call him *Sungura*, the Nyanja *Kalulu*, the Tonga *Sulwe*, the Basuto *Mutlanyana*, etc. For the Basuto, the cleverest animals are the hare and the jackal who are taken over from the Hottentot tales. They are also favoured by the Galla and Somali in Northeast Africa. These nations, however, (mainly the Hottentots) consider the hare a stupid animal and also the chameleon. Another hero is the tortoise or turtle; he is slow, but patient and able to outwit even the elephant, the largest animal of all.

The tortoise-race theme is well-known in East, Central and South Africa. The defeated racer may be the antelope. For the Kamba it is the eagle; for the Bonde, the falcon; for the Kondo, the elephant, etc. These animals are referred to in the masculine gender. Thus: The tortoise and the elephant argued over which of them was the faster runner. The elephant wished to start the race immediately but the tortoise said: "Not today. I am rather tired after a long walk. Will you come tomorrow?" The elephant agreed. They fixed the place of the race and said they would start at sunrise. The tortoise went home and called his wife and children. He spent the whole night gathering his relatives whom he placed at intervals along the race-course. Then he told all of them what to do.

The elephant arrived early in the morning. They greeted each other and started the race. The elephant began trotting at once. After a while he cried: "Where are you?" He thought that the tortoise was far behind him and he was surprised to hear the tortoise's voice in front of him: "I am here!" This was repeated again and again till the elephant finished the race only to discover that the original tortoise was already there awaiting him. And so the elephant was beaten by the wise tortoise.

There is some doubt as to whether these tortoise fables come from Bantu territories. Their origin is said to have been in West Africa, from where they came to the Bantu tribes. But there is no reliable evidence of this assertion. In the Congo, where there are no hares, the nseshi, a small antelope, is regarded as the cleverest animal. African folklore chooses small animals as its heroes, as it is believed that the strongest ones need not necessarily be the cleverest ones. The lion and elephant are considered to be stupid, cruel beasts. The hyena usually represents the worst character. The crocodile is not always evil; he often helps other animals. In the south-eastern Bantu folklore of the Pedi, the Venda and the Zulu in the Republic of South Africa, and of the population of Angola, there are two arch-fellows called *Hlakanyana* and *Hweana*. The former (in Zulu, he is known as *Uhlaka-nyana*) is a very cunning, astute little man the size of a weasel; for this reason he is called *Icakide* (weasel) or *Ucakijana* (little weasel). He resembles the weasel in all respects. Originally it might have been a weasel, corresponding to the other Bantus' hare, but later this fact was probably forgotten and tradition personified it as a man. *Hweana* is *Hlakanyana's* father or creator.

An important role in African fairy-tales is also played by various talismans, possessing supernatural powers and capable of advising their owner in the worst possible situations, and even of turning their owners instantly into any person, animal or object.

When the black American woman writer, who wrote under the name of Joel Chandler Harris, published, more than eighty years ago, her collections of African folk-tales, *Uncle Remus* and *Nights with Uncle Remus,* which are still fairly popular, some experts said that the tales were directly or indirectly taken over from the Amazonian Indians; others affirmed that the Indians had taken them over from the Negroes of Brazil. Finally it was proved that these tales had originated in Africa from where they had been brought by black slaves to America. Simultaneously, it was possible to determine the place of their origin through the "hero" of the tale. While the hare or the antelope prevail in the southern states of America, the spider is the hero of the West Indies, which shows that Bantu Negroes from East Africa and the Congo were brought into the southern states, while the West Indies received West African blacks (the Yoruba and Ibo from Nigeria, the Fante from the Gold Coast, etc.), whose favourite animal was the spider *Ananse*.

Joel Chandler Harris was naturally obliged to adapt African fauna to the American milieu, introducing Brer Rabbit instead of the African hare, Brer Wolf and Brer Fox instead of the African hyena, etc. The usage of such forms as Brer Rabbit or Mrs. Cow for most animals is no innovation, but an ancient African custom. The denomination Brother Hare (*Ndugu Sungura*) or Mr. Leopard (*Bwana Chui*) or Mrs. Cow (*Bibi Ng' ombe*) is in current usage in Swahili, as well as in the other Bantu languages.

Tales about the African "clever hare" can be compared with those of the European "sly fox". Similar folk-tales spread throughout Europe in the 12th and 13th centuries. In this way, the animal epos arose as cyclical poems, which were gradually extended thanks to their popularity. This was how the French *Roman de Renart* or the Low German epos *Reinke Vos* originated. But the essential difference lay in the fact that the European medieval animal epos was essentially a satire on the political, religious and social situation (the Fox was a robbing knight or a clever bourgeois; the Lion, a king; the Donkey, an archbishop, etc.), whereas in Africa folklore never inserted these cryptonyms (allegories) in the animal world. But this opinion could be erroneous and it is possible that folk fables such as those dealing with the clever hare may eventually be developed into an epos, naturally, by some African author.

Among the purely Bantu tales, fables and short stories, one often meets with those whose origin is not African, but rather European or Oriental. However, they are so skilfully adapted to the African situation that their foreign origin is completely disguised. For instance the Swahili collection *Kibaraka* includes the tale about Siyalele and her sisters, in which we can safely recognize our own Cinderella.

We can easily comprehend how European and Oriental tales were taken over by the Africans, especially in modern times. Andersen's, the Grimm brothers' and other European collections of fairy-tales were translated into many other languages. Then an African author or translator knowing European languages modified and adapted these tales, while changing the names, to the African situation, and his new fairy-tale was ready to start circulating throughout the African continent.

The origin of many fairy-tales cannot always be easily determined. "The Magic Mirror, the Magic Carpet and the Water of Life" comes from the Orient; it is difficult to say from which country—India, Persia or Arabia, perhaps. Henri A. Junod in his collection *Chants et contes des Baronga* (Songs and Tales of the Baronga, 1897) published, under the title "The Three Vessels", the same tale which he had discovered in the Congo and in the Ivory Coast. Some versions of this tale suggest that it originated in Central and West Africa. It can briefly be summarized as follows: Three brothers go out into the world. The first of them has a magic mirror, the second has a magic carpet (mat or basket) and the third has the water (elixir) of life. The first brother sees in his mirror a lovely girl with whom all three brothers fall in love. But the girl is dying. So the second brother, using his magic carpet, transports all of them, just in time before the girl's burial. The third brother uses his elixir to raise the girl from the dead. Now the question arises: Which of the brothers has done the most to rescue the girl and which of them should marry her? In the Congolese version, the narrator interrupts his tale and asks his listeners to solve this problem. The solution naturally varies.

If one considers that numerous ancient Bantu tales, fables and short stories (as well as modern ones) have been preserved until today, one feels great respect for those ancient black narrators and their descendants who have preserved these wonderful treasures. It would be incorrect, unjust and unscientific to assert that Bantu (and generally Negro) folklore is more primitive than American, European or Asian folklore from which it differs in character. For a relatively long time, Africa was regarded as a continent without a history. It would be highly inaccurate and insulting to add that that continent also lacked its own mythology and literature, when it is fully apparent that precisely the opposite is true.

X. LITERATURE OF THE CONGO AREA AND RWANDA

1. Literature of the Congo and Zaire

Black African French-written literature does not have a long tradition in Central Africa. Its development started only in the 1940's, in both Congo states, and still later in Chad, Rwanda and the Central African Republic where no national literature has as yet been constituted. Nevertheless, gifted artists are emerging in these countries as well.

Although we shall distinguish between the writers of Zaire and those of the Republic of Congo (Brazzaville), their country of origin is not very relevant to an evaluation of their works. In fact, the authors of the two Congo states have much in common.

Jean Malonga (b. 1907) represents the old generation of writers in the Republic of Congo (Brazzaville). In his novel *Le coeur d'Aryenne* (The Heart of Aryenne, 1954) and in *La Légende de M'foumou Ma Mazono* (The Legend of M'foumou Ma Mazono, 1955), he demonstrated his knowledge of the Congolese countryside and traditions. Descriptions of scenery, love episodes and the praising of agricultural work reflect the influences of folklore. *La Légende* depicts the origin of Malonga's tribe. Ma Mazono's mother was a wealthy noblewoman who loved a slave and fled from her husband to a valley, where she sought the protection of the gods and nature. Her son found later allies in his father's slaves, dethroned his father and ensured a happy life for his tribe.

Antoine-Roger Bolamba (born in 1913 in Bomo) is of Mongo origin. He started his journalistic and literary career in Zaire and became chief editor of the well-known monthly *La Voix du Congolais*. His first collection of poems *Premiers essais* (First Attempts, 1947) shows the strong influence of French Parnassianism. More surprising was his second collection *Esanzo, chants pour mon pays* (Esanzo, Songs for My Country, 1956), which was practically free of any imitation of European examples. The collection took its motifs mainly from tropical nature. Vivid imagery results from his juxtaposition of various concepts. Bolamba is content to find those that suit the general rhythm of his poems and certain effective acoustic details are probably accidental. His range of ideas is rather limited. He repeatedly praises his native country's march towards freedom, but presents this idea in variegated, fantastic images. Apart from French, Bolamba has also used his vernacular language—Mongo. Senghor considered Bolamba a *négritude* poet, but the philosophy and pathos of the Dakar intellectuals are rather remote from Bolamba's way of thinking. He has chosen his own, independent path and only the ideology of post-World War II African nationalism can be said to link him to the *négritude* writers.

The young generation of Zaire writers has for the most part abandoned lyrical patriotism, preferring openly political poetry (e.g. Henri Lopes and A. Tusikama).

The most original and accomplished poet of the Republic of Congo (Brazzaville) is Gérard Felix Tchicaya U Tam'si (born in 1931 in Mpili), who came to France in 1946 to study in Orleans and Paris. He was impressed by Césaire's verses and was influenced by the French Surrealists, as can be seen in his first collection *Le mauvais sang* (Bad Blood, 1955). Very successful also were his following collections: *Feu de brousse* (Bush-Fire, 1957), *A triche-coeur* (A Game of Cheat-Heart, 1960), *Epitomé* (1962), *Le ventre* (The Belly, 1964) and *L'Arc musical* (Bow Harp, 1969). Some of these collections used central symbols derived from the poet's contrasting impressions during his sojourns in Africa and Europe. Apart from the usual praising of nature, one finds in his collections successful love poems and poems celebrating woman's beauty and faithfulness. In his later collections, his poems embark upon bold formal experiments. Like Dylan Thomas, Tchicaya U Tam'si has elaborated his own system of symbols linked with concepts, according to a certain key.

Gerald Moore characterized *Epitomé* in the following words: "*Epitomé* grows more from the immediacy of the poet's position as a black man and a Congolese in Paris and Leopoldville through the disastrous summer months of 1960. From August to October of that year, he worked, at the invitation of Thomas Kanza, as chief editor of the new daily *Le Congo*. In Leopoldville, he was close to the centre of affairs which left a deep wound in the consciousness of modern Africa; he watched Patrice Lumumba's virtual imprisonment in his own capital, the ambiguous role of the United Nations in that affair, and its disastrous culmination in the Prime Minister's attempted escape, capture and subsequent death. The poetry of those months is full of the special and immediate anguish imparted by those events. Back in Paris, Tchicaya feels intensely the falsity of the smiles he is himself obliged to give, reflecting the diplomatic smiles of Leopoldville." (G. Moore, Introduction to his translation of Tchicaya U Tam'si's *Selected Poems*, 1970, p. XII).

Théophile Obenga (born in 1936 in Brazzaville) and Martial Sinda (M'Bamu Kinkala) represent different characteristic tendencies in Congolese poetry. Obenga is a radical who follows in the path of David Diop's romanticism, while Sinda is strongly influenced by French aesthetic thinking. His collections are *Premier chant du départ* (First Song of Departure, 1955) and *Chants pour une jeune Congolaise* (Songs for a Young Congolese Woman, 1955). Jean-Baptiste Tati-Loutard (born in 1938 in Pointe Noire) published two collections, *Poèmes de la mer* (Poems of the Sea, 1968) and *Les racines congolaises* (Congolese Roots, 1968).

Prose-writing in the Belgian Congo (now Zaire) gained some reputation thanks to Paul Lomani-Tchibamba (b. 1914) who was awarded a prize in Brussels (1948) for his book *Ngando, le crocodile* (Ngando, the Crocodile, 1948), and to Dieudonné Mutombo (which is the pseudonym of Jean Mathieu), who scored in the Brussels literary contest with his novel *Victoire de l'amour* (The Victory of Love, 1957). It tells the love story of two young people who meet in Kinshasa. He also wrote *Consultation du midi* (Noon-time Consultation, 1955), *Les hommes de l'aube* (Men of Dawn, 1956) and *Deux chômeurs* (Two Unemployed Men, 1957).

Paul Mahamwe Mushiété (born in 1934 in Kinshasa) writes chiefly critical surveys and compiles anthologies. He organized some literary competitions in his newly-independent country. His collection of tales, songs and sayings bears the title *Quand les nuages avaient soif* (When the Clouds Were Thirsty, 1968).

The most promising playwright of Zaire is Valérien Mutombo-Diba (b. 1944). After his comedy *Beau Michel* (Handsome Michael, 1966), he wrote *Tamouré et les seigneurs du Garengazé* (Tamouré and the Lords of Garengazé, 1966), a serious drama about a young man who tries to avenge his family.

The three-act play *Un trône à trois* (A Throne for Three, 1969) is based on a conflict between Queen Luedja and her disinherited brothers in the Lunda Empire.

Adieu Eloli (1968) is a love story of two young people who get married without asking their parents' consent. Topical social questions are discussed in his following drama *Son Excellence Boumba* (His Excellency Bumba, 1969), which reminds us of Achebe's novel *A Man of the People*. This is another portrait of a ruthless careerist who changes his wife and his manners in private life. Mutombo-Diba criticizes not just one problem. His most recent plays show his increasing experience in handling dramatic action, resulting from his own acting in classical plays which have been increasingly staged in recent years (e.g. Corneille, Molière, Gogol) parallel with modern plays.

2. Writing in Rwanda

J. Saverio Naigiziki (b. 1915) wrote a simple but sincere autobiographical book *Escapade ruandaise* (Ruanda Escapade, 1949) and *Mes transes à trente ans* (My Delusions at Thirty, 1955). In them, he describes his early jobs, love affairs and difficulties.

Alexis Kagame (b. 1912) is a Roman Catholic priest who analyses philosophical and sociological problems in his *La philosophie bantouruandaise de l'Etre* (The Bantu-Rwanda Philosophy of Being, 1952). He collected traditional poetry in *Introduction aux grands genres lyriques de l'ancien Rwanda* (Introduction to the Great Lyrical Genres of Ancient Rwanda, 1969) after his studies entitled *Bref aperçu sur la poésie dynastique du Rwanda* (Brief Survey of the Dynastic Poetry of Rwanda, 1950) and *La poésie dynastique au Rwanda* (Dynastic Poetry in Rwanda, 1951). His *La divine pastorale* (The Divine Pastorale, 1952) is equally well-known for its method of handling traditional texts.

Only one play from that country has been published: J. Saverio Naigiziki's *L'optimiste* (The Optimist, 1954).

XI. OTHER LITERATURES OF CENTRAL AND EAST AFRICA

1. Tanzania and Uganda

While French-language authors of Rwanda belong to the Congolese cultural sphere, English-language authors are oriented towards the east. John Nagenda (born in 1938 in Gahini), a missionary's son, came to Makerere, Uganda, at the age of nineteen. At the Makerere University College in Kampala, a significant centre of English-language authors had arisen. Nagenda was one of the editors of the journal *Penpoint,* with which many writers were associated.

However, if we wish to trace the beginnings of East African writing, we shall have to go back to Badibanga of Zanzibar, who published his French-written fables *L'éléphant qui marche sur les oeufs* (The Elephant which Walks on Eggs, 1931). But this is an exception, since English is the preferred language for the literary works of the authors of Kenya, Uganda, Tanzania, Malawi and Rhodesia. Prose prevails in all these countries, both quantitatively and qualitatively. Poems and theatrical and radio plays are written almost exclusively by young authors. Gabriel Ruhumbika described the process of modernization in his novel *Village in Uhuru* (1969). Innocent K. Kayombo wrote *Stories of Our Tanganyikan Forefathers* (1952), while Harley Manson was the author of *The Festival* (1957), an interesting drama. Peter R. Palangyo in *Dying in the Sun* (1968) discussed problems of life, happiness and death. Barbara Kimenye portrayed the life of a Buganda village in *Kalasanda* and *Kalasanda Revisited*. Leban Erapu (b. 1944), who studied at Makerere and Edinburgh, is a journalist who writes plays and poetry. He used mythological and historical subject-matter in his novel *Restless Feet* (1959).

Another Ugandan writer, Robert Serumaga (b. 1939), graduated from the University of Dublin in 1965. He wrote for the National Theatre in Kampala *A Play* (first performed in 1968) and *Elephants* (1969). His first novel *Return to the Shadows* (1969) told about Joe Musizi who flees from his country after a coup in which his enemies assume power.

Davis Sebukima (b. 1943), whose main subject is political science, used in his novel *A Son of Kabira* (1969) folklore themes in order to present a true-to-life picture of the village Kabira: Lukuza, the chief's son, was educated overseas and is attracted by the modern way of life. He is respected by the other villagers, who do not know of his weaknesses. Technically the novel is only average level, but the author's sense of humour and irony makes it a piece of amusing reading.

Bonnie Lubega (b. 1930), who after some journalistic practice published the short novel *The Outcasts* (1971), dedicated it to the "fertilizers" of East Africa's so-called literary desert. He describes in it the interrelationship between a herdsman and rich cattle-owners in Buganda.

Okot P'Bitek (b. 1931) is one of the most active representatives of artistic life in Uganda. He published a novel in Lwo in 1953 and a number of good English-language poems. He lectured in America, as did Taban lo Liyong (b. 1938), who popularized Lwo poetry in his original adaptation *Eating Chiefs* (1970). He has produced literary criticism, short stories in the collection *Fictions* (1969) and his own poetry in *Frantz Fanon's Uneven Ribs; Poems More and More* (1971).

In his novel *Prostitute* (1968), Okello Oculi approaches the experimentation of his Nigerian colleagues; his heroine also shows the contrasts between the old and the new, between village life and city life. Another Ugandan author, Enrico Seruma, devoted *The Experience* (1970) to similar problems.

2. The Literature of Kenya

2.1 *Mau Mau*

The literature of Kenya began to develop only after World War II, when the Kenyans fought for freedom and their land which had been taken by the white owners who had turned the Africans into mere "tenants". The African Union set up in 1945, which used the method of passive resistance, sent delegations to London. The British government tried to satisfy the population by unimportant concessions and by modernizing the constitution. In 1952, the "Unity" movement using the code name Mau Mau (this Kikuyu expression means "to devour a goat") began its activities. The British press at that time regarded it as a secret religious organization whose members were admitted during "beastly" magic rites, after having taken oaths and having promised to drive the white man out of Kenya and to punish its black quislings. One part of the world press wrote ironically about these fantastic fabrications, while some newspapers remained serious. The Mau Mau attacked the European landowners and burnt down their houses. The British governor declared a state of emergency and closed all the tribal schools. Well-armed troops arrived and terror dominated the whole country.

In 1953, the African Union was officially denoted as an illegal organization and its chairman, Jomo Kenyatta, and other leaders were sent to jail for directing "the Mau Mau rebellion". About eighty thousand Kenyans (mainly Kikuyus) were imprisoned in jails or detention camps in 1953—1960. In 1958, the *Kiama kia muingi* (meaning in Kikuyu "party of numerous people", i.e. a mass organization) was established. Although it used only peaceful, political means, it was also declared unlawful. These facts can be confirmed by Kariuki's and Ngugi's autobiographical novels and by articles published in the journal *Nyota Afrika* (African Star).

The firm attitudes of the Kenyan people and their leaders, who insisted on independence, equal rights and the abrogation of racist legislation, enabled them to resist both terror and promises. The emergency ended on January 12, 1960, and, after some delay caused by Britain, Kenya became independent on December 12, 1963.

The development of Kenyan literature was influenced by the East African Literature and Publication Bureau, founded in Nairobi in January 1948. It supported morally and materially young authors writing in English or in the vernacular languages. The ancient Swahili traditions mentioned in the chapter of his work dealing with old Bantu literature had a retarding effect on English-language writing. Few Kenyan authors have used the vernacular languages; e.g. Henry Kuria and James J. Mbotela write in Swahili, while John S. Mbiti writes in Kamba. Most English-writing authors are Kikuyus, the most significant and numerous nationality of Kenya.

Josiah Mwagi Kariuki (b. 1929) studied at Makerere College and became a teacher. After a short interruption, he continued his studies at the University of Cambridge. Working for the BBC, he gained valuable experience. After his return to Kenya, he taught at the Kangaroo School and did not write systematically. Apart from some average-quality verses, he published his autobiographical book *Mau Mau Detainee. The account by a Kenya African of his experiences in detention camps, from 1953 to 1960* (London, 1963). This book is of considerable historical value, as it presents the African view of the events which led to bloodshed. Two episodes have still not been cleared up: the death of eleven "unsubmissive" prisoners in the Hola camp, caused by African guards in 1959, and the massacre of the Lari villagers by the Mau Mau. Kariuki denies that the massacre was a planned action of the Mau Mau. Despite some inaccuracies, his book is a frank and instructive account written in an anti-colonialist spirit.

2.2 Literary Development

Jonathan Kariara (b. 1935) graduated from Makerere College and became a publications officer at the East African Literature Bureau in Nairobi. Unlike Kariuki's bitter document, Kariara's writing excels in psychological analysis and in the description of the decay of ancient social norms.

R. Mugo Gicaru (b. 1921) is a son of a Kikuyu medicine-man (*mugo*). He studied law at United States and British universities and married an American woman. During his stay abroad, he wrote autobiographical portrayals of Kenyan life before the Mau Mau rising. His short stories in his book *Land of Sunshine* (1958) are rather idealistic and full of nostalgia resulting from his experiences in America and London.

In his second collection of stories *Child of Two Worlds* (1964), he attempts to compare life in New York and London with that in Kenya. His comparison is partly ingenious and ironical, partly tedious. The most interesting passages deal with the difference between Kikuyu medicine-men and American psychoanalysts, the Mau Mau movement which fully confirms Kariuki's explanations, and his discussion of polygamy in African society. This last-mentioned theme gave the author an opportunity to judge the traditional development of African social structures. But this "Westernized" author was probably content to offer a somewhat shallow treatment of the essential problem.

Joseph Waiguru (born in 1939, in Nyeri) studied at the Kangaroo School and then at Makerere College (1959—1964), where his main subjects were English, economics and political science. His verse constitutes an average-standard description of the countryside, scenery, natural beauty, etc. But his stories, e.g. *The Untilled Field*, are more sophisticated. *The Untilled Field* was included in David Cook's anthology *Origin East Africa* which also contains Peter Nazareth's satirical play *Brave New Cosmos* and other short stories, poems and plays by Kenyan authors.

In 1962, Peter Nazareth graduated from Makerere, where he had edited the journal *Penpoint*. He wrote criticism and radio plays. In the 1960's, Nazareth studied at the University of Leeds. In *Brave New Cosmos* (1965) he ridicules the haughtiness and selfishness of the graduates, whom he contrasts with a good-natured village teacher who is completely free of snobbery. Nazareth demonstrates the increasing "gap" between the educated sons and their uneducated parents living in African villages. The "new cosmos" of the élite is the civilized world of technological devices and luxurious cars.

Rebecca Njau published her play *The Scar* (1963) in the journal *Transition*, while another woman writer—Grace A. Ogot (1930)—revealed her impressive style in her short stories and in the novels *The Promised Land* (1966), *Land without Thunder* and *The Other Woman*.

James T. Ngugi (born in 1938 in Limur) is a well-known prose writer and playwright. Now he uses the name Ngugi Wa Thiongo. When he was attending the government school at Karinga (the Kikuyu tribal school was closed at the time of the rising), his teacher lent him Robert Louis Stevenson's books. He liked most *Treasure Island*, which he read many times, both in English and in Swahili. He longed to write such a novel. In 1955, he went to the Alliance High School, where he wrote his first longer story in a year. The story, which betrayed the influence of Edgar Wallace's writings, was rejected by a local journal. Ngugi was desperately unhappy that he could not become a writer. In 1959, he started his studies at Makerere and wrote four short stories, which were then published by *Kenya Weekly News*. The most interesting short story is *The Fig Tree*, which describes the fate of Mukami, a young woman married to an old, rich farmer, whom, however, she must share with two other co-wives. Her love and self-sacrifice during the first three years turn to suffering, because she is barren. She is ridiculed and held in contempt by the other wives, who constantly quarrel with her. Her husband also behaves differently: he ceases to visit her hut and beats her. The unhappy Mukami decides to flee from her husband's hut to the sacred fig tree, to ask for the aid of her forefathers' god. The tired woman falls asleep under the fig tree. At sunrise she awakes to discover that she is pregnant. She realizes she should go back to her husband in order to give the baby to her tribe.

During his university studies, Ngugi worked as an editor of the journal *Penpoint* and sent his political articles to *The Sunday Nation*. Other short stories of his were published in *Transition* and *The New African*. Altogether, he has produced about fifteen short stories, most of which have appeared in African reviews.

As an undergraduate, he wrote the theatrical play *The Black Hermit* (published in 1963), which was first performed by the National Theatre of Uganda on November 16, 1962, on the occasion of that country's independence. He worked as a journalist after 1964, and then continued his studies at the University of Leeds.

His extraordinary talent can best be seen in his novels. *Weep Not, Child* (1964), awarded a prize at the World Festival of Negro Arts in Dakar, portrays Ngotho, the father of four sons, three of whom have gone to the mountains to fight against the white man. Ngugi shows the villagers' difficult path to education at a time when knowledge is becoming increasingly significant in the process of political and cultural emancipation. He also illustrates the economic causes of the Mau Mau rising. The restless atmosphere dominating Kenya is well described, and the role of the force of violence is explained in a convincing manner.

Even more impressive is his next novel *The River Between* (1965). which was awarded first prize in the literary competition of the East African Literature Bureau in Nairobi. In it, Ngugi tries to generalize certain characteristics of the Mau Mau movement. The conflict between the old traditions and Christianity is symbolically presented as a conflict between villagers inhabiting the opposite banks of a river. The tension rises after the death of Muthoni, a Christian preacher's daughter, who—against her father's will—attends the "heathen" circumcision rites. On the opposite side of the river, a rumour is circulating to the effect that the unhappy girl has been poisoned by the missionaries who are trying to achieve their aims as easily as possible. The villagers have been used to identifying the white man's colonization with education. Therefore, they reject schools, which they do not consider useful, and rely solely on traditional tribal wisdom. Thus, the struggle against the white man acquires distinct conservative features in their culture.

Some of these questions are developed in Ngugi's third novel *A Grain of Wheat* (1967), which deals with the later development of Kenya. Although Ngugi is a technically advanced author, he still keeps to his well-tested simple descriptive style. He seems to be eager to present as much information as possible. For this reason, there is some journalistic superficiality in certain passages of *A Grain of Wheat*. Moreover, he does not write sufficiently economically.

Hazel Murgot (pen-name) published her novel *Black Night of Quiloa* in the late 1960's. The year 1972 was particularly fruitful in Kenyan literary life. The first Kenyatta Prizes were awarded both in the Swahili section (Ahmed Nassir's poems edited by Shihabuddin Chiraghdin) and in the English section (Okot P'Bitek's *Two Poems*).

Almost equally successful were *The Burdens*, a play by John Ruganda, and *Son of Woman* (Charles Mangua's novel). Jared Angira acquired a considerable reputation thanks to his collections of poetry *Juices* and *Silent Voices*. Other popular books of 1972 were *In a Brown Mantle* by Peter Nazareth, *What a Life* by Mwangi Ruheni, *Mashetani* by Ebrahim Hussein and *Rosa Mistika* by Euphrase Kazilahabi. It should be noted that some of these recent works owe their commercial success to their attractive content. Thus, for instance, *Son of Woman* was acclaimed by readers, though some critics refused to appreciate it or even called it "near pornography". On the other hand, a number of books gained the experts' respect.

The press of Kenya devotes some attention to contemporary imaginative writing, but more significant discussions occur in academic circles. They are at present centred on two basic questions: the prospects of Swahili as the unifying East African language and the topicality of subject-matter chosen by the authors. Some writers (e.g. Grace Ogot) feel that English is still the best language through which the readers from different tribes can be reached. In her interview for *The Sunday Nation* (November 28, 1971) she said:

"After all, we are often patient enough to wade through some literary works which are written in cockney English, because the story is good. My plea has never been for personal gain, but it has been mainly to encourage up-coming writers who may not be fluent in English but who have fantastic stories to tell. Quite a number of people assume that when we write in English we are only concerned with attracting the outside market. This is not so. Sometime we just want to communicate within East Africa itself, where quite a number of African people can only communicate in English and not in Kiswahili yet."

Discussing the problem of topicality, some Kenyan authors claim to deal with traditions and folklore, whose relevance is felt even at the present time, and refuse to identify topical subjects with "purely contemporary" ones. For this reason, there is no over-concentration on city topics; on the contrary, there are quite a few books describing the past and the present of the Kenyan village.

Khadambi Asalache in *A Calabash of Life* (1967) follows the tribesmen's efforts to secure the chieftainship. The action of the novel takes place in ancient times, before the era of colonization. Most of the more recent novels, however, deal with contemporary problems. Among them are *A Curse of God* (1970) by Stephen N. Ngubiah, *The Land is Ours* (1970) by John Karoki, and *Ordeal in the Forest* (1968) by Godwin Wachira, which analyzes the "Mau Mau psychology". One of the more recent women writers—Charity Waciuma—tells in *Daughter of Mumbi* (1969) about her difficult path to knowledge and modern thinking. The book is also notable for her lucid style.

There has been a substantial increase, both in number and quality, of dramatic writing in East Africa since the early 1960's. There are, of course, fewer plays in Kenya and Uganda than in West Africa, but analogical differences may also be seen in poetry and prose writing. After all, it is the artistic standard that matters most. One might think that it is too early to arrive at any conclusions concerning the development of East African dramatic writing, because of its obvious lack of professionalism.

The tribal and linguistic problems of Kenyan playwrights can hardly be overestimated. Some of them began learning English rather late. Elvania Namukwaya Zirimu (born near Entebbe in 1938), the author of the play *Keeping Up With the Mukasas*, learned no English till the age of ten.

Most African playwrights have been inspired by European dramatic works. "The African amateur was, and still is, to be found in schools and universities: there, however, he tends to produce plays with an eye to school certificate examinations. Thus, in some schools, an annual production of Shakespeare, with African boys dressed in the costumes of 16th century England, has become—like Speech Day—a ritual." (J. Ngugi, in his preface to *The Black Hermit* (1968). It follows from Ngugi's words that there should be two different kinds of stages in East Africa: one for the educated, the other for the masses of the population. So far, East African authors have produced plays mainly for intellectuals. Some of them, however, have realized that they will need a wider audience in the future.

Ngugi mentions the Makerere Students' Dramatic Society, which, in 1966, "set up a travelling company which toured many parts of Uganda and Kenya—playing in village-halls, in churches and in the open air" (ibid.).

Ganesh Bagchi (b. 1926) studied in Calcutta and taught in Uganda, where he was awarded prizes at the Uganda Drama Festivals. Bagchi's *The Deviant* follows a conventional "triangular" pattern: Lalit, his mistress, and his friend live in Kampala. Lalit's mistress asks him to marry her, but he refuses, stating his objections to marriage. She is so much influenced by his opinions that later on, when talking to Lalit's friend, Dibu, who wants to marry her, she uses the same arguments.

Having failed to demonstrate his courage, Lalit comes home rather distressed. Paradoxically enough, Dibu succeeds in soothing him. As Lalit's mistress thinks of marriage "in moments of stress and strain" in her own "fantasy world", Lalit finally wins over the cynical Dibu. In Bagchi's plays, personal and social elements are interwoven.

Kuldip Sondhi was born in 1924, in India, where he studied. His family then left for Kenya, but he obtained his higher education in the United States. He works as an engineer in Mombasa. His play *The Undesignated* won the first prize in a Kenya Drama Festival. Sondhi's play *With Strings* is esssentially a study of the interrelationships between the Indians and the Africans living in Kenya. Dev, the retired Indian engineer, tells his son: "In real life, the Indians, Africans and Europeans are three different races. God made them so. Not me; God! Let us live as equals and be fair to each other, but keep marriage out of it, for God's sake. "But his son loves an African girl and the situation gets complicated when a letter from an American uncle arrives, promising 10,000 pounds to the family, if Mohan "gets married and produces an heir within the next twelve months". When the African girl learns this, she refuses to marry Mohan, though she loves him. Everything ends well as a telegram, announcing the uncle's death, comes just in time to ensure the happiness of the young couple.

Sondhi's characters are sometimes schematic, sketchy and flat, like some other characters in East African plays. Their sketchiness may result from the shortness of such works. David Cook tries to see them in a more positive way: "East African restraint and economy of wording may surprise some readers, while the deliberate, forceful rejection of melodrama in the unwinding of many of the stories may be misinterpreted by those who look for the 'well-made' dramatic *dénouement* so common in European tradition." (David Cook, editor, *Origin East Africa*, Introduction, p. XI).

There is a dénouement in most East African plays, but in some cases it is not "well-made". The reason for this is not only the authors' restraint and economy of wording, but mainly their efforts to resolve certain topical problems in the final parts of their plays. Generally speaking, the play should provide theatre-goers with entertainment and its conclusion should offer some instructive advice, as well. Thus, East African drama has acquired a role in the educational process.

James Ngugi's black hermit—Remi—loves Toni and is greatly disappointed when she marries his brother. But six months after her marriage, her husband dies in a crash and—according to an ancient custom—she becomes Remi's wife. But Remi is not happy as he is jealous of his own deceased brother who has won his wife's love before him. Consequently, Remi leaves for the city where he works as a clerk. He wishes to forget all about the past and becomes a "hermit". He tells Jane, his mistress in the city: "I came here in search of solitude". Jane asks him: "At night-clubs and wild parties?" This is the main paradox of the hermit's life. Both Jane and Remi's wife are deceived. Jane learns too late that he is married and Remi returns to his tribe (the Marua) to find his wife there.

Ngugi criticizes tribalism and Christianity here—just as he does in his novels. When the elders from his native village tell him to come back and lead them, Remi realizes the limitations of tribalism. They want their own tribal party, a district officer or prime minister from their own tribe. He refuses, saying: "Has our nationalist fervour that gave us faith and hope in the days of suffering and colonial slavery been torn to shreds by such tribal loyalties? All my life I believed in the creation of a nation." (*The Black Hermit*, p. 41). It is only the pastor who is able to exert more influence upon him. Finally, however, Remi refuses his help and repudiates the Christian religion. The Pastor says: "You joined the Africanist Party and became lost in politics. You put all trust in yourself and in man, not God". Remi replies: "Pastor, you and your religion never did anything for our people. It's only divided them and made them weak before the white man" (*ibid.*, p. 74).

There is a broad variety of topics and methods in East Africa. Although realism still prevails, there are also a number of symbolical plays, which, however, seem to be more successful as broadcast plays, as they have little action and require more concentration than stage productions. Unlike the West African plays, most of which constitute a synthesis of folklore and modern elements and which sometimes utilize the combination of music, dance and texts, East African plays are mostly one-act works with relatively few characters (an exception being *Encounter*) and a drawing-room setting.

3. The Literature of Malawi

Samuel Yosia Ntara (b. about 1900) wrote two biographical works, *Headman's Enterprise* (1930) and *Man of Africa* (1934), in which he used the method of critical realism. The poet David Rubadiri (b. 1930) studied at Makerere College and Cambridge, later becoming Malawi's representative at the United Nations and Ambassador to the United States. His verses express sympathy for suffering people.

The most popular post-World War II novelist of Malawi is Aubrey Kachingwe, the author of *No Easy Task* (1956). Kachingwe studied in Tanganyika and spent a long time in Kenya, subsequently becoming chief editor of the Malawi Broadcasting Corporation. The main character of his novel is also a journalist: Jo Jozeni intends to study law in London, just at the time when the nationalist movement in his country is reaching its climax. The novel describes the dramatic events preceding independence, disclosing particular details resulting from the writer's insight into the background of political life.

Legson Kayira's *I Will Try* (1965) is less satisfactory from the artistic point of view, but it is a frankly-written novel. Kayira describes his own complicated path to education, leading from his native country to Washington and Cambridge. Moreover, the book presents an African's impressions gained during his stay abroad.

4. The Literature of Rhodesia

The best-known writer is Doris Lessing, who, however, belongs rather to English literature. She was born in Persia in 1919 and came to Rhodesia together with her parents as a child. Lessing's first novel *The Grass Is Singing* (1950) describes the unhappy married life of Mary Turner, who lives through a love affair with her black servant, who finally kills her. Lessing analyzes the psychological roots of the relationship of the white lady and her servant in connection with the moral decay resulting from the worsening economic conditions.

The technical skill of the writer can well be seen in her short stories *This Was the Old Chief's Country* (1951), *Five* (1953) and *The Habit of Loving* (1957), discussing both racial and sexual problems. The cycle of novels *Children of Violence* contains the novels *Martha Quest* (1952), *A Proper Marriage* (1954), *A Ripple from the Storm* (1958) and *Landlocked* (1965). Martha, the heroine of the cycle longs for sweet life and is at first attracted by the delights of Salisbury debauchers but she dislikes their reactionary views and grows more progressive, chiefly due to the rapid social development in World War Two. Finally Martha takes part in communist activities. The writer gradually proceeds from psychological analysis to large-scale social criticism.

This tendency is visible after Lessing's arrival to Britain. She deals with English life, e.g. in her novel *Retreat to Innocence* (1956). She also published *Fourteen Poems* (1959), the plays *Each in His Own Wilderness* (1959) and *Play with a Tiger* (1962), the novels *In Pursuit of the English* (1960) and The *Golden Notebook* (1962) and the collection of short stories *A Man and Two Women* (1963).

The psychological portraits of the white middle-class living in Africa, as we find them in her early works, exerted some influence on South African protest writing. The background of racial conflicts is revealed either with realistic faithfulness or with psychoanalytical openness, whenever she chooses to explore an individual's feelings "in the jail of the dark complexion", if we may use the words of James Matthews.

Among the few works of the native Rhodesians we can appreciate the novel *The Lonely Village* (1951), written by Sylvester Masiye. On the whole, Rhodesian imaginative writing is underdeveloped owing to the existing political and social situation.

XII. BLACK LITERATURE OF THE PORTUGUESE TERRITORIES IN AFRICA

0. Introduction

The territories that are still dominated by the Portuguese, i.e. Angola, Guinea-Bissau, the Cabo Verde Islands, Mozambique and São Tomé, were discovered in the 15th century by Portuguese seamen or by foreign sailors serving Prince Dom Henry of Portugal. These territories were soon settled by merchants and missionaries. In order to obtain a cheap labour force for the settlers' newly-established plantations and roads, the administration turned the local population into slaves. Each chief was responsible for providing a prescribed number of slave labourers from the villages.

The inhabitants were divided into two categories: *indigenas* (natives, the uncivilized) and assimilados (the civilized), i.e. those who had mastered Portuguese, owned a prescribed amount of property and had abandoned all tribal customs. These *assimilados,* who today represent only about three per cent of the total number of the population, are considered traitors by the rest of the people. For this reason, even well-educated blacks who could join the *assimilados,* refuse to do so. This division deprives about ninety-seven per cent of the inhabitants of all social and political rights. No wonder the only possible reaction to such inhuman treatment has always been revolts and uprisings. Some riots were quickly suppressed, others lasted longer and ended only after the Portuguese military interventions, which were sometimes unsuccessful.

After World War II, mass resistance developed in the form of a national liberation movement. Political parties and organizations were formed to carry out their programme of eliminating Portuguese colonial rule and gaining independence. The rising movement was repressed by the Portuguese authorities. Many leaders were imprisoned and others left the country in order to direct the struggle for national liberation from their exile abroad.

In 1961, a well-organized insurrection started in Angola and in Guinea-Bissau. The guerilla troops attacked Portuguese garrisons and important centres and occupied or controlled large areas in both colonies.

In the recent period, two political parties were formed—the MPLA and the FRELIMO. Additional troops had to be sent from Portugal. Although the colonial army has resorted to terrorist methods—burning villages and killing inhabitants—it has not been able to defeat the insurrection.

The Portuguese colonies in Africa lie rather far apart and have many different, but also many common, features. Mozambique, Angola and São Tomé are inhabited by Bantu blacks,

Guinea-Bissau by Sudanese blacks, the Cabo Verde Islands mostly by a mixed Creole population speaking Creole Portuguese. Many forms of their original culture and the desire to put an end to colonialism are common to all of them.

Generally speaking, African culture has always been subjected to persecution, so that it is more or less illegal at present. Nevertheless, much original music and many dances (e.g. in Mozambique) have been preserved until now. The *mornas*—song-dances—of the Cabo Verde Islands are still very popular. They are usually highly nostalgic, expressing the performers' love of and longing for their native country. The dancers, accompanied by singers, move slowly and melancholically. At present, there are in actual fact two cultures existing in the Portuguese territories: that of the African nationalities and that of the Portuguese colonizers. African written literature is today in its initial historical period.

Although the black inhabitants have their oral traditions, their legends and tales are not permitted to be disseminated. The vernacular writers have acquired a European education, but literate blacks in these countries constitute only about one per cent of the population. Out of the eleven million inhabitants of Angola, Mozambique, the Cabo Verde Islands and São Tomé, only one hundred thousand have been able to attend Portuguese schools. In these schools, the teaching language is Portuguese, and only that which has a definite relation to Portugal is taught; no mention of the African countries is made.

Ronga is the written language in Southern Mozambique, but only limited numbers of people can read and write, as the use of African languages at schools is forbidden. A few Protestant missionary schools teach in Ronga, but only a relatively few privileged Africans can attend them.

All black writers are obliged to write their works in Portuguese. Today, they are facing a difficult problem: should most African nationalities remain illiterate, i.e. without any knowledge of reading or writing either in Portuguese or in their vernacular languages, or not? The above-mentioned countries' writers are not confining themselves only to national interests; on the contrary, they are trying to establish contacts with the entire world. Although they still must use Portuguese, they are also beginning to write in the vernacular languages, which enables them to establish close spiritual ties with their brothers and to acquaint the rest of the world with their native countries.

1. The Cabo Verde Islands

Since 1924, literature marked with a specific local colour has been developing in the Cabo Verde Islands. Jorge Barbosa, Manuel Lopes and other poets who formed the Claridade Group (1936) have portrayed in their works the dramatic life of their native country. That whole generation of poets was inspired by tragic subject-matter preserved by oral folk traditions: flights from the islands, imprisonment, poverty, droughts and resulting famines. More contemporary topics include efforts to escape to the vast expanses of the ocean, suffering from colonial oppression and the inability to become free.

Young poets, such as Antonio Nunez, Gabriel Mariano or Aguinaldo Fonseca, are trying to develop the tragic theme of oppression more deeply and in more detail. But the difficult conditions under colonial rule have prevented any real blossoming of Negro writing.

Osvaldo Alcantara (a pseudonym—his real name is Baltasar Lopes; he was born in 1904), a lawyer and headmaster of the São Vincente lyceum, belonged to the Claridade Group. He writes poems and philological and sociological essays, and some of his works have been published in Brazilian journals. His main works are *Chiquinho* and *O dialecto crioulo* (The Creole Dialect, 1958).

Jorge Barbosa, a poet and civil servant in the Cabo Verde Islands and one of the founders of the Claridade Group, cooperates with local and Portuguese journals. He has published a collection of poems entitled *Arquipélago* (Archipelago); his *Caderno de nu ilhéu* (The Diary of an Island, 1955) was awarded the Camil Pessanha Prize.

Aguinaldo Fonseca (b. 1922), a functionary in Lisbon, writes for the Portuguese literary reviews *Seara Nova, Atlântico* and *Mundo Literário*. His collection of poems, *Linha de horizonte* (Line of the Horizon), was published in 1951.

Manuel Lopes has published a book of short stories, *O galo que cantou na baïa e otros contos cabo-verdeanos* (The Cock which Sings to the Bay and Other Cabo Verde Short Stories, 1959) and a novel, *Os flagelados do vento leste* (Battered by the Eastern Wind, 1960).

Gabriel Mariano (b. 1928), a lawyer, writes Creole poems for Cabo Verde journals. Ovídio de Sousa Martins (b. 1928) published his lyrical poems under the title *Caminhada* (The Long Walk) and a collection of short stories called *Tutchinha* (1962).

2. Guinea-Bissau

Terencio Casimiro Anahory Silva (born in 1934 in Boa Vista, Cabo Verde Islands) studied at the Lisbon Faculty of Law. He has published his poems and short stories in the *Buletin de Cabo Verde* and in the Guinean review, *Bolanense*.

3. São Tomé

Francisco José Tenreiro (1921—1963) took an active part in the neo-realist movement that originated in Lisbon. He published *Novo Cancioneiro* (New Song-Book) in 1941—1944. In the Portuguese capital, Tenreiro published (in 1943) a number of poems under the title *Ilha de nome santo* (Island with a Holy Name). In it, he described the historical, pre-colonial life of the inhabitants, as well as the contemporary life of the Portuguese exploiters and the common people living in São Tomé. Tenreiro tried to write in a pure style, introducing into his poetry Negro imagery, characteristic rhythm and popular songs. Although he wrote in Portuguese, he was a great bard of his native country. He cooperated with Mário de Andrade in editing *Caderno de poesia negra de expressão portuguesa* (A Collection of Negro Poetry in the Portuguese Language, 1953).

One of his predecessors with respect to the content of his works was Costa Alegra (1864—1890, Alcobaca, Portugal) whose *Versos* (Verses, 1916) appeared in Lisbon. A contemporary of Tenreiro is Alda do Espirito Santo (1926), a professor who teaches on his native island. He publishes his poems in local and Portuguese journal and is represented both in *Caderno* (1953) and in Andrade's *Anthology* (1959).

4. Angola

The oldest writer in Angola today is Oscar Bento Ribas (born in 1909 in Luanda). He studied in Luanda. At the age approximately of twenty, he began to lose his sight and became blind when he was twenty-one. He has written one novel, several collections of short stories, ethnographic texts and literary essays: *Flores e Espinos* (Flowers and Thorns, 1948), *Uanga* (1951), *Ecos de Minha Terra* (Echoes of My Country, 1952), *Divindades e Ritos Angolanos* (Angolan Gods and Rites, 1958), *Literatura Traditional Angolana* (Angolan Traditional Literature, vol. 1, 1961). His short story "In Prague", published in *Ecos de Minha Terra*, was awarded the Margaret Wrong Prize in 1952. He published his short story "Medelhao" (The Medallion) in an anthology comprising the works of various Angolan authors, the title of which was *Contos d'Africa* (African Tales, 1961). It describes an event which really took place in Luanda in 1905: Aunt Zente discovers that her gold medallion has been stolen. First, she consults the medicine-men; and then she "imprisons" the statue of St. Anthony by binding a ribbon round his leg. St. Anthony tells her the name of the thief—her niece, Fuxi, who needs money and therefore sold the gold pendant. The pregnant Fuxi suffers from pangs of conscience and fears a scandal. Thinking of her baby's health, she regrets her offence and counts on God's help. She also promises to buy back the medallion. Zente then begs St. Anthony to nullify the evil charm over her niece's baby, and this really happens. Fuxi's baby is born safe and sound and the medallion is bought back.

Another writer and poet is Geraldo Bessa Victor (born in 1917 in Luanda), a lawyer who lives in Lisbon. His prose and verse have appeared in Portuguese and overseas reviews and journals. Thus far, he has produced a book of essays *A poesia e a Política* (Poetry and Politics, 1937), two collections of poems *Ecos dispersos* (Dispersed Echoes, 1941) and *Debaixo do Céu* (Under the Sky, 1949), a book of chronicles and essays of African literary problems *Minha Terra e Minha Dama* (My Country and My Lady, 1952) and two collections of poems having African motifs *Ao Som das Marimbas* (To the Sound of the Marimbas, 1943) and *Cubata Abandonada* (The Abandoned Hut, 1958).

A very promising and favourable recent phenomenon in Negro poetry in the Portuguese language was the movement initiated by the Angolan poet. Viriato da Cruz (born in 1928 in Porto Amboim) under the slogan: *Vamos descobrir Angola* (Let's Discover Angola). The movement tries to show the values and shortcomings of the Angolan culture and customs. Viriato da Cruz publishes his poems in journals in Angola and Mozambique. His verses have also appeared in *Caderno* (1953).

Social problems are reflected on by another great Angolan poet, Agostinho Neto (born in 1922 in Icolo e Bengo), a physician and now one of the leaders of the MLPA. He has published his poems in Angolan and Portuguese journals. Showing mastery over the language, he has expressed the theme of a riot with great vigour.

Since World War II, the younger poets have been trying to approach more closely their national folklore—the source of their people's oral traditions. They also deal with topical aspects of colonial reality. Mário Pinto de Andrade (born in 1928 in Golungo Alto) studied sociology in Paris. He has published his critical literary and sociological essays in Angolan, Portuguese and Brazilian journals. In cooperation with Tenreiro of São Tomé, he edited *Caderno de poesia negra de expressão portuguesa* (1953). In Paris, he edited *Antologia da poesia negra de expressão portuguesa* (Anthology of Negro Poetry in the Portuguese Language, 1959), the introduction to which is his study "Negro African Culture and Assimilation". He has also written essays under the title *A literatura africana contemporanea* (Contemporary African Literature). In connection with his function as the chairman of MPLA, he went to Guinea in 1959. Andrade's verses are more refined, but they are equally effective.

Mário António Fernandez de Oliveira (born in 1934 in Luanda) is a state functionary who publishes his poems in the Lisbon journal *Távola Redonda* and in the press of Angola and Mozambique. His collection of poems *Poesias* (Poetry) appeared in 1956.

5. Mozambique

The literature of Mozambique was initiated by two journalists—João Albazini and Estacio Dias—in the 1920's. In Lourenço Marques, they started editing the monthly *Voz Africana* (The Voice of Africa), which has existed until the present time. The journal, which is published partly in Ronga, propagates the interests of the African nations.

Rui de Noronha (1909—1943, born in Lourenço Marques) began his artistic career a little later. His collection *Sonetos* (Sonnets) closely approximates folk poetry. After World War II, the poetess Noémia de Sousa (born in 1927 in Lourenço Marques) produced her first verses. Her poem "Deixa pasar o meu povo" (Let My People Go) appeared in *Caderno* (1953) and others were subsequently published in Andrade's *Antologia* (1959). Miss Sousa tries as much as possible to approach oral traditions and indigenous folklore. She clearly formulates the aspirations of the African people and knows how to encourage them in their struggle for freedom. Her poems suggest the black man's better future. Strengthening her people's national consciousness, Noémia de Sousa is continuing the best traditions of her native land. Folk-songs resound in the poetry of Lilinho Micaya (b. 1930). This young Mozambican poet describes the tragedy of Africa most convincingly in his remarkable "Shangana" (the name is said to be as common among Bantu blacks as "John" is in England and America), which contains a rousing appeal to overthrow the colonizers and liberate the nation.

Marcelino dos Santos (born in 1929 in Lumba), who has used the pseudonym Carlos Kalungano, studied sociology in Paris. He cooperates with *Présence Africaine* and is one of the leaders of FRELIMO. His poems have been published in *Brado Africano* and *Itinerário*.

José Craveirinha (born in 1922, in Lourenço Marques) is a journalist who publishes his poems in *Brado Africano* (The African Cry), *Itinerário* (Itinerary) and *Notícias* (News). They have also appeared in Andrade's *Antologia*.

XIII. THE LITERATURE OF MADAGASCAR

0. Introduction

Madagascar belongs to the African continent both geographically and owing to the fact that one part of the original population came from the continent. There were later Malayan migrations and the unification of tribes led to the formation of the Malagasy nation with its language, Malagasy, belonging to the Malayan linguistic group. It is interesting that the Comoro Islands, which politically belonged to Madagascar (now the Malagasy Republic), have preserved their own Bantu language, with a few dialects, which is closely related to Swahili on the nearest coast of the African continent. Moreover, Swahili has become a commercial language on the northern coast of Madagascar, mainly at the ports and in business centres. It has been assumed that the island was settled by Bantu tribes in pre-Malayan times, but this is not certain. The fact is, however, that a great number of Bantu words have penetrated into Malagasy vocabulary.

The old Malagasy literature could develop freely under the reign of the local rulers who encouraged this development. The old literature was based on folk forms (*hain-teny, ohabolana, fabliaux,* dynastic poems, etc.) which were perfected by Malagasy popular bards—*mpilalao.* Even today, some poets are endeavouring to continue in the spirit of folk poetry (e.g. Rasamuela, Ranaivo, et al.).

1. Ancient Literature

Ancient Malagasy literature was not directly recorded, but it was disseminated by oral tradition and passed on from one generation to the next. According to the old local custom, popular or wandering bards and troubadours (*mpilalao*) spread their *hain-teny* and stories, and especially their highly popular rhymed *fabliaux,* throughout the country. They recited poems or sang songs accompanied by music. Their subjects were taken from everyday life (rulers, wars, birth, circumcision, death, etc.).

The clasical form of poetry is the *hain-teny* (literally meaning "skilful speech"), a short poem in a dialogue form in which two reciters compete eloquently in a dispute interlaced with proverbs. The replies are sharp but hidden in exuberant imagery. Thus the orator's struggles develop—together with their elegiac or satirical character, they also always contain some humour. This form, which is very much in favour even today, is applied to such subjects as love, one's neighbours' disputes, etc. Flavien Ranaivo still writes poems inspired by the *hain-teny.*

Another form of folk poetry are *ohabolana,* popular sayings, proverbs and aphorisms, which are widespread not only in Madagascar, but throughout Africa. Human weaknesses, miserliness, sentimentality and great and small rulers are ridiculed, e.g.: "If a rich person does not eat, he is not his own master, but a hoarder of his stores"; "Kings resemble fire: he who is near them gets burnt, he who is far from them catches cold"; "One finger is not enough for a man to kill a louse," etc.

Tales are the most widespread genre of educational literature. Some of them explain various problems relating to the birth of man, gods and animals, the origin of death, illness and hostility—transferring listeners to the unreal world of giants, dwarfs, fairies or other supernatural beings.

Rhymed fables, the so-called medieval style of *fabliaux,* which are, in fact, shorter or longer realistic or satirical novelettes usually dealing with social subjects and love plots, are still very popular. Their aim is to make people laugh; therefore, they ridicule human stupidity and praise wisdom. They may be parodies or hyperboles, but they are usually comical and—stressing, as they do, the weaknesses of the human character—and they are closely related to folklore. The *fabliaux* are sung and dancers express their content in pantomime. Transient forms of these rhymed romantic tragic and lyrical tales paved the way for the future development of drama.

2. Modern Literature

In the 19th century, Malagasy intellectuals began—after the introduction of script and printing into the country—editing Malagasy newspapers, books and journals. In 1866, missionaries began to print the journal *Teny Soa* (Good Words), publishing not only religious tracts, but also articles in prose. Since 1886, the official journal *Ny Gazety Malagasy* has been issued.

Later on, general interest was centred on the history of the island. Kabaras, royal laws, and descriptions of Malagasy customs were published. The first historical work written on the island in Malagasy was *Tantara sy fombandrazana* (The History and Customs of Our Ancestors), whose author was Rainandriamanapary. That period can be characterized as one of flourishing writing.

The Malagasy nation, with its united territory and language, started to develop its political, economic and cultural independence. However, the French occupied the island in 1895. Right from the outset, they fought against the Malagasy culture relentlessly and systematically. The Malagasy language was banned at schools and only French was permitted as a teaching language. It was not permitted to teach the history or geography of Madagascar, as this was considered harmful and politically dangerous. The publication of Malagasy-language newspapers, journals and books was forbidden for the same reason. Research activities were centralized in the Malagasy Academy, established by French scientists in 1902. Gradually, especially after 1920, the French scientists' jobs were taken by Malagasies. The situation improved only in 1936 when the Popular Front won the French

elections. The Malagasy national liberation movement was strengthened in 1936—1939.
The Malagasy section of the Communist Party of France was founded and progressive
Malagasy-language newspapers were published, e.g. *Ny firénena Malagasy, Ny Ráriny,*
etc., which called for the country's independence. Shortly after the beginning of World
War II, both the Communist Party of France and French progressive newspapers were
banned.

The national liberation movement in Madagascar—as in other colonial countries—became successful, particularly towards the end of World War II and during the immediate
post-war years. The political party known as the MDRM, which arose from this movement,
became so powerful that the colonizers were afraid of its possible victory in the elections
in April 1947. Before the elections, the French government and army provoked a rising
(1947). The deputies of the National Assembly (including poet J. Rabemananjara)
were deprived of their immunity, imprisoned and most of them (17) sentenced to death.
Rabemananjara was sentenced to life imprisonment and deportation to France. Thanks to
the intervention of the progressive public abroad, the death sentences were mitigated to life
imprisonment. The rising, in which one million Malagasies took part, was drowned in blood
within three years. According to official statistics, about one hundred thousand Malagasies
were killed, while about twenty-five thousand patriots suffered in jails and concentration
camps. The political leaders interned in France were promised that they would be allowed
to return as soon as Madagascar achieved its independence (in 1960). But in October 1959,
the National Assembly gave amnesty to all patriots who had been imprisoned and deported
by the French colonial regime.

From the beginning of the French occupation, Madagascar was closely linked with
France, politically as well as culturally. Old and modern French literature exerted—and
still exerts—an influence on Malagasy poets, who were affected by the Romantics,
Baudelaire, the Parnassians, especially Symbolists and Surrealists. Only in the period of the
struggle for freedom and independence did Malagasy poets let themselves be inspired by
ancient folk poetry. One may ask whether French literary trends—particularly Symbolism
and Surrealism—exerted a positive influence on Malagasy poets. This question is usually
answered in the affirmative, as these trends gave the poets an opportunity for expressing
their sensitive souls' nostalgia and rich imagery. Moreover, the French language has been
advantageous for the purpose of informing the world of their problems, efforts and their
fight against colonialism, neocolonialism and French domination.

At the beginning of the 20th century, when the French influence affected the life of the
population of Madagascar relatively strongly in all its forms and institutions, chiefly in
schools, a new generation was growing up. These young intellectuals mastered the French
language and literature but were dominated by French thought and by all forms of
French literature, particularly French poetry. The same was true of drama, while
novel-writing was still rather weak.

Havana Ramanantoamina (b. 1910) is a predecessor of the great Malagasy poets. He likes
to use the archaic language of the ancestors in his elegiac and lyrical poems. He adheres to
exact numbers of syllables, rhythm and rhyming (often internal rhyming). His poems and

songs are still recited and sung all over Madagascar, especially on festive occasions, at weddings and other family ceremonies. He was one of the first poets to criticize in his works the French domination.

Three great poets, who wrote mostly in French, can be said to have adhered to European trends (Symbolism, etc.), but sooner or later they attempted to adopt the traditions of their native country.

Jean-Joseph Rabearivelo (1903—1937, Tananarive), who came from an impoverished aristocratic family, used both French and Malagasy for his works. At the age of thirteen, he was expelled from his secondary school. By working hard, he mastered the French language and literature, as well as Spanish and Latin. He was extraordinary poet, neither Malagasy nor French but something in between. Friends avoided meeting him, from which he suffered very much, considering himself a spiritual outcast. He was employed at the Imerina Printing-house. Like Charles Baudelaire, his favourite poet, he was adicted to drugs and finally committed suicide.

Rabearivelo's work is extensive and many-sided. His first collections *La coupe des cendres* (The Cup of Ashes, 1924), *Sylves* (1927) and *Volumes* (1928) show the unlimited influence of the French Parnassians and Neo-Romantics in terms of form (the sonnet), dreamy melancholy and content. The tragic cleavage of the poet's soul, resulting from his sensibility to French poetry, can clearly be observed here. This insoluble conflict exists in all his works. The talent of this frustrated poet was so much affected by foreign culture that he could not penetrate into his own national traditions. Many of Rabearivelo's verses are deeply moving. They reveal his frank but unsuccessful efforts to reach to the roots of national life. In the sonnets "Aviavi" and "Filao", describing the contrasting symbols of two different trees, both an example and a warning are given. Aviavi shows how a foreign palm-tree can adapt itself to new soils, while the filao withers away, as it cannot adjust to a foreign environment. This implies, of course, a sort of admonition to those whose poems consist of foreign cadences only. The two sonnets are written in an ancient, imitated form, but they faithfully express the poet's wish to be closer to the traditions of his country and they underline his failure.

Later, Rabearivelo imitated the French Surrealists by using free verse in his collections of poems *Presque songes* (Almost Dreams, 1934) and *Traduit de la nuit* (Translated by Night, 1935) which contains translations of Imerina poems. Here the poet's imagination is linked to the realm of dreams which rule out the force of life. His imagery often springs from ancient legends and myths, but it is too artificial and spontaneous, like that of the Surrealists. It is ironic that in trying to enrich Malagasy culture, Rabearivelo translated Paul Valéry's formalist verses into Malagasy.

Only the last collection *Vieilles chansons d'Imerina* (Old Songs of Imerina, 1939), written in Malagasy and French and published posthumously, can be said to derive from Madagascar's national tradition. His laconic poems in prose reveal the poet's attempts to imitate the popular *hain-teny* form.

Rabearivelo edited his own journal *Calepins bleus* (Blue Notes) and also produced one novel—*L'Aube rouge* (The Red Dawn). His works were published in the newspapers and journals of Madagascar, Mauritius, France, Belgium, Austria and South America. His talent was unquestionable. His poetry has impressive musicality, melancholic depth and fresh rhythm. Each successive collection of poems betrays the poet's efforts to come closer to folklore. But he was unable to employ French poetic techniques to express the contemporary progressive ideas of his native country. He loved trees, and saw himself as a filao withering away in the dry winds of foreign culture, as he was not able to find "the water of life".

Jacques Rabemananjara (born in 1913 in Tananarive) is a poet and playwright whose name is well known at home and abroad. He studied at the Jesuit grammar school in Tananarive. In 1939, he joined the Colonial Administration Service and took a job at the Ministry of Colonies in Paris. There he remained during World War II, studying philosophy and law. After the liberation in 1944, he returned to Madagascar and founded a cultural movement guided by the slogan: "Write like the French, but in your heart remain Malagasy!" The movement published *La Revue des Jeunes* (Young Authors' Journal). Rabemananjara was elected a member of the French National Assembly to represent Madagascar. During the rising of 1947, he was arrested, sentenced to life imprisonment and interned in France where he spent nine years. He was released in 1956, but was permitted to return to his native country only in 1959, when the National Assembly of Madagascar granted amnesty to all patriots who had been sentenced by the French colonial regime in 1947. Shortly afterwards, he was elected a member of Parliament and appointed a government Minister.

His first collections of poems L'éventail de rêve (The Dream Fan), *Aux confins de la nuit* (Within the Confines of Night) and *Sur les marches du soir* (On the Steps of Evening, 1942) are strongly influenced by the French Romantics and Symbolists of the 19th century. But the poet soon followed his predecessor—Rabearivelo. Rabemananjara arrived at indigenous folk traditions by way of the Negro literary movement known as *négritude*.

A borderline between these two stages is represented by his collections *Lyre à sept cordes* (The Seven-String Lyre, 1948), first published in Senghor's *Nouvelle Anthologie de la poésie nègre et malgache d'expression française* (New Anthology of Negro and Malagasy Poetry in the French Language, 1948), *L'Apothéose* (Apotheosis), *Ode à Ranavalona* (Ode to Ranavalona, 1952) and *Rites millénaires* (Millennium-old Rites, 1955) showing the conflict between two cultures, Malagasy and French, multiplied by nostalgia (the poet was interned in France at that time).

In *Lyre à sept cordes*, Rabemananjara contrasts cold, old, war-damaged Europe with his beautiful, legendary homeland. He lauds the heroism of his native country, its glorious past and its infinite beauty. Despite their stylistic differences, Rabemananjara and Senghor are close to each other in their enthusiastic emphasis on their lands' "noble" historical traditions, which they term "royal", in reference, of course, not only to kings, but also to the medieval independent states existing in their countries in pre-colonial times. Their poems are full of nobility, exaggerated imagery and solemn intonation, recalling French neo-Romantic verse. This can also be seen in the love poems of *Rites millénaires*, with their numerous literary associations, names of heroes and gods, Dianas and Mona Lisas.

This eulogy on love for a white woman from the North becomes rather tedious due to its artificiality and over-refinement. These were the observations of the critics, but we should try to ascertain the causes of such influences. Rabemananjara reveals in all his collections a special interest in solemn, romantic and exalted poetry. Consequently, he praises the strength and beauty of sentiments, which he raises to legendary heights. Unfortunately, his example was again somewhat ornate, artificial French neo-Romantic poetry.

Rabemananjara's lyrical collections *Antsa* (1948, 1956) and *Lamba* (1956), written during the period spent in prison and in exile, are professions of love in praise of freedom and Madagascar. The *lamba*, the Malagasy national costume, is the poet's symbol for his native country when he lives far from it. Both collections overflow with patriotic feelings, descriptions of his homeland's natural beauties, eulogies on the undefeated nation, and justifications for its failure in the struggle against the French colonial army in 1947—1956. They call for Malagasy's independence. Although containing many vague and artificial images, they constitute genuine patriotic poetry, as serious and heroic as the poet's life itself.

Rabemananjara also published the following dramas: *Les Dieux malgaches* (Malagasy Gods, 1947), *Les Boutriers de l'Aurore* (The Sailors of Dawn, 1957) and *Les Agapes des Dieux* (Feasts of the Gods, 1962). His political essays *Témoignage malgache et colonialisme,* 1956 (Malagasy Testimony and Colonialism, 1956) and *Nationalisme et problèmes malgaches* (Nationalism and Malagasy Problems, 1958) are also well known. Rabemananjara, whose verses are rich in imagery and noble in ideas, employs in his works old traditions which originated and developed under the Malagasy rulers and is therefore called "the poet of royal traditions".

Flavien Ranaivo (born in 1914 near Tananarive) is a modern French-language poet, folklorist and author of works dealing with art and linguistics. He spent his youth in Imerina, where his father was a governor. Ranaivo came from an intellectual family and acquired a university education (natural sciences, literature) in his native country. Later, he became a member of the Malagasy Academy.

Ranaivo has loved French poetry since his youth. The natural, skilful usage of French in his verses and his subtle irony prove this. But unlike other African and Malagasy poets, Ranaivo soon escaped from the direct influence of French poetry. He was inspired by specific forms of Malagasy folklore, chiefly by *hain-teny,* which form a basis of his extraordinarily sonorous collections *L'ombre et le vent* (The Shadow and the Wind, 1947), *Mes chansons de toujours* (My Long-Known Songs, 1955) and *Le retour au bercail* (Return to the Fold, 1962). The poet tries to preserve the genuinely national specificity of his forms. He does not endeavour to merely repeat them, but prefers to refine and enrich folklore forms, while simultaneously avoiding mysticism. In his handling of these forms, he differs essentially from other modern poets.

Ranaivo also wrote two unusual poems, "The Song of a Truly Loving Man" and "Advice to the Newly Married". The critics wondered what their relationship to the great national liberation struggle of Africa and Madagascar could be. There undoubtedly is some relationship, since the poet attempts to preserve the characteristic qualities of poetic forms, under the very powerful pressure of the colonizers' culture. His "Song" is remarkable for its conciseness, while "Advice", full of proverbs and sayings, offers malicious instructiveness, jokes and witty inuendos.

In addition to poems, Ranaivo has published literary, aesthetic and linguistic studies in various journals at home and abroad. In 1956, he spoke at the First Congress of Negro Writers on Malagasy Folklore, which folklore, due to its long isolation, had remained untouched by foreign influences up to the 20th century. He stressed that proverbs, sayings, fables, *hain-teny*, etc. were essential parts of folklore. In the opinion of Malagasy researchers, common people possess a peculiar belief in the power of the word and love and respect for oratory. One proverb says that the Malagasy who can speak nicely is able to fulfil any activity successfully. The "soul" of the *hain-teny* consists of the special force of proverbs and sayings. Definitions of the *hain-teny* vary. Some consider it a poetic form of debate, a dispute (Faublée says that a *hain-teny* is not recited, that it is used in arguments). Others emphasize its jocose or erotic character or its inseparable connection with music. Ranaivo regards these definitions as too one-sided and thinks that despite the variety of *hain-teny*, their conciseness, rich alliteration, musicality of words and excessive use of proverbs and sayings are their most significant qualities. Popular *hain-teny* not only include old proverbs and sayings, but form and coin new ones. It should be stressed that *hain-teny*, like Ranaivo's verses, are unrhymed. Ranaivo's works mark a new stage in the development of the modern French-language poetry of Madagascar. Henceforth, it was no longer to be affected by French trends or movements, but was to use national traditions in an original manner.

3. Other Genres

Few novels have been written in Madagascar. In the existing ones, their authors usually praise the virtues of their ancestors, ancient traditions, or the sense of duty, but they rarely deal with topical questions of the liberation struggle. They describe, rather than solve, problems. A. Rina, in *My fasan' Ibéby sahondra* (The Grave of the Beloved), tells of a young girl from a noble family who sacrificed her love and life because of her respect for traditions and her father's honour.

Rodlish in *Ranomody* (Return to the Source) describes another young girl also from a noble family who, despite the desires of her parents and the entire family, refuses to marry a physician from a lower-class family. In the end, they marry. After their wedding, the reconciled pair wish to devote all their energies to the fight against leprosy. But the physician catches the disease and dies. His wife swears on his grave that she will continue helping the suffering social outcasts, disregarding all ancient prejudices.

There is no theatre in Madagascar in our sense of the word. Not because the Malagasies would not understand drama, but because no theatrical tradition has been established. Their contemporary plays are a strange mixture of ancient *hain-teny*, tales and choirs in verses, historical or political drama and music. The authors of these remarkable plays are

Ravelomoria, Riberalegue, Dondavitra and others. The modern and fashionable plays written by playwright Ratsimiseta are, in fact, Montmartre cabaret shows and revues transferred to Madagascar.

Antso (The Voice) caters to the new generation of intellectuals who are trying to revive the national literature and defend and enrich the Malagasy language. Another such journal is *Iarivo* (One Thousand).

The Malagasy Academy was established by French scientists in 1902, but Malagasies have prevailed in it since the 1920's. Its task is to perpetuate the country's traditions and protect its cultural heritage. The origin of the Malagasy population has been investigated and determined by ethnographers Rabary, Ranjavoly, Ratrema and Raveliojoana, linguists Rakotonirainy and Razafintsalama, anthropologist Rokoto-Ratsimananga, et al. The Malagasies have also achieved good results and world-wide recognition in medicine, anatomy, physiology, biochemistry, engineering and agriculture.

XIV. THE LITERATURE OF SOUTH AFRICA

1. Introduction

South African writing, in both the vernacular languages and English, has an extraordinary position among the literatures of Black Africa. It possesses what other literatures lack—a tradition extending over several generations. Despite this fact, for a long time it was not thought of as an independent national literature, and those interested in its development had to rely on scattered, fragmentary comments occurring in handbooks dealing with the British Empire in more general terms. As a branch of English literature it is comparatively young (its development could begin only after the establishment of British imperial power in South Africa) and has hardly been able to compete with the other, more developed branches of British writing. Generally speaking, English literary historians have paid little attention to the works written in the overseas territories. Only recently has the so-called Commonwealth literature been more systematically studied. But even in comparison with the literatures of Australia and Canada, etc., it has suffered considerable handicaps. Many South African books were written in Afrikaans or other African languages (e.g. Sotho, Xhosa, Zulu). Creative writing in English only rarely touched on British reality and was not regarded as very interesting. Moreover, the competition with other English-writing authors was so great that certain South African "classics" have remained almost unknown outside the Anglo-Saxon world. Another handicap resulted from the fact that South African writing has never been produced by a single race. The literature of South Africa is a product of a multi-racial society and has been developed by white, coloured and black writers. Some critics doubt whether it should be discussed as one of the literatures of Black Africa. There have been obvious tendencies to separate white authors from the rest.

As some white people born in Africa do not call themselves "Africans", many authors writing about "Africans" mean chiefly black Africans. It is incorrect, though it is frequently done, to treat African culture entirely on a racial basis.

It should be noted that this cultural separatism has been practised by the whites as well as blacks. Even though its causes may be understood, it seems now that a well-balanced survey of South African writing must be based on the inclusion of writers belonging to all racial groups living in that country. The difference between writing in the vernacular languages and writing in English lies in the fact that the former group will hardly include any white man, or "European", to use the term more often employed in South Africa. However, an omission of white authors from South Africa's English-written literature would distort its picture.

It has been observed that the early creative writing of South Africa was not readily appreciated overseas, or one might better say, in Europe. But the country itself was considered fairly promising, even in the last century, and many Europeans wished to visit it. The English began to show an increasing interest in South African affairs in the last quarter of the 19th century.

There was much interest in that part of the world, particularly during the Boer War; South Africa was "discovered" through newspaper reporters. In the sphere of creative writing, romantic ideas still prevailed and the novels of Rider Haggard (1856—1925) were widely read. Some doubts must be expressed concerning his position in the literary sphere, however, and in a study of this sort they might well be mentioned only in passing for Haggard's works are, strictly speaking, a part of English literature. This more or less exceptional mention, therefore, is due both to his originality and to the fact that he dealt in many works with South Africa. Writers of historical tales and pioneer romance reacted in some way or another to his narrative manner. Haggard was very idealistic and eager to invent plots full of adventure. He attracted young readers by showing the black African as a proud warrior. One of the main objections to Haggard's work is that the author looked back too often, in his effort to idealize the primitive tribesmen. His Africa was an unknown, uncivilized land, full of mystery and strange customs.

Modern studies in South African writing have rightly found that there is a danger in an over-concentration on the white man's image of South Africa. An insufficient knowledge of the Bantu languages and the peculiarities of vernacular writing prevented many serious students from obtaining an "inside" view of South Africa, while some English writing about South Africa was rather superficial, or even biased. It is natural, therefore, that a growing interest should develop in hearing the real voice of Africa and knowing the other version of the story. Parallel with the activities of ethnographers, anthropologists, historians and folklorists, those of the linguists developed, enabling each generation of them to penetrate more deeply into the nature of indigenous thinking and writing in South Africa. Although some of their early findings were rather unilaterally conceived, as they lacked an adequate evaluation of literary history, criticism, aesthetics, etc., they attracted public attention to hitherto ignored artistic values.

Numerous studies dealt exclusively with South African vernacular writing. Obviously, this writing is worth scholarly treatment, but the emphasis placed upon it was sometimes excessive, especially when discussed by those who were pursuing a definite political purpose: namely, to show it in contrast to English writing, as a native, truly South African creativeness. This approach, which tended to consider English as a "foreign", imported language, was not too remote from the nationalists' exaggerations. English has played an important role not only from the artistic standpoint, but also from the ideological one. As a widespread language, it has been used by many writers who wished to express their own attitudes toward burning social issues and to reach readers both in South Africa and abroad. No other written language of South Africa has fulfilled this function better than English.

English has often been used by journals and magazines supporting the South African

Negro, while Afrikaans has been chosen by those nationalists who were interested in propagating the white man's racist propaganda and backing up the official reactionary doctrines. Such has been the situation in the sphere of journalism.

In the field of fiction, the situation has been more complicated. Here, the number of anti-apartheid English-writing authors is indeed large. This fact in itself is not surprising; it results logically from the historical development of South Africa. Many factors revelant to an evaluation of the literary development of that country are identical with those referred to in our previous discussion on other parts of Black Africa. Christianity is one of these factors; however, a few words should be added at this point, to illustrate its role in the South African milieu. Owing to the relatively long activities of the South African missions, Christianity influenced South African writers more than their West African colleagues. Such traces can be discovered mainly in the works of many vernacular authors. If one takes into account the various causes of the slow development of vernacular writing, one discovers that its decreasing social significance was somehow connected with its excessive religious didacticism. This writing has developed partly in another direction than English-written protest literature, and it is, therefore, discussed in a separate chapter of this book. For a surprisingly long time the Christianity introduced by the white missionaries was mechanically connected with the technological progress of modern civilization. On the other hand, the Church sometimes interpreted resistance to political and economic oppression as "a lack of gratitude" on the part of South Africa's Negroes. Of course, Christianity has played a rather ambiguous role in South Africa and elsewhere. Religion was a very significant component in the spiritual life of the Boer farmers who were highly conservative, both in economic and political matters. There have been church authorities who favoured apartheid, but also clergymen who rejected that racist doctrine.

For the above-mentioned reasons and due to the extraordinary wealth of South African writing, we shall discuss this subject in two chapters: first, the vernacular literatures, and second, English-language writing. Both tendencies have been in constant contact and have reacted to the same conditions in the country. Consequently, they must be considered in connection with South Africa's political life.

2. South African Writing in the Vernacular Languages

2.0 In comparison with other African countries, the situation in South Africa is much more complicated, owing to its linguistic as well as political aspects. That country's official language has always been English and this is still the predominant language. (The Boers' Dutch was for a long time merely tolerated.) Only in 1925 was Afrikaans (a mixture of the Dutch, Bantu, Hottentot and Bushman languages) legally recognized as the second official language, in place of Dutch. There are many African vernacular languages in South Africa—e.g. Sotho, Tswana, Zulu and Xhosa, etc.—and these became standard languages in the middle of the 19th and beginning of the 20th century.

The country's political development was affected by the large number of wars waged by the Bantu tribes (the Kaffirs, i.e. Xhosas and Zulus) against the Boers and the English. These wars had varying results, ending in victories and defeats on both sides. The conflicting interests of the Boers and the English led to the Boer War (1899—1902), in which the Boers were defeated. But a few years later a period of reconciliation followed, as Britain promised not to interfere into South African affairs. It was during this period that the military campaigns against the Zulu King Dinizulu began in Natal (1907). But soon after that war, a large part of the territory was occupied, and in 1910 the Union of South Africa emerged from the original Cape Town Colony, the Orange Free State, the Transvaal and Natal. The new Union was declared a British dominion. A period of relatively tranquil political development followed; this was also the period during which the cultural activities of the English, Afrikaaners and Africans began. The most disturbing years of this period were, of course, those of World War I, however, the field of literature was not much affected by them. A worse period began after the elections of 1924, when the Nationalists' party won and its leader, General Hertzog, became the Prime Minister of the Union of South Africa. Under him, certain racist laws introducing discrimination and segregation were passed; these were directed not only against the Bantu population, but against all kinds of cultural activities. During this wave of repression, some missionaries, as the owners of publishing houses, also became involved. Their attitudes affected, among others, the Basuto writer, Thomas Mofolo, author of the novel *Shaka*. The missionaries saw in this work the author's return to a pagan faith and managed to delay its publication for twenty years. South African writing in African vernacular languages, the beginnings of which date from the middle of the 19th century, was not particularly comprehensive or varied, as it was too much concerned with tribal history.

Among the Xhosa writers, one should mention those collectors of short stories, essays and proverbs who produced their literary adaptations: T. Soga (1831—1871) and W. W. Gqoba (1840—1888). Soga translated a part of *Pilgrim's Progress* (Uhambo lo Mhambi), while Gqoba described the famous Xhosa historical traditions in Mongqavuse. Many works from the initial period of Xhosa writing may be found in the anthology *Zemk'Inkomo Magwalandini* (Keep Your Heritage, 1906), compiled and edited by W. B. Rubusana, and in the later collection, *Imibengo* (Delicacies, 1936), edited by W. G. Bennie.

2.1 Sotho Writing

Before Thomas Mofolo (1873—1948), there were two outstanding Basuto writers: Everitt Lechese Segoete (1858—1923) and Zakea D. Mangoaela (1883—1963) who compiled collections of folk traditions and wrote short stories. But Mofolo was unquestionably the greatest author in all of Bantu literature. He was brought up in a mission school and became a Christian. After finishing his higher school education, he worked as a teacher and later at the Sesuto Book Depot (the Basuto Publishing-House) of Morija. Having written his novel *Shaka*, the publication of which was so much delayed by the missionaries, he became disillusioned, as he lacked understanding. Turning away from Christianity, he stopped writing and teaching, and devoted himself first to trade and then to agriculture. In his works, he used the Sotho language. He is generally regarded as the first great African novelist of the 20th century.

His first novel *Pitseng* (In a Pot, 1910) described a South African's childhood, education and behaviour in the Christian spirit. His second novel *Moeti oa Bochabela* (The Traveller to the East, 1912) deals with a boy who goes out to seek an "unknown saviour". The novel can be considered a Christian parable of the boy's serious efforts to find God who condemns hatred, violence and who dwells in all human beings and societies. Viewed from a different angle, the novel can be understood as a description of a painful search for new Christian ideals.

His third novel *Shaka* (1925) tells of the Zulu king who founded the Zulu empire in the 19th century. It does not present any detailed biography of the famous warrior or of the history of his empire. The author makes use of all accessible sources (memoirs, legends, eulogies, poems, songs, oral traditions) as a historical basis for his narrative about the human selfishness and passionate ambitions which drive Shaka to his tragic end. He does not try to idealize or excuse Shaka's cruelty, nor does he declare him to be an "unredeemed savage", as some writers do. Mofolo understands Shaka as an extraordinary military commander, one of the Caesar-Napoleon-Shaka breed, and this approach is undoubtedly the correct one.

The author mentions certain customs followed and respected in Shaka's time by all members of the tribe, including the chief. Thus, we can learn that the fighter who killed his enemy in a battle was allowed to "purify" himself by coitus with an unmarried girl; then he could return to his normal life, if the girl agreed and if she did not become pregnant before her wedding.

As a consequence of such a "purification action" by Chief Senzangakhona (1757—1816) and the girl, Nandi, this couple got married and soon after the wedding (1787) a boy, whose name was Shaka, was born. The Chief was delighted, as this was his first-born son. When Shaka grew older, the chief's principal wives bore the following sons: Mfokazana, Dingane, Mhlangana and Mpande. The wives then asked Chief Senzangakhona to drive Nandi and Shaka out of the court. Otherwise, they threatened, they would betray to King Jobe (who ruled the Thetwa tribe) and to the entire Ifanilendja tribe the fact that Nandi had become pregnant before her wedding. Consequently, Senzangakhona, though he loved Nandi and Shaka, had to repudiate them. They returned to her native village, but the local inhabitants despised them. Shaka's life was embittered particularly by the shepherds, boys of his own kind, who thrashed him whenever they met him. Shaka soon got used to receiving blows, but he also learnt how to thrash these boys thoroughly. For this reason, he was very much feared by the youngsters, who then decided to elect him their leader, *Mampoli*. In this way the author wished to show how Shaka's harsh younger days hardened him and turned him into a bold, fierce fighter. Mofolo inserts in his narrative, according to customary practice, the folk-songs and legends about Shaka which have been preserved by oral traditions down to the present time.

Once Shaka killed a lion and saved a girl carried away by a hyena. He was much admired by the girls and women, who celebrated him in their songs. On another occasion, Shaka came to a nearby cave. As he was walking through its caverns, he heard a strange voice coming from an unknown place. Suddenly he came to the bank of a lake to listen to the voice predicting his splendid career as a powerful ruler. One day he came to Dingiswayo, Jobe's successor, and asked him for his protection. He became a warrior in Dingiswayo's army and displayed so much boldness and courage that the king promoted him to the post of commander (*induna*) of one of his best regiments (*impi*). When in the next battle Shaka succeeded in taking prisoner the enemy chief, Zwide (of the Ndandwa tribe), Dingiswayo appointed him commander-in-chief of all his regiments.

At Dingiswayo's court, Shaka met the king's sister, Noliwe, and fell in love with her. The king approved of their love, as he wished to use the marriage to bind Shaka to his own tribe. He hoped that Shaka would succeed him as ruler. The battle against the Ngwana followed. In the meantime, Zwide (who had been liberated soon after his imprisonment) attacked the Thethwa, took Dingiswayo prisoner and had him executed. After the decapitation, Dingiswayo's head was displayed at the gathering place of his former residence. Shaka was just returning from a victorious battle. Instead of welcoming him, the people looked fearfully at Dingiswayo's head. All the fighters and other tribesmen asked Shaka to become their chief (*inkosi*) and protector. Shaka accepted and immediately set out on his punitive expedition against Zwide. The result was the sanguinary destruction of the enemy. Zwide himself was pursued and had to flee to the Pedija tribe, where he soon died. Thus, Shaka became a victorious commander and ruler at a relatively young age. He was feared by all the neighbouring tribes and his name was sufficient to frighten other peoples.

According to legend, Isanusi, who was both a sorcerer and an evil spirit, suggested to Shaka that he choose a new name for his Ifanilendja and Thethwa tribes. This name, he said, should express the power of both the king and the tribe. Shaka was said to have chosen the name, "Zulu, Amazulu" (sky, sky people, i.e. the invincible). Moreover, the legend states that Isanusi advised Shaka to kill his sweetheart, Noliwe—that is, Shaka had to choose: either Noliwe, or great fame. Shaka chose fame.

It is certain that Shaka's behaviour was dramatically changed after the death of his pregnant mistress, Noliwe. His kindness disappeared and he thought only of murder, which completely preoccupied his mind. He could no longer feel friendship or love. He formed his "girls' regiment" and his harem of twelve thousand "sisters", but he did not marry. He was even considered the murderer of his own mother, Nandi.

After careful military preparations, Shaka launched his conquering expedition against all the neighbouring tribes. His enemies in battles were surprised by his powerful attacks. They never resisted, but fled to save their lives, while their villages were being pillaged and burnt. The young people were taken prisoners. They could join the Zulu army, if they wished. But if they refused, they had to work as slaves in the fields. After these battles, Shaka used to call his fighters together to check their weapons. Those who did not have their own assagais and those taken from the enemy formed a special group, as did the cowards who had deserted the battlefield. These two groups were killed in front of the gathered warriors. In this way, Shaka tried to strengthen his men's fighting spirit and his own personal power. Thus, he created a unique Zulu state with a strict military organization and a powerful army dominated by its cruel discipline, ensuring its position with its well-controlled rear. The respect enjoyed by Shaka among his fighters and the common people is well seen in Mofolo's eulogy.

Shaka continued his military expeditions in all directions and forced the submission of many tribes. There was much confusion in Southeastern Africa. The strong tribes resisted and fought Shaka, but they were destroyed; the weak ones greatly feared him and moved from one place to another, fleeing him. This migration was rather unusual in the history of South Africa.

The year 1825 was the worst period in Shaka's life. His best commander, Mzilikazi, persuaded his fighters to take Zulu women with them when setting out on an expedition. They were told to leave Shaka behind. Shaka, however, learned about this plan and immediately sent his commander Manukuza to punish and kill Mzilikazi. Manukuza also deserted and led his fighters to the other bank of the Limpopo, where he founded a new empire. When some of Manukuza's fighters returned together with their commanders with their task unfulfilled, Shaka, enraged at this situation, ordered the commanders of the regiments burnt alive.

Shaka sent several plundering expeditions to the north and the south, where the Zulu warriors clashed with enemies more dangerous than themselves. Thousands of Zulu fighters were killed, while the rest barely escaped. Shaka's power already seemed to be declining: his name no longer frightened his enemies, as in earlier days.

The Zulu people, weary of these continual wars and disturbances, found the slaughter of numerous women and children repulsive. They even expressed this idea in their proverb: "A boy is an ox assigned to the vultures." Shaka obviously sensed the decline of his power and glory and therefore furiously had his people killed under any pretext. His fighters ceased to admire him and grew increasingly discontent.

Shaka's brothers, Dingane and Mhlangana, went with the army to defeat the enemy in the north, but they returned, pretending that they were sick. Both of them had seen that the tribes were dissatisfied and tired and that they obeyed the orders unwillingly. They came back with the intention of killing Shaka and assuming power. Shaka was sitting in front of his hut, dreaming... One of his brothers came up to him, while the other approached the ruler from behind; they stabbed Shaka with their assagais... At that moment, Shaka felt the pain and awoke. Dingane and Mhlangana ran off, frightened... Shaka's prophetic words uttered before his death in 1828 allegedly foresaw the white man's domination in the future.

In Shaka, Mofolo criticized and condemned "pagan" customs, clearly illustrating their harmful efects. However, the missionaries who owned the publishing house persisted in seeing in Shaka the author's return to paganism and therefore permitted the publishing of the book only twenty years later. Even so, Shaka, as well as Mofolo's two preceding books, were censored and their texts slightly altered. The authorities and the Roman

Catholic Church permitted the books' publication only on condition that religious and political problems would be avoided, especially if the author were an African. Even though Mofolo was forced to write his books in conformity with the existing conditions of the ruling regime, he exerted a strong influence on his own generation and on the following authors writing in African languages. His period is considered the golden epoch of Bantu literatures.

Tswana writing of the initial period is represented by Solomon Tshekisho Plaatje (about 1900 to about 1940). In the early period, he translated a number of Shakespeare's plays, e.g. *Julius Caesar, A Comedy of Errors, The Merchant of Venice, Othello* and *Much Ado About Nothing* into Tswana, his mother tongue.

Plaatje was one of the first fighters for the rights of the South African Negroes against Boer domination. He wrote in English *The Mote and the Beam,* which sold eighteen thousand copies. In this way, he succeeded in financing his trip to the United States. As a politician, he presented a long English-written account of the difficult situation of black Africans living in the Union of South Africa, describing a number of striking episodes under the title *Native Life in South Africa,* before and since the European War and the Boer rebellion (1916, 352 pp).

His novel *Mhudi* was written before 1920, but for unknown reasons it was published only in 1930. In this novel about love and struggle, the Rolonga fight the Zulus, who in turn resist the Boers, assisted by the Rolonga. The action takes place near the Vaal, in the 19th century. The novel's main character is Mhudi, an unmarried girl from the town of Kunana. She is a reaper from the Rolonga tribe. Shaka's former commander, Mzilikazi, crosses the Dragon mountains to find new lands for his Ndebele (Matabele) tribe. He plunders Kunana, thus taking his revenge for the murder of his two tax-collectors. Gubuzu, Mzilikazi's able, cunning officer, openly admits that the plundering and burning of Kunana was a cheap victory over its powerless people. Mhudi flees from her native town, far from her slaughtered fellow citizens, and accidentally meets Ra-Thaga, who has also succeeded in escaping from Kunana. Although they did not know each other before, they fall in love and get married in the peaceful country of Chief Moroka. Moroka wants to help the Boer, Sarel Cilliers, most members of whose family were killed by Mzilikazi's Ndebeles. One day, Ra-Thaga is caught just as he is about to take revenge for the murder of his and Mhudi's compatriots at Kunana. Fortunately though, he escapes death and, together with his wife, Mhudi, he is able to devote himself to the education of their children.

In Plaatje's novel, his black characters—who are often described as cruel rulers, stupid fellows, faithful slaves or rebellious servants by European writers—are common people. They possess normal qualities as well as loyalty, confidence and sometimes a clever intellect. They are also cowards, filled with desire for revenge, sensuality and cruelty— typical representatives of the human race. The author sees the Boers as representatives of the European civilization, who make use of superior, dangerous military techniques and who resort to terror to make the Africans submissive and temporarily resigned.

Plaatje was a politician and historian rather than a novelist. Despite the fact that he was a member of a nation whose territory was devastated by the Zulus (Ndebele) and the Boers, he injected neither envy nor cruelty into his writing. As a traditional narrator, he inserted poems into his prose work. The first South African author, he was aware of the need to preserve traditional folk-poems, folk-tales, proverbs and sayings—before they were lost in oblivion. He compiled and edited *Sechuana Proverbs and their European Equivalents* and *Bantu Folk-Tales and Poems*.

Zulu writing started with M. M. Fuze's first book *Abantu Abanyama Bapha Travela* (Negroes and Where They Came From, 1922). Largely historical in character, it served as an example for such later writers as J. L. Dube and B. W. Vilakazi.

If one follows the general trends in the modern vernacular writing of South Africa, one may arrive at the conclusion that the period from the 1920's to the 1940's could be considered the beginnings of the racist and reactionary tendencies initiated by Hertzog's cabinet. But these facts did not excessively affect literature. That period saw the publishing of Zulu, Sotho and Tswana newspapers, journals and books, all of which exerted a strong influence on African intellectuals. It was also a period of the development of national literatures in the vernacular languages.

The African National Congress, founded in 1912, was the first mass organization of the Bantu people fighting against the government's racist policies. The democratic forces found favourable conditions for their development during and shortly after the end of World War II. But in the elections of 1948, Malan's Nationalist Party won as the representative of the most reactionary whites, and a period of darkness set in. Apartheid became the official governing doctrine. In 1950, the government banned the Communist Party of the Union of South Africa, in accordance with the Suppression of Communism Act. In that same year, The Group Areas Act and The Immorality Amendment Act were issued. These acts started not only the forceful relocation of the black and coloured population but they also banned mixed marriages and sexual intercourse between Europeans and non-Europeans, i.e. the coloured and the natives. This meant in practice that Africans would henceforth not be allowed to enter most hotels, theatres or cinemas, that they could take only seats especially reserved for them in public transport vehicles, that they could use only special counters in post-offices, and separate entrances to public buildings, and that higher education would be almost inaccessible to them. In 1959, the many strikes and demonstrations against the government, which took place all over the country, were brutally suppressed (e.g. about seventy Africans were killed in Sharpeville). In 1953, a new era started in South African writing when African authors were warned that their manuscripts had to be suitable for educative purposes and that they must not deal with political or religious problems.

The first black Afrikaans-writing author was Arthur Nuthall Fula. He obeyed the rules and regulations and produced in "the new spirit" the novels *Johannie giet die beeld* (Johannie Casts a Statue, 1954) and *Met erbarming, o Here* (Mercy, My Lord, 1957). His heroes from Johannesburg are entirely "exemplary", they succeed in overcoming the temptations of dancing, the cinema and drunkenness, the three amusements and vices officially permitted South African natives. They discuss no religious or political problems. This "exemplary writing for schoolboys" never mentions racial discrimination and is directed by the principle: the Negro is a sinner, the white man is an angel.

The other literatures, in Zulu, Xhosa, Tswana and Sotho, proceeded to develop in accordance with this regulation. Although some authors, including Herbert Dhlomo, Rolfes R. R. Dhlomo, Silas M. Molana, D. D. T. Jabavu and Katie Mandisodza, also used English for their works, they were nevertheless affected by the harsh decision of 1953. These authors found no other choice than to seek their escapist subjects in history, to write hunting stories, travel books, fables or eulogies, or to leave South Africa altogether (like Peter Abrahams, Ezekiel Mphahlele, and others) in order to present true descriptions of the situation there.

It need not be stressed that all these political changes in South Africa have been directly or indirectly reflected in vernacular literature, and especially in poetry. The three following periods in South African writing can be clearly distinguished.

1. Up to the 1930's (already discussed herein).
2. From the 1930's to 1953 (tightening of the racist regime).
3. From 1953 until today (the period of darkness).

All these periods (especially the last two) are characterized by different degrees of freedom for the author, with respect to his possibility to choose subjects and develop them.

2.2 Zulu Writing

The Zulus, who are well aware of their famous past, excel among the many South African black authors, owing to their fight for freedom and for equal rights and to their radical opposition to racist legislation. They frequently celebrate their famous kings as well as Shaka, Dingane, Tsetshwayo and Dinizulu and their fathers and ancestors, in historical and biographical legends, novels and plays written in the Zulu language.

John Langalebalele Dube chose the period of Shaka for his novel *Insila kaShaka* (Shaka's Chamberlain, 1933) and historian Rolfes Reginald Raymond Dhlomo discussed the period ranging from Senzangakhona—Shaka's father, Dingane and Mpande to Tsetshwayo—Mpande's son, in his series of historico-biographical novels *UDingane kaSenzangakhona* (Dingane, Senzangakhona's Son, 1938), *UShaka* (Shaka, 1937), *UMpande kaSenzangakhona* (Mpande, Senzankakhona's Son, 1938) and *UCetshwayo* (Tsetshwayo, 1952). Because of the strict law of 1953, Dhlomo's novel describing conflicts and disturbances between the blacks and Indians in Durban, in January 1950, could not published.

Historical novels are very much in favour among the Zulus; one of them was written by the great poet, B. W. Vilakazi. His *UDingiswayo kaJobe* (Dingiswayo, Jobe's Son) described the period of the unification of different tribes (the Thethwa, Ifanilendja, Ndwandwa, Ngwana and others) into the Zulu nation, which was successfully realized by Shaka only after Dingiswayo's death.

Folk legends, songs and poems about Shaka are equally popular. The Zulu recite them every year at the grave of the "great lion and elephant" Shaka, at Stanger, the little town about forty miles northeast of Durban and about four miles from the coast of the Indian Ocean, in Natal (near Shaka's former residence at Gungudlovu).

The greatest modern Zulu author, Benedict Wallet Vilakazi, represents an important trend in protest writing. Born at Groutville in Natal (1906), he died in Johannesburg (1947). After finishing school at Groutville, he studied at the College of Education at Mariannhill. From 1923 on, he worked as a teacher. He was particularly interested in philology and literature and studied, in particular, the oral traditions of the South African Bantu nationalities (Zulu, Xhosa, Sotho, Tswana etc.). Without leaving his job, he succeeded in obtaining his B.A. degree at the University of Witwatersrand (1934). In 1935 he published his scholarly work *The Origin and Development of Zulu Poetry,* obtained his M.A. degree for it. In 1936—1947, he lectured at the University of Witwatersrand in the Department of Bantu Languages. In cooperation with Professor Clement M. Doke, a South African researcher in Bantu linguistics, he wrote and published a Zulu-English Dictionary (1945). In 1946, his research work *Oral and Written Literature of the Nguna* (Nguna and other Bantu nationalities) was published and Vilakazi obtained his Ph.D.

Vilakazi began his activities at the end of the 1920's when racist legislation was just starting to be applied in his country. He wrote in Zulu, and could not—and did not want to—give up his mother tongue. He wrote for his fellows with whom he had spent his youth at Groutville and during his twelve years' teaching at Mariannhill. Vilakazi felt immense respect for the culture of his nation which had been deliberately humiliated by the colonizers. As a scholar, he understood that a people's true national literature, and especially their poetry, is closely connected with the language and history of their nation.

Vilakazi's poetry is the truthful statement of a courageous man; his protest against racial oppression, it is also his emotionally expressed appeal to struggle. In his *Missionaries' God,* he exposes the white man's God as an instrument of deception: the black man has always been deprived of his riches and lands, "with God's assistance" or "in the name of God".

Vilakazi sees the only path to liberation as struggle, a cruel fight which, the poet firmly believes, will be victorious. Each of Vilakazi's poems includes his central idea of the fight for freedom, stimulating and encouraging its readers and listeners. The poet admits the difficult fate of the black man and shows the need for a patient waiting for the time of victory.

Vilakazi was a Zulu national poet of genuine talent. His verses are closely linked with Zulu national poetry. Their form often imitates folk-songs but their imagery is sometimes taken over from national eposes. He published two collections of poems: *Inkondlo kaZulu* (Zulu Songs, 1935) and *Amal'ezulu* (Zulu Horizons, 1945). Vilakazi's historical novel *UDingiswayo kaJobe* (Dingiswayo, the Son of Jobe, 1939) and contemporary novels *Noma nini* (Whenever, 1935) and *Nje-nempela* (Quite a Lot, 1955), which were written under the influence of J. L. Dube and R.R.R. Dhlomo, were devoted to the same burning problems that had excited the older writers. In them, the author celebrates his nation's famous past and describes their contemporary poverty and lack of rights. Vilakazi died too young. Although his life was hard in the country of racism and segregation, he succeeded in overcoming poverty and humiliation thanks to his persistence, courage, belief in his own powers and love of work. As a scholar, poet and novelist, he greatly contributed to the development of South African vernacular writing in the Bantu languages.

Recognizing the strictness of South Africa's racial laws, the younger Zulu writers try to say everything in parables. They choose inconspicuous, often escapist subject-matter and develop it in such a way that the censorship cannot interfere, but their readers can understand the authors' slight allusions. It is not an easy way, but it is necessary...

Like historical novels, contemporary and historical plays were much in favour before 1953, and present-day Zulu writers often continue along these lines. For their novels and plays, they mostly choose historical topics, e.g. Kenneth Bengu in his novel *UKadebona iqhawe lenkosi* (The Chief's Hero is an Experienced Man, 1958), James Ngumbi in *Ukuzalwa kuka-Muntukaziwa* (The Birth of Muntukaziwa, 1957), J.E.S. Tchamase in *UNsingizi* (Nsingizi, 1959), Elliot Zondi in *Ukufa kukaShaka* (The Death of Shaka, 1960) or L. M. Mbulawa in *UMamfene* (Mamfene, 1952).

Truly "escapist" are those novels, short stories and plays which have neutral subjects but which use parables for veiling contemporary problems, e.g. Maduna's novel, *Lemuka izwe elihle* (The Beautiful World Vanishes, 1957), Jordan K. Ugubane's novel *Uvalo lwezinhlonzi* (Eternal Fear, 1957) and Cyril Lincoln Sibusiso Nyembezi's satirical novel *Inkisela yaseMgungundlovu* (The Brag of Pietermaritzburg). The same is true of the play by Jeremiah Andries Blose, *Uqomise mina uje uqomisa iliba* (If You Fall in Love with Me, You Will Love Best, 1960) or *Inkinga yomendo* (Troubles with the Wedding, 1961) by Benjamin John Dube, as well as Leonhard L. J. Mncwang's plays *Kusasa umngcwabo nami* (Tomorrow Your and My Revenge Will Come, 1969), *Ngenzeni?* (What Have I Done?, 1959) and *Mhla iyokwendela egodini* (The Day I Was Engaged to the Grave), etc. The short stories, *Emhlabeni, nezinye izindaba* (On the Earth and Other Stories, 1963) were written by Simeon Thandindawo Zeblon Khwela and Otty Ezrom Howard Nxumalo.

John Charles Dlamini published his collection of poems Inzululwana (Great Sensation, 1958) and James Shadrack Mkhulu Matsebula presented his poetry in *Iqoqo lezinkondlo ziqoqwe sahlelwa* (The Council's Discussions are Over, 1957). An anthology of children's verse compiled by Cyril Lincoln Sibisiso Nyembezi was published under the title *Imisebe yalanga; imilolozelo nezinkondlo* (Sun Rays: Lullabies and Poems, 1959—1961, 3 volumes).

2.3 Xhosa Writing

Samuel Edward Krune Mqhayi belonged to the old generation which dealt with almost all literary genres. Mqhayi never wrote plays but he produced a number of other works. *Ityala lama-wele* (The Trial of the Twin Brothers, 1914) is a novel based on a real case (it was republished in 1931 and 1953). Mqhayi also published *Imihobe nemibongo yokufundwa ezilkoweni* (Cheerful Songs and Lullabies for School, 1927), the historico-biographical novel

U-Mqhayi wase-Ntab'ozuko (Mqhayi from Prayer Mountain, 1936—republished in 1957) and the collection of poems *I-uzuzo* (The Reward, 1942—republished in 1957).

A.C. Jordan (b. about 1912) lectured in the African Department of the University of Cape Town until 1964. Today he is working at the University of Wisconsin, USA. The themes of Jordan's novel *Ingqumbo yeminyanya* (The Wrath of the Ancestors, 1940—republished in 1951), which was written originally in Xhosa and then translated into English, is the conflict between modern thinking and tribal traditions. Two fellow students from a mission school get married and come back home. One of them is a hereditary chief. His wife goes mad because the tribe persecutes her. The tribesmen think that her Christian way of living offends their sacred tribal traditions. Ezekiel Mphahlele mentions in his criticism that hereditary chiefdom no longer exists, so that there is little topical relevance in Jordan's incident. But in other parts of Africa, hereditary chiefdom is still preserved; old customs have been maintained to the present time and will undoubtedly exist in the future, though under altered conditions.

3. South African Writing in English

Thomas Pringle (1789—1834) was a romantic poet who came from Scotland to Cape Town in 1819. He returned to London after six years spent in South Africa, but most of his books were inspired by South African reality. His *African Sketches* (1834) include the well-known poem "The Bechuana Boy". His *Narrative of a Resident of South Africa*, written in prose, is very interesting but non-fictional. The Scottish poet, who became active in the anti-slavery compaign, liked the South African native as a passive creature and created pleasant portraits of South African scenery. His Negro remains a noble victim of the white man's "barbaric civilization", which can be seen in *Ephemerides* (1828) and in *Afar in the Desert and Other South African Poems* (1881).

In 1867, diamonds were discovered near Kimberley. New waves of settlers had come there before Cecil Rhodes amalgamated the diamond diggings (the De Beers Company, 1880) and introduced more advanced machinery and railway transport. Other important discoveries provoked the Transvaal gold rush but neither the British colonies (Cape Town and Natal) nor the Boer Republics could achieve prosperity at that time, because of the frequent clashes with the African tribes (the Zulu War was won by Britain in 1880, but the Basuto uprising followed) and the conflict between Britain and the Transvaal (which was won at Majuba Hill in 1881). It is not necessary to describe here the increasing tension between the British imperialists and Kruger's conservative Transvaalers who had owned gold deposits at Witwatersrand (called the Rand) since 1886. The Boer Republics became richer, but at the same time experienced troubles with their immigrants (the Uitlanders) who had no franchise. Their dissatisfaction was made to serve the purpose of Rhodes' imperialist expansionist schemes. Rhodes wished to create a united South Africa and gradually added territories to those already ruled by the British Crown. His dream was to build up and control a railway line from Cairo to Cape Town. He became the Prime

Minister of the Cape Town Colony, but lost his political position after the failure of Dr Jameson's raid in 1895. Dr. Jameson, Rhodes' ruler in Rhodesia, started an attack on the Transvaal before the surprised Uitlanders could organize their own uprising. The political crisis, affected by the different attitudes of the European powers (England, Germany, France, Portugal, etc.), led to the Boer War (1899—1902), which ended with Britain's victory and the Peace of Vereenining (May 31, 1902).

South Africa's racial problems have always had a social background. They could not be solved by the government of the Union (which came into being as a result of the amalgamation of the four colonies in 1910, as a British dominion). The temporary cooperation of the pro-British wing of the white bourgeoisie, led by Prime Minister Botha and General Smuts in cooperation with Hertzog, did not last long. In 1912, Hertzog, representing the nationalist trend in cultural and educational policies (equal opportunities for Afrikaaners) left the government and established his own party, which was strongly opposed to Smuts' Holism, the ideology of the South African Party.

The period of World War I witnessed the laying of the foundations of the segregationalist policy which was to be carried out intensely in the late 1920's. The nationalist leaders opposed the government which had supported the British cause in World War I. They even organized riots and campaigns and actually succeeded in gaining the favour of the rural Afrikaaners. After Botha's death (1919), Smuts' position was also weakened, owing to the revolutionary spirit of the proletariat. The Labour Party, partly inspired by the newly-established Communist Party (founded in 1921), organized a significant strike in 1922. But even before that there had been strikes of Bantu workers (in 1920) and conflicts between Kadalie's Industrial and Commercial Union and the police. The post-war period, which was influenced by the Great October Revolution and was filled with class struggles, led to a new situation in South African political life. While the government had been able to rely on the support of the Labour Party before World War I, now many workers were joining the opposition. This, of course, was utilized by the leading opposition force—Hertzog's nationalists. Thus, the post-war economic depression and workers' actions indirectly helped to strengthen the more reactionary wing of the white politicians. The general dissatisfaction of the proletariat was comprehensible, but it was precisely at that time that the chances of democracy were lost.

This turbulent period found a few women writers in the realm of literature, who were, however, still being influenced by the Late Victorian tradition. One of them was Olive Emilie Albertina Schreiner (1855—1920). Her father was a missionary at Wittebergen in the Cape Colony. In 1872, Olive Schreiner went to visit her brother, Theo, one of the numerous diggers during the Kimberley diamond rush. Other experiences were gained when she worked as a governess. She began her career as a creative writer in the 1870's. Her novel, *Undine*, was finished probably in 1876. *The Story of an African Farm* was completed in 1878. It was mainly *The Story of an African Farm* that made her famous. *Undine* was published only after the author's death (in 1928).

While *Undine* sees protection from injustice in diligent work and activity, the positive characters in *The Story of an African Farm* are unable to find any remedy and resort to their prayers. *Undine* deals more deeply with topical questions and, in particular, with the rapid social changes taking place during the period in which the novel was written. Olive Schreiner wrote essays and fiction. Her famous novel *Trooper Halkett of Mashonaland* was completed in 1896.

During the Boer War, Mrs. Schreiner had to spend some time in a concentration camp, despite her poor health (she suffered from asthma) where she was interned for about eighteen months. During World War I, she lived in England, returning to South Africa in 1920, the year of her death.

Undine certainly contains some autobiographical features. This lovely girl likes reading as much as Olive Schreiner did, and she also leaves for England. Her brother Frank studies at the Medical Faculty, just as the author had planned to do. Undine experiences a tragedy: her brother is drowned and his fiancée goes mad. As Undine is a pretty woman, the gentlement court her, especially George Blaire and his male relatives. Finally she marries George Blaire but relatively soon becomes a widow. After a series of dramatic events she comes to her native country, South Africa, in the period of the diamond rush. There she finds the only man whom she has ever really loved: Albert Blaire, who is now married and is being deceived by his wife. Both Undine and Albert die during the same night with Undine feeling a strage kind of happiness, though she meets her great love in the man who is already dead. Mrs. Schreiner describes the backwardness and obscurantism of the Boer villagers, who conserve their archaic system of life. The idyllic aspects of rural life are made memorable through successful descriptions which are so characteristic of pioneer works in all literatures.

Olive Schreiner's moving story *Trooper Peter Halkett of Mashonaland* was appreciated by readers not only because it was skilfully narrated, but mainly because its characters could easily be understood.

The story of a black African who is to be executed for espionage is intended not only to expose the violence of the white invaders, but also to celebrate the noble hero, who sacrifices his own life for the sake of the black African, and is killed by the English. As in her other works, the writer's attention is concentrated here upon the psychology of the white hero, while the black African plays only a minor role. The story is only partly devoted to the racial conflict, devoting more attention to the rivalry between the English and the Boers.

In some of her works, Olive Schreiner discloses her philosophical and lyrical power. Her *Dreams* (1890) remind us of Oscar Wilde, both with respect to its calm reflexion and for its suberb manner of story-telling. This book should not be confused with *Stories, Dreams ad Allegories*, published only after the writer's death, as was her less well-known work *From Man to Man* (1926).

Mrs. Schreiner's essays do not belong to the realm of fiction, but they are just as compelling as her novels. *Woman and Labour* (1911) was published by herself, *Thoughts on South Africa* was published by her husband in 1925. *The Political Situation in* 1895 was written by both of them.

Her essays show how the author understood such important events in South African history as the Great Trek and the Boer War. She knew the hatred of the rural Boers who were fighting against the native tribes in the border regions; she knew the prejudiced indifference of the English-speaking townspeople and she also knew the efforts of her contemporaries, the enlightened white intellectuals, who regarded the Negroes as their fellow citizens. However, she usually exaggerated the significance of psychology and underestimated the economic factors. This was due to the fact that she was never really in contact with the black population.

Sarah Gertrude Millin (b. 1889), a South African Jewish writer, represents the following generation. In comparison with Mrs. Schreiner, she took more interest in racial relationships within South African society, however she did not understand the coloured people as an active force. Miss Millin's true-to-life description helped to reveal hidden relationships among social groups. However, as she did not believe in the possibility of transformations resulting from the activities of the non-white population, she finally arrived at the rather fatalistic idea of the rigidity of social development.

Sarah Millin attended a secondary school at Kimberley. She could have entered the university, but was more attracted by creative writing. There has never been a more prolific writer in South Africa than she; Miss Millin produced a new novel every year or every second year: *The Dark River* (1919), *Middle Class* (1921), *Adam's Rest* (1922), *The Jordans* (1923), *God's Stepchildren* (1924), *Mary Glenn* (1925), *An Artist in the Family* (1928), *The Coming of the Lord* (1928), *The Fiddler* (1929), *The Sons of Mrs. Aab* (1931), *Three Men Die* (1934), *What Hath a Man?* (1938), *The Herr Witch-doctor* (1941), *King of the Bastards* (1950), *The Burning Man* (1952), *The Wizard Bird* (1962). She also wrote biographies: *Rhodes* (1933) and *General Smuts* (1936), autobiographies: *The Night Is Long* (1941) and *The Measure of My Days* (1955), and essays: *Man on a Voyage* (1930). *South Africa* (1941) and *The People of South Africa* (1951).

Sarah Gertrude Millin spent most of her life in Johannesburg, where her husband worked. One of the central problems in Sarah Millin's novels is miscegenation. In *God's Stepchildren*, the Reverend Andrew Flood is an Anglican missionary among the Hottentots. In order to show them that there are no real differences between them and himself, he decides to marry a Hottentot woman. He hopes to persuade the Africans more easily in this way, as he does not agree with the usual approach to "the natives". But his married life is not happy and his wife finally leaves him. His daughter, Deborah, who has a lighter skin colour than her mother, has a baby with a white man (the Boer, Hans Kleinhans), who refuses to marry her; she goes to Griqualand West. But when the coloured people are pushed out of that region, they start their own trek. The novel then goes on to describe the life of Deborah's son, the old missionary's grandson, at Kimberley during the diamond rush. He does not succeed in marrying a white woman, and his eventual wife is a coloured woman. The position of the family in "white surroundings" is rather difficult. This also affects their daughter, who has to keep her origin a secret. Her marriage (to a very old white man) is also unhappy and she leaves her husband, just as her Hottentot great-grand-mother had done many years before. Once again, the "old sin" causes the suffering of her son, who marries an Englishwoman but, finding it unlawful, agrees to live in South Africa alone, separated from his wife who has returned to England. The isolation of the individual, the disaster of so many marriages in a single family, the unpleasant social position of the coloured people—all these facts are the result of their ancestor's (Andrew Flood's) original error. Like Olive Schreiner, who also treated the problem of the Coloureds from an idealistic viewpoint, Sarah Millin cannot see any help for these unfortunate people.

Her outlook is largely pessimistic; her characters are all driven by fate, feeling that nothing can be changed. This is applied to the South African social scale, as described in *Adam's Rest,* one of her earlier novels.

King of the Bastards (1950) deals with the position of the coloured people on the basis of their past experience. This book contains numerous descriptions of clashes between the whites and the Bantu tribes. Entering the field of history, the author becomes an investigator who tries to discover the true nature of old events. In the story of Conraad Buys, however, some of the ideas discussed above occur again. Having a coloured wife and child, this white man, though descended from the French Huguenots, cannot be accepted by the white society. Conraad Buys is a man of principle and consequently must trek away from the civilized lands. He lives with his three wives and his large family (during their trek towards the frontier of Portuguese East Africa, they meet Dingiswayo). One of the novel's dramatic episodes describes the development of the Cape Colony in 1803—1806, when England had to give it up for a few years. The writer appreciates the enlightened rule of the De Mists in those years, when Conraad Buys lives in the Cape Colony. After the new invasion by the English in 1806, he has to leave for Bechuanaland.

Although Sarah Millin's biographies of Cecil Rhodes (1933) and J.C. Smuts (1936) have been highly appreciated, she seems to have expressed her opinions most frankly in her autobiographies.

In South Africa (in *The British Commonwealth and Empire,* p. 172), she wrote: "The fairest suffrage in South Africa (and the world) would be to make the vote dependent on a very high intellectual standard and then attainable by all who could reach it. There would be then fewer fools for tools. 'Education and knowledge', Hitler rightly says, 'endanger the maintenance of a slave class'…".

The whites could be outvoted by the blacks in this case also, but the author evidently supposed that fewer black people would be able to reach "a very high intellectual standard". As only the ruling racial group could make education accessible to the others, obstacles would be created to provide both fair suffrage and a higher education. It seems justifiable to predict that as long as the white man fears the black man, he will not remove the existing inequality of opportunities.

While there is much unclarity in her essays dealing with internal issues, Sarah Millin displayed her firm support for the democratic anti-Nazi forces in her comments on World War II. Her middle-class attitudes prevented her from understanding the historical role of the South African black people, yet she identified herself with the British cause in the war, and with those forces in South African political life which desired the defeat of Hitler's Germany. Similarly sound are the writer's ideas concerning the development of South African culture.

Pauline Smith's collection of short stories *The Little Karoo* (1925) reminds us of Olive Schreiner; in it, the picture of the countryside farms owned by the Boers occurs very frequently. Her novel *The Beadle* (1926) would probably excite even overseas readers: A pretty, honest girl (Andrine) experiences a passionate love. Left by her lover, she bears a baby and faces many difficulties. Her luck finally improves at a pace with her father's (the beadle's) psychological evolution.

The new literary magazine *Voorslag* ("Voorslag" means the end, the front tip, a "sweep" of a "sjambok") was edited by William Plomer, Laurens Van der Post and Roy Campbell.

William Plomer (born in 1903 in Pietersburg) studied in England, but later lived in Zululand. He also spent a short time in Japan. Apart from several volumes of poetry, one volume of essays (*Four Countries*), two autobiographies (*Double Lives* and *At Home*) and two biographies (*Cecil Rhodes* and *Ali the Lion*), he published five novels (*Turbott Wolfe, Sado, The Case is Altered, The Invaders* and *Museum Pieces*) and four collections of short stories (*I Speak of Africa, Paper Houses, The Child of Queen Victoria* and *Four Countries*). But his fame rests chiefly on his first novel *Turbott Wolfe*. Turbott Wolfe secretly loves a married native woman, Nhliziyombi. Naturally, the action of the novel takes place at a time when marriages between partners belonging to different racial groups were still legally possible (today they are prohibited). Apart from Turbott Wolfe's vain love, there is another, more tragic affair. The white missionary, Friston, goes mad, having joined in marriage a black man (Zachary Msomi) and a white girl (Mabel van der Horst), whom he has loved. Before this tragedy, the three of them had established an organization based on their belief that Africa was not the white's man country and that miscegenation was inevitable, right and proper for the future coloured world.

It is clear why the book was considered so provocative at the time of its publication. Moreover, it is clear why the novel still makes the reader think over the painful problems of South Africa. Martin Tucker summed up the author's approach in the following lines: "Plomer's view is radical but pessimistic. The two liberal, sensitive heroes, Wolfe and Friston, fail to achieve their desires or a sense of the fullness of their own beliefs. Both die with the taste of failure on their tongues; Wolfe dies a few days after telling his story to the first-person narrator, who, with a realistic touch, is referred to as "William Plomer". The novel in fact seems to be an indictment of Wolfe as a weak liberal, a man without the courage of his convictions. He is not able to declare his love for the native girl through fear of losing caste, yet ironically he is called a "nigger-lover" and is accused of "hobnobbing with the blacks". The tag "Chastity Wolfe", with which the natives label Turbott (because he seems to shun sexual activity), is an apt symbol: his life has been a rejection of experience, and that rejection has led to the void that encloses him. Miscegenation in *Turbott Wolfe* is not only condoned—it is encouraged and demanded as a condition of health. "Eurafrica"—the union of the two races—is the novel's pervasive image.

"Today, it is easy enough to understand why *Turbott Wolfe* stimulated much controversy when it was first published. And, because the novel calls for the abolition of the colour bar in a violently sexual manner, the book has remained controversial". (M. Tucker, 1967, p. 210).

In the early stages of the development of South African fiction in English, either no Negro characters occur at all, or, if they do, they play only minor roles (servants, passive creatures, etc.). It was only in the 1920's that the black man became more significant as a literary character and, more or less occasionally, turned into a central figure, thus gaining the position he has firmly occupied in many post-World War II prose works. It is very characteristic of Plomer's revolutionary mind that when writing his *Ula Masondo* he somehow anticipated this direction and showed more understanding and concern for the black African than the majority of writers of his time. For, if it was difficult to bridge the gap between the white and black workers, it was by no means easier for a white intellectual in the 1920's to understand the native underdog.

Plomer's novelette *Ula Masondo* (1927) is almost as well-written as *Turbott Wolfe*. The main character this time is a young native who comes to Johannesburg. He must change his way of life and, together with his new comrades, takes to drinking and housebreaking. He is not able to adapt himself to the new circumstances and tries to imitate the white man's behaviour, but in vain, as his place in the existing society is determined by the colour of his skin. Moreover, the white man's city cannot improve him morally, being itself in a state of decay. The most moving tragedy in *Ula Masondo* is perhaps the suicide of the hero's mother.

Ula Masondo exerted a certain amount of influence on some of the later authors, particularly the development of its main character who comes to the white man with considerable admiration and some youthful ideals, and then is deceived. This deception—together with the bad influences of the company he keeps and his surroundings—turns the young native into a criminal.

For this reason, William Plomer can be considered a predecessor of the naturalists who began to use similar methods in the 1960's. They too are linked with Plomer through their concern for the causes of the violence existing in South African life.

Laurens Van der Post (b. 1906) is the author of matter-of-fact accounts of his own journeys to the African interior—*Venture to the Interior* (1954), *The Lost World of the Kalahari* (1958) and *The Heart of the Hunter* (1961). *Venture to the Interior*, which describes his expedition in 1949 to Nyasaland, is remarkable for its vivid images of African nature. *The Lost World of the Kalahari*, unquestionably Van der Post's most popular book, deals with the life of the Bushmen and shows the author's humanistic, anti-racist attitudes. This work, based on the journey he made in 1957, contains valuable material, chiefly from the ethnological standpoint. *The Heart of the Hunter* is closely related to the preceding work.

This same author wrote about Japan and the Far East in *The Seed and the Sower* (1963), his "Christmas trilogy" which bears the title of the second of these three novelettes, the other two being *A Bar of Shadow* and *The Sword and the Doll*. Laurens Van der Post's comprehensive knowledge of the Far East was not gained during his early stay in Japan but considerably later, when he was taken prisoner by the Japanese during World War II. It was only after that dramatic experience that Colonel Van der Post was able to begin his famous post-war research expeditions in Africa. While *The Face beside the Fire* (1953) and *Flamingo Feather* (1955) belong to the realm of fiction, *The Dark Eye in Africa* (1955) is a volume of Laurens Van der Post's lectures. Among his fiction works only one (the first) novel *In a Province* (1934) is written entirely in the "Voorslag spirit". Its theme is the following:

Van Bredepoel, a white shipping clerk, becomes the friend of Kenon, a young African. Both of them lack experience with city life, but their general approach to practical affairs is different. The white man comes from a milieu of individualism, while his black friend comes from a background of collectivism. Kenon, who has joined a political organization, refuses to tell the police the names of his fellow members and is arrested. The black man's moral decline and his personal dissatisfaction and violence are all well explained by the writer. It is the social situation that prevents Kenon and Van Bredepoel from understanding each other.

The individual's isolated life is frequently examined, both by Plomer and by Van der Post; it was the latter who indicated the direction for South African protest writing. One characteristic should be stressed here: isolated individuals can be found among the whites as well as among the blacks, despite the basic difference in their milieux' social structures.

Roy Campbell (1901—1957) published the following collections of poetry: *The Flaming Terrapin* (1924), *The Waysgoose* (1928), *Adamastor* (1930), *The Gun Trees* (1930), *The Georgiad* (1931), *Choosing a Mast* (1931), *Mithraic Symbols* (1932), *Flowering Reeds* (1933), *Flowering Rifle* (1939), *Songs of the Mistral* (1941) and *The Mamba's Precipice* (1954). Some of his verse is bitterly satirical. Campbell also wrote stories; his favourite subject was bullfights. During the Spanish Civil War, he sympathized with General Franco's camp and became reactionary towards the end of his life.

Guy Butler (1918), a professor at Rhodes University in Grahamstown, edited *A Book of South African Verse* (1959), which places excessive emphasis on racial differences. His own collections are *Stranger to Europe* (1960) and *South of the Zambezi*. He also wrote two plays—*The Dam* (1953) and *The Dove Returns* (1956).

After a long period of opposition to Hertzog's government, Smuts decided to join it. This new coalition, however, provoked an angry reaction on the part of some Afrikaaner nationalists, who formed a "purified" party headed by Dr. Malan. In the 1930's, there were also other political groups whose views approached those of the European Nazis and fascists (e.g. Broederbond, Ossewabrandwag and Reddingsdaadbond) but the position of the United South African National Party (formed from Smuts' South African Party and Hertzog's nationalists) was not shaken. The split came only during the dramatic voting which determined that South Africa would fight as a British ally in World War II. Smuts then won over Hertzog, the advocate of neutrality, and held the post of Prime Minister until the nationalists' victory in the post-war elections (1948).

The World War II government headed by Smuts was supported by English-speaking South Africans and by a minority of Afrikaaners, but was opposed by the nationalists. Smuts' victory in the war-time elections (1943) encouraged the working people, including the Bantu proletariat. The non-whites achieved a considerable degree of unity but the miners' strike (1946) was repressed by the police. The government, which was not able to satisfy the working-class and thus to ensure a powerful ally for the following elections, was becoming weaker. Malan's nationalists, propagating their apartheid programme, finally won in 1948 and introduced new legislation. Since 1950, marriages and sexual intercourse between members of different racial groups have been considered crimes. The situation of the Bantu population became much worse, owing to the Popular Registration Act and the Group Areas Act. In order to separate the racial groups, the government recommended their parallel development. This meant, in practice, that non-Europeans often had to leave their houses and lands in the so-called white zones and were forced to settle farther from the big cities, making their position disadvantageous. The phrase "parallel development" was utilized in order to maintain the existing inequality.

Just at this period, *The Drum* magazine appeared (in 1960) in Johannesburg, bringing to South African journalism "a new vitality which none of the white writers had seemed capable of achieving" (L. Nkosi, Home and Exile, p. 19). Among its reporters were many authors who later became popular; among them, Casey Motsisi, Bloke Modisane, Arthur Maimane, Ezekiel Mphahlele, Can Themba, Todd Matshikiza and Lewis Nkosi.

Casey Motsisi's work is typical of South African journalistic writing. His usually short vignettes record the scene around him in true-to-life dialogues. His stories are sometimes witty, sometimes too superficial. He is one of those few artists who are still capable of laughing at the absurd reality.

Bloke Modisane (b. 1923) left South Africa without a permit and came, via Tanganyika, to England in 1959. Before that, he had been a jazz critic in Johannesburg (for *The Golden City Post*). His satire "The Dignity of Begging" published in *The Drum* is based upon a commonplace paradox: a beggar can earn more than a hard-working man. The main character, Nathaniel, refuses to change his way of life, for he does not want to stop begging. He refuses to return to his family. Moreover, he is ready to write a book on begging and to organize a United Beggars' Union.

Modisane's short story "The Situation" tells about Caiaphas Sedumo, who works as a psychologist for an advertising firm. His only handicap is the dark colour of his skin. He is attacked by Afrikaaner villagers but is not helped by the police. Modisane attempts primarily to present "social facts". The most serious picture of the Sophiatown ghetto can be found in Modisane's book *Blame Me on History* (1923).

Arthur Maimane (b. 1932) left South Africa for Ghana in 1958. In the 1960's he lived in London. One of his best short stories, "The Kaffir Woman", describes the tragic consequence of the sexual intercourse between a Boer farmer and his "Kaffir" maid-servant: the girl gradually loses her original respect for the white's man power; finally the lovers are caught in flagranti by the farmer's wife. The fact that her husband has deceived her with a girl belonging, according to her, to an inferior race makes her leave him. The farmer shoots himself.

Can Themba (1924—1968) studied at Fort Hare University and became a reporter on *The Drum*. His detached manner of depicting violent life was strengthened all the more by his occasional cynical remarks. But sometimes he tries to avoid a repetition of frequently-used patterns of protest writing by turning to other aspects. Can Themba taught in Swaziland. He died in Manzini. His works appeared in *The Will to Die* (1972), which contains largely realistic sketches and short stories.

Todd Matshikiza is not only a journalist, but also a musical composer. His musicals *Mkhubane* and especially *King Kong,* based on the story by Bloom, were successful. He spent some time in London but later moved to Zambia where he now works in radio broadcasting.

Lewis Nkosi (b. 1936) was employed as a journalist in Johannesburg. Later, he left South Africa and in London became a literary editor of The New African. His only play is entitled *The Rhythm of Violence* (1964). His volume of essays *Home and Exile* (1965) is a good source of information about South African life in 1950's. *Home and Exile* contains several essays which have been reprinted and have become well-known as valuable pieces of critical writing. In them, Nkosi explains in a convincing way what *négritude* has meant in South Africa. He discovered his Africanness when he learnt that he was not only black, but non-white.

South African writing of the 1950's was affected first by the Suppression of Communism Act (1950) and then by the regulations concerning literature for school-children (1953).

Uys Krige (b. 1910) graduated from the University of Stellenbosch and now lives in Cape Town. He translated works from English, French and Spanish into Afrikaans and comparatively soon joined the anti-fascist movement. He took part in the Spanish Civil War, fighting against Franco. During World War II, he worked as a correspondent until his capture by the Germans at Tobruk. Escaping from the Italian prison in which he was held, he made his way to the Canadian lines. In 1944, Krige served in the American Army in Europe. In the final weeks of the war, he broadcast in five languages for the British Broadcasting Corporation.

Krige's own works were written partly in English, partly in Afrikaans. The author's personality is most vividly described in his English-written autobiography *The Way Out* (1955), which deals chiefly with his flight from the prisoners' camp. His narrative ability can also be seen in his collection of short stories *The Dream and the Desert* (1953) and in his collection of short stories, *The Dream and the Desert* (1953) and in his plays *Wall of Death* (1960) and *The Sniper and Other One-Act Plays* (1962) in which one appreciates his ability to create convincing characters. The basic progressive idea of his works is usually directed against the conservative upper-class Boer intellectuals.

Stuart Cloete was born in Paris. This author, whose attitudes are rather conservative, comes from a Dutch family of original South African settlers. After World War I, he became a farmer in the Transvaal. He published a number of novels: *Turning Wheels* (1937), *Watch for the Dawn* (1939), *The Hill of Glory* (1941), *Congo Song* (1943), *The Curve and the Tusk* (1952), *Mamba* (1956), *The Mask* (1957), *The Fiercest Heart* (1959), *Rags of Glory* (1963). He also wrote collections of short stories, e.g. *The Soldiers' Peaches* (1959) and *The Writing on the Wall and Other African Stories* (1968), as well as a volume of biographical sketches, *African Portraits* (1948).

Beginning with *Turning Wheels*, which tells of the Boer great trek (1837), Cloete's bias can be observed. The whole event is understood from an idealistic viewpoint, without showing its real economic or political causes. History is often treated as an adventure, rather than as a result of relevant conflicts. Cloete sometimes blindly accepts racist attitudes (e.g. the Zulus in *The Mask* are seen as an "inferior race").

Cloete's literary technique is fairly advanced, both in his historical novels and in his "hunting stories". Like Rider Haggard, he depicts the beauties of nature, exciting wild life, the freedom of the vast uninhabited areas, and charms and magic, in order to gain his reader's favour.

The socially committed stories narrated by Attwell Sidwell Mopeli-Paulus (b. 1913), who had published the lyrical poem "Ho Tsamaea ke ho bona" (To Travel Means to See, 1945) and short stories under the title, *Lilahloane oa botho* (The Poor Lilahloane, 1950), were adapted by Peter Lanham (a pseudonym; his real name is C.J.L. Parker) and Miriam Basner. The latter co-author participated in writing the novel, *Turn to the Dark* (1956), while the former published *Blanket Boy's Moon* (1953). Both of these English-written adaptations were successful, though only *Blanket Boy's Moon* became popular, thanks to its content and composition.

The novel describes the dramatic events in 1950 when the authorites restricted the number of cattle on the reserves. The hero of the book, Monare, observes how political intrigues lead to bloodshed between the Africans and the Indians, and compares the political situation in the Union with that in Mozambique.

The novels of the following three English-writing authors are fairly typical of the protest tendency of the 1950's. All these writers took a great interest in the political developments in South Africa.

Phyllis Altman showed in *The Law of the Vultures* (1952) very concrete forms of racial discrimination, in order to persuade her readers of the need for the anti-apartheid struggle. The hero of the novel spends some time in jail and lives through another bitter experience. Only then does he realize that he must take part in this fight. Miss Altman undoubtedly succeeded in creating a realistic character in typical circumstances. The action of the novel takes place in Johannesburg, where an African group prepares a revolt with the aim of setting up a new African society. Naturally, such an attempt is defeated.

Gerald Gordon's novel *Let the Day Perish* (1952) was published in the same year as Phyllis Altman's *The Law of the Vultures*. The beginning of this novel also describes the promising career of a member of an unprivileged racial group. The hero is Anthony Graham, a coloured man whose skin colour is relatively light. Graham's fall becomes inevitable only when his real origin is discovered. Anthony's brother, who is handicapped by a darker skin and who gradually becomes involved in the struggle against the system of apartheid, is a positive character, though insufficiently developed.

Ronald Harwood's novel *All the Same Shadows* (1961) also spiritually belongs to the 1950's though it was published later. Tabula, a young Zulu, works as a servant in a white family. He suffers from racial discrimination as much as Peter Abrahams' heroes did but reacts to his experiences in a different way: he mocks and laughs at them. The existing colour bar seems to him absurd, for all people have the same shadows. He joins a secret organization which is trying to attack the police. When the plan is betrayed, Tabula hides for some time but is then arrested—as are the other members of the organization—but for another offence.

While the whole tendency of the novel is typical of the 1950's, Harwood's creative method is nearer to that of the 1960's. As will be seen in the passages dealing with later fiction, naturalism was slowly beginning to penetrate into South African prose works.

Alan Paton (born in 1903 in Pietermaritzburg) studied in his native town and became a teacher and later the Principal of Diepkloof Reformatory for young delinquents in Johannesburg. His novel *Cry, the Beloved Country* (1948) is also concerned with the problem of criminality and, in particular, juvenile delinquency. While his works are inspired to some extent by the ideology of Christian passive suffering, Paton himself has been a critic of apartheid and the head of the South African liberals. As a result, *Cry, the Beloved Country* has had its admirers as well as opponents. Objections to it have been raised not only by conservatives and nationalists, but also by some Bantu intellectuals who do not regard the idea of suffering profitable under the existing political conditions.

It tells the story of the black priest, Stephen Kumalo, who leaves his village and travels to Johannesburg. His stay there is one continuous bad experience. Respectable and honest believer that he is, he suffers to see this world of sin, fear and pain, where it is very difficult for him to find his own son. He is distressed to learn that the boy has been arrested as the murderer of a young white negrophilist.

Racial interrelations are also discussed in Paton's second novel, *Too Late the Phalarope* (1953). Paton believes in the individual's freedom as well as in the possibility of finding some solution. Paton's optimism can clearly be seen in his collection of short stories *Debbie Go Home* (1961), which is based on his personal experience gained during his work as the Principal of the Diepkloof Reformatory.

Pursuing his educational ideas, he attempted to analyze the psychological background of young delinquents' behaviour and to illustrate how the pedagogue's approach may succeed or fail in various cases. As in his second novel, he touches on the "father-son" relationship as one of the determining factors.

All of Paton's works have shown that their author has never ceased to place his hopes in man's basically good nature. Concerned primarily with the fate of the individual, he describes those methods which may be effective in certain particular cases, although the general problem of his society cannot be solved by applying these methods. Some critics have appreciated his simple "biblical" style which corresponds very well both to his subject-matter and to his moral intentions. Alan Paton is certainly a writer of world-wide reputation. His musical plays have been successful (*Sponono* was presented on Broadway). He was awarded the American Freedom Award in 1960.

Peter Abrahams (born in 1919 in Vradedorp) spent some time as a boy in the Transvaal, at Elsenberg, and then returned to attend St. Peter's in Johannesburg. His collection of short stories *The Dark Testament* (1942) and his book *Tell Freedom* (1954) are autobiographical. Abrahams' profession was teaching, but even in the late Thirties he was more attracted by travelling and a journalistic career. His relatively short experience with the Cape Town period is reflected in the initial part of *The Path of Thunder* (1948). Abrahams worked as a journalist even later, when he moved from Great Britain to Jamaica where he became the editor of the journal West Indian Economist. Technically weak though interesting, the first part of *The Dark Testament* contains the writer's early reminiscences and autobiographical sketches. Being a coloured man himself, Abrahams often deals with the injustice resulting from the existing colour bar. He likes to portray common people, not only the black man, but also persecuted Jews or white liberals who are trying to come into contact with the South African non-white population (Henry and Martha). The second part of the book includes true short stories (e.g. "Hatred"). Most of them betray a lack of experience on the part of this young author.

The same is true of his novel *Song of the City* (1945). As a novel, this book is more extensive and more complex, but it would have been more successful as a piece of creative writing if the author had not failed in his efforts to make his characters typical. As it is, one must be satisfied with two heroes who are worth mentioning here: Dick Nduli, a young Bantu servant, and Van der Merwe, a Cabinet Minister responsible for solving native problems. Probably the most notable passages of the novel are those describing the slums, where the humiliated Africans live, in contrast to the fashionable upper middle-class milieu. The action of the novel takes place in the dramatic period at the beginning of World War II, when South African politicians had to decide if their country would support Great Britain or not. Van der Merwe wants South Africa to remain neutral, though his wife, Myra, takes an anti-Nazi standpoint. Consequently, the conflict between the great powers leads to the breakdown of the Minister's married life.

Song of the City revealed the author's concern for the life of the poor. This line can be traced in his next novel *Mine Boy* (1946) which describes the development of the young black village boy, Xuma (a more convincing character than Dick Nduli), who comes to work in the gold mines. Hardly any other South African writer has illustrated the monotonous rhythm of the miner's life so impressively as Abrahams has in *Mine Boy*. Practically the only joy in Xuma's life is derived from his drinking illicit alcohol. Under cruel working conditions, solidarity between the white and black miners, is born because they work side by side every day. Abrahams describes the gradual process in which their class-consciousness increases, so that finally Xuma becomes one of the leaders of the striking miners. *Mine Boy* follows the line established by Plomer (*Ula Masondo*), but while Plomer presented primarily a personal tragedy, Abrahams attempts to show the social conflict in the broad sense of the word. Xuma's increasing self-confidence is determined by the increasing conflict between the miners and their employers.

His following novel *The Path of Thunder* (1948) describes the tragic conflict of an ardent idealist who goes out to the countryside to introduce learning among the common people, with their crude Boer *baases* (i.e. bosses). Lanny Swartz, a coloured teacher, returns from Cape Town to his native village. He would have felt his intellectual isolation, living among these illiterate villagers, if he had not met there Meka, an African teacher. Through Meka, Abrahams expresses many valid views concerning the colour bar. He understands the non-whites' efforts to imitate the white man as an expression of their mental bondage. The black man recognizes his inferior social position if he tries to obtain a lighter colour for himself or his children (by painting himself or by intermarrying). Meka objects to mixed marriages, as they represent only a "compensation" for the fact that a person is non-white. He indicates that he would not object to them if there were racial equality in South Africa.

The central problem of the novel is undoubtedly the love of Lanny Swartz and Sarie Villier, who is related to one of the most prejudiced Afrikaner *baases*. Swartz becomes a victim of the racial hatred that has brought the ruling class to forbid sexual relations between members of different racial groups. But *The Path of Thunder* is not intended merely to provoke the reader's pity for the suffering non-white hero; it is also a condemnation of people like Gert Villier, who, in addition to the book's hero and heroine, also dies. The author clearly shows that the segregationist blindness brings disastrous consequences upon themselves.

His following novel *Wild Conquest* (1950) deals with the period of the Boer great trek, but it nevertheless raises a number of very topical problems. Peter Abrahams did not choose a historical subject in order to avoid contemporary problems; on the contrary, he undertook this journey into the past mainly in order to give his contemporaries some information.

Abrahams devotes much attention to the causes of the Boers' great trek and finds them mostly in the economic sphere. He shows the Boer trekkers as double-faced people, who are on the one hand suppressed by the British expansion, and on the other hand greedy for land, and therefore ruthless conquerors of African territories. During their invasion of the uncivilized regions, they use not only weapons but also tricks. They are contrasted—from the moral viewpoint—with the heroic Matabele.

After a volume of essays *Return to Goli* (1953) and the above-mentioned autobiographical work *Tell Freedom* (1954), Peter Abrahams published the novel *A Wreath for Udomo* (1956), the most controversial book he has written so far. Udomo, an African politician, begins his activities after his return from London to his native country, the fictitious name of which is Panafrica. Udomo fights against reactionary opponents and tries to utilize the dock-workers' strike. He is then arrested but still retains his popularity among the masses. Upon his release from prison, he organizes political life in a liberated country but fails in his dealing with traditional patterns and comes into conflict with his previous followers. Finally, he is murdered by those who had helped him gain political power.

Abrahams anticipates the possible development of a liberated African state, at a time when there was no independent country as yet in the part of Africa he is dealing with (he seems to be concerned with some West African country, but at the time of the publication of his novel only Liberia was independent, and it certainly was not his model; Ghana only became independent in 1957). The novel shows clearly the contradiction existing between political dreams and realities. Once Udomo becomes a ruler, he no longer feels bound by moral principles. Rather, he regards his personal desire as a political necessity. *A Wreath for Udomo* can be and has been understood as Abrahams' original contribution to the question of whether African countries can do without dictators. Abrahams was certainly aware of the need for a strong force for solving urgent problems immediately after liberation. The masses of people are portrayed in an oversimplified manner, though it is precisely the standard of class differentiation that is relevant for the possible success of the tribalists in Africa.

The style of this novel, unlike the preceding ones, is surprisingly concise; the author's attitude is more detached than heretofore. *A Night of Their Own* (1965) tells about the Indian population living in Natal. Richard Nkosi, a black artist, comes to that province in order to organize the illegal activities of the anti-apartheid groups. The book devotes special attention to relations between the Africans and Indians in South Africa. One of the best developed characters, Sammy Naidoo, reveals the hypocrisy of certain "liberals" and tells Van Ase, who serves the government, though he does not share the idea of racial segregation, that the violent fanatic proponents of apartheid could not retain power without the assistance of the Van Ase kind of "liberal". Abrahams rightly sees that there are still several stages between moral resistance and real conflict. His latest novel *This Island Now* (1966) discusses the post-independence political development of a Caribbean island.

Jack Cope (b. 1913) became a journalist after finishing his studies. In 1935, he left South Africa to work as a political correspondent in London. His creative writing, however, dates mostly from a later period. In 1940, he returned to Natal where he started writing various genres. Apart from a number of poems and plays, he has produced several novels and collections of short stories.

After *The Fair House* (1955), he published *The Golden Oriole* (1958) and *The Road to Ysteberg* (1959), as well as two collections of short stories: *The Tame Ox* (1960) and *The Man Who Doubted* (1967). *The Fair House* uses the background of the Zulu rising of 1906 in order to illustrate some topical aspects of South African reality. Full of humanistic spirit, the novel describes the last great attempt of the South African natives to liberate themselves. The love-story, written relatively well, contrasts with the brutality and ruthlessness of the penal expedition sent to crush the Zulus' resistance.

The novel was influenced by the doctrine of non-violence that has had a long tradition in the history of South Africa. The question remains of why Jack Cope chose such historical material as the basis for his first protest novel. Cope's second novel *The Golden Oriole* is notable chiefly for its true-to-life portrait of a young Zulu intellectual (Glanvill Peake), who attempts to play an important role in white literary circles in the Thirties. At that time this was a rare phenomenon. Peake longs for fame, but at the same time he does not try to become a professional politician, though he speaks on behalf of the workers. He finally dies, shot by white racists. *The Golden Oriole* analyzes the social situation in the period when the black intellectual could hardly acquire confidence in the eyes of the white middle-class whose moral decline was about to commence. Glanvill Peake is also rather remote from the average non-white man because of his higher education and social aspirations. The latest collection of Cope's short stories, *The Man Who Doubted*, shows him to be a very skilful writer, possessing an admirable story-telling technique.

Dan Jacobson (born in 1929 in Johannesburg) studied at a Kimberley secondary school and at the Witwatersrand University. His Jewish origin made him very sensitive to racial discrimination even during his school days.

Jacobson has written mainly novelettes and novels—*The Trap* (1955), *The Price of Diamonds* (1955), *A Dance in the Sun* (1956), *Evidence of Love* (1961) and *The Beginners* (1966)—as well as short stories published in the following collections: *A Long Way from Home* (1958), *The Zulu and the Zeide* (1959) and *Beggar, My Neighbour* (1964). Apart from his creative writing, he has produced a certain amount of non-fiction during his journalistic career. He also worked as a teacher and spent some time in the United States and Israel before settling in London.

His novel *The Beginners* is an exciting account of the Glickman family living in South Africa. Jacobson examines the experiences of the Jews in very different countries (Israel, England, etc.). To the detriment of his novel, however, he tries to cover too vast an area, both geographically and ideologically, and has to abandon his former economy of style. His earlier novels, though simpler in structure, were more effective from the artistic viewpoint.

This is particularly true of his *Evidence of Love*, which describes the love affair between a white woman and a coloured man. The novel has a definite social message; it not only shows their case being made tragic by the apartheid laws, but also the psychological causes of the existing unnatural relationship on both sides of the colour bar. Jacobson was similarly successful with *The Trap* and with his story *Beggar, My Neighbour,* which, perhaps, reflects childhood reminiscences (the meeting of white and black children in the street).

Jacobson is by no means a typical protest writer. In his best passages he strikes remarkable lyrical tones, in his poorest stories he more closely approaches superficial journalism. In his second creative period, Jacobson shifted from a protest type of writing with dramatic suspense (in the 1950's) towards more synthetic realistic prose. It is possible to compare the role of dialogue in his early novels with that in his later works. *The Trap* is a very short work, which really deserves to be classified as a novelette rather than a novel. A marked characteristic of Jacobson's early prose works (*A Dance in the Sun, The Price of Diamonds*) was that they contained much action and little reflection.

Nadine Gordimer (b. 1923) has spent most of her life in Johannesburg where she lives with her family. She has visited some European countries (England, Italy, Germany) and many parts of Africa and America.

In her novels *The Lying Days* (1953), *A World of Strangers* (1958), *Occasion for Loving* (1963) and *The Late Bourgeois World* (1966) and in her short stories collected in the volumes *The Soft Voice of the Serpent* (1952), *Six Feet of the Country* (1956), *Friday's Footprint* (1960) and *Livingstone's Companions* (1966), she attacks the apathy with which individual racial groups regard the development of South Africa.

The method of Mrs. Gordimer's novels remind one of some of the works of Jack Cope. Only a limited area is portrayed, which enables the author to concentrate on an analysis of carefully chosen heroes. She has unquestionably implemented her aesthetic principles, being aware of their difference from the topical needs of the political protest movement.

In her novel *A World of Strangers,* a young Englishman comes to Johannesburg where he develops his talent for shrewd observation. He perceives the members of different racial groups living as "strangers". Particularly effective are Mrs. Gordimer's portraits of women. This novel has an additional, more noteworthy symbolical level. Her short stories possess a kind of stylistic conciseness, e.g. "The Last Kiss" in the collection *Friday's Footprint*. Each sentence is as meaningful as those in Guy de Maupassant's best short stories.

Although this authoress was probably influenced by European short stories, she has certainly revealed one characteristic quality of modern South African prose writing—a matter-of-fact, almost journalistic presentation—and it is precisely this quality that was to be further developed by the youngest fiction writers in the Sixties. As we shall see in subsequent passages dealing with their works, a general trend has evolved toward increasing authenticity, from the late Fifties until today.

But unlike her literary disciples, Nadine Gordimer treats emotions more often than facts. Her central topic in such books as *Occasion for Loving* or *Not for Publication* (the collection of short stories that was not permitted to be published in South Africa) is the lack of human communication.

Mrs. Gordimer's novel *The Late Bourgeois World* partially abandons the sphere of psychology in order to go more deeply into several political and ideological problems, how can the relations between racial groups be solved?, how should democracy be understood?, the question of African socialism, etc. There has been a remarkable development in this authoress' writing: she started her literary career by analyzing the "master-servant" relationship in modern South African society and has gradually become a socially committed writer par excellence, though she has never abandoned her profound concern for the individual, which can well be seen in her short stories *Livingstone's Companions* (1966) and in her latest novel *A Guest of Honour* (1971).

Ezekiel Mphahlele (born in 1919 in Pretoria) spent his childhood in the countryside and in Pretoria's slums. His alcoholic father left his family, and his mother had to ensure a bare subsistence for herself and her children. The future writer also had to start earning a living very early.

Mphahlele began his literary career with his collection of short stories *Man Must Live and Other Stories* (1947), which describes the sufferings and humiliation of black people in South Africa. In the Fifties, Mphahlele took an active part in public life and helped to organize such significant protest campaigns as the struggle against the Verwoerd Education Bill. He joined the African National Congress and worked on the editorial board of the Johannesburg monthly *The Drum* (founded in 1950). Although this author wrote a successful thesis and obtained several university degrees (B.A. and M.A.), he experienced many difficulties in his native country. When he was forbidden to teach, he decided to go abroad. He first worked in Ibadan, Nigeria, then became head of the African Department of the Congress for Cultural Freedom in Paris. Subsequently, he became Director of Chemchemi in Nairobi and afterwards worked for some time with the University of Denver (Colorado) in the USA.

His autobiography *Down Second Avenue* (1959), which describes the author's impressions and criticizes the social situation in South Africa, is perhaps Mphahlele's best-known work. In it, he discusses the conditions existing in that country's educational, artistic and political life, confirming what other South African writers have already said before him: South

African relationships are more complicated than the idea of the colour bar can suggest. A lack of consciousness and moral poverty also exist among the blacks, while a number of active, unselfish fighters for racial equality are to be found among the so-called Europeans. Their handicap results chiefly from the fact that they lack political power and cannot influence those actually wielding such power.

Mphahlele's collection of short stories *The Living and the Dead and Other Stories* (1961) marked the beginning of a new period in his creative career. The evil faced by his heroes is more concrete than in his preceding works of fiction. Simultaneously, the author's conviction is strengthened that weak human force is incapable of overcoming it. This pessimism, resulting from cruel personal experiences, is reflected in this collection, as it is in the works of the prose writers emerging at the beginning of the Sixties. It is further emphasized by Mphahlele's crudeness of expression. Mphahlele presents the black man's literary portrait, painted by himself, and discusses such important issues as *négritude*, the African personality, etc. More than his colleagues, Mphahlele has become aware of the position of South African writing in the literature of the present-day world. His generalizations are based chiefly on his own analyses of other literary works by black Africans.

In his collections of short stories *In Corner B* (1967), Mphahlele is well aware of the relationship between form and content, the necessary balance between descriptive passages and dialogue, etc. This collection shows not only the author's increasing interest in the technical aspects of fiction writing, but also his keen sense of linguistic experimentation and modern expression. Yet unlike some of his colleagues, he has never abandoned a realistic, true-to-life portrayal of reality. His latest novel *The Wanderers* (1970) is partly autobiographical. Moreover, Mphahlele is an adviser of young African authors who are about to set out into the sphere of creative writing. Mphahlele, who does not believe in magically inspired talent and who tries to be as practical as possible, feels that a writer should listen closely to his people's speech and should capture the mood, atmosphere and verbal pictures or images evoked by what a character says or does, in the character's own language.

This author is also interested in writing in the African languages (which he analyzed during his stay at Chemchemi, Kenya), though he himself writes in English. According to him, the standard of African vernacular writing should be raised, both by seeking more perfect ways of expression and by choosing more suitable subject-matter. More than once, Mphahlele has drawn attention to the fact that it is those traditional qualities of African culture which are no longer topical that have been strengthened. Both as a critic and as a writer, he stresses the social function of literature and considers its principal task to be the interpretation of contemporary problems. This, in his opinion, ought not to lead to any kind of uniformity. On the contrary, African authors should differentiate their subjects, as well as their individual styles. In this way, Mphahlele hopes, culture may become more widespread and cease being limited to the so-called intellectual élite.

Harry Bloom, the author of *Episode* (1956), has few illusions concerning the future development of South Africa. Being a Jew himself, he has a sensitive feeling for the injustice existing in that society, and particularly for the evil of racial prejudice. There can be no peace between the races, he implies, and he analyzes the different attitudes of whites and blacks. Those characters who fail completely are best depicted by him, for example the white superintendent, Hendrik du Toit, and the black politician, Mabaso, representing the African National Congress.

From the beginning of his novel, Bloom sets himself the task of portraying the atmosphere of a specific location and therefore devotes attention to descriptive details. The tranquility of the entire scene at the beginning makes the contrast all the more powerful later on, when hatred turns into violence. By stressing that the name of the place is purely fictitious, Bloom seems to suggest that similar situations could suddenly occur in any South African city.

The separated Negro location inhabited by masses of poor people is situated at Nelstroom, a fictitious small South African town. The white administrator achieves no improvement with his "reforms". On the contrary, the tension between the whites and blacks becomes even more intense. No wonder a single incident is enough to provoke a storm. The secret organization, the African National Congress, organizes the resistance of the black masses, whose actions gradually grow into a real riot. Du Toit, who has to flee from the location, is replaced by a ruthless police officer whose opinions are not too different from those expressed in the racist doctrine of the Nazis.

As Bloom's *Episode* is full of violent action, most of its characters, even the "flat" ones, are intriguing. A well-known lawyer, journalist and author of musicals, Harry Bloom, has not surpassed the success of his first novel with his following books *Sorrow Laughs* (1959) and *Whittaker's Wife* (1962). His *King Kong; An African Jazz Opera* (1961) undoubtedly deserves special attention, but it is unrelated to the subject under discussion here.

In the Fifties, when relationships between the Europeans and other racial groups became further aggravated and more complicated, naturalistic elements began to penetrate into the realm of South African fiction. In the opinion of some critics, it no longer sufficed to present a mere record of facts; some authors began to choose those facts that were most expressive and most drastic, painting them in rich colours. But only in the Sixties was this development of naturalistic writing accomplished by the young generation of prose writers, who were able to describe things in an almost scholarly, sober, detached manner.

The South African writer continually comes up against phenomena resulting from apartheid. Under these conditions, most of his personal experiences contribute to the evolution of protest writing; but one question still remains to be answered: how can the doctrine of racism be most effectively fought? Needless to say, progressive authors have been materially handicapped, persecuted and often forced to flee from South Africa. South African protest literature has also experienced a "generation problem". Most writers belonging to the old generation believed—as we have seen—that much could be improved by means of patient education and persuasion. They protested against apartheid in the name of the moral renascence of their society. The characteristic trend of their works, which usually stressed their moral instruction, also resulted from this attitude.

Most young authors who began to publish their English-written works at the end of the Fifties and especially in the Sixties are convinced that nothing can be improved by a mere appeal to sympathy, common sense or a feeling for justice, etc. They describe poverty, the consequences of discriminatory measures, serious contradictions and violence in a dispassionate, unbiased way and in great detail, like biologists describing animal and plant life. They do not preach, for they believe that their readers will understand the main ideas of their works, even when they are not precisely spelled out. Their naturalistic, often stark works confirm their authors' intention to present chiefly a revelation and an analysis of the facts. They seem to ask: what can be done? It is up to the reader to try to answer this question.

Protest could be heard in South African life for over twenty years, but without positive effects. Alex La Guma, the main representative of South African naturalism, who took part in the writer's conference in Beirut in 1968, expressed there the desperate feelings of his colleagues who knew that they had to write chiefly for foreign readers. According to him, those who wanted to read their works in South Africa had to do so secretly.

Today's realistic prose works still approach journalism. This can be seen both in their content and their form. Some works are actually on the borderline separating the novel from the reportage. In comparison with the Fifties, purely fictitious elements are today vanishing or else exist only in the background. This situation contrasts sharply with the contemporary efforts of West African writers to distinctly delineate the above-mentioned borderline. These efforts may lead to a certain dispersion of themes as well.

One may well imagine the isolation of very gifted authors after a sojourn of several years outside South Africa. Many of them live in London and base their works mainly on their reminiscences. If they were able to return home, they could acquire many new impulses for their creative writing.

South African writers and other artists who live in exile usually tend to gradually absorb foreign, non-African (or at least non-South African) inspiration, though they know very well that if this foreign inspiration persists, they will sooner or later no longer differ from those around them in their new countries; few of them, therefore, are willing to cut themselves off from their original cultural mileux. Political themes and folklore are most often utilized for keeping alive the old ties.

The collection *Quartet* (1963) contains sixteen short stories written by four authors. The book is divided into four parts having characteristic names "Without Justice", "The Dispossessed", "The Possessed" and "The Outsider". The order of these sections is significant, as it shows the gradual decline of the South African outcast. Each of the authors contributed one story to each of the above-mentioned sections. Consequently, we can find in this unusual book not only a unity of purpose, but also a variety of style, which makes reading it more attractive.

One of the authors is Alex La Guma (b. 1925), who is probably better known than the other three writers: Alf Wannenburgh (b. 1936), James Matthews (b. 1929) and Richard Rive (b. 1931). The reputation of the first two is based chiefly on their participation in *Quartet* and on their stories published in African and non-African journals.

Alf Wannenburgh studied at the University of Cape Town. He worked as a land-surveyor's assistant, salesman, clerk and window-dresser. Apart from serious fiction, he has also published commercial short stories for trade publications. An extraordinarily gifted writer, his economy of style logically requires a very careful choice of words. His "Echoes", published in the section called "The Dispossessed" and reprinted in Rive's anthology *Modern African Prose* (1964), describes the tragic impact of the Coalbrook mine disaster on the African miners. The genuine serious atmosphere of his "Awendgesang" could hardly be grasped without the author's skilful handling of linguistic means.

While Wannenburgh's approach to reality seems to be more rational, James Matthews' attitudes are rather emotional. Unlike Wannenburgh who is a white man, Matthews tends towards sentimentality and melancholy, particularly in his short story "The Park" which tells us about a coloured boy who is not allowed to play in the part that is reserved for white children only.

It is highly probable that James Matthews' writing resulted from his own bitter experience in childhood. He was the eldest son of a large poor family and had to earn his living at first selling newspapers and then as a messenger-boy. Owing to the colour bar restrictions, he could not get better jobs than those of a telephone operator and receptionist. As a writer he has been more successful, publishing his own collection of short stories in Sweden. The name of the collection—*Azikwelwa*— is also the name of one of his stories included in *Quartet*.

Equally remarkable is "The Party", which has some features in common with "The Park". This time he shows the frustration of a coloured intellectual who seeks social recognition among the whites, but in vain. The story also explains the specific problems of South African literary life. Matthews' forte is his psychological analysis of his characters, which can be seen in his story "The Portable Radio".

Richard Rive studied at the Teachers' Training College and at the University of Cape Town. He became a teacher of English and Latin at a Cape Town secondary school. His collection *African Songs* (1963) was published in English and Swedish. His best stories can be found in it, as well as in *Quartet*. Rive's method is considerably different from that of James Matthews. From the creative point of view, Richard Rive is closer to Alex La Guma's naturalism. His analysis of the so-called low life is based primarily on his dialogues which faithfully reproduce the ordinary people's ways of speaking. Rive's famous "Resurrection" is the first story of the section "The Dispossessed", for which the author chose a characteristic saying of Matthew Arnold: "Our inequality materializes our upper classes, vulgarizes our middle classes, brutalizes our lower classes".

Sometimes Rive appears to approach very closely the bordeline between journalism and creative writing, e.g. in his novel *Emergency* (1964), describing the Sharpeville events. On March 28, 1960, about ten thousand Africans demonstrated in Sharpeville against the humiliating laws limiting their freedom. Following a brutal police attack, about seventy of them lay sprawled on the pavement, dead.

Rive is interested not so much in characters as in actions and situations. He recalls certain modern painters who create a characteristic atmosphere by bizarrely applying different colours on the canvas, without caring for details. There is, of course, one disadvantage in this creative method. Rive's works will have documentary value, even

258

at the end of this century, but at that time they will hardly possess the emotional appeal they unquestionably contain for Rive's contemporaries.

As we have said, *Quartet* originated from the cooperation of very different personalities, but all these writers share the same basic idea about the function of South African writing in the Sixties. Although it is not advisable to hastily generalize, one feels that they see this function as the describing of reality (particularly interracial relations) without preaching. As Ezekiel Mphahlele, to whom *Quartet* is dedicated, has explained several times, modern prose works in South Africa should let the readers think and then come to their own conclusions. As this function sharply contrasts both with the approach of the pre-war protest writers and with the Afrikaaners' ideas about the development of South African literature in general, we can say that *Quartet* represents a qualitatively new step in South African literary history. It should be stressed here that this new approach in the Sixties to the function of South African writing has nothing to do with dividing this literary production into progressive and reactionary trends. Undoubtedly, the older writers who preferred realistic descriptions of South African life were no less progressive than *Quartet's* writers. They believed that the tendency of their social message should be more explicit and they published their works—and this is also significant—under political conditions which differed from those of the Cape Town writers of the early Sixties. The continual tightening of the system of apartheid ever since the late Forties influenced the literary arena as well. While in the earlier period a greater variety of themes had been dealt with developments in the late Fifties made progressive authors concentrate on the racial situation, other subject-matter being more or less exceptional.

Alex La Guma (b. 1925) describes the moral decline of people caused by the pressure of racial discrimination, e.g. his short story "Out of the Darkness", which speaks of a teacher who kills a man and goes mad in jail. The cause of his tragedy is his sweetheart, who has a lighter skin colour and who begins to behave like a white girl; she shows contempt for him, calling him "a black nigger". When someone tells the teacher that she is a whore playing at being a white woman, he kills him.

La Guma, like other naturalist writers, usually stresses details, trying to increase the credibility of his stories. *A Walk in the Night* (1962) as well as *And a Three-fold Cord* (1964) describe the slum regions on the outskirts of South African cities and their inhabitants whose happy dreams result only from the merciful state of drunkenness after a few gulps of secretly-produced liquor. The heroes of *A Walk in the Night* feel an almost instinctive aversion to the traditional tribal way of life, as they suffer from a continuous fear of being pushed back to the native reserves. According to the system of apartheid, black Africans must leave the South African cities (except for a small number of servants, etc.); this is supposed to lead to a more perfect separation of racial groups. La Guma shows these black Africans desperately clinging to their city life to which they have become accustomed, although precisely this city life implies a continual lack of economic security. In La Guma's underworld, powerless figures stagger between hunger and crime, while drunkards and prostitutes live in constant fear of the police. La Guma touches on many social questions, but does not try to solve any of them. His genuine force lies in his ability to combine description of the fates of individuals with those of the contemporary social milieu.

And a Three-fold Cord is lengthier than La Guma's first long short story. The action takes place in the slums of Cape Town. Here, too, the author has succeeded in creating the atmosphere of restlessness, insecurity and humiliation surrounding his non-white characters. Unlike the pessimistic conclusion of *A Walk in the Night, And a Three-fold Cord* contains an appeal for solidarity. The optimism of this book is all the more remarkable, since the author wrote it under the very difficult conditions of house arrest and police supervision. *And a Three-fold Cord* is not an autobiographical book, though it emerged essentially from the writer's own experiences. It describes events in a South African ghetto: The large Paul family must work hard in order to earn their living. If they are not able to organize mutual cooperation, they will completely fail.

La Guma's next book *The Stone Country* (1956) is dedicated "to the daily average of 70,351 prisoners in South African gaols in 1964". The novel describes the life of prisoners who spend their time together: political rebels can be found side by side with murderers and burglars. Although the novel recalls ordinary thrillers, it is not concerned only with problems of human humiliation and prison brutality (the author himself also spent some time in jail). Rather, La Guma attempts primarily to show the decay of a society ruled by a racial doctrine and to draw from his narrative some sort of generalization, which obviously is impossible to perceive, unless one takes into consideration the novel's symbolical level.

The Stone Country is certainly better elaborated than his preceding books. The straightforward presentation of social criticism in *A Walk in the Night* especially appears rather primitive in comparison to La Guma's latest work, or some of his best short stories.

Alfred Hutchinson graduated from the University of Fort Hare. Like the well-known critic, Ezekiel Mphahlele, he became a teacher but did not teach for long. Like Mphahlele, he took part in the struggle against the reactionary education bill. He was subsequently forbidden to teach and was accused of high treason. In 1956, he was sent to jail together with many other members of the African National Congress. In *The Road to Ghana* he revealed the background of the infamous trial of 156 opponents of the official doctrine. Eventually, Hutchinson was fortunate enough to flee to Tanganyika. In Malawi, he met his future wife. After a year-and-a-half's stay in Ghana, he moved to Great Britain. His novels *The Road of Ghana* (1960) and *The Rain-Killers* (1964) are rather journalistic.

Peter Clarke (born in 1929 in Simonstown) finished secondary school and went to work on the docks. Later, he began to establish his reputation as a painter. His pictures were exhibited and he continued his educational career at the Academy of Amsterdam. He entered the realm of literature after winning a literary contest organized by *The Drum* magazine. In the story "Eleven O'clock: the Wagons, the Shore", which was awarded first prize in the Encounter competition (1958), Clarke describes Simonstown pupils who spend their leisure time at the seaside, at various times of the year. Sitting around the wagons, they watch the sea-gulls. The image itself is clearly escapist. We can feel how much Clarke wishes to forget all about his surroundings.

Sylvester Stein (b. 1920) is remembered equally for his novel Second-Class Taxi (1958) and for his work in the editorial office of *The Drum*. Ezekiel Mphahlele correctly compares Staffnurse in Stein's novel with the character of Mr. Johnson in Joyce Cary's novel of the same name.

Ronald M. Segal, who founded and edited the progressive quarterly *Africa South,* which was later banned, was concerned with politics rather than literature. But his autobiography *Into Exile* (1963)—though it cannot be called a piece of fiction—provides worthwhile reading.

Nathaniel Nakasa and Barney Simon worked successively as editors of the literary magazine *The Classic*. Nathaniel Nakasa (1937—1965), formerly a journalist in Johannesburg, lived in the United States. Although he started a successful journalistic career in America, he found no happiness there and committed suicide in New York. William Plomer's poem "The Taste of the Fruit" was written in memory of Nakasa and Ingrid Jonker, who also died tragically. Bessie Head wrote the novel *When Rain Clouds Gather* (1969), describing the flight of a South African political prisoner to Botswana, where he goes on fighting for progress.

Barney Simon is an almost exceptional writer. He spent four years in London and then at the age of twenty-five returned to Johannesburg where he began to cooperate with Athol Fugard, the foremost playwright and author of *The Blood Knot* and *Hello and Goodbye*. Their common objective was to set up a multi-racial theatre which would produce socially significant plays. Simon's "The Fourth Day of Christmas" is a short story in which the author's keen sense of staging can be discerned. Ordinary speech in his dialogue does not satisfy him; he has introduced into his story a fairly long part (over one page) in which the page is divided by an imaginary vertical line which enables him to present the swiftest conversation possible: neither of the two speaking characters says more than three or four words, including monosyllabic replies. Indirect speech is, of course, omitted only in this part of the story. The unusual form of the story would deserve a better subject; nevertheless, Simon's talent is very promising. *Familiarity is the Kingdom of the Lost* (1970) was this playwright's adaptation of the text of Dugmore Boetie (d. 1966).

Sidney Clouts left South Africa for London in 1962. His modern verse is included in *One Life* (1966). Ruth Miller, a Cape Town teacher, was awarded the Ingrid Jonker Prize in 1966. Her collection of poetry *Floating Island* (1965) is rather melancholic. Douglas Livingstone, who works as a bacteriologist in Durban, has published two collections of poems *The Skull in the Mud* and *Sjambok*. His poetry was awarded the first prize at the Cheltenham Festival of English Literature.

Mazisi Kunene (born in 1930 in Durban) graduated from the University of Natal. In 1959, he went to London. He wrote poetry and drama in Zulu and was awarded first prize in the Bantu literary contest in 1956. He also treats the theory of Zulu poetry.

Dennis Brutus (born in 1924 in Salisbury, Rhodesia), a South African coloured poet, studied at Fort Hare College and at the University of Witwatersrand. He is at present professor at Northwestern University in the United States. During his studies at Witwatersrand, he was awarded second prize in the Mbari literary contest. His collection of poems

Sirens, Knuckles, Boots (1963) is notable for its anti-apartheid content. After an unsuccessful attempt to get to Europe via Swaziland (he was sent back to South Africa by the Mozambique police) he was sentenced to eighteen months' hard labour. This gruelling experience inspired his *Letters to Martha* (1968).

Having finished his prison term, he left for London and then settled in America, where he has been director of the South African Non-Racial Olympic Committee (SANROC) and the World Campaign for the Release of South African Political Prisoners. His latest collection is *Poems from Algiers* (1970). In February 1970, he explained the aesthetic reformation he underwent in prison, addressing the undergraduates of the University of Texas in Austin, in the following way:

"The first thing I decided about my future poetry was that there must be no ornament, absolutely none. And the second thing I decided was you oughtn't to write for poets; you oughtn't even to write for people who read poetry, not even students. You ought to write for the ordinary person: for the man who drives a bus, or the man who carries the baggage at the airport, and the woman who cleans the ashtrays in the restaurant. If you can write poetry which makes sense to those people, then there is some justification for writing poetry. Otherwise you have no business writing.

"And therefore, there should be no ornament because ornament gets in the way. It becomes too fancy-schmancy; it becomes over-elaborate. It is, in a way, a kind of pride, a self-display, a glorying in the intellect for its own sake, which is contemptible.

"I don't know whether I would hold the same position now. I am only trying to explain how I arrived at that position then.

"So I said, 'You will have to set the thing down. You will tell it like it is but you will let the word do its work in the mind of the reader. And you will write poetry that a man who drives a bus along the street can quote, if he feels like quoting.' Very ambitious indeed.

,,But this is based on the idea that all people are poets. Some are just ashamed to let it be known, and some are shy to try, and some write but don't have the guts to show it to others. But we all are poets because we all have the same kind of response to beauty. We may define beauty differently, but we all do respond to it." (*Palaver*, "Interviews with Five African Writers in Texas", 1972, p. 29.)

Among the most recent novels by South Africans is Modikwe Dikobe's *The Marabi Dance* (1973), a typical account of the author's reminiscences, the revision of which was carried out by several of the foremost experts. The writer received only an average formal education. He was born in the Northern Transvaal in 1913 but has lived in Johannesburg since 1923. The setting of his novel is a pre-World War II suburban district inhabited by black people. The story, centred round the character of Martha, is written in a true-to-life manner with numerous vivid details.

Many more topical problems and more interest in politics is shown by D. M. Zwelonke, representing the younger generation of writers. His raw narrative *Robben Island* (1973) is totally based on his personal experience as a South African political prisoner. The novel expresses his political convictions, combined with drastic descriptions of that much feared prison. He follows the behaviour of the prisoners and warders in a way reminiscent of

Alex La Guma, but dwells more on the problem of the disintegration of a tortured personality. The main character, one of the prisoners, suffers from the harshness of solitary confinement, hunger and constant humiliation. Finally he dies, after long-endured torture. Equally appalling are the passages devoted to some aspects of homosexuality and violence in prison. The period of imprisonment, according to the author's evidence, is full of harshness, obscenity and wild sexual fantasies on the part of men who have to lead this unfortunate, unnatural life, without joys or satisfactions.

Athol Fugard is a contemporary playwright, whose plays *Hello nad Goodbye* and *The Blood Knot* were successful in the United States. The latter drama deals with two brothers having differing skin colours. Fugard follows their love and hatred in both their individual and social relationships.

After his collections of poems *An Unknown Border* (1954) and *The Last Division,* Anthony Delius (b. 1916) surprised readers with his versified political satire *A Corner of the World* (1962). He also produced a play and a travel book. The Cape Town teacher Perseus Adams was awarded a prize in 1965 for his collection of poems *The Land at My Door* (1965).

An obsession with the question of race has never ceased to make itself felt throughout South African writing. But the difference between pro-apartheid and anti-apartheid writers is more significant than skin colour. While pro-apartheid authors are usually white, many white writers, we should not forget, are non-conformists.

The close connection between politics and literature is the main reason why the content of South African literature has usually been examined more carefully than its form. But different stages of its development can be discerned, when the inseparable unity of content and form is borne in mind.

The following books are typical of their respective periods, not merely owing to their content but also to their form: Olive Schreiner, *The Story of an African Farm* (1883); William Plomer, *Turbott Wolfe* (1926); Alan Paton, *Cry, the Beloved Country* (1948) and *Quartet* (1963).

Thus we could divide South African writers into four distinctive groups, as follows:

— Olive Schreiner, Pauline Smith, Sarah Gertrude Millin;
— William Plomer, Laurens Van Der Post;
— Alan Paton, Peter Abrahams, Jack Cope, Nadine Gordimer, Dan Jacobson, Ezekiel Mphahlele, Harry Bloom;
— Richard Rive, Alex La Guma, David Lytton.

Although as creative individualities they differed, the authors in each of these periods have had to react to certain common problems. During the first period, South Africa was, portrayed as a "wide veldt", as a country of Boer farmers, romantic girls and passive black servants. The prevailing philosophy was that of Christian idealism, and if ever a black man appeared as a character in literature, he was shown as a humble creature (the psychological analysis of the "master-servant" relationship comes only in the third period). The prevailing form in the first period was the full-length novel, while in the fourth period it is short novels and short stories, novelettes (long short stories) and sketches. The above-men-

tioned periods obviously correspond to such important historical events in South Africa as:
The increasing of political tension after the diamond rush and the battle of Majuba Hill
(Rhodes-Kruger-non-whites);
Hertzog's Nationalists rise to power after the 1924 elections;
Smuts' defeat in the 1948 elections and the launching of Malan's programme of apartheid;
The Republic (formerly the Union), now no longer a member state of the British Common-
wealth of Nations, intensified its policy of apartheid and prevents many progressive
authors from publishing their works in South Africa (many writers already are in exile).

South African writing (not only journalism) has invariably reacted to topical issues in the
the sphere of politics. This also has affected creative methods, styles and forms. The
prevailing method used by South African English-writing authors has been critical
realism. However, as in Europe, there have been a variety of creative methods, including
romanticism and naturalism.

The Soviet critic Saratovskaya regards the main realistic trend in South African fiction
as contrasting with "novels of adventure and exoticism". Although we may try to cate-
gorize large numbers of works in several successive periods, a word of warning must be
expressed to the effect that any purely chronological division of South African writing will
prove ineffective, if the personal attitudes of the individual writers are examined. A wide
variety of opinions and tendencies appear in each period. Therefore, in this connection
literary historians and critics sometimes propose other kinds of classification, namely that
categories should be established on the basis of criteria applied to the content of literary
works and their writers' approaches.

Apart from chronological, typological and ideological criteria we can use also statistical
methods, e.g. the measuring of the number and length of works in certain periods, thereby
determining "booms and depressions".

Like other literatures of Black Africa, South African writing has been systematically
followed by experts. Soviet critic Kartuzov and Lewis Nkosi, a South African critic living
in exile, adopt typical viewpoints with respect to the present-day situation of South
African literary activities. Kartuzov appreciates social and political commitment, positive
heroes, and the art of story-telling. He also praises a matter-of-fact relating of contemporary life—e.g. Richard Rive's *Emergency* and David Lytton's *The Freedom of the
Cage* (1966). The former novel, which concentrates on the period following the Sharpeville
events, has already been mentioned; the latter is documentary, based on the investigation
of the attempted murder of Vorster, a leading nationalist politician, by an alleged lunatic.
Kartuzov rightly stresses a negligible influence of the aesthetics of folklore on South African
creative writing (in which South Africa differs from West Africa, for example). On the other
hand, Nkosi realized that the black South African writers' concern for telling the story has
not actually freed them from the traditional patterns. He finds some recent books un-
interesting, their themes commonplace and the artistic treatment of these themes un-
imaginative. He dislikes Rive's *Emergency* and books having a similar artistic orientation.

As we have said, Kartuzov appreciates positive heroes. Novels and stories, he feels,
should provide the reader not only with a certain amount of entertainment, but should

above all be instructive or should carry a "message". According to him, certain social models are followed and imitated and the ideas discussed in books are incorporated into practical life. A positive character embodies an ideal of a certain epoch. The introduction of positive heroes is undoubtedly one method by which writers generally should attempt to affect reality. Moreover, the author's opinions are more easily ascertained if they can be identified with those of his positive characters. The occurrence of such characters and various other qualities seem to suggest that some South African novelists (Altman, La Guma, Abrahams in *A Night of Their Own,* etc.) employ certain elements of the method of socialist realism. This does not mean, however, that there are South African writers who are under Eastern European influence. On the contrary, if foreign influences are to be sought, it can be clearly seen that since the very beginning South African English-written fiction has been primarily influenced by the literatures of other English-speaking countries, in particular by British and American writing. Kartuzov mentions the Sinclair Lewis' montage method utilized in Rive's *Emergency,* E. M. Remarque's influence on Alex La Guma, and Gerald Gordon's and Anton Chekhov's influence on Ezekiel Mphahlele (Bloke Modisane's idea). But many foreign influences are concealed and the attempts to discover them usually lead to results of doubtful validity. To give one example: the Anglo-Saxon literary origin of Rive's *Emergency* is incontestable. One is certainly reminded of Sinclair Lewis, but his influence has not yet been proved. On the contrary, Lewis Nkosi feels that James Joyce's novel *Ulysses* was Rive's inspiration.

Since contemporary problems of literary criticism cannot be discussed in connection with the South African literary scene, a special chapter of this book devoted to the role of criticism will present additional facts concerning South African and other sub-Saharan literatures in order to illustrate the most topical ideas prevalent in that region.

XV. THE ROLE OF LITERARY CRITICISM

There is a very close relationship between modern Black African writers and their critics. In fact, many authors deal in criticism themselves, while the critics sometimes present concrete examples of their theoretical ideas. They also meet quite often at conferences, festivals, etc. This relationship results partly from the general scarcity of intellectuals in Black Africa, and partly from the fact that a number of questions having to do with creative methods and aspirations have not yet been cleared up. While many European and American theorists devote their attention to the classics and works written long ago, African critics concentrate mostly on contemporary production and its topical aspects. Naturally, one of their tasks is to give young authors advice and basic instruction and sometimes even encourage them a bit. But this relationship is not so one-sided. The critic's opinion is not always blindly accepted and obeyed by the writer. As a matter of fact, some literary works constitute a polemic reply to the critic's view; this reply may not be explicit, but merely indirect or implied. Such an exchange of opinions is necessary in the dynamic, passion-charged atmosphere in which the literature of Africa is developing.

In the 1950's, Janheinz Jahn based his interpretation of African culture on his mystical philosophy of vital forces. He has been both admired and criticized since the publication of his *Muntu*. Generally speaking, Jahn's "defence" of Africa's past implies a more favourable appreciation of politically non-committed works, as in his eyes aesthetic criteria rank higher than content. Considerable attention was devoted to artistic form also by Ulli Beier, who spent a long time in Nigeria. Interested in literature, painting and sculpture, he tried to analyze the sources and inspiration of Black African works of art. More than Jahn, Beier was influenced by the thinking of anglophone Africa. He rejected the revolutionary romanticism and pathetic rhetorical qualities of a certain part of *négritude* poetry. B. H. Atkinson (Canada) gave inexperienced writers useful instruction concerning the technical aspect of modern prose-writing exclusively. In his *Fiction-Writing for West Africans* (1962), he summed up his impressions gained during his editorial work and described the most typical shortcomings and errors committed by beginners writing short stories. Needless to say, advice concerning narrative technique has been offered by various other authors, including Ezekiel Mphahlele, the author of *A Guide to Creative Writing* published by the East African Literature Bureau in 1966. In it, he recommends the use of idiomatic dialogues and stresses the social function of literature. As a scholar, Mphahlele started out with his analysis of the black hero in *The African Image* (1952). He compared the way white authors have portrayed black characters with their portrayal by black writers themselves. Mphahlele's comments are often highly personal, but his general attitude to European culture is positive. He is well aware that modern African writing should be viewed within the scope of world literature and judged by universal critical criteria. He dislikes the idea of creative writing giving only information about the "exotic continent" or serving as material for sociologists. In his opinion, its main objective is to raise present-day artistic standards, which he rightly understands as a unity of aesthetic and social values. He believes that uniformity may be harmful and wants new writing to be more differentiated and varied.

One of the most frequently discussed questions is that of the African writer's commitment. The expression "commitment" necessarily implies "an engagement restricting freedom of action". We may ask what kind of restriction is characteristic of the writer's commitment, as this problem becomes very topical, for instance, in South African writing, which must take into account the official doctrine of apartheid. As the writer constantly comes across facts resulting from the application of the doctrine of racism to practical life, he must deal with it.

In most cases, the author's political commitment seems to be a gradual process in which the author consciously and deliberately abandons his former position and begins his struggle for a certain cause. The former position might be that of an unbiased thinker, dispassionate observer or neutral commentator. Whoever is familiar with the present-day political situation in South Africa will understand its black writers' increasing political commitment, which results from the fact that progressive writers have often been materially handicapped, persecuted, or forced to leave their native country. This kind of commitment now unquestionably exists among those who are still living in South Africa, even though their works may be neither published nor quoted. It also exists among those who are living in exile and are continuing their creative activities. As far as their themes are concerned, these are chosen on the basis of what is most effective for the purpose of the struggle against apartheid. The restrictive quality of their commitment is apparent in the fact that the committed author's attention is never centred on all aspects of reality, but only on certain ones, while other aspects remain more or less neglected. Consequently such commitment invariably implies selectivity.

The South African writer's political commitment—especially during the 1960's—intensified the matter-of-fact, true-to-life, non-fictitious elements in prose writing, i.e. in novels and short stories, while fiction in the literal sense of the word was relegated to a more modest position in the background. Topicality was very characteristic of the books that appeared in the 1960's. But such topicality is objected to by those critics who attempt to discredit realistic works by describing them as "pieces of political propaganda". Tucker, for instance, wrote in his article "The Headline Novels of Africa" (*West Africa*, 1962, p. 829) that topicality was ruining the modern novel written in English about Africa.

But such direct accusations proved to be completely ineffectual and they therefore took a disguised form. Some Black African authors have also been found guilty by the critics of sensationalism, i.e. of exaggerated efforts to attract the readers' attention. This so-called sensationalism does not merely mean that the author wishes to reach the public at any cost. Such an approach implies an identification of sensationalism with gross commercial writing. The sensational element in creative writing is that which is calculated to produce a violent impression on the reader. But thus far, this label has been used by critics in its pejorative sense, since creative works should not produce a violent impression. Moreover, the author is not expected to play tricks, and the reader likes to form his own impression. Therefore, these pejorative implications seem to result from a rationalist perception which is prevalent in this era of realism.

If such expressions as "political commitment" or "sensationalism" are to contribute anything to our studies, they should be used in their precisely defined, "natural" meaning. Some South Africans, who have had to work under very difficult conditions, have expressed their scepticism about the possibility of changing reality by means of protest appeals in imaginative writing. Some of them have been publishing and writing for many years, during which there has been no improvement in South African reality. On the contrary, the regime has become more rigid during the last decade. Now they are starting to ask themselves: What is the use of writing under these circumstances? Does our society need us? The critic, playwright and commentator Lewis Nkosi was particularly sceptical in his comments at the African-Scandinavian Writers' Conference in Stockholm (1967), saying that he was not even sure, in fact, that they were absolutely necessary to society (*The Writer in Modern Africa*, 1968, p. 46). He himself does not understand the South African writer's commitment as a "political commitment", as a concentration on some selected subject-matter which serves the purposes of the anti-apartheid struggle, but rather as a commitment to the republic of letters. Chiefly concerned with the problem of increasing the artistic standard of South African writing, he remarks that "there is a lot of committed literature which is simply bad literature" and that "our commitment as writers is a commitment to the craft, to being good writers" (*ibid*. p. 27).

Nkosi separates "the man" from "the writer", yet in fact any writer's work is in some way connected with his non-literary activities. If Nkosi were right, we should not have to go to the pains of studying the biographies of writers. Actually sometimes a biography is immensely relevant to the evaluation of a creative work. Nkosi admits, however, that expressing the truth is a decisive atribute of any art, and he asserts: "A writer's special commitment is to language and its renewal, and to the making of a better instrument for the delineation of human character—it is a commitment to craftsmanship. This is not at all a romantic notion. After all, language is not unrelated to those human concerns that we speak of as freedom, the preservation of human life, etc. I certainly find no contradistinction between language as a method or form and the content of what is being expressed—these two are inseparable. If a writer were to write a poem about slavery, and I found in it an image like 'as happy as a slave', I should judge that poem a failure, especially if it were full of lines like that" (*ibid*, p. 48).

Nkosi's conception of the South African writer's commitment is closely connected with his idea of artistic freedom. We have already observed that commitment restricts freedom of action, but that this restriction is willingly accepted by writers who sense their urgent tasks under specific social conditions. It is true that Nkosi, when using such expressions as "language", "speech" and "vocabulary", usually means something more than artistic means and linguistic material. But his primary concern is that of creative freedom and the writer's possibility for total self-expression in the broadest sense of the word, and therefore he is rather sceptical about "political commitment". *In Home and Exile* (p. 121) he writes as follows:

"What we so clearly need in South Africa is a vocabulary which bears witness to our variousness as a people, but which may also do more, securing us an individuality, a sense of repose in our completeness as a nation. For such a task we direly need the maximum freedom of speech and the untrammelled functioning of our writers and intellectuals. South African whites cannot—and I am speaking as an African—become full human beings until they have dealt, however painfully, with their fear of black people, and their power, both economic and social."

Nkosi artificially separates "artistic freedom" from "social freedom" and for this reason the conception of the "political commitment" of the South African poet and critic Dennis Brutus is preferable. He said at the above-mentioned conference: "In South Africa, commitment is not a problem. You do not have to be a hero to be committed, you are compelled to be committed, you are involved in a situation so fraught with evil that you are brought into collision with it. That is the only way of asserting human values and the fundamental value of freedom, freedom of expression—what else is he seeking in his writing but precisely the freedom? (*The Writer in Modern Africa*, p. 33—34). But this freedom—like the freedom conceived of by socialist artists and critics—is not absolute or unlimited; this is clearly understood by Brutus. Brutus is primarily concerned with the position of those South African authors who are still living under the shadow of apartheid, and consequently "commitment" appears to him as the political content of literary works. He believes that "...writers must necessarily be in some way or other expressive of certain human values and therefore they are in a sense committed to precisely these values. If they fail to assert these values, they not only betray the values, but their own functions as writers" p. 33). Brutus rejects all kinds of escapism and feels that writers living in exile must continue their anti-apartheid struggle and constantly remind the public in all parts of the world of the existence of racism in the present-day world.

Brutus never asks whether writers are necessary to society or not. He understands their task in the present-day world, their function and their duty. For him, political commitment is not only desirable, but even necessary. For him, Nkosi's problem of *how* to write is certainly less significant than that of *what* to write about. He says that he is not concerned with how a man expresses his involvement, but he is "desperately concerned" that he should (*ibid.*, p. 50). While Nkosi feels that the author's commitment is to the republic of letters, and while he does not consider political commitment as a relevant or necessary quality in literary evaluation, Brutus feels that the very fact of being a writer should strengthen and emphasize the citizen's political commitment. This idea is developed by Alex La Guma, another South African writer in exile, who considers writing as only one of a variety of possible methods of the anti-apartheid struggle. If his method is no longer adequate, the writer usually decides to use other means of struggle.

This thinking is typical at present of certain writers living in countries that have not achieved their political independence (e.g. the Portuguese overseas territories). In La Guma's opinion, actual fighting is an extension and logical continuation of literary activities. This opinion is based on his belief in the essential unity of "the man" and "the writer". La Guma says:

"The South African artist finds himself with no other choice but to dedicate himself to that movement which must involve not only himself, but ordinary people as well. So that I say that in our society we are prepared to run guns and hold up radio stations, if it is necessary; I say this because I believe that, whether we are European writers or African writers or American writers, all human activity which does not serve humanity must be a waste of time and effort" (*ibid.*, p. 24).

The above-mentioned statements explain why, in the 1960's, South African protest literature developed towards naturalism and social realism, why many works approached the borderline between creative writing and journalism, and why topicality was their most characteristic feature. Unlike the older generation of writers, the younger authors know that it is no longer sufficient to protest against apartheid in the name of the moral renascence of their society, that nothing can really be changed by mere appeals to one's sympathy, common sense, or sense of justice, etc. Today for the most part, they describe poverty, the consequences of discriminatory measures, serious social contradictions and violence, with some of them choosing methods that remind one of biologists describing animal and plant life. This "scientific" approach is fairly characteristic of natural scientists. This also indicates that so-called sensationalism has not found any significant roots among these writers. The fundamental approach of the younger generation of writers in South Africa is a rationalist one, resulting from a curious mixture of social pessimism and "scientific" optimism. Most African authors, it seems, are aware of the fact that no profound changes in South African society will take place in the near future; on the other hand, their optimism is generally based on their belief that social reality can be objectively recognized.

Those who have had to leave their native countries must face other, by no means simple, problems. Many authors have lived in London since their departure and have lost all direct contact with the situation at home. Consequently their works are fed with reminiscences. Probably the only way of acquiring new inspirations and fresh impetuses would be to re-visit South Africa, which, of course, is impossible at present. These authors often tend to absorb foreign, non-African (or at least non-South African) elements. As they are not prepared to cut themselves off from their original cultural milieux, they often make use of political themes and folklore to keep up the link.

In the 1960's, Soviet research with regard to Black African writing increased. Although most Russian scholars seem to be mainly interested in oral literature, some of them are concerned almost exclusively with Black African contemporary writing. With only a few exceptions, these Soviet essays and papers are published in Russian, and consequently may escape the attention of those Western students who do not regularly follow Russian-language publications.

F. M. Breskina believes that the originality of rising African literature connected with their democratic and collectivist traditions, which are strengthened by the national liberation movement. She emphasizes "committed anti-colonialist literature" as opposed to extreme individualism. Moreover, she does not agree with Ulli Beier who characterizes David Diop as a "romantic" poet. Rather, she suggests replacing the theory of a "clash of cultures" with her own "clash of epochs" theory, affirming the basic unity of literature and politics, aesthetic and social values, form and content, etc.

V. V. Ivasheva states that most (and probably the best part of) African novels are written by authors who use the method of critical realism. She notes the penetration of folklore elements into modern writing, but considers folklore only one of the traditions of African literatures. She believes that this critical realistic method of modern African authors (e.g. Achebe, Ekwensi, Beti, Oyono, Conton, Mphahlele) more closely approaches that used by the European classical critical realists (Flaubert, Dickens, et al.). While S. P. Kartuzov traces the beginnings of socialist realism in Africa (e.g. in Abrahams' novel *A Night of Their Own*), V. V. Ivasheva feels that it is too soon to speak of any genuine application of this method, certain elements of which may be observed in some of the works of Sembène Ousmane.

V. N. Vavilov thinks that "certain critics are attempting to lead West African novelists away from the urgent topics" by accusing them of writing "propaganda" and by wanting them to make the informative part of their books dominate the rest (the colonial exotic type of writing). Criticizing *Black Orpheus*, this critic shows that African poetry is oriented towards modernism, which permits some critics to assert that the specificity of African creativity is irrational. Since this magazine represents, in V. N. Vavilov's opinion, a platform for *négritude,* this scholar tries to prove that African folklore has a privileged position within the sphere of human oral expression. Consequently, conservative elements were praised by the bourgeois editors of *Black Orpheus* and interpreted as an expression of the African's exceptional psyche. Vavilov's essay "Zhurnal Chornyy Orfey" (in *Literatura stran Afriki*, Moscow 1964, pp. 91—109) is directed chiefly against the tendency to present the mystical and irrational elements in some African books as the African's "eternal qualities". He describes the lack of Ghanaian novels to their authors' efforts to disseminate their own works as much as possible in Ghana, where short stories are very popular. In addition to Ghanaian writing, Vavilov discusses most of the Nigerian novels.

S. P. Kartuzov in *"Literatura protesta v Juzhno-afrikanskoy respublike"* (pp. 147—177) is concerned with South African prose writing, which he divides into roughly two categories: reactionary colonial writing and democratic literature. By South African "protest literature", he means the books that appeared in the last quarter of the 19th century (!) as a reaction to the exploitation of the masses of the South African population by the colonialists. "Protest literature" reflected the rise of Bantu self-consciousness, but it was also written by white liberals. Of course, some kind of protest has been expressed in South African journalism and literature since their beginnings, but it would be preferable to date modern liberal protest writing from 1926, the year of the publication of William Plomer's *Turbott Wolfe*. Protest writing has existed as a distinct literary trend ever since. Kartuzov considers the choice of the hero as the main problem encountered by the South

African writer. Progressive authors try to find a hero who will serve as a means of asserting human dignity. The individualism of bourgeois society produces a feeling of pessimism on the part of some African authors. S. P. Kartuzov stresses once again the idea of the positive hero in South African novels, showing the need for an aesthetic ideal which will strengthen the educative role of literature.

The well-known concept of the African personality has been raised in counterdistinction to the belief that African art and culture cannot be thought of as a single entity, and that there exists only art, which is expressed differently by different tribes, etc. If applied to literary studies, this concept of ethnical isolation would mean that there can be no national literatures in tropical Africa because the frontiers of the present-day countries do not correspond to the areas inhabited by the individual tribes. But the situation is not so simple.

"When we speak of preserving the traditional African culture", says E. A. Veselkin, "we should not forget that it is not what it could have been. It is a 'frozen' culture whose development had been braked or which had received a one-sided development. So the desire to preserve it in its virgin form is looking back at the past, looking back at yesterday—and even the day-before-yesterday's Africa. It constitutes a refusal to look into the future.

"Intensive ideological exchange is an objective process today. A wish to shut oneself off spiritually is nothing but fear of the difficulties of growth, a desire to avoid the need of solving complicated tasks of the times. Such sentiments would tally with the interests of neo-colonialism.

"But events break down the prejudiced schemes drawn up by many of the Western scientists. The nascence of new forms of art in Africa, the development of the theatre, the film industry and the opera parallel with the traditional forms of art show that the African personality seeks new means of expression to go with the old. To refuse these new means would impoverish language, culture, psychology and degenerate the African personality. I have no intention of saying that the African should speak the language of Western art. But to express his own ideas, he must select and digest all that is best in the cultural heritage of the East and the West." (E. A. Veselkin, *The African Personality in Essays on African Culture,* 1960, pp. 85—86).

The concept of a "national literature" is in itself a relative one south of the Sahara. Moreover, it is complicated by the varying stages of cultural development achieved by the various nations, peoples, tribes, etc. at different stages of their material development. The usual approach to a study of European literatures—the study of a national litsrature, as it has developed within the framework of a given political context—is least effective where there are striking ethnic differences, where tradition in the colonial and post-colonial periods remains strong, where the vast expanse of territory concerned entails the isolation of cultural phenomena, and where artificial barriers exist hindering closer contacts.

In addition to the division into territories, the division into spheres of power must be considered; the linguistic zones correspond to the former division of the continent among the European colonizing countries (anglophone, francophone etc.). One must also bear in mind the degree of urbanization in a given area, for naturally modern writing has developed in the larger urban centres. An important role in literary life is played by the towns of sub-Saharan Africa where universities have been established.

The native intelligentsia of West Africa, who were educated, for the most part, at British universities, have gradually become acquainted with the classical and modern European literatures and have accepted the structures of values formulated by Europeans. In South Africa, on the other hand, the tendency to segregate the different racial groups has become more and more pronounced. The black South African suffers from serious social handicaps even if he is well educated. In some respects his position is very similar to that of the uneducated blacks and coloureds. The situation in West Africa is very different. For instance, after Nigeria became independent, her intellectuals took over the positions held by colonial officials, earned high salaries and acquired considerable social prestige. They worked in many spheres, for the new state wanted to Africanize the more important positions.

What opportunities were offered to their South African counterparts on the same intellectual level at that time? They were limited indeed. Some of them might become teachers, traffic inspectors or librarians, with modest salaries and even less prestige. In the eyes of the authorities, however, they continued to be an undesirable element, a potential threat to the racist regime. Their conflict-ridden situation was revealed most starkly in urban environments,towards which the African's interests and tendencies inclined him and from which the authorities would sooner or later expel him into the rural areas, especially if he aired his political views.

The urbanized South African evidently clings to his city milieu also out of fear of being transferred to the native reserves with their poor soils and rather primitive way of life.

In the first half of the 1960's, educated Nigerians gathered in Ibadan and Lagos to consider how best to further their country's economic and cultural development. Most of them, including Nigeria's best writers, took an active part in public affairs and propagated the modern way of life. Many of the books written during that period reflect the conflict between this way of life and the traditional social norms.

Some South African blacks had entered the political arena much earlier, but they could not expect any material advantages from their actions, such as the careers that their Nigerian counterparts might enjoy. The South African blacks' social commitment and interest in public affairs are still necessarily the outcome of the need to defend that country's oppressed majority. Race relations constitute such a key social problem for South African writers that they are hardly likely to attack tradition. The significant exception, of course, is the system of tribal chiefs, whose actual function is to serve the ruling classes in their subjugation of the rural blacks. In the attitude of Nigerians towards traditions, one can discern two fundamental tendencies: the dominant tone of criticism heard in the works of those who consider tradition a hindrance to progress, and the occasional idealization to be found in the works of those who worship the "good old days". The latter are few, however—decidedly fewer than are to be found in the *négritude* movement. This mood of criticism may also have had something to do with the hard-dying illusions concerning the possibility of following the British model of democracy in Nigerian life.

The intellectuals of South Africa, perhaps enlightened by decades of parliamentarism, have not shared these illusions. In many cases, they have even passed through a period of disenchantment over the existence of social wrongs and over the various ways by which individual liberty has been restricted (and not only in Africa). In most cases, they came to the conclusion that a mechanical imitation of foreign models had nothing to offer. Nevertheless, they did not work out any theory on how to improve things. Their critical yet reserved attitude does not seem to be due only to an understandable resignation arising from the impossibility of achieving profound reforms in the foreseeable future. It is also a reflection of their frequent difficulty in earning a living and the practicism characteristic of a situation in which they have no hope of sharing in the governing of the country.

With no possibility of finding their outlet in the political and economic spheres, South African black intellectuals are seeking a refuge in cultural work, where they have perhaps some slight opportunities. This has given South African literature one of its most powerful, if enforced, impetuses over the last twenty years. We have already pointed out that in South Africa there is relatively little vertical differentiation among the black intelligentsia. On the other hand, the Nigerian intellectuals seem to be a much less compact entity; their writers deal with a far broader range of subjects and very different philosophical outlooks. The new élite of Nigeria embraces a remarkable range of personalities who differ in terms of position, function, prestige, financial situation and demands.

In South Africa after World War II, the social significance of literature in the native languages decreased. It was to some extent characterized by religious didacticism and was little suited to the needs of the anti-apartheid movement. Works with a protest message were written in English for another reason: it gave them greater hope of attracting an international audience. At a time when waves of nationalism were inundating Nigeria, the cultural atmosphere of South Africa was being subjected to a highly variegated selection of philosophical influences.

There were still a number of questions awaiting clarification. For a surprisingly long time, for instance, Christianity, which had been introduced by the whites, was mechanically connected with the technical progress of modern civilization. It is paradoxical that the Church encouraged this view, interpreting resistance to political and economic oppression as ingratitude on the part of the South African blacks with regard to all that the Western countries had done to civilize them. What Mphahlele and other black intellectuals mainly reproach the Church for is its passivity, indifference and formalism.

Before the outbreak of the tragic civil war in 1967, the literature of Nigeria gave cause for optimism, in sharp contrast to the hopelessness and occasional expressions of cynicism in the works of South Africa black writers, which in some cases was openly anti-white in sentiment. In Nigeria, the liberals were to be found mostly among the nucleus of élite writers, whereas in South Africa they stood aside from the mainstream of protest, which was highly radical, both at home and in exile. Sociological differences between the readership in the two countries might well merit a separate analysis.

The rapid increase in the number of novels written in Nigeria from 1958 to 1966 can be traced to reasons of prestige (while at the same time these writers neglected the lesser forms) and to a feeling of material security and increased self-confidence on the part of their authors. It is also clear that Nigerian writers have been aiming at an overseas audience. Few South Africans would dare risk writing a novel without prior guarantee of publication. Both monotony of subject-matter and political difficulties oblige the South African to keep the native reader in mind—as long, of course, as he is not an emigrant who can rely on a foreign market. Differences between the works emanating from these two countries are also to be seen in the nuances of language; these are probably due to differences in the mode of expression of the various social strata.

Some critics have observed that the literary differences between Europe and Black Africa lie in their differing traditions of epical forms and genres and, more generally, in their varying aesthetic norms. These provocative complex problems may be mentioned here in passing, but they cannot be dealt with in great detail, due to lack of space. The African art of oral language is based on collectivist tribal traditions, which date back countless generations.

Analyses of West African creative writing have often dealt with its significance with respect to contemporary social requirements. Such authors have been advised not only to examine the past. Their excessive concentration on traditional subject-matter has led to the false assumption that African culture is essentially religious and mystical, thereby forming a counterpoise to European materialism. Such errors, which can easily be refuted by sociologists and historians, result from generalizations about African philosophy which is regarded as a compact whole. But the recent development of African literatures stems from a remarkable variety of ideological trends. Thus, certain concepts which are quite clear in Europe become rather vague in African discussions. Only one example might be mentioned—the very complicated, and at times confusing, treatment of the subject of socialism by non-Marxist Africans.

Many Black African thinkers and practical politicians have been sceptical about the existence of a class structure in tropical Africa. Although they could easily perceive the gap between their own bourgeoisie and the masses of the peasants, they have tended to overlook it, for the sake of national unity. Stressing, for example, the difference in interests existing between European workers and trade-unionists, on the one hand, and the inhabitants of the former African colonies, on the other, they have attempted to show that the concept of a class conflict cannot be applied to Africa. In Senghor's opinion, Karl Marx underestimated the revolutionary role of the peasantry in the underdeveloped countries, and predicted the victory of socialism in the most advanced industrial countries because he could study only the earliest stage of colonialism. Others consider a future revolution of African peasants to be a logical and radical probability. They anticipate that the poorest people—those in the countryside—will become a leading force, similar to the Chinese model, while the role of the urban proletariat is frequently underestimated. The romantic, unrealistic aspect of this approach results from the fact that such excessively "optimistic" ideologists do not realize that the process of class differentiation cannot be halted, and that the proletariat is the class that plays an historical revolutionary role, since it becomes the best-organized class when it is led by a Marxist party. As the most politically conscious class, the workers find their allies among the peasantry. In the developing countries, the revolutionary forces expect to be assisted by the revolutionary parties and classes of the former metropolises.

Folklore has always had a specific function in society, serving the needs and purposes of large masses of people. The origin of written literatures in tropical Africa under foreign, chiefly European, influences logically also implied the introduction of unusual, foreign forms of artistic expression. New genres in prose and poetry were not readily accepted everywhere, however. Their arrival affected both writers and readers and brought forth varying reactions. The classical European type of novel did not correspond to the tribal art of the spoken word, as the former proved to be highly individualistic. The African novelist's initial identification with his work naturally led to an impressive increase in autobiographical writing in sub-Saharan Africa. Moreover, much of the early Black African poetry, which was so outspoken and so subjective, could hardly attract overseas audiences, not only due to its technical deficiencies, but mainly because of its unfamiliar content. The ordinary reader in Europe and America, lacking sufficient information about African social, religious and other structures, did not understand very clearly these messages coming from another continent.

Black African writing has had to "swallow" all at once the European aesthetic experience that has been gathered for ages. All the aesthetics of Romanticism, the importance of which for European literatures is undeniable, had been practically ignored and avoided by Africans. Consequently, present-day literature in Africa, lacking this experience, treats many aspects of reality in a different manner. Take, for instance, the image of nature, which has played an important role in European aesthetic thinking. It has been vital since Antiquity in painting, writing, etc. Although one might think of Africa as being closer to Nature, an examination of this image in modern African literatures shows that most sub-Saharan authors' relationship to nature is by no means immediate. There is, however, an obvious similarity between the intellectuals among both sorts of authors, mainly in the following three aspects which are more or less equally important:

1) Nature as a life-giving force outside the context of human society;

2) Nature as a concrete part of one's surroundings;

3) Nature as a mere coulisse for mythological, legendary and imaginary characters and subjects.

At the risk of over-simplification, one may nevertheless suggest that modern European authors definitely prefer the image of Nature as a concrete part of their surroundings (2), whereas they rarely introduce it as a mere coulisse (3).

Much has been said and written about the differences between black and white aesthetic norms, yet precisely this problem still requires special study. A number of typical examples could be mentioned, drawn from the recent development of modern drama, because this type of art produces an immediate contact between the actors and their audience (or listeners to broadcast plays). The texts of some theatrical or radio plays are never published, or else they are circulated in a limited number of copies, serving exclusively the purposes of the theatrical companies in question. Some types of African drama are also recorded with the help of modern auditory techniques.

Africans reject European fixed ideas of what is "dramatic" (and what is not) and seldom respect the traditional doctrines of dramatic composition, unities, etc. They often utilize typically epical subject-matter, stressing the non-dialogical forms of artistic expression (dance, music, pantomime, etc.). African drama often deals with superstitions, religious rites and traditional thinking. African playwrights feel more intensely than their European colleagues the social justification for giving their plays an instructive conclusion of moral significance. However, the educative function and responsibility of the theatre is not understood in this way in all countries south of the Sahara. Africa has not gone through that long period of realism which contributed to the authenticity and validity of dramatic action on European stages.

The African theatre can absorb more easily any mixture of facts and fiction, as it has been developing in the present era of the strong modernist, anti-realistic influences of Western Europe and America. As folklore is still alive in Africa, it can be more profitably used for the stage than in Europe, yet the above-mentioned use of non-dialogical forms of artistic expression decreases relatively the role of the dramatic script in Africa. No wonder, then, that literary criticism is, on the whole, more tolerant and less strict in judging the shortcomings of African theatrical dialogues. Needless to say, the power of the word is more intensely felt in radio plays.

According to the importance of the dramatic script, we can roughly distinguish two kinds of sub-Saharan drama: the published (often philosophical) type, which is sometimes unsuitable for theatrical performances, and scripts for performances, which are often unpublished and display all the characteristics of the spoken form of the language. The classical European stage was rather strict with respect to its basic principles, the actors' discipline, the solemnity of the performances and the respect and prestige enjoyed by the whole realm of literature. The European spectator has been taught to accept well-tested conventions, while the stage has had its own system of acoustic aids and procedures corresponding to the graphic division and symbols used in printed books.

The dance, drumming, singing, pantomime and music, together with the text produce in Africa a "synthetic" theatre which has no parallel in Europe. As African performances are sometimes freely linked with traditional rituals, one could expect these "shows" to be "naturalistic". But the opposite is true: the present-day African stage is usually highly stylized, full of symbols and avoids any detailed presentation of drastic scenes. Here again, the question of stage illusion and authenticity would deserve serious analysis, in order to discern the existing differences in aesthetic approach. The African spectator, who has been taught by traditional folk gatherings round village fires to be more active and more spontaneous than his European counterpart, can scarcely conceive of the imaginary or real borderline separating the artists from their audience as something never to be crossed. He will hardly accept European conventions, but he does not miss the lack of theatrical properties, as he is used to relying on his own imagination.

Those interested in the role of literary criticism in sub-Saharan Africa will find much valuable information in certain special literary reviews (*Présence africaine, Black Orpheus, Transition,* etc.), which today are overcoming their handicaps and are discussing broad problems that are quite remote from literary studies. Numerous collections of critical essays, conference reports, book reviews and monographs have been published in various countries. Detailed bibliographies (e.g. the MLA Bibliography) and systematic surveys of works in progress (published in *Research in African Literatures*) have facilitated the possibilities for international cooperation in this sphere.

Equally significant are the plans of the main publishing houses which are publishing new works by sub-Saharan writers. Heinemann's *African Writers Series* has introduced over 140 books which have by now become a part of the basic treasury of African creative writing. But much is being done by many other publishing houses. Janheinz Jahn in "Modern African Literature: Bibliographical Spectrum "(in *Black Africa, Review of National Literatures,* Vol. II, No. 2, Fall 1971, pp. 224—242) gives statistical data for modern literature. Thus, 38.6% of modern African works were published in 51 vernacular languages, 34.5% in English, 20.4% in French, 5.8% in Portuguese and 73% of the works of literary criticism were written in English, 22% in French and 5% in Portuguese; 15.4% of this criticism deals with general subjects, 42% with writing in English, 26% with writing in French and 8% with writing in Portuguese. We can see that both imaginative writing and criticism correspond to the traditional use of languages in the spheres formerly (or still) controlled by the colonial powers.

XVI. CONTEMPORARY APPROACHES TO AFRICAN WRITING

The present-day development of national literatures requires a discussion of the close connection between modern African writing and ideologies, linguistics, aesthetics and other spheres. In this volume, as well as in other works, fairly detailed descriptions have been presented of what has been written by African authors and critics; still lacking, however, are sufficient analyses of inter-disciplinary cultural relationships. In the initial stage of our examination, we attempted to describe the subject itself as completely as possible, but further progress in literary studies can be achieved mainly through reliable generalizations of broader questions in this sphere than those discussed thus far.

The origins of written literary works in the countries lying south of the Sahara and the rapid development of these literary activities are relatively rare phenomena in the history of world culture. A vast section of that continent has undergone a transition from the pre-literary to the literary era. However, there still remain societies which have not yet experienced such profound changes in their cultural evolution. We may suppose that if the nature of this process is properly analyzed, the analytical methods thus used could be subsequently applied to various underdeveloped societies outside Africa. Before we commence this effort, however, a number of pertinent questions concerning African writing should be answered or explained. In raising these questions, we can simultaneously orientate our attention towards a future analysis.

Such general considerations may be found helpful in analyzing the formation and evolution of national literatures in Europe, where analogical processes took place centuries ago. It should be pointed out that many essays dealing with the impact of the colonial powers on the countries of Asia and Africa have been based—for the sake of establishing a simplified model— on the theme of the active, progressive West altering various structures of the passive East. So much attention has been concentrated on these modifications of Asian and African structures that the less evident modifications of the West have been more or less left aside. But dialectical thinking cannot accept interpretation of such an impact as a process leading in one direction only. This process should be understood as a long series of changes taking place both in industrially advanced countries and in economically backward regions. Without denying the obvious aggressiveness of the West, we can, at the same time, observe a considerable feedback of this impact, i.e. the fact that the West has not only changed Asian and African structures, but that it itself has been modified as well.

This idea may be profitably applied to studies of ideological systems and the history of social and economic changes, as well as to art and literature. Revolutionary changes in the cultural life of the developing countries have not been due only to education, but also to technological progress, more intense contacts between peoples living in remote regions, rapid development of the mass-communication media, etc. The political emancipation of many African countries led first to the rise, and later to the strengthening, of their own ideological, educational and artistic institutions as well as to a so-called cultural democratization. This process is frequently observed in economically advanced countries as well, but it is naturally more striking in those parts of Asia and Africa in which large sections of the population are now overcoming their illiteracy dating from time immemorial.

The implementation of large-scale literacy campaigns requires more serious research into the relationship between literature and language in sub-Saharan Africa. The achievements of African writers depend on their education and skill, but also on their material prerequisites. African authors have never been able to afford to neglect the commercial orientations of literary journals and magazines and therefore have sometimes succumbed to doubtful "slanting". The development of truly national literatures is supported everywhere by public demand, as a market economy exists in culture as much as in other spheres of African life. Modern sub-Saharan writers spend much time and effort on becoming professionals, but this does not depend merely on their personal desires. An author pursuing his career must devote due attention to the political situation in his country, while simultaneously taking into account the material and ideological needs of his society.

Nation-building and the phenomenon of class differentiation in modern Africa cannot avoid a search for identity resulting both from a gradual discovery of traditional cultural roots and from an increasing awareness of differences between one's homeland and foreign influences in various spheres.

Thus *négritude,* which has so often been analyzed by the critics, is usually understood as a rediscovery and strong assertion of the black man's values, historical roots and accomplishments, etc. Its excessive emphasis on the racial aspect, however, has entailed serious disadvantages, as the two sides of the Atlantic are too remote from each other, both actually and figuratively, for the black people to unite. Moreover, Africa is a multi-racial continent. It is natural that modern groupings, such as the Organization of African Unity, do not favour concepts implying disunity. On the contrary, the typical post-independence idea of the African personality as a force overriding existing political frontiers is far more acceptable to English-speaking intellectuals of Black Africa, despite its dire need to be redefined.

As a concept, the African personality is frequently distorted when it is thought of on a single level only. Any discussion of the African personality would be useless if we were to identify it only with Pan-Africanism or cultural nationalism, merely because of an incomplete understanding of its implications. Our view of such concepts as these can be complete and satisfactory only when all their aspects are taken into consideration. Thus, the concept of the African personality is logically based on the existence of the dynamic process of social change and cannot be accepted by those who believe—or wish to believe—in the possibility of preserving tribal structures. We could never deal with

African national literatures if we were convinced that the highest possible unit in Sub-Saharan cultural life is the tribe. The process of social integration is going on everywhere, although serious local mental reservations cause some resistance to it. This gradual integration, which is also manifested in the economic and cultural spheres, should not be interpreted as complete uniformity, however.

Such striking similarities exist between the two above-mentioned concepts—*négritude* and the African personality—that any explanation of them undoubtedly requires the stressing of their distinctive features, rather than their common ones. *Négritude*, as we have mentioned, derives from cultural roots and an approach to it is necessarily essentially historical. Owing to its philosophical and anthropological bases, it has become highly abstract and theoretical in nature. After all, it originated outside Africa, in the colonial era and therefore it possesses a speculative character which was influenced by the general orientation of its forefathers.

In contrast to *négritude,* the concept of the African personality was introduced into the area of practical political affairs by the late President of Ghana, Dr. Kwame Nkrumah, at the first African Conference (1958). At that time, Ghana was already independent and newly emerging African concepts were directed towards the most topical problems of that continent: the national liberation struggle and the strengthening of Black Africa's spirit of independence. Although both of these concepts originated in quite different situations, they would be inconsistent and ineffective if they did not respect the necessary dialectical unity between the past and the present. Consequently, the concept of *négritude* cannot completely avoid topical questions of daily concern, while the idea of the African personality partially owes its origin to a certain philosophical interpretation of African history, namely that of colonialism. Unlike *négritude,* the African personality has been considered an explicitly anti-colonialist concept ever since its origin. On the other hand, traditions have played a decisive role in the entire development of *négritude.* It is evident that in the sphere of culture, *négritude* implies separatism, while the African personality implies a search for new ways of expression and, therefore, more willingness to "borrow" for the sake of enrichment. This is in accordance with the emphasis on the common aims of sub-Saharan Africa and North Africa, so typical of the African personality. Due to its internal contradictions and basic limitations, *négritude* could not, practically speaking, work as an all-African concept. Thinkers spreading the concept of the African personality have had this ambition, resulting from the changed conditions under which the younger concept arose.

Although the left-wing black intellectuals adhering to the ideas of *négritude* had been interested in politics since the time of their studies, they had no hopeful prospects in this field before or during World War II. For this reason, *négritude* has been orientated towards the spheres of ideology and culture, exerting a strong influence mainly on art and literature. On the other hand, the African personality, as a direct result of the struggle for independence, has been asserted on a number of different levels, among which the political level has continued to maintain its primordial importance.

Clarity is undoubtedly commendable in redefining African and/or Negro concepts. But it is most useful also in the cases of foreign, "imported" ideas which are occurring in increasing numbers. Practically all basic concepts of public life possess a double meaning: one native, the other "imported". Thus for instance, democracy and socialism may mean either a complex of more or less egalitarian attitudes existing in traditional tribal societies of Black Africa or our usual sense of the word. One can easily imagine the confusing character of discussions, unless the speakers clarify exactly which meaning they are giving a particular concept. Moreover, urgent practical needs sometimes do not permit devoting valuable time to developing theoretical approaches. The analysis of essential characteristics of social structures, the class struggle and existing contradictions may conflict with the intentions of African nationalism and with the frequent appeals to national and all-African unity.

Despite this fact, many African authors may become involved in a criticism of the ruling regimes; they do so, since they feel that the writer should consider it his task to expose the errors and vices existing around him. The original, more didactic and informative function of African writing has now been replaced by this increased sense of social responsibility. This evolution is typical of societies entering their literary era, not only in Africa but also elsewhere. The position of the African writer working under political pressure in South Africa is obviously very difficult, but that of writers living in the newly independent states which are the fruit of national liberation struggle is not entirely free from difficulties. The new, well-educated élite enjoy high posts in those countries which are trying to Africanize their superstructures, and they maintain relatively close relations with those in power. The literary efforts which pursue the line of social commitment may, therefore, be characterized by a certain degree of compromise between conformist and non-conformist attitudes. There have been attempts to separate the sphere of art and aesthetics from that of propaganda and criticism. The difference between imaginative creative writing and journalism, i.e. the committed sphere of the press, has often been discussed precisely for this reason. Nowadays, however, few people adhere to the idea of art for art's sake, of "pure" literature completely devoid of propaganda.

Discussions on the foreign impact have been centred on the impact of the European colonial powers, although the countries lying south of the Sahara have also been affected by the philosophy and religion of the Arab world. Islamic civilization penetrated into the interior of Black Africa very early and influenced its various regions. The Arab ideological impact could be felt in the press, in social relationships, in education and in art and literature. The Islamic faith has become deeply rooted in certain countries of West and East Africa and modern Arab political ideas (anti-colonialist and anti-imperialist attitudes, applications of socialist elements to public life, etc.) have left some traces in the thinking of different Black African countries (Tanzania, Ghana, Senegal, Guinea).

The main components in sub-Saharan creative writing are, of course, African and European. Critics sometimes look for African specificity, as if it could exist in a pure state. It can be discerned in folklore more easily than in written works. European elements can be discovered on several different levels, as has been shown earlier in this book. They are very clearly seen in the imitations of European classics. One can come across themes and forms established in European writing and also observe typical viewpoints, which were lacking before this impact.

Western liberal thinking may have influenced the African author's increasing desire for creative freedom, which he certainly enjoys more in the sphere of imaginative writing than in that of ideology. The individual is today attaining his artistic self-expression. However, the African writer need not regret that this foreign impact has invariably made itself felt in a rather incomplete and distorted form, since he has enough scope to selectively absorb these foreign qualities. Precisely because of this feeling for selection on the part of African intellectuals, these imported European values never remain unchanged. Their modification undoubtedly results from the fact that in this African environment they have lost their original cultural context and have acquired a new one, which will give them a different position. Thus, for instance, the transplanting of European literary trends and creative methods has affected both the cultural climate of Black Africa and the trends and methods themselves. The same is true of imported literary forms.

A highly characteristic example of this transformation is that of the tragedy. As a genre of drama, it did not exist before the impact of colonialism on Black Africa, not because there were no tragic elements in ancient tribal life, but because the theatre developed under the European influence only in the most recent period. In earlier times, its function had been fulfilled by rites. Islam-controlled areas did not achieve much progress in this respect, because of the retarding effects of the religious doctrine. Man's creation by Allah was a strictly respected belief and, therefore, any other act of creation—even in the form of a theatrical representation—was unacceptable. The evolution of drama under Christianity was somewhat easier: the atmosphere was never quite free of prejudice, but the missionaries usually had more modern outlooks. Nevertheless, tragedy had no bright prospects in an animistic milieu, as the traditional African's conception of what is or is not tragic differs from the recognized principles of the European stage. Thus, for example, death, which is understood as tragic by the white man, is viewed differently by the natives who believe in the essential union of the living and the dead. Death acquires a special imagery in African poetry, into which, however, many "borrowed" elements also penetrate. Such a symbiosis also formed a basis of the modern African tragedy, which necessarily departs from our conventions. But even if "tragedy" is not understood as a kind of drama, but in its broad and rather vague meaning, its application—outside the sphere of dramatic writing—may be puzzling. The tragic element in a novel or poem becomes all the more effective, the greater the relevance of the conflict chosen by the author. But this also depends on the nature of the society in which this conflict is perceived. Judith I. Gleason (*This Africa*, Evanston, 1965, p. 141) remarks:

"Our critics claim that we can no more have tragedy for various reasons: because of Christianity with its redemptive features, because, romantics that we are, we attach too little importance to this world's goods and honours, and thus underestimate the real loss that a hero's fall means (delighting rather too much in the intensity of his sufferings), or because we are no longer a community. It would seem this last is most relevant to the notion of African tragedy."

Analogical speculations could be made with respect to what subjects are considered comic and humorous, or with regard to the changing nature of the novel in African writing. Although originally understood more as an autobiographical account, at present this literary form enables the author to illustrate the gradual separation of the individual from the traditional community. At the same time, the novel as a literary form is assuming new qualities, which we find unusual, as "it still preserves to a considerable degree the immediate epical nature of the folkloric subject, narrating the fate of the whole tribe and of the folklore hero who is closely linked to the tribal collective." (F. M. Breskina, in *Aktualnye problemy izucheniya afrikanskikh literatur*, 1969, p. 74).

The impact, which works in both directions, may be conceived as a clash between two cultural systems, each possessing its own characteristic hierarchy of values. The elements deriving from the more advanced system appear to be modified and differently situated in the less advanced system. Considering, for instance, various genres of European prose-writing—didactic, picaresque, sentimental, detective, etc.—we find that they have a certain structural arrangement. They occur in certain periods, in certain national literatures, in certain phases of literary development. The intrinsic structure of the European system has been established for centuries, whereas its individual elements have been introduced into Africa only during a short period of time. As a result, the above-mentioned genres can be found in modern Ghanaian literature, where they exist in parallel or mixed forms, without constituting the kind of hierarchy established in Europe. Even where individual components of the system happen to be the same, their organization and hierarchy is never identical with that of the "donating" system. In fact, the components themselves differ, since there has always been a dialectical unity between the acceptance and rejection of European elements in modern African writing. This unity has given rise to a large-scale integration of traditional and foreign elements. Thus, for example, rhythm in modern African poetry has been affected both by the traditional use of drums and other musical instruments and by our own familiar concept of rhythm as an essential component of human speech.

The process of integration enables African authors to employ folk subject-matter simultaneously with modern impulses from overseas to form a synthesis. This synthesis may be achieved not only by writers having a traditional village background and a certain amount of knowledge of folk customs, but also by so-called entirely urbanized and detribalized Africans who never deal with the life of péasants or shepherds. The power of folklore elements in modern African writing stems from the fact that the traditional art of the word is still alive in many areas of that continent. Moreover, folklore does not disappear with the villagers coming to the town. Actually, it exists—in a different form— in the large cities as well, providing a rich source of artistic inspiration.

Other characteristics which contribute to the richness of sub-Saharan national literatures should be considered in future analyses. Apart from additional facts, more efficient methods and approaches will facilitate the perception of basic patterns of this process. This important task cannot be fulfilled by a single person; it calls for the combined efforts of a team of specialists who have mastered a relatively large number of disciplines and languages.

BIBLIOGRAPHY

Abraham, W. E. 1962: *The Mind of Africa*, Chicago

Abrahams, Lionel and Gordimer, Nadine 1967: *South African Writing Today*, Harmondsworth

Abrash, Barbara 1967: *Black African Literature in English since* 1952, New York

Achebe, Chinua 1965: The Novelist as Teacher. In: *J. Press (ed.) Commonwealth Literature*, London: 201—205

Adams, R. F. G. 1947: Obɛri Ɔkaimɛ: A New African Script. In: *Africa* 7: 24—34

Adeley, R. A. and El-Masrī, F. H. 1966: Siffofin Shehu: An Autobiography and Character Study of 'Uthman B. Fūdū in Verse. In: *Res. Bull., Inst. of Afr. Studies* (Center of Arabic Documentation). vol. 2, No 1: 1—13

Ademola, Frances (ed.) 1962: Nigerian Prose and Verse. In: *Reflections*, Lagos
Aktualnye problemy izucheniya literatur Afriki 1969, Moskva

Alexandre, Pierre 1961: Problèmes linguistiques des états africains à l'heure de l'indépendance. In: *Cah. Et. Afr.* 2/6

Alexandre, Pierre 1963: Les problèmes linguistiques Africains vus de Paris. In: *John Spencer (ed.) Language in Africa*, London: 53—59

Alexandre, Pierre 1972: *An Introduction to Languages and Language in Africa*, London

Aliyu, Yahya and Scharfe, Don 1967: The Tradition of Hausa Poetry In: *Black Orpheus* No 21 31—40

Amonoo, R. F. 1963: Problems of the Ghanaian Lingue Franche. In: *Language in Africa:* 78—85

Andrade, Mario Pinto de (ed.) 1958: *Antologia da poesia negra de expressão portuguesa*, Paris

Anozie, Sunday O. 1970: *Sociologie du roman africain*, Paris

Ansre, Gilbert 1968: The Need for a Specific and Comprehensive Policy on the Teaching of Ghanaian Languages. In: *The Study of Ghanaian Languages*, Accra: 5—11

Ansre, Gilbert 1971a: Language Standardisation in Sub-Saharan Africa. In: *Current Trends in Linguistics* 7: 680—699

Ansre, Gilbert 1971b: The Influence of English in West African Languages. In: *John Spencer (ed.) The English Language in West Africa*, London: 145—164

Arnott, D. W. 1957: Proverbial Lore and Word-Play of the Fulani. In: *Africa* 27: 379—396

Arnott, D. W. 1968: "The Song of Rains": A Hausa Poem by Na'ibi S. Wali. In: *African Language Studies* 9: 120—147

Atkinson, B. H. 1962: *Fiction Writing for West Africans*, London

Awoonor, Kofi and Adali-Mortty, Geormbeeyi 1971: *Messages*, London

Ba, Oumar 1962: Dix-huit poèmes peul modernes (présenté par P. F. Lacroix). In: *Cah. Et. Afr.* 2(8): 536—550

Ba, Oumar 1965: Poèmes peul modernes. In: *Etudes mauritaniennes*, Nouakchott

Ba, Oumar 1968: Trois poèmes poular. In: *Cah. Et. Afr.* 8 (22): 318—322

Babalọla, Adeboye and Albert, Gérard S. 1971: A Brief Survey of Creative Writing in Yoruba. In: *Rev. Nat. Literatures* 2: 188—205

Bamgboṣe, Ayọ 1965: *Yoruba Orthography: A Linguistic Appraisal with Suggestions for Reform*, Ibadan

Bamgboṣe, Ayọ 1966: *A Grammar of Yoruba.* (West African Language Monographs No 5), Cambridge

Bamgboṣe, Ayọ 1971: The English Language in Nigeria. In: *The English Language in West Africa,* London: 35—48

Barth H. 1857: *Reisen und Entdeckungen in Nord- und Zentralafrika in den Jahren 1849—55,* Gotha

Bassir, Olumbe 1957: *An Anthology of West African Verse,* Ibadan

Beier, Ulli (ed.) 1964: An Anthology of African and Afro-American Prose. In: *Black Orpheus,* London

Beier, Ulli 1964: Public Opinion on Lovers: Popular Nigerian Fiction Sold in Onitsha Market. In: *Black Orpheus*

Beier, Ulli (ed.) 1967: *Introduction to Africa Literature,* London

Beneš, Eduard and Vachek, Josef 1971: *Stilistik und Soziolinguistik, Beiträge der Prager Schule zu st. Sprachwissenschaft und Spracherziehung,* Berlin

Benn, Gottfried 1955: *Lyrik des expressionalistischen Jahrzehnts,* Wiesbaden

Benton, P. A. 1911: *Kanuri Readings* (including facsimiles of Mss). Repr. in: Benton, *The Languages and Peoples of Bornu* II, London, 1968

Berry, Jack 1953: Problems in the Use of African Languages and Dialects in Education. In: *African Languages and English in Education,* UNESCO, Paris: 41—49

Berry, Jack 1958: The Making of Alphabets. In: *Proc. 8th Intern. Congress of Linguists:* 752—770

Berry, Jack 1962: Pidgins and Creoles in Africa, *CSA—CTL Symposium on Multilingualism,* Brazzaville: 215—220

Berry, Jack 1970: (African) Language Systems and Literature. In: *J. N. Paden and Edward Soja* (eds.) *The African Experience* vol. I (Essays): 80—98

Berry, Jack 1971: Pidgins and Creoles in Africa. In: *Current Trends in Linguistics* 7: 510—536

Boadi, L. A. 1971: Education and the Role of English in Ghana. In: *John Spencer (ed.) The English Language in West Africa:* 49—65

Bol, V. P. and Allary, Jean 1964: *Littératures et poètes noirs,* Léopoldville

Brauner Siegmund 1968: Bisherige Ergebnisse bei der Schaffung von Transkriptionsystemen für die nationalen Sprachen der Republik Mali. In: *Mitteilungen des Instituts für Orientforschung,* vol. 14, No. 3, pp. 375—380

Brauner Siegmund 1973: Zur Herausbildung nationaler Sprachen im subsaharischen Afrika. In: *Asien, Afrika, Latein-Amerika,* Sonderheft 1 (Beiträge zur Afrikanistik u. Orientalistik, herausgegeben von S. Brauner u. Wolfgang Reuschel), pp. 5—29

Breskina, F. M. 1964: Nekotorye voprosy razvitiya afrikanskikh literatur. In: *Literatura stran Afriki,* Moskva: 5—38

Breskina, F. M. 1966: Traditionalisme et modernisme. Métamorphose d'une théorie. In: *Essays on African Culture,* Moscow

Butler, Guy (ed.) 1959: *A Book of South African Verse,* London

Cartey, Wilfred 1969: *Whispers from a Continent,* New York

Cassirer, Thomas 1965: Profile of a Jester. In: *African Forum,* vol. 1, No 4: 128

Cassirer, Thomas 1967: Politics and Mystique—The Predicament of the African Writer. In: *African Forum,* vol. 3, No 1: 26—33

Césaire, Aimé 1955: *Discours sur le colonialisme,* Paris

Cook, David 1965: *Origin East Africa,* London

Cook, David and Lee, Miles (eds.) 1968: *Short East African Plays in English,* London

Cook, David and Rubadiri, David (eds.) 1971: *Poems from East Africa,* London

Cook, Mercer 1963: *Five French Negro Authors,* Washington

Cornevin, R. 1970: *Le théâtre en Afrique Noire et à Madagascar,* Paris

Creighton, T. R. M. 1965: An Attempt to Define African Literature. In: *G. Moore (ed.) African Literature and the Universities,* Ibadan: 84—88

Dadié, Bernard Binlin 1964: Folklore and Literature, translated by C. L. Paterson. In: *The Proceedings of the First International Congress of Africanists — Accra 1962*, Evanston: 119—129

Dalby, David 1967: A Survey of Indigenous Scripts of Liberia and Sierra Leone: Vai, Mende, Loma, Kpelle and Bassa. In: *African Lang. Studies* 8: 1—51

Dalby, David 1968: The Indigenous Scripts of West Africa and Surinam: Their Inspiration and Design. In: *African Lang. Studies* 9: 156—197

Dalby, David 1969: Further Indigenous Scripts of West Africa: Manding, Wolof and Fula Alphabets and Yoruba "Holy" Writing. In: *African Lang. Studies* 10: 161—181

Damas, Léon (ed.) 1947: *Poètes d'expression française*, Paris

Daneš, František 1968: Einige soziolinguistische Aspekte der Schrift-Sprachen. In: *Die Welt der Slawen* 13, 1: 17—27

Dathorne, O. R. 1965: African Writers of the Eighteenth Century. In: *Black Orpheus* No 18: 51—57

Dathorne, O. R. and Feuser, Willfried 1969: *Africa in Prose*, Harmondsworth

Davidson, Basil 1961: *Black Mother*, Boston

Davidson, Basil 1964: *The African Past*, Boston

Decker, Thomas 1964: Three Krio Poems. In: *Sierra Leone Language Review* 3: 32—34

Decker, Thomas 1965: Julius Caesar in Krio. In: *Sierra Leone Language Review* 4: 64—78

Decker, Thomas 1966: Udat di Kiap Fit—a Krio Adaptation of As You Like It. In: *Sierra Leone Language Review* 5: 50—60

Delafosse, Maurice 1899: Les Vais, leur langue et leur système d'écriture. In: *L'Anthropologie* 10: 129—151; 294—296

Delavignette, Robert 1931: *Les paysans noirs*, Paris

Dhlomo, Herbert I. E. 1939: *Nature and Variety of Tribal Drama*, Durban

Diop, Anta 1954: *Nations Nègres et Culture*, Paris

Dipoko, Mbella Sonne 1968: Cultural Diplomacy in African Writing. In: *Africa Today* 15, No 4: 8—11

Diringer, David 1948: *The Alphabet, a Key to the History of Mankind*, New York

Dokulil, Miloš 1971: Zur Frage der Norm der Schriftsprache und ihrer Kodifizierung. In: *Beneš—Vachek* 1971: 94—101

Dugast, I. and Jeffreys, M. D. W. 1950: *L'écriture des Bamum*, Dakar

East, N. B. (ed.) 1970: *African Theatre: A Checklist of Critical Materials*, New York

East, R. M. 1941: *A Vernacular Bibliography for the Languages of Nigeria*, Zaria

Edgar, Frank 1911: *Litafi na Tatsuniyoyi na Hausa*, Belfast

Ekwensi, Cyprian 1964: African Literature. In: *Nigeria Magazine* No 83: 294—299

Eliet, Edouard (ed.) 1965: *Panorama de la littérature négro-africaine (1921—1962)*, Paris

Encyclopaedia of Islam

Essays on African Culture 1966: Moscow

Fafunwa, A. B. 1969: The Importance of the Mother-Tongue as Medium of Instruction. In: *Nigeria Magazine* No 102, 539—542

Ferguson, Charles A. 1962: The Language Factor in National Development. In: *Anthropol. Linguistics* 4: 23—27

Ferguson, Charles A. 1964: *Diglossia*. Repr. in: *Dell Hymes* (ed.) *Language and Culture in Society:* 429—439

Ferguson, Charles A. 1968: Language Development. In: *Language Problems of the Developing Nations, Ferguson—Fishman—Das Gupta eds.*, New York: 27—35

Fiawoo K. F. 1973: *Tuinese. Fia Yi Dziehe*. Two plays in Ewe and English. German Introduction: H. Jungraithmayr. Marburg an der Lahn, Marburger Studien zur Afrika- und Asienkunde, H. J. Greschat, W. Heenisch, H. Jungraithmayr eds.

Fishman, Joshua 1971: National Languages and Languages of Wider Communication in the Developing Nations. In: *W. H. Whiteley (ed.) Language Use and Social Change*, London: 27—56
Folklor i literatura stran Afriki 1970, Moskva
Following the Sun 1960, Berlin
Frobenius, Leo 1937: *African Genesis*, New York

Galperina, E. 1959: Problemy realizma i modernizma v sovremennoy literature Afriki. In: *Voprosy literatury* No 12: 67—96
Galperina, E. 1962: Literaturnye problemy v stranakh Afriki. In: *Sovremennaya literatura za rubezhom*, Moskva: 164—208
Garvin, P. M. 1964: The Standard Language Problem: Concepts and Methods. In: *Language and Culture in Society:* 521—526
Gérard, Alain 1971: *Four African Literatures*, Berkeley
Gérard, Alain (ed.) 1972: *Black Africa*, New York
Gleason, Judith Illsley 1965: *This Africa*, Evanston
Goody, Jack (ed.) 1968: *Literacy in Traditional Societies*, Cambridge
Gorer, Geoffrey 1945: *Africa Dances*, London
Graft-Johnson, J. C. de 1954: *African Glory*, London
Graham-White, Anthony 1967: A Bibliography of African Drama. In: *Afro-Asian Theatre Bulletin 3*, No 1: 10—22
Greenberg, J. H. 1947: Arabic Loanwords in Hausa. In: Word 3: 86—97
Greenberg, J. H. 1949: Hausa Verse Prosody. In: *Journ. Amer. Orient. Soc.* 69: 125—135
Greenberg, J. H. 1963: *The Languages of Africa.* Bloomington
Griaule, M. and Dieterlen, G. 1951: *Signes graphiques Soudanaises*, Paris
Grunebaum, G. E. von 1964: *French African Literature*, The Hague
Guirao, Ramón 1937: *Orbita de la poesia afro-cubana*, Habana
Gukhman, M. (ed.) 1960: *Voprosy formirovaniya i razvitiya natsionalnykh jazykov*, Moskva

Hair, P. E. H. 1963: Notes on the Discovery of the Vai Script (with a Bibliography). In: *Sierra Leone Language Review* 2: 36—49
Hair, P. E. H. 1967: *The Early Study of the Nigerian Languages: Essays and Bibliographies.* West African Language Monographs No 7, Cambridge
Hall Jr., Robert A. 1966: *Pidgin and Creole Languages*, Ithaca
Harries, Lyndon 1962: *Swahili Poetry*, New York
Hau, Kathleen 1959: Evidence of the Use of Pre-Portuguese Written Characters by the Bini. In: *Bull. I.F.A.N.* 21 (Série B): 109—154
Hau, Kathleen 1964: A Royal Title on a Palace Tusk from Benin (Southern Nigeria). In: *Bull. I.F.A.N.* (Série B), 26: 21—39
Hau, Kathleen 1967: The Ancient Writing of Southern Nigeria. In: *Bull. I.F.A.N. (Série B)* 29: 150—178
Haugen, Einar 1966: *Language Conflict and Language Planning (The Case of Modern Norwegian)*
Havránek, Bohuslav 1966: Zur Problematik der Sprachmischung. In: *Travaux Linguistiques de Prague* 2: 81—95
Havránek, Bohuslav 1971: Die Theorie der Schriftsprachen. In: Beneš—Vachek 1971: 19—37
Heine, Bernd 1970: *Status and Use of African Lingua Francas*, München
Herms, I. 1973: Die Yoruba-Sprache im Bildungswesen Nigerias. In: *Zeitschrift für Phonetik* 26: 581—590
Herskovits, Melville J. 1962: *The Human Factor in Changing Africa*, New York
Hill, Archibald A. 1967: The Typology of Writing Systems. In: *Papers in Linguistics in Honour of Léon Dostaert*, The Hague: 92—100

Hintze, Ursula 1959: *Bibliographie der Kwa-Sprachen und der Togo-Restsprachen*, Berlin

Hiskett, M. 1965a: The Song of Bagauda: A Hausa King List and Homily in Verse. In: *Bull. S.O.A.S.* 27: 540—567; 28: 112—135, 363—385

Hiskett, M. 1965b: The Historical Background to the Naturalisation of Arabic Loan-Words in Hausa. In *African Lang. Studies* 6: 18—26

Hiskett, M. 1968: Hausa III. Hausa Literature. In: *Enc. of Islam* (New Edition), Leyden: 280—283

Hodgkin, Thomas 1957: *Nationalism in Colonial Africa*, New York

Holub, Jan 1962: *Jižní Afrika v dílech anglicky pišících autorů* (unpublished diploma work), Praha

Horálek, Karel 1966: *Filosofie jazyka* (The Philosophy of Language), Praha

Houis, Maurice 1967: *Aperçu sur les structures grammaticales des langues négro-africaines*, Lyon

Hughes, Langston (ed.) 1960: *An African Treasury*, New York

Hymes, Dell (ed.) 1971: *Pidginization and Creolization of Languages*, Cambridge

Ismagilova, R. N. 1971: *Etnicheskiye problemi i nek. aspekty yazykovoy politiki v sovr. Afrike.* Moskva

Italiaander, Rolf 1957: *Neue Kunst in Afrika*, Mannheim

Ivasheva, V. V. 1964: Roman Sovremennoy Nigerii. In: *Literatura stran Afriki*, Moskva; 39—74

Ivasheva, V. V. 1967: *Literatura stran zapadnoy Afriki*, Moskva

Jahn, Jahnheinz 1957: *Rumba Macumba,* München

Jahn, Janheinz 1957: *Schwarze Ballade*, Düsseldorf

Jahn, Janheinz 1958: *Muntu*, Düsseldorf

Jahn, Janheinz 1965: *Bibliography of Neo-African Literature from Africa, America and the Caribbean*, London

Jahn, Janheinz 1968: *A History of Neo-African Literature: Writing in Two Continents*, London

Johnson Kuawovi G. 1947: *"Kuawovi" be Gɛ̃gbe Hɛ̃hlɛ̃* (Nouvelle Méthode "Kuaowi" pour apprendre à lire et à écrire la langue Gɛ̃ (Mina-Popo), Anecho

Jones, Eldred 1957: The Potentialities of Krio as a Literary Language. In: *Sierra Leone Language Studies*, N. S. 9: 40—48

Jones, Eldred 1964: Krio in the Sierra Leone Journalism. In: *Sierra Leone Language Review* 3: 24—31

Jones, Eldred 1965: Jungle Drums and Wailing Piano: West African Fiction and Poetry in English. In: *African Forum*, vol. 1, No 4: 93—106

Jones, Eldred 1965: Nationalism and the Writer. In: *J. Press* (ed.) *Commonwealth Literature*, London: 151—156

Jones, Eldred 1971: Krio: An English-based Language of Sierra Leone. In: *The English Language in West Africa:* 66—94

July, Robert W. 1967: *The Origins of Modern African Thought*, London

Kagame, Alexis 1951: *La poésie dynastique au Ruanda*, Bruxelles

Kagame, Alexis 1956: *La philosophie bantou-ruandaise de l'être*, Bruxelles

Kaufmann, Herbert 1958: *Nigeria*, Bonn

Kejzlar, Radko 1952: *Historický a politický vývoj Jižní Afriky a odraz v literatuře* (unpublished diploma work), Praha

Kenyatta, Jomo 1953: *Facing Mount Kenya*, London

Kesteloot, Lilyan 1963: *Les écrivains noirs de langue française*, Bruxelles

Kesteloot, Lilyan (ed.) 1967: *Anthologie négro-africaine*, Verviers

Killam, D. G. 1968: *Africa in English Fiction 1874—1939*

Killam, D. G. (ed.) 1973: *African Writers on African Writing*, London

King, A. V. 1966: A bòorìi Liturgy from Katsina (Introduction and Kíráarìi Texts). In: *African Lang. Studies* 7: 105—125

King, A. V. 1968: The Song of Rains: Metric Values in Performance. In: *African Lang. Studies* 9: 148—155

Kirk—Green, A. H. M. 1964: The Hausa Language Board. In: *Afrika und Übersee* 47: 187—203.

Kirk—Green, A. H. M. 1971: The Influence of West African Languages on English. In: *The English Language in West Africa:* 123—144

Klíma, Vladimír and Ortová, Jarmila 1969: *Modern Literatures of Sub-Saharan Africa,* Prague

Klíma, Vladimír 1969: *Modern Nigerian Novels,* Prague

Klíma, Vladimír 1971: *South African Prose Writing in English,* Prague

Kloss, H. 1968: Notes Concerning the Language-Nation Typology. In: *Language Problems of the Developing Nations:* 69—85

Knappert, Jan 1967: *Islamic Poetry,* London

Kunene, Daniel P. 1968: Deculturation—The African Writer's Response. In: *Africa Today* 15, No. 4: 19—24

Labouret, H. et Rivet, P. 1929: *Le royaume d'Ardra et son évangélisation au XVIIe siècle,* Paris

Labov, William 1971: The Notion of "System" in Creole Languages. In: *Dell Hymes (ed.) Pidginization and Creolization of Language*

Lacroix, P. F. 1965: Poésie peule de l'Adamawa, 2 vols, Paris

Laya D. 1971: Utilisation des Langues Africaines au Niger. Paper presented to the UNESCO-sponsored meeting of experts in Dar-es Salaam, Roneo

Lebeuf, Jean-Paul et Rodinson, Maxime 1952: Les Mosquées de Fort-Lamy (Manuscrit kanouri avec traduction). In: *Bull. I.F.A.N.* 14: 970—974

Lepsius, R. 1880: *Nubische Grammatik. Mit einer Einleitung über die Völker und Sprachen Afrikas,* Berlin

Lindfors, Bernth 1967: A Preliminary Checklist of Nigerian Drama in English. In: *Afro-Asian Theatre Bulletin* 2, No 1: 22—25; No 2: 16—21

Lindfors, Bernth 1968: Additions and Corrections to Janheinz Jahn's Bibliography of Neo-African Literature (1965). In: *African Studies Bulletin* 11, No 2: 129—148

Lindfors, Bernth 1969: The African Politician's Changing Image in African Literature in English. In: *The Journal of Developing Areas* No 4: 13—28

Literatura stran Afriki 1964, Moskva

Liyong, Taban lo 1972: *Popular Culture of East Africa,* Nairobi

Mafeni, Bernard 1971: Nigerian Pidgin. In: *The English Language in West Africa:* 95—112

Margarido, Alfredo 1962: The Social and Economic Background of Portuguese Negro Poetry. In: *Diogenes,* No 37: 50—74

Marsh, Zoe 1961: *East Africa through Contemporary Records,* Cambridge

Mayssal, Henriette 1965: Poèmes foulbé de la Bénoué. In: *Abbia* 9/10: 47—90

Meinhof, Carl 1911: Zur Entstehung der Schrift. In: *Zeitschrift für Ägyptische Sprache und Altertumskunde* 49: 1—14

Meloné, Thomas 1962: *De la négritude à la littérature négro-africaine,* Paris

Menezes, Flinto Elisiode 1949: *Apontamentos sobre a poesia de Angola,* Luanda

Mohamadou, Eldridge 1963: Introduction à la littérature peule du Nord-Cameroun. In: *Abbia* 3: 66—76

Mohamadou, Eldridge 1956: Contes foulbes de la Bénoué. In: *Abbia* 9/10: 11—45

Moore, Gerald 1962: *Seven African Writers,* London

Moore, Gerald and Beier, Ulli (eds.) 1963: *Modern Poetry from Africa,* Harmondsworth

Moore, Gerald 1965: Mots anglais, vies africaines. In: *Présence Africaine,* No 54: 116—126

Moore, Gerald 1969: *The Chosen Tongue,* New York

Moore, Gerald 1972: The Debate on Existence in African Literature. In: *Présence Africaine,* No 81: 18—48

Moser, Gerald M. 1970: *A Tentative Portuguese-African Bibliography*, Pennsylvania

Mphahlele, Ezekiel 1962: *The African Image*, London

Mphahlele, Ezekiel and Komey, Ellis Ayitey 1964: *Modern African Stories*, London

Mphahlele, Ezekiel 1966: *A Guide to Creative Writing*, Nairobi

Mphahlele, Ezekiel (ed.) 1967: *African Writing Today*, Harmondsworth

Muhammad, Liman 1966: Comments on John N. Paden's Survey of Kano Hausa Poetry. In: *Kano Studies* 2: 44—52

Murdock, George P. 1959: *Africa: Its Peoples and Their Cultural History*, New York

Mutiso, Gideon and Cyrus, M. 1970: *Messages, Upper Montclair*, New Jersey

Neves, João Alves das (ed.) 1963: *Poetas e contistas africanos de expressão portuguesa*, Capo Verde, Guiné, São Tomé e Principe, Angola, Moçambique, São Paolo

Niekerk, Barend van 1970: *The African Image in the Poetry of Senghor*, Cape Town

Nketia, J. H. Kwabena 1971: Surrogate Languages of Africa. In: *Current Trends in Linguistics* 7 699—732

Nkosi, Lewis 1965: *Home and Exile*, London

Nwoga, Donatus 1965: Onitsha Market Literature. In: *Transition* 19

Obiechina, E. N. 1967: Transition from Oral to Literary Tradition. In: *Présence Africaine*, No 63: 140—161

Obiechina, E. N. 1968: Cultural Nationalism in Modern African Creative Literature. In: *African Literature Today*, No 1: 24—35

Ohly Rajmund 1974: *Języki Afryki* (The Languages of Africa) Warsaw

Okhotina, I. V. (ed.) 1965: *Afrikanskaya filologiya*, Moskva

Olderogge, D. A. 1960: *Zapadnyy Sudan v XV.—XIX. vv.*, Moskva—Leningrad

Olderogge, D. A. 1969: O nekotorykh etnolingv. problemakh Afriki. In: *Voprosy socialnoy lingvistiki*, Pp. 135—56

Olderogge, D. A. and Potekhin, I. I. 1964: *Narody Afriki*, Moskva

Olivera, José Osirio de 1944: *Poesia de Cabo Verde*, Lisboa

Ologunde, A. 1969: The Yoruba Language in Education. In: *Nigeria Magazine* No 102, 532—539

Orth. Mem. 1927: Practical Orthography of African Languages. In: *Memorandum*, International African Institute, London

Ortová, Jarmila 1971: *Étude sur le roman au Cameroun*, Prague

Ortová, Jarmila 1971: *The Art of the Word in the Culture of Sub-Saharan Africa*, Prague

Otoo, S. K. 1962: The Growth of Fante Literature. In *New Orient Bimonthly* 3: 164—166

Otoo, S. K. 1969: The Bureau of Ghana Languages: Its Operation and Difficulties. In: *The Study of Ghanaian Languages*, Accra: 43—45

Paden, J. N. 1965: A Survey of Kano Hausa Poetry. In: *Kano Studies* 1: 33—39

Paden, J. N. 1966: Letter of Reply to L. Muhammad's Comment on My Survey of Kano Hausa Poetry. In: *Kano Studies* 2: 53—55

Pageard, Robert 1967: *Littérature négro-africaine*, Paris

Palaver. Interviews with Five African Writers in Texas 1972, Austin

Páricsy, Pál 1967: A Supplementary Bibliography to Jahn's Bibliography of Neo-African Literature from Africa, America and the Caribbean. In: *Journal of the New African Literature and the Arts* No 4: 70—82

Páricsy, Pál 1969: *A New Bibliography of African Literature*, Budapest

Páricsy, Pál 1971: *Studies on Modern Black African Literature*, Budapest

Pfeffer, G. 1939: Prose and Poetry of the Fulbe. In: *Africa* 12: 285—306

Piault, Marc H. 1970: *Histoire Mawri*, Paris

Pieterse, Cosmo (ed.) 1967: *Ten One-Act Plays,* London
Pieterse, Cosmo and Munro, Donald (eds.) 1969: *Protest and Conflict in African Literature,* London
Pike, K. L. 1966: *Tagmemic and Matrix Linguistics Applied to Selected African Languages,* Ann Arbor
Piłaszewicz, St. 1972: Wypisy z literatury Hausa. Warszawa
Plaatje, Solomon 1916: *Native Life in South Africa,* London
Potekhina, G. I. 1968: *Ocherki sovremennoy literatury zapadnoy Afriki,* Moskva
Povey, John F. 1968: The Quality of African Writing Today. In: *Literary Review* No 11: 403—421
Press, John (ed.) 1965: *Commonwealth Literature,* London
Price-Mars, Jean 1956: *Survivances africaines et dynamisme de la culture noire outre-atlantique,* Paris
Priebe, Richard 1972: *Letters and Manuscripts from Southern Africa,* Austin
Prietze, Rudolf 1924/25: Wüstenreise des Haussa-Händlers Mohammed Agigi. (in Gesprächen geschildert von Hažž Ahmed aus Kano). In: *Mitt. des Sem. für Orient. Sprachen* 26/27: 1—37; 28: 175—247
Prietze, Rudolf 1927: Lieder des Haussavolks. In: *Mitt. Sem. Orient. Spr.* 30: 5—172
Prietze, Rudolf 1930: Bornu-Texte, mit Ms in arabischer Schrift. In: *Mitt. Sem. Orient. Spr.* 33: 82—159
Prietze, Rudolf 1931: Dichtung der Haussa. In: *Africa* 4: 86—95
Pujman, Petr 1959: *Doris Lessingová* (unpublished diploma work), Praha

Ramsaran, John A. 1965: *New Approaches to African Literature,* Ibadan
Ray, Punya Sloka 1963: *Language Standardisation: Studies in Prescriptive Linguistics,* The Hague
Reed, John 1964: *A Book of African Verse,* London
Res. Review Ghana 1965: A Report on Arabic Manuscripts. In: *Res. Review,* Institute of African Studies, Univ. of Ghana 1: 15 ff.
Rial, Jacques 1965: *Littérature africaine d'expression française,* Léopoldville
Ritter, E. A. 1955: *Shaka Zulu,* London
Rive, Richard (ed.) 1964: *Modern African Prose,* London
Robinson, C. H. 1896: *Specimens of Hausa Literature,* Cambridge
Robinson, C. H. 1953: *Hausa Grammar⁵,* London
Rowlands, E. C. 1963: Yoruba and English: a Problem of Co-existence In: *African Lang. Studies* 4: 208—214
Rowling, F. and Wilson, C. E. 1923: *Bibliography of African Christian Literature* (with a Supplement, published in 1927), London
Rutherfoord, Peggy (ed.) 1958: *Darkness and Light,* London
Růžička, Karel F. 1960: *Zpěvy černé Afriky,* Praha
Ryauzova, E. A. 1972: *Portugaloyazychnye literatury Afriki,* Moskva

Sadji, Abdoulaye 1955: Littérature et colonisation. In: *Présence Africaine* No 6: 139—141
Saint-Amand, Edris 1952: *Bon dieu rit,* Paris
Saratovskaya, L. B. 1969: Etapy razvitiya literatury YAR. In: *Aktualnye problemy izucheniya literatur Afriki,* Moskva. 116—127
Sartre, Jean-Paul 1956: *Situationen,* Hamburg
Sayers, E. F. 1928: In Praise of the Faith of Futa. A. Fula poem with introductory notes and translation. In: *Sierra Leone Language Studies* 13: 35—53
Senghor, Léopold Sédar (ed.) 1948: *Anthologie de la nouvelle poésie nègre et malgache de la langue française,* Paris
Senghor, Léopold Sédar 1964: *Négritude et humanisme,* Paris
Seydou, Christiane 1967: Majaado Alla gaynaali: poème en langue peule du Foûta Djallon. In: *Cah. Et. Afr.* 6, 4 (24): 643—681
Seydou, Christiane 1967: Essai d'étude stylistique de poèmes peuls du Foûta Djallon. In: *Bull. I.F.A.N.* 29 (Série B): 191—233

Sithole, Nadbaningi 1959: *African Nationalims*, Cape Town

Skinner, A. N. 1968: *Hausa Readings: Selections from Edgar's Tatsuniyoyi*, Madison

Skinner, A. N. 1971: Realism and Fantasy in Hausa Literature. In: *Rev. Nat. Literatures* 2: 167—187

Slater, F. C. 1951: *The New Centenary Book of South African Verse*, London

Sow, A. I. 1965a: Poetic Construction in Foûta Djallon. In: *Prés. Afr.* 26/54: 185—200

Sow A. I. 1965b: Notes sur les procédés poétiques dans la littérature des Peuls du Foûta Djallon (Guinée). In: *Cah. Et. Afr.* 5, 3 (19): 370—387

Sow, A. I. 1966: *La femme, la vache, la foi: écrivains et poètes du Foûta Djallon*, Paris

Soyinka, Wole 1966: And After the Narcissist? In: *African Forum* vol. 1, No 4: 53—64

Stewart, Gail 1967: Notes on the Present-Day Usage of the Vai Script in Liberia. In: *African Language Rev.* 6: 71—74

Stikhi poetov Afriki 1958, Moskva

Sulzer, Peter 1955: *Schwarze Intelligenz*, Zürich

Sulzer, Peter 1958: *Christ erscheint am Kongo*, Heilbronn

Sutherland, Efua 1968: Textbooks for the Study of Ghanaian Languages. In: *The Study of Ghanaian Languages*, Accra: 24—42

Swanzy, Henry (ed.) 1958: *Voices of Ghana*, Accra

Taiwo, Oladele 1967: *An Introduction to West African Literature*, London

Taylor, F. W. 1929: *Fulani-Hausa Readings in the Native Scripts, with Transliterations and Translations*, Oxford

Tempels, Placide 1956: *Bantu Philosophie*, Heidelberg

Tenreiro, Francisco (ed.) 1953: *Poesia negra de expressão portuguesa*, Lisboa

Tibble, Anne (ed.) 1965: *African English Literature*, London

Tucker, A. 1971: Orthographic Systems and Conventions in Sub-Saharan Africa. In: *Current Trends in Linguistics* 7: 618—653

Tucker, Martin 1967: *Africa in Modern Literature*, New York

UNESCO Report, 1953: African Languages and English in Education. In: *UNESCO Educational Studies and Documents*, Paris

Vachek, Josef 1939: Zum Problem der geschriebenen Sprache. In: *Travaux du Cercle Linguistique de Prague* 8: 94—104

Vachek, Josef 1948: Written Language and Printed Language. In: *Recueil Linguistique de Bratislava* 1: 67—75

Vachek, Josef 1959: Two Chapters on Written English. In: *Brno Studies in English* 1: 7—36

Vavilov, V. N. 1973: *Proza Nigerii*, Moskva

Velten, C. 1908: *Suaheli Wörterbuch*, Berlin

Vernacular in Education 1953: The Use of Vernacular Languages in Education. In: *UNESCO Educational Mon.* No 8, Paris

Wake, C. H. 1964: African Literary Criticism. In: *Comparative Literature Studies* 1: 197—205

Wali, Na'ibi and Haliru, Binji 1959: *Mu koyi Ajami da Larabci. Gaskiya*, Zaria

Ward, I. C. 1945: *Report of an Investigation of Some Gold Coast Language Problems*, London

Warner, Alan 1963: A New English in Africa. In: *Review of English Literature* 5, 2

Wästberg, Per (ed.) 1968: *The Writer in Modern Africa*, Uppsala

Wauthier, Claude 1966: *The Literature and Thought of Modern Africa*, London

Welmers, W. E. 1971: Christian Missions and Language Policies. In: *Current Trends in Linguistics* 7: 559—569

Westermann, Diedrich 1907: Zeichensprache des Ewe-volkes in Deutsch-Togo. In: *Mitt. des Sem. für Orient. Sprachen* 10 (3. Abt.): 1—14

Westermann, Diedrich 1927: Zum Andenken an Missionar B. Schlegel In: *Monatsblatt der Norddeutschen M.—ges.* 88: 142—143

Westermann, Diedrich 1950: *Die Volkswerdung der Hausa,* Berlin

Westermann, Diedrich and Bryan, M. A. 1952: *A Handbook of African Languages Part II. Languages of West Africa,* London (a second edition with an extended bibliography, prepared by D. W. Arnott, appeared in 1970)

Westermann, Diedrich 1954: *Wörterbuch der Ewe-Sprache,* Berlin

Westermann, Diedrich 1965: *The African Today and Tomorrow* 3, London

Whiteley, Wilfred H. (ed.) 1964: *A Selection of African Prose,* Oxford

Whiteley, W. H. 1969: *Swahili, the Rise of a National Language,* London

Wiedner, Donald L. 1962: *A History of Africa South of the Sahara,* New York

Wiegräbe, Paul 1960: Neuere Literatur in Ewe. In: *Afrika und Übersee* 44: 132—135

Wolf, Hans 1954: *Nigerian Orthography,* Zaria

Works in Ghana Languages 1967: *Bibliography of Works in Ghana Languages Compiled by the Bureau of Ghana Languages,* Accra

Wright, Edgar 1966: African Literature I: Problems of Criticism. In: *Journal of Commonwealth Literature* No 2: 103—112

Yankowitz, Susan 1966: The Plays of Wole Soyinka. In: *African Forum* vol. 1, No 4: 128—133

Yarzeva, V. N. 1969: Social Changes and Function of the Literary Languages. In: *Proc. Intern. Days of Sociolinguistics,* Rome: 227—241

Yarzeva, V. N. 1971: The Problem of the Development of the Literary Languages. In: *Social Sciences,* Moscow 4 (6): 151—164

Young, Peter 1971: The Language of West African Literature in English. In: *The English Language in West Africa:* 165—184

Zahan, Dominique 1950: Pictographic Writing in the Western Sudan In: *Man* 50: 219

Zell, Hans and Silver, Helene 1971: *A Reader's Guide to African Literature,* New York

Zima, Petr 1961: The Language Situation in the New States of West Africa. In: *New Orient Bimonthly* 2: 180—181

Zima, Petr 1964: Some Remarks on Loan-Words in Modern Hausa. In: *Archiv Orientální* 32: 522—528

Zima, Petr 1966: *Tamtamy dosud zní,* Praha

Zima, Petr 1968: Hausa in West Africa: Remarks on Contemporary Role and Functions. In: *Language Problems of the Developing Nations,* New York: 365—377

Zima, Petr 1969: Language, Script and Vernacular Literature in West Africa. In: *African Language Review,* London 8: 212—224

Zima, Petr 1974: Digraphia (The Case of Hausa). In: *Linguistics* No 124: 57—69

Zima, Petr 1975: Is a General Typology of Language Standardisation Feasible? To appear in: *Acta Universitatis Carolinae* (Prague)

Addendum

Klingenheben, August 1933: The Vai Script. In: *Africa* 6: 158—171

Monod, Théodor 1958: Un nouvel alphabet ouest-africain: le bété (Côte d'Ivoire). In *BIFAN, sér. B* 20: 432—553

Schmitt, A. 1963: *Die Bamum-Schrift,* Wiesbaden

Welmers, W. E 1974: *African Language Structures. UCLA*

INDEX OF PERSONS

INDEX OF AFRICAN LANGUAGES AND DIALECTS

1. Remarks on African Language Systems and Their Classification

1.0. As the present book is oriented toward an analysis of the relationship between African languages and literacies or literatures, its task is by no means either to describe the most typical African language systems or to discuss the intricacies of their genetic classification within the respective families, branches or sub-branches. As it is supposed, however, that this work will be read, and hence its index of African languages and dialects also consulted, by literary historians and other specialists of disciplines, who are not acquainted with the basic linguistic facts and their theoretical backgrounds, a few introductory words preceding such an index may not be altogether out of place. Such introductory remarks are obviously not intended to replace any detailed introduction of the study and description of the language systems of Africa or of the rich and still largely disputable field of their genetic grouping. Those readers who wish to be introduced fully to the details of the field of description may well be referred to several contemporary works written by Maurice Houis (1967), Pierre Alexandre (1972), W. E. Welmers (1974) and Rajmund Ohly (1974). On the other hand, an authoritative survey of up-to-date attempts at genetic classifications of the African languages may be found in one of the most recent volumes of *Current Trends in Linguistics* (Volume 7: *Linguistics in sub-Saharan Africa*, edited by Thomas Sebeok in cooperation with Jack Berry and J. H. Greenberg, Associate Editors, and D. W. Crabb and Paul Schachter, Assistant Editors, 1972). An historical outline of the African classification saga may be found — with many constructive critical remarks and additional analyses — in the paper contributed to that volume by D. T. Cole (pp. 1—29); Paul Schachter's paper (pp. 30—37) attempts to analyze certain questions raised by the most recent classification presented by J. H. Greenberg.

1.1. A linguistic analysis of the area of Sub-Saharan Africa was started — primarily owing to historical, non-linguistic factors — from three different geographical directions. The western coast of Africa, and especially its area covering approximately the southern parts of what is today the Ivory Coast, Ghana, Togoland, Dahomey and Nigeria, were among the first targets of the early buccaneers and some of their forts testify even today to their historical interest. The Congo basin and the southern and south-eastern areas of the African coast also came to the fore and obviously left their traces along the road of exploration of the African languages. Last but not least, the areas adjacent to the Sahara desert had always served as the final (or initial) points of trans-Saharan itineraries and thus offfered a third gateway to the recognition of Africa's languages.

1.1.1. The western coast, and especially the above-mentioned area of it, displayed to the early explorers a type of language system which was completely different from the usual "classical" IE pattern. The languages of that region display few, if any, formal grammatical features manifested by morphemes consisting of segmental phonemes (consonants and vowels) or the corresponding categories of classical grammar in the mechanical sense. They have no case and no gender expressed by means comparable to the IE model, and hence no case ending and no gender concord, etc. exist. The grammatical relationships of morphemes (words) in constructions are expresesd by their behaviour, combination and position in constructions, but partly also by modifications of their phonemes (vowel alternation); their tonal systems are highly developed to an extent rarely discovered in conventional flective grammars. Moreover, their tone is distinctive also at the morpheme — and word-level: thus, morphemes or words may be identical as far as their construction from consonants and vowels is concerned, but only their different tone may distinguish their often completely different meanings. Yoruba, Ewe, the Akan languages, Ibo, Gã, Nupe and many languages of this area belonging to what was later labelled the *Kwa* branch offer examples of such a type of language system.

1.1.2. The central, southern and south-eastern coasts of Africa confronted the early explorers with a completely different type of language system. These were, in fact, languages having a highly developed system of formal grammar, expressed by morphemes which mostly consisted of segmental phonemes (although the tonal systems often played their role, as well). In place of the "classical" binary or triadic categories of gender, the nouns are grouped into several so-called noun classes: the semantic equivalents of such noun classes did not cover the mere "sexual" gender field (as in the classical grammars), but extended, rather, to such fields as human beings, animals, plants, liquors, etc., etc. The formal repercussions of the existence of many such noun-class categories in a given language are even more important: in fact, these categories deeply penetrate the entire grammar and syntax of the language system in question, especially through prefix- or suffix- concords, initial alternation, etc. According to D. T. Cole (l.c.p. 3 ff), this grammatical category known as noun class was first analyzed by the Italian Capuchin Giacinto Bruscioto, who introduced it into his early analysis of the Kongo (kikongo) language (*Regulae quaedam pro difficillimi Congensium idiomatis faciliori captu ad grammaticae normam rectae, 1659*).

From the Congo basin, attention was shifted toward the languages of the southern and south-eastern coasts, such as Tswana, Zulu, Xhosa, Swahili, etc. All these languages manifested striking similarities of noun-class systems, in terms of both their forms and their functions, and thus their genetic relationship could not escape attention. It was W. H. I. Bleek, apparently, who first use dthe term "Bantu", and it was also he who elaborated the bases of comparative Bantu philology. In the last decades of the 19th century and the first two or three decades of this century, the basis of its theory was moulded by the eminent German scholar, Carl Meinhof, and his pupils, while more recent decades have seen its further development both in the London school by Malcolm Guthrie and his colleagues and in Africa itself by Clement T. Doke and his followers. Both in Leningrad and in Moscow, several Bantuists, trained mostly by D. A. Olderogge, have started to develop a fruitful approach towards the intriguing field offered by the Bantu type of language system (I. V. Okhotina, E. N. Myachina, N. V. Gromova and others).

1.1.3. The opportunities offered for the linguistic exploration of Africa through the areas adjacent to the Sahara desert did not display any such striking typological similarity as those in the west or south. A belt revealing a clear diversity of language systems was found to be scattered along the borders of the desert, but at least in the Chad area there was an opportunity to analyze a language type (represented by Hausa) which offered certain typological and lexical similarities with the Semitic languages of North Africa. The existence of the category of grammatical gender, based supposedly upon the binary (sexual-oriented) schema, was evident in many languages of that area. Even this category operates throughout the entire respective systems, being manifested (as noun classes) by way of concord in most grammatical and syntactic constructions. It was only much later that it was discovered that Hausa uses — besides gender — also other important categories, and that its system was described by adequate methods of contemporary linguistics (F. W. Parsons, Claude Gouffé, C. T. Hodge, D. A. Olderogge, J. V. Osnitskaya, and many others). It was also discovered that a more appropriate classification of the languages of the Sub-Saharan Chad area may be offered only if the other so-called Chadic languages are analyzed and their systems mutually compared. This immense task of drawing attention away from "surface" similarities towards "deep" genetic ties could have been accomplished in recent decaces only against the background of a patient analytical and comparative effort which was accomplished in the Chad area by such scholars as Johannes Lukas, H. Jungraithmayr, C. Hoffmann, P. Newman and many others.

1.2. Historical coincidence thus confronted early attempts at a genetic classification of the languages of Africa with examples of an extreme typological diversity. Thus, while at the end of the last century and during the first decades of this century, the rudiments of knowledge about the *Kwa* languages in the west and the *Bantu* languages in the centre, south and south-east were available, a knowledge of those systems which share some of the features of both typological extremes and which are spoken in the "interior" was limited, if it existed at all. No wonder, therefore, that the available knowledge of typological extremes led automatically to a certain overestimation of typological criteria for the purposes of genetic grouping. Thus, theories were formulated at that period concerning the existence of four genetic language families in Africa: *Bantu, Hamitic, Sudanic* (inserted between the first two, mostly in the form of a geographically scattered belt) and *Bushman* in the south-west. The prestige of Carl Meinhof, rightly earned from his respectable work in the Bantu field, gave these theories their general justification for a relatively long period of time. Moreover, while supposing, on the basis of the merely supposed existence of the grammatical category of gender, that the Hausa, Masai, Fula and Nama Hottentot languages could well be included in the Hamitic family, he opened the way even to non-linguistic (anthropological or even racial) interpretations of his theories.

For many decades, the basic orientations of such a classification of African languages have survived in manuals, textbooks and introductions to linguistics or anthropology of Africa. If they were interpreted creatively, with reason and restraint, they served relatively well the purposes of a general classification of languages during their time. Moreover, it is important to realize that neither an over-estimation of typological criteria, nor possible non-linguistic (anthropological or even racial) simplifications were the sole origins of such "classical" theories. An ignorance of data on language systems inside the African contine nt was, together with the availability of incorrect or incomplete data, certainly at the origin of these over-simplifications. It was undoubtedly not by chance that two distinguished pupils of Carl Meinhof, August Klingenheben and Diedrich Westermann, both of whom started from Meinhof's original plat form, ultimately contributed to the clarification of its errors, especially by providing new, adequate, linguistically reliable data and material on certain "key" language systems which were either unknown in Meinhof's time, or else the knowledge of which was only partially correct, or even altogether incorrect. Klingenheben realised the analysis of Fula to the level of serious linguistic research (his synchronic analysis of this language having been surpassed only recently by the systemic approach used in the works of D. W. Arnott and P. F. Lacroix). His comparison of this language and its noun-class and permutation syste ms with the systems of related West Atlantic languages has dispelled any possible doubts about their ge netic relationship. Westermann, for his part, analyzed several languages of West and Central Africa, whether or not they displayed the noun-class system and he showed beyond any doubt their mutual relationship, thus opening the way to a broader comparison. In fact, both of these pupils of Meinhof (together with innumerable other linguists working in the same or related fields) paved the way for a general revision of the traditional classification — a step which they were prevented from taking perhaps, only due to their modesty and restraint. This task, however, was accomplished by J. H. Greenberg (1963).

1.3. Greenberg has proposed the following revision of the language families of Africa (indexes and symbols are also used identically in the present index as characteristics added after the name of each language):

A. Niger-Kordofanian family

Branches: I. Niger-Congo

Sub-branches: 1. West Atlantic
2. Mande
3. Gur
4. Kwa
5. Benue-Congo (including the entire Bantu languages area)
6. Adamawa Eastern

II. Kordofanian

B. Afro-Asiatic family

Branches: I. Semitic
II. Berber
III. Cushitic
IV. Ancient Egyptian
V. Chadic

C. Nilo-Saharan family

D. Khoisan family

This classification provoked particular discussion and several points in connection with it are still being debated. Thus, while the incorporation of Fula into the West Atlantic languages was almost universally welcomed, the incorporation of the whole Bantu area (previously listed as an independent language family) into the Benue-Congo sub-branch of the Niger-Congo branch, of the Niger Kordofanian family, met with particular opposition, especially from the Bantuists (M. Guthrie). Instead of accepting the idea of a genetic relationship between the Bantu languages and several languages of West Africa, the Bantuists tend to explain the existence of comparable systemic features shared by the Bantu languages and several so-called class languages of West Africa (to an analysis of which the works of Gabriel Manessy and S. Sauvageot have contributed recently) by the possible massive language contact of the originally unrelated West African languages with certain Pre-Bantu groups, which might have migrated in this direction. Similarly, the analysis of the Afro-Asiatic language family as falling into five equal branches has destroyed the notion of Semito-Hamitic dualism propagated by the Semitists who have been traditionally oriented toward a knowledge of the languages of North Africa and those of the Middle East. Greenberg's analysis of this family has, however, strengthened in several respects the views formulated earlier, by D. A. Olderogge.

1.4. In general, one may criticize this or that aspect of Greenberg's classification, which is easier to do now than it was ten years ago, as the filling in of linguistic gaps on the map of Africa has progressed considerably since the time of the original conception of this classification. In general, however, this classification brings to light certain new possible interrelationships; moreover, it unquestionably reflects the contemporary stage of our knowledge about Africa and its languages better than the "traditional" classification. This is why we have also used it as a basic frame of reference for the following language index. The languages of non-African origin (such as Afrikaans, Krio, Pidgin, Malagasy) are indicated in this index only if they occur in a regional, African variety or context, their genetic origin being labelled by other abbreviations (IE — Indoeuropean). It is unnecessary, perhaps, to point out that only the names of the languages mentioned in the text of this book appear in this index. In a way, the index thus reflects the necessary incompleteness af any such undertaking, as has been mentioned in the preface.

2. Index